Also by Fiona Rule …

The Worst Street in London

Foreword by Peter Ackroyd

● The remarkable untold story of Dorset Street in Spitalfields, the worst street in London, from its 17th century beginnings through its descent into vice and violence.

'Fiona Rule's fascinating microhistory of the life and grimes of a long forgotten place … powerful and well-researched.' LEO HOLLIS, *THE INDEPENDENT ON SUNDAY*

Published 2009 | Paperback | 198mm x 129mm | 234 pages | ISBN 978 0 7110 3363 4 | **£8.99**

London's Labyrinth: The World Beneath the City's Streets

● Explores the visionary, ground-breaking and sometimes dark history of the world beneath London's streets.

● Includes not only London Underground but also the forgotten Post Office railway, tunnels for underground rivers and waterways, foot tunnels, vast complexes of sewers and politicians' bunkers.

Published September 2012 | Hardback | 978 0 7110 3544 7 | 229mm x 152mm | 192 pages | ISBN 978 0 7110 3544 7 | **£19.99**

FIONA RULE

LONDON'S DOCKLANDS

A History of the Lost Quarter

Ian Allan
PUBLISHING

First published 2009

This impression 2012

ISBN 978 0 7110 3716 8

All rights reserved. No part of this book may be reproduced or transmitted in any form or by any means, electronic or mechanical, including photocopying, recording or by any information storage and retrieval system, without permission from the Publisher in writing.

© Fiona Rule 2009

Published by Ian Allan Publishing

An imprint of Ian Allan Publishing Ltd, Hersham, Surrey KT12 4RG.
Printed and bound by CPI Group (UK) Ltd, Croydon, CR0 4YY

Visit the Ian Allan Publishing website at www.ianallanpublishing.com

Copyright
Illegal copying and selling of publications deprives authors, publishers and booksellers of income, without which there would be no investment in new publications. Unauthorised versions of publications are also likely to be inferior in quality and contain incorrect information. You can help by reporting copyright infringements and acts of piracy to the Publisher or the UK.

For Harry Mann – Thank you for inspiring me.

ABOUT THE AUTHOR

Fiona Rule was born in Hertfordshire in 1967. After attending the University of the Arts in Charing Cross Road, she spent many years working in marketing for major industrial and retail companies. Over the past 15 years, Fiona has written numerous articles for magazines and journals and has also collaborated on books. She lives in London with her husband, Robert. Her first book, *The Worst Street in London*, is also published by Ian Allan Publishing; her latest title, *London's Labyrinth: The World beneath the City's Streets*, will see publication in September 2012.

ACKNOWLEDGEMENTS

I am indebted to the helpful staff at the National Maritime Museum, the Museum in Docklands, the National Archives in Kew, the British Library and the Metropolitan Archives for their assistance with my research. Thanks are also due to Bruce Watson and Lynn Blackmore at the Museum of London for their help in uncovering the lost world of the Hanseatic League.

Special thanks to Dick de Kerbrech, Alan Richardson, Brian Metherell, Brian Powell and, of course, Harry Mann for sharing their personal reminiscences of dock life with me.

Finally, I would like to thank my agent, Sheila Ableman, for her wise advice and support, Catharine and Adrian Edwards for their help with my talks and presentations, Jay Slater, Nick Grant and Sue Frost for their faith in me as a writer and last but by no means least, my husband Robert, for putting up with me.

CONTENTS

	Introduction	8
1	Ad Initium	11
2	A New Era	42
3	The Rebirth of London	56
4	Merchants and Monopolies	66
5	Plague and Politics	88
6	Voyages of Discovery	97
7	Black Gold	129
8	Fire	142
9	Mr Lloyd's Coffee House	159
10	Fur, Whales and New Developments	165
11	The Pros and Cons of Prosperity	173
12	The Canal Boom	186
13	The Great 19th Century Docks	195
14	The Age of Steam	207
15	The Rise of the Wharves	224
16	Life in the Victorian Docks	233
17	Boiling Point	252
18	The Beginning of the End	267
19	Crash, Depression and Conflict	281
20	The Demise of the Docks	298
	Select Bibliography	326
	Index	330

INTRODUCTION

3 May 1993 brought torrential rain to London and its surrounds. By the time I drove down the industrial lane that led to the front gate of Wood Bros.' furniture factory, the road was almost totally submerged under large pools of water, in places over 1ft deep. I manoeuvred my car to where I thought the kerb lay, slowly ground to a halt and opened the door to find water lapping at the sill.

'The Lea's burst its banks again.' A tall man with grey hair, whom I would later discover was George the gateman, called across to me. The path to the factory gates was entirely submerged; an inauspicious welcome to the premises of my new employer.

'Do you want a piggyback, love?' shouted one of a group of men congregated next to George, watching my reaction to my dilemma with macho relish. Cursing the fact that I was wearing a new pair of suede heels but determined not to conform to the female stereotype so hoped for by my masculine audience, I rolled up my trouser legs and waded through the murky water.

It transpired that my watery welcome was not the only surprise I received that day. After squelching into reception and being shown my desk by the sympathetic but amused office manager, I was given a tour of my new workplace by a cheerful chap named Peter, with whom I would be working on marketing campaigns. We toured a line of offices, meeting and shaking hands with people whose names I almost instantly forgot, despite making a concerted effort not to. Finally, Peter led me to a door behind which I could hear an almighty cacophony of machinery whirring, clunking and clacking. In the vast room that lay beyond stood a huge printing press, spewing sheets of paper from its bowels in a steady, rhythmic stream, diligently watched over by a grey-haired man dressed in green overalls who distractedly waved at us as we approached. 'This is Harry,' said Peter. 'You'll be working with him on the print.'

Before walking into Wood Bros.' print shop, I knew absolutely nothing about the art of printing and was horrified to learn that I would be responsible for overseeing the production of the multitude of brochures, price lists, posters and advertising flyers that the company dispatched to its retailers. However, Harry proved to be a patient and hugely knowledgeable teacher. As I embarked on my crash course, he taught me much about the complex facets of the process, from selecting paper to how plates were made for the press. However, it was our chats about an entirely different subject that would ultimately lead me on an adventure of discovery into a part of London that has now almost totally vanished.

During our tea breaks, Harry would tell me about his life, which began in September 1934 in West Ham, East London. When he was very young the family moved to Canning Town, an area dominated geographically, economically and socially by three vast expanses of water occupying nearly 250 acres of what had once been Plaistow Marsh.

Known collectively as the Royal Docks, the Victoria, Albert and King George V Docks formed the most visually impressive section of the Port of London; a sprawling network of quays, ancient wharves, deep canals and high-walled basins that stretched along the River Thames from the City to Tilbury. Walking the length of the Victoria and Albert Docks alone would take up to an hour, the total length of these massive bodies of water being over three miles. When constructed in 1880, the Royal Albert was the largest dock in the world, running 1¾ miles along the north bank of the mighty Thames. At the western edge, a lock connected it with the Royal Victoria Dock, a deep water monster-structure measuring 3,000ft long by over 1,000ft wide – enough to fit seven football pitches with room to spare. Along its warehouse-lined quayside, enormous jetties, complete with their own railway sidings, stretched out into the centre of the basin, allowing myriad goods from the four corners of the globe to be unloaded onto trucks and conveyed to an increasingly prosperous and consumerist nation.

The London docks provided employment for over 100,000 men and Harry's father and numerous neighbours and friends all worked at the waterside. Work was physically demanding but plentiful and dockworkers' pay, while not a king's ransom, was sufficient to raise a family (albeit in less than idyllic surroundings), and keep a bit back for beer money. Naturally enough, Harry always assumed that the docks would eventually provide him with his own living until a conversation occurred that had a profound effect on the rest of his life. A short time before his 14th birthday, the boy's father announced that he had secured him an apprenticeship with a local printer. Harry was bewildered by this resolution; why would his dad eschew Canning Town's major employer in favour of a trade he knew nothing about? His father's response was remarkably prescient: 'There's no future in the docks,' he told his son.

Until Harry told me his story of a lost London community, I knew little about the docks or the people that once lived there. However, a visit to the Royal Victoria Dock showed that his father's prediction was utterly and undeniably correct. The terrace of the ExCel event centre, built over what was once the dock's North Quay, overlooked a placid expanse of redundant water, used only by the occasional canoeist. Over on the South Quay, a new development of luxury flats sat alongside the long-deserted, empty hulk of Spiller's Millennium Mills; a relic of the dock's commercial past. Further eastwards, the shimmering glass walls of an empty office block reflected the ripples running across the deserted waters of the Albert Dock. Occasionally, the tranquil atmosphere was interrupted by the engines of a short-haul plane landing on a windswept runway that stretched along the Albert's south quay. To erstwhile residents of Canning Town, many of whom, including Harry, moved northwards to Essex after the war, the scene is as unrecognisable today as it was unimaginable 50 years ago. Intrigued at how evidence of what was until very recently such an integral part of London had been so quickly swept away, I began to explore the history of the area.

1

AD INITIUM

London's docks are as old as the city itself. The city's first harbour, founded by the Romans, grew up around the foot of an ancient river crossing on the north bank of the Thames, roughly where London Bridge stands today. At first, the dock was relatively small but as Roman Londinium increased in size and importance, so did its port with ships arriving from all over the Roman empire bearing a plethora of goods, from silks to olive oil, to be consumed by the prosperous populace. The Port of London represented an essential facet of London's economy and its location at the heart of the city reflected its status.

For centuries, Londinium's port boomed but when the Roman Empire went into inexorable decline, so did the docks and following the Romans' departure from the British Isles in circa. 410AD, the first incarnation of the Port of London was left to slowly disappear along with the sophisticated way of life that had previously dominated the city. For well over 100 years, the old Roman dock lay disused and deserted until the Anglo-Saxons, fleeing attacks from aggressors, sought sanctuary within the crumbling remains of the old city walls. Thus, Roman Londinium became Saxon Lundenburh and the city and its docks entered a new period of prosperity.

By the dawn of the eighth century, the port of Lundenburh had once again established itself as an international trading centre with vessels from distant lands arriving at the riverside, their holds laden with exotic cargo. As the centuries passed, prosperous Lundenburh and its busy dock began to attract the attention of acquisitive noblemen from the European mainland and following his victory against King Harold in 1066, the Duke of Normandy finally succeeded in taking the coveted city.

Lundenburh became London and its port entered a new era that would prove to be both long and fruitful.

Throughout the ensuing centuries, the Port of London played a vital role in the financial, commercial and social life of the city, attracting wealthy merchants and ship owners from Europe and beyond, most notably the mighty Hanseatic League – northern Europe's most powerful trading alliance. The League established their London headquarters in the heart of the port and built a forbidding, high-walled fortress known as The Steelyard on the north bank of the Thames within which they lived and worked. For centuries, their grand trading centre stood as a symbol of the Hanseatic League's international power and status but, like the Romans before them, the alliance's stranglehold on northern European trade gradually loosened and today the once-magnificent Steelyard lies forgotten beneath the foundations of Cannon Street Station.

The growing importance of London throughout the Middle Ages meant that its thriving port was often at the epicentre of battles for control of the coveted city. In the mid-13th century, the docks were at the heart of Simon de Montfort's valiant bid to wrest control of the kingdom from Henry III. One hundred years later, the people of the port struggled with a threat of a very different kind as the city was ravaged by the Black Death – a frighteningly contagious and ruthlessly fatal plague that was spread by flea-ridden rats living on board the ships that made their way up the Thames. But despite these and countless other challenges, the Port of London continued to expand and the men and women who traded there became hugely influential. Taking inspiration from the Hanseatic League, the English merchants gradually formed a coalition, first known as the Merchant Staplers and later the Merchant Adventurers – a group of individuals who were to play a vital role in the formation of the British Empire.

By the end of the 1400s, London was handling over 60% of the kingdom's overseas trade and the shipyards that had gradually grown up on the south bank of the Thames to serve the busy port caught the attention of the great Tudor monarch, Henry VIII, who developed the yards into majestic royal docks where state-of-the-art warships such as the *Henri Grace* a Dieu were built. Simultaneously, the Merchant Adventurers embarked on a lengthy search for new international markets. Under the direction of Sebastian Cabot, son of the great mariner, John

Cabot, they set forth on expeditions to the east, opening up lucrative markets with the vast Russian Empire. The resulting increase in trade at the docks and the sheer amount of vessels jostling for position at the ancient waterfront prompted Elizabeth I to restructure the way the port was run and resulted in the introduction of 'Legal Quays' – a series of landing stages along the north bank of the Thames through which all imported goods had to pass under the watchful eye of customs officials. Each quay specialised in a particular commodity and the system proved so effective that they remained at the centre of London's overseas trade for centuries. Today, virtually all trace of them has been erased.

Throughout the 16th century, the Port of London played a fundamental part in the development of Britain as a world power. The Merchant Adventurers extended their expeditions into Asia where they found lucrative markets offering great riches. In order to finance return voyages, they formed the East India Company, which was destined to become the most powerful commercial organisation in modern history, governing immense territories in addition to overseeing all trade with the region. The Merchant Adventurers also journeyed south to the west coast of Africa where they embarked on the Port of London's most shameful enterprise, transporting human cargo to plantations in the Americas where the unlucky prisoners were subjected to a life of slavery.

The questionable activities of the East India Company and the dreadful trade of the slave merchants only served to increase the prosperity and status of the Port of London. Throughout the 16th and early 17th centuries, the Legal Quays heaved with ships waiting to discharge their goods and the Thames was a teeming mass of vessels jostling for position along the ancient waterfront. However, the landscape of the docks was about to be changed forever. In September 1666, a fire broke out in the premises of a ships' biscuit maker in Pudding Lane, close to the docks. The resulting conflagration totally destroyed the port and much of the city beyond it. With no insurance against this catastrophe, the owners of the ancient quays that lined the north bank of the Thames ploughed their life savings into rebuilding this most essential part of the city. Amazingly, it took just six years to rebuild not only the docks but also much of the city. Grand plans to create a new port were mooted but the complex pattern of land ownership that had existed for centuries rendered any wholesale redevelopment impossible. By the mid-1670s, the newly rebuilt docks traced much the same footprint as they had done before the destructive conflagration. However, the landowners vowed to protect themselves financially from such a catastrophe ever occurring again and thus the concept of fire insurance was born. Soon the dock merchants began to devise ways of applying insurance to their businesses and summits to discuss this novel idea were held in the new coffee houses that had recently sprung up on the city streets. Several of these establishments became regular meeting places for dock merchants and ship owners and the coffee house proprietors found themselves privy to valuable intelligence involving the shipping industry. The owners of Lloyd's Coffee House seized the opportunity to disseminate the information they gleaned and began to publish newssheets detailing the safe arrival of ships. These sheets ultimately evolved into Lloyd's List, which is still today the leading daily newspaper for the maritime industry. Some of the coffee house's regular clientele also capitalised on the demand for maritime insurance and became the first Lloyd's underwriters, skilfully marrying investors with ship owners and merchants to great profit.

As trade in the docks became more organised throughout the 18th century, the city gained strength as he country's centre of commerce. During the 1700s, the population of London doubled from 400,000 to 800,000 as thousands of families relocated from the countryside to the city, where the manufacturing industry was rapidly becoming a major source of employment. As manufacturing increased, the docks thrived as all manner of products arrived at the port for export to mainland Europe and beyond. The old Legal Quays struggled to cope with the sheer volume of shipping arriving in the Thames and the merchants and ship owners began to discuss potential solutions to the problem of congestion. Thus, the model for London's first enclosed docks – leviathan structures that were to dominate the perimeter of the Thames in London for over 150 years – was devised. The first of these new maritime innovations, the West India Docks, was built on land at the northern tip of the Isle of Dogs in 1799. The complex provided a template on which all future enclosed docks in the city would be built, comprising massive basins in which ships could berth, accessed via huge locks leading from the river. The basins were surrounded by warehousing in which goods could be stored and were cut off from the outside world by towering walls running the entire length of the site's perimeter.

The success of the West India Docks and the effect it had on easing traffic on the perennially congested Thames prompted a wave of imitations throughout the first half of the 19th century. First came the London Docks in the ancient seafaring district of Wapping, then the East India Docks at Blackwall followed by the (later amalgamated) Surrey and Commercial Docks across the river at Rotherhithe. Each of these developments proved financially successful and were quickly followed by a further development close to the Tower of London known as the St Katharine Docks. Later in the century, the vast size of the new steam ships plying their trade at the Port of London prompted speculative developers to create even larger basins further east, where they could be more easily accessible to the huge vessels. The Port of London acquired the Victoria and Royal Albert Docks on the Plaistow Marshes, the Millwall Docks on the Isle of Dogs and the Tilbury Docks on the Thames estuary in Essex. These colossal waterside developments were complimented by (and were in direct competition with) numerous wharves that lined both sides of the river from London Bridge to Silvertown, occupying a staggering 3,000 acres of land.

Unsurprisingly, the docks and wharves became the major employers in Rotherhithe, Deptford and the whole of East London adjacent to the river. Literally thousands of Londoners worked at the port in a wide variety of jobs. Demand for housing in the dock areas was such that entire districts – for example, Cubitt Town on the Isle of Dogs – were built specifically to accommodate dock workers. However, despite the neverending supply of work and the unceasing, frenetic activity that surrounded the docks, there was trouble afoot. Poor pay and extremely tough working conditions prompted the workers to collectively rise up against their avaricious employers and the docks became inextricably linked with the embryonic trades union movement that was beginning to gain momentum by the 1880s. As the 20th century dawned, the dock owners were becoming overwhelmed by strike action by their increasingly militant workers. This problem was exacerbated by the fact that as ships increased in size, the ancient Port of London was gradually becoming inaccessible. In addition to these two problems, competitive warehousing rates offered by the Thames wharves meant that many of the enclosed dock companies faced bankruptcy if the situation was not improved. In a dramatic move, the government resolved to nationalise all of London's enclosed docks and in 1909, overall control of these gigantic structures was given to the newly-formed Port of London Authority, otherwise known as the PLA. This drastic measure initially paid off and despite the disruption of two world wars, by the late 1950s, the Port of London had entered its final boom period.

In the end, the ultimate cause of death for London's docks was not unionisation or competition from the wharves, but containerisation. As container ships began to replace smaller, more traditional vessels, it became impossible for the Port of London (with the exception of Tilbury) to accommodate them. The River Thames was simply not deep enough for these giant vessels to safely navigate. What had originally been the deciding factor in the docks' location – the river – now proved to be the Port of London's downfall. As ship owners eschewed the historic port in favour of the great seaports, the docks gradually closed. One by one, these hives of industry shut down leaving desolation in their wake. Families who had earned a living at the waterside for generations moved out to the new towns of the northern Home Counties in search of alternative employment. By the mid-1980s, the docks were a wasteland and any visitor to the deserted streets that surrounded them would have been hard pressed to imagine how the areas had once played such a key role in the development of one of the world's most celebrated cities.

***

The events that led to the foundation of the great city of London and its docks are shrouded in both mystery and myth. One of the first accounts appears in the *Historia Britonum*, an ancient tome attributed to a ninth-century Welsh monk named Nennius who took it upon himself to assemble a collection of historical stories for posterity. Once he began his research, the scholarly monk quickly realised that he had set himself an onerous task. For centuries, myriad tales of the history of Britain had been handed down orally from generation to generation, gradually becoming embellished and altered along the way. Finding proof or even a vague provenance for these tales was virtually impossible and no doubt tantalising and frustrating in equal measure. Nennius himself admitted, '[I], pupil of the holy Elvodug, have undertaken to write down some extracts that the complacency of the British cast out; for the scholars of the island of Britain had no skill ... I have therefore made a heap of all that I have found.' That said, Nennius' 'heap' of information survived the test of time and his account of the foundation of London was retold over 200 years later by Geoffrey of Monmouth, in his *Historia Regum Britanniae*.

According to the two texts, the name 'Britain' was coined by Brutus, a Roman consul and descendant of the legendary hero Aeneas. In true classical fashion, Brutus was banished from his homeland after accidentally killing his father. He fled to Greece where he recruited a crew of Trojan ex-slaves and from thence sailed to a Mediterranean island where he discovered an abandoned temple to Diana, goddess of hunting. Brutus was exhausted after his voyage and after making a sacrifice to the deity, he fell asleep at the foot of her statue where he dreamt of a far-distant land inhabited by giants – the place in which he was destined to settle. Following this premonition, Brutus and his men continued on their journey westward. After briefly settling in Gaul, where they fell out with the King of Aquitaine, they escaped across the channel to Albion (the ancient name for Britain) – an island, so legend has it, populated by a race of giants. Convinced that this was the land in his premonition, Brutus renamed the island Britain and declared himself king, bequeathing the land covering present-day Cornwall to his second-in-command, Corineus.

Life in the new kingdom proved difficult, not least because the Trojans were constantly harassed by the resident giants, but after a series of bloody battles, they managed to slay every one of the creatures except for their leader, Gogmagog, who was challenged to wrestle Corineus. The ensuing fight resulted in the last giant of Albion being thrown from the Cornish cliffs into the sea. This legendary event was later immortalised in the magnum opus of the poet Michael Drayton, *Poly-Olbion* (1613):

> *Amongst the ragged cleaves those monstrous giants sought:*
> *Who (of their dreadful kind) t'appal the Trojans brought*
> *Great Gogmagog, an oake that by the roots could teare;*
> *So mighty were (that time) the men who lived there.*

But, for the use of armes he did not understand
(Except some rock or tree, that coming next to land,
He raised out of the earth to execute his rage),
He challenge makes for strength, and offereth there his gage,
Which Corin taketh up, to answer by and by,
Upon this sonne of earth his utmost power to try.

Having defeated the enemy, the Trojans turned their attention to establishing settlements throughout the country and their leader Brutus chose the site of today's City of London as his headquarters, naming it Troia Nova or New Troy. A royal palace was built where the Guildhall now stands and a temple to Brutus' guide and protector Diana was built on the site now occupied by St Paul's Cathedral. The London Stone, an ancient piece of masonry now sited at 111 Cannon Street, is said to be part of the temple altar and legend has it that 'so long as the stone of Brutus is safe, so long shall London flourish.' When Brutus died, he was buried in a temple on Tower Hill and his lands were divided between his three sons – Locrinus taking what is now England, Albanactus Scotland and Kamber Wales.

Sadly, there is no evidence that the heroic characters in Nennius and Geoffrey of Monmouth's stories ever truly existed and archaeology has as yet yielded no signs of Brutus' royal palace, temple or tomb. Curiously though, the giant Gogmagog makes an appearance in another piece of British folklore, this time specifically concerning London. From circa 1500, huge 14ft effigies of two giants named Gog and Magog were paraded at the head of the procession during the annual Lord Mayor's Show. According to legend, these two giants were descendants of the Roman Emperor Diocletian's daughters, who were banished to Albion after killing their husbands. The original model giants were made from wicker and plaster and stood guard at the Guildhall when not in use. Over time, the figures began to rot and were finally destroyed during the Great Fire of 1666. In the early 1700s, they were replaced with two wooden effigies, but these proved too heavy to be paraded around at the Lord Mayor's Show and the yearly ritual ceased. However, nearly 300 years later, basket maker Olivia Elton Barratt took on the challenging task of re-creating the two figures and, in 2006, the leviathans once again took their place at the head of the parade.

If Brutus' New Troy ever did exist, all evidence of it had been lost by the time the great Roman Emperor Claudius arrived on British shores in AD43. At the time of his arrival, there were no major settlements on the marshy flood plains of the River Thames. The site of the modern city was occupied by just a few humble farmsteads and, as one archaeologist pointed out, the entire population of 'London' would probably have fitted inside a double-decker bus.

The sparsely populated banks of the first-century Thames are described in Cassius Dio's account of the Roman invasion, written over 100 years after the actual event in about AD175. In the first known reference to the area, Dio describes how the native Britons were chased to 'the River Thames at a point where it empties into the ocean and at flood-tide forms a lake' by Roman soldiers and were attacked 'from several sides at once' resulting in many casualties. Some of the Britons managed to escape, with the Romans in hot pursuit. However, the invaders' inferior knowledge of the terrain proved to be their downfall and 'they got into swamps from which it was difficult to make their way out, and so lost a number of men.'

Dio's description of a watery wasteland does not suggest that the area was an ideal situation for the founding of a city and dock. However, even then, the mantra 'location, location, location' prevailed. Following Claudius' successful invasion, the Romans immediately set about creating an infrastructure across the wild landscape of south-eastern Britain and began to construct commercial and military routes through the area. A capital was established at present-day Colchester named Camulodunum that served as a base from which the Romans could gradually spread their control west and northwards. Further south, they built a fort and dock on the banks of the Thames with the intention of using the site as a distribution centre for goods shipped into the country from other parts of the empire.

The new dock was well positioned. Ships carrying civilian cargo and military supplies weighed anchor in a natural harbour at Richborough in Kent. The goods were then loaded onto smaller vessels, which sailed a short distance around the coast and up the Thames to the new dock where they could be unloaded, warehoused and finally distributed by land to other settlements. The fort, dock and nearby warehouses rapidly became busy and soon people were flocking to the area in search of work.

What had initially been a small hamlet grew into a busy, prosperous and strategically important town known as Londinium.

The Roman invasion of Britain was, by necessity, gradual. At the time, the island was a mishmash of roughly defined areas governed by various Celtic tribes, all of whom were understandably reluctant to hand control over to the Romans. One such tribe was the Iceni, who occupied what is now Norfolk, Suffolk and part of Cambridgeshire. Archaeological evidence suggests that the Iceni were a wealthy clan who had been established in the area for over 500 years. According to the historian Tacitus in his *Annals of Imperial Rome*, their leader Prasutagus brokered a deal with the invaders and his lands became a 'client kingdom', meaning that overall control was submitted to Rome but the region continued to be governed locally. Initially, this arrangement seems to have worked but once Prasutagus died, *circa* AD60, the uneasy peace between the Romans and the Iceni was shattered. Tacitus explained:

> Prasutagus, king of the Iceni, after a life of long and renowned prosperity, had made the [Roman] emperor co-heir with his own two daughters ... But it turned out otherwise. Kingdom and household were plundered like prizes of war ... As a beginning, his widow Boudicca was flogged and their daughters raped. The Icenian chiefs were deprived of their hereditary estates as if the Romans had been given the whole country. The king's own relatives were treated like slaves.

Unsurprisingly, the Iceni were incensed by this betrayal and, supported by other aggrieved tribes, marched on the capital at Colchester led by Prasutagus' feisty widow Boudicca, hell-bent on revenge. Having razed the capital to the ground, Boudicca's army quickly headed south towards Londinium. Very little is known about the Icenians' warrior queen. Cassius Dio described her as 'most tall, in appearance most terrifying, in the glance of her eye most fierce and her voice was harsh', which seems fitting enough until one remembers that Dio was born almost a century after Boudicca's death and so was not imparting first-hand recollections. There is no doubt, however, that she was a courageous woman who earned the respect of not only her people but also other Celtic leaders.

The arrival of Boudicca's army in Londinium was well timed as the military governor, Suetonius, and a large proportion of troops were many miles away in Wales fighting the Druids. According to Tacitus, whose future father-in-law was serving as a military tribune in Britain during time of the rebellion, Governor Suetonius led his men back to Londinium after hearing about the destruction of Camulodunum. However, after seeing the vast numbers of Celts waiting there, he made the brave and difficult decision to sacrifice the town and wait to confront the enemy in a more strategically advantageous place. His actions had dreadful consequences for many inhabitants, who pleaded with him to save Londinium. Tacitus wrote, 'unmoved by lamentations and appeals, Suetonius gave the signal for departure. The inhabitants were allowed to accompany him but those who stayed because they were women or old, or attached to the place, were slaughtered by the enemy.'

Boudicca's army were relentless in their destruction. Venting their fury at the Romans, they mercilessly massacred all who stood in their path, leaving a scene of utter carnage in their wake. Then, perhaps appalled at the monstrous sight that lay before them, they lit torches and set fire to the fragile, wooden buildings that lined the streets, razing Londinium to the ground. Their work done, the army quickly regrouped and departed towards their next target, Verulamium – a Roman town of strategic importance that occupied part of modern-day St Albans in Hertfordshire.

At this point, legend has it that on departing the smouldering remains of Londinium, Boudicca's forces were attacked by an army hastily dispatched by Suetonius at the spot where King's Cross station now stands. It was here that the Iceni uprising was stopped in its tracks. Realising there was no chance of victory, Boudicca committed suicide by drinking poison. She was buried at the battle site, in an area now occupied by platforms 9 and 10 of the mainline station. Many centuries later, the battle site was commemorated in the naming of Battle Bridge Road, which is situated to the north of the station. Of course, this rather unlikely story is almost certainly untrue. Placing the battle at King's Cross dates back to the 1930s when a folklore expert named Lewis Spence identified the area as the location for the final conflict between the Romans and the Iceni. In the following decades, Spence's theory (which was based on extremely flimsy evidence in the first place), was embellished; the part about the burial site being under platforms 9 and 10 was probably added as a joke.

The true location of the Icenian's final battle remains a mystery. Even Tacitus does not give a location in his account of the battle, remarking only that the battleground had a narrow approach and a backdrop of dense woodland. Wherever its location, the Romans chose the site wisely. Despite being severely outnumbered, they managed to slay up to 80% of Boudicca's army, leaving the remaining Celts to flee from the battlefield or suffer the ultimate indignity of being taken prisoner. It is reported that Boudicca and her two daughters survived the battle but unable to face the inevitable humiliation at the hands of the Roman soldiers, the three women poisoned themselves. Their burial site has never been found.

Although the Celts could be seen as the injured party at the start of the rebellion, their contempt for civilians combined with their avarice and ruthlessness during their campaign does little to engender sympathy. Tacitus noted, 'the natives enjoyed plundering and thought of nothing else.' They avoided attacking heavily protected military buildings in favour of private property where goods and possessions could be looted with little resistance. An estimated 70,000 civilians were killed during the uprisings at Camulodunum, Londinium and Verulamium and Tacitus lay the blame for this firmly on the Celts who 'did not take or sell prisoners, or practise other wartime exchanges. They could not wait to cut throats, hang, burn and crucify – as though avenging, in advance, the retribution that was on its way.'

The Celtic uprising left the Romans with three major settlements destroyed and no capital, but Londinium was destined to rise again, bigger and stronger than before.

At this point, it is perhaps an opportune moment to take a look at some of the theories on how the town first got the name from which London is derived. Geoffrey of Monmouth claims an ancient king of Britain named Lud first coined the name: '… he surrounded the capital with lofty walls and with towers built with extraordinary skill, and he ordered it to be called Kaerlud, or Lud's city, from his own name. Thereafter, we are told the town was renamed by the legendary King Lud as Kaerlundein, and eventually London.' According to legend, when King Lud died, he was buried on the mount of one of the town's two hills, which subsequently became known as Ludgate. No evidence of either King Lud or a tomb on Ludgate Hill has been found, but that did not stop the myth becoming widely believed in the 1500s. Wooden effigies of Lud and his two sons were commissioned and placed on the hill to commemorate the city's namesake. They survive to this day and can now been seen in the churchyard of St Dunstan in the West in an extremely sorry state.

Another popular hypothesis is that the name is derived from the Celtic personal name Londinos, which itself is from the word 'lond' meaning 'wild', suggesting that the land was once owned by a wealthy Celtic family. An interesting recent theory was proposed in 1998 by linguistics professor Richard Coates, who suggested that the name could derive from an Old European word – Plowonida – roughly meaning 'wide flowing river', a description of the pre-Celtic Thames as it travelled through the area. When the Celts built a settlement on the banks of the 'Płowonida' they named it after the river, adding the place name suffix of 'on' or 'onjon', thus making the settlement name 'Plowonidon' or 'Plowonidonjon'. To British Celts, the letter 'P' was silent so the settlement would have been referred to as 'Lowonidon' or 'Lowonidonjon' and this gradually corrupted into 'London', which in turn was altered by the Romans to 'Londinium'.

Whatever the true history of the name 'Londinium', Boudicca's army succeeded in almost totally destroying it. To this day, a layer of ash and remains of burnt debris can be seen in the soil layer dating to the first century. The Celts may have been defeated, but they literally left their mark on London. However, shards of pottery found very close to the ash layer suggest that the Romans began to rebuild London very quickly after its devastation.

Before the Celtic insurgence, Londinium had been gradually developing a reputation as a busy and convenient port. In addition to being situated at an expedient distribution point, it was also sufficiently inland to discourage sorties by sea pirates that lurked in the English Channel. It was also easily accessed from three major rivers on the Continent – namely the Rhine, the Elbe and the Seine – which made transportation of goods reasonably simple. Its location was so desirable that the Romans decided that, not only was the town worth rebuilding, but the previously small dock area was also worthy of major redevelopment. With this new phase of building came London's first dockland community.

The first London docks straddled the north end of the Roman bridge, which ran across the Thames from today's church of St Magnus the Martyr in Lower Thames Street to Hay's Galleria on the south bank. The original harbour was tiny by modern standards, stretching roughly from King William Street to Billingsgate. That said, the whole of Londinium was not much larger than Hyde Park, so the dock represented a fairly sizeable chunk of the settlement. At the centre of the harbour was a wooden landing stage measuring around 57 metres (187ft) long with a small jetty protruding from it. The land immediately behind the jetty was covered with large warehouses, known to the Romans as 'horrea', where goods were stored and beyond them stretched a network of roads and tracks leading to the residential part of Londinium.

Archaeological evidence suggests that, at first, the harbour was purely a place of work, with its employees commuting on foot from their homes a little further north along Cornhill, Poultry and Cheapside. However, its instant popularity as a port meant that the area rapidly developed. During the early decades of the second century, the landing stage was enlarged to accommodate more ships and the old timber warehouses were replaced with more durable masonry constructions.

As Londinium expanded, hundreds of people flooded into the area looking for work and soon the limited accommodation north of the harbour proved insufficient. In response, new homes appeared along the riverside, the most impressive of which was the governor's palace, which stood close to the site now occupied by Cannon Street Station. The palace, known by the Romans as the 'praetorium', was designed to impress both the inhabitants of the town and visiting dignitaries, many of whom were familiar with the opulence of Rome. Needless to say, no expense was spared in its construction. Despite being close to the noisy, sometimes malodorous docks and the chaotic, lively forum complex, the palace was spacious and airy, with panoramic views across the waters of the Thames. The building was designed for both private and state use – it combined living quarters for the governor, his family and staff with offices and large meeting halls used for formal entertaining. The halls were elaborately decorated with intricate mosaic floors and led to an elegant terrace that descended to the banks of the Thames. On warm summer evenings, guests could discuss civic matters while strolling amid calming fish pools or watch the sun set over the fields and forests beyond the river's south bank. The location of the governor's palace proved so pleasing that a formal residence remained on the site for over 200 years, by which time Londinium had grown into an important and wealthy city.

The first site that the town had become a valued part of the Roman Empire came in about AD122 when the Emperor Hadrian visited the city while on a tour of his northern provinces. In the months prior to his visit, many towns in Britain had been thrown into chaos following a major rebellion in the north. Although Londinium was largely unaffected by the events taking place hundreds of miles away, the governor was no doubt keen to present a united front to his commander-in-chief. Thus it is highly likely that the town received a major overhaul in anticipation of the imperial visit, with new buildings erected and shabby streets tidied up. In the event, Hadrian's visit to Londinium was brief and largely uneventful, perhaps because the Emperor was more concerned with the construction of his eponymous wall stretching from Segedunum near Wallsend, north Tyneside, to the Solway Firth in the west. Despite this, his arrival would have been met with great excitement as it was rare for Londinium to receive high-ranking Roman officials, let alone the Emperor himself.

The improvements to the town in anticipation of Hadrian's visit proved to be disastrously short-lived. Soon after the Emperor's departure, a major fire swept through Londinium, wiping out a large part of the city including most of the dock building on the west side of the bridge. The cause of the fire remains shrouded in mystery as no mention of it is made in existing classical sources. We shall probably never know if it was the result of another uprising or simply began by accident like the Great Fire of 1666. However, what we do know is that it provided the catalyst for a massive development programme which continued for the next 30 years.

By the mid-second century, Londinium had established itself as a thriving cosmopolitan port city and was at the peak of its powers. Tacitus described how its streets 'thronged with great numbers of merchants and abundance of merchandise' and it is even mentioned in Ptolemy's

Geography, the great gazetteer of the Greco-Roman world, that 'in the island of Albion, Londinium has its greatest day of 18 hours'. The city was finally on the Roman map.

One of the men responsible for Londinium's rise in fortune was Julius Classicianus, who, in his capacity as Procurator, was responsible for reviving the city's fortunes following the Celtic revolt. As part of his job, Classicianus oversaw all manner of civic activities from construction to communications. Archaeologists have found the Procurator's official mark 'PP BR LON' (*Procurator Provinciae Britanniae Londinii*) on a diverse range of items dating from this period, from bricks through to metal stamps and writing tablets, giving some idea of the wide realm of activities in which the Procurator was involved.

A large quantity of the bricks ordered by Classicianus were used to enlarge the forum complex that stood on top of Corhhill, directly behind the docks. The forum was an integral part of day-to-day life in Londinium and represented the centre of the city both geographically and socially. It occupied a massive site and contained offices, shops and temples set around a large central courtyard. The most prominent building in the forum complex was the basilica, a huge edifice over 500ft long, which was used for a variety of civic affairs from court cases to political meetings. Although no detailed descriptions of Londinium's basilica exist, studies of other examples from a similar period reveal that it would have been a tall stone building with an open plan interior bordered by rows of column-lined arcades from which members of the public could watch proceedings. In the centre lay a large raised area finished with smooth marble floor tiles. At one end stood a dais from which magistrates delivered their verdicts, politicians squabbled and orators addressed their audience. Outside the basilica, the interior of the forum complex provided a convenient meeting place where friends and colleagues could sit on the piazza watching their neighbours buzzing in and out of the shops that lined the perimeter or disappearing into one of the temples that stood within the courtyard for a few moments of peace and solitude.

Outside the forum, houses stretched westwards towards Ludgate Hill. Unlike British homes of today, Roman houses were long, low and usually positioned end-on to the road. By the middle of the second century, Londinium's wealth and status were such that most homes were built of brick and stone rather than wood, although there is little doubt that those built for poorer inhabitants would have been constructed from cheaper, less durable materials. Roofs of the properties were either thatched or covered with fine terracotta tiles. Wealthier citizens who could afford more land built impressive villas set around a rectangular courtyard complete with fountains, mosaic floors and walls painted with elaborate murals. The intemperate British climate was made more bearable with hypocausts – underfloor central heating systems – that must have come as a great relief to visitors from the more southerly parts of the Roman Empire.

The residential areas were interspersed with small parades of shops and towards the outskirts of the city lay several industrial areas. Tanneries and leather-workers' shops have been found along the banks of the Walbrook, which at the time flowed from Finsbury out to the Thames near what is now Cannon Street railway bridge. One excavation site even revealed the remains of an abandoned Roman hide still pegged out on the ground after being tanned. The area now occupied by the Bank of England was once the domain for several bone and antler workshops within which craftsmen whittled the raw materials into handles for knives, beakers and even hinges. Nothing was wasted at these workshops. Even the discarded chips of bone were recycled as a surface material for roads. In recent years, archaeologists have found bone deposits on Roman thoroughfares that still bear the impressions of the thousands of hobnail boots that marched over them nearly 2,000 years ago. Further west, near the site of St Paul's Cathedral, lay the potteries where thousands of cups, bowls and cooking vessels were crafted from the indigenous London clay and fired in smoky kilns.

Across the Thames, pieces of lamb skulls and butchers' remnants are all that remains of the numerous slaughterhouses that once stood among the taverns and wooden shacks that lay in this poor district just outside the city boundary. The area we now know as Southwark held two main purposes for Roman Londoners. Firstly, it seems to have been the site for activities that, for one reason or another, the Romans preferred to keep outside the city walls: abbatoirs provided the residents with meat without them having to endure the blood-curdling noises of animals being slain, the stench of the blood and excrement, and the mess of the detritus. The area also held a large cemetery to which the dead were brought from across the water. However, the south bank of the Thames was not only a place of death. Its streets were also places to which Roman Londoners came to eat, drink and make merry. Numerous clues to the Roman taverns of the south bank have been unearthed over the centuries, including flagons from which ale was swigged and plates, pots and cutlery from the inns' kitchens. Roman cooking equipment such as saucepans was often made from bronze and so was very durable and lay for many centuries under the thoroughfares of Southwark, long after their owners had discarded them. With them lay the knives and spoons with which the Romans ate their food (they did not use forks) and the long skewers onto which meat was threaded before cooking. Roman taverns did not have names like today's pubs. Instead they were identified by their location, which was advertised on the vessels used by their customers (these advertisements also served as property stamps). For example, one large jug found in Southwark is imprinted with the words 'LONDINI AD FANUM ISIDIS', which means 'In London by the temple of Isis.'

At the docks across the water, the old wooden landing stage was eventually replaced with a sturdy new quay, capable of holding several sea-going ships side by side. Immediately behind the wood-planked quayside lay a collection of low, stone stores into which the ships' cargoes were temporarily deposited prior to dispatch. Behind these buildings lay much larger warehouses which stored imported supplies for the town. As part of a vast empire, Londinium played host to a large number of Roman merchants, sailors and officials who hankered after goods from their homeland. Consequently, a huge variety of non-perishable commodities arrived in the port. During excavations, storage jars were found bearing inscriptions such as 'Lucius Tettius Africanus' finest fish sauce from Antipolis' and '250 ... of green olives transported by Gaius ... of Avernus.' Africanus' fish sauce – colloquially known as 'garum' – was an immensely popular condiment used to accompany a variety of foods in much the same way as tomato ketchup is used today. It was made by boiling whole fish until they had disintegrated into a paste, which was then decanted into jars and retailed both at the port and at shops throughout the province. Garum was a particularly popular accompaniment to oysters – a Roman delicacy farmed along the Thames estuary in Kent and Essex and brought by boat into the port to be sold fresh or pickled and put into storage. Oysters were eaten as snacks or hors d'oeuvres and were also believed to have miraculous medicinal properties. Roman apothecaries regularly prescribed a dose of oysters for complaints as diverse as sore throats, constipation and abscesses.

With the arrival of hundreds of Roman families in Londinium came the demand for high-quality pottery. The Celts had made their own earthenware for centuries but it tended to be rather roughly executed and was certainly too provincial for Roman tastes. Therefore the port warehouses became stacked with Samian ware (so called because it was originally made on the island of Samos) imported from Rome and Gaul. Samian pottery was a distinctive rich red/brown colour and was often decorated with classical designs in relief. It was vastly more expensive than locally produced pottery so Roman families tended to use it as tableware only, especially if important guests were visiting, in the same way as families use Wedgwood or Spode china today. The cheap locally produced pots were used for cooking where their low cost was seen as a positive boon – in the days before detergents, it was almost impossible to clean cooking vessels so once they became too dirty, the family simply threw them away and bought a new one.

Other household items imported into the dock were textiles such as silk damask, fine linen, ceramic ornaments, glassware, lamps, toys and votive offerings to the gods. Building materials from elsewhere in the British Isles were also imported to satisfy the almost constant development of the Roman city. Ragstone was brought up the Thames from Kent, tiles and brick came down from Bedfordshire and Northamptonshire, and Purbeck marble was shipped in from Dorset. In return, ships were loaded with diverse cargoes ranging from corn to large hunting dogs. Not surprisingly, one of the most successful exports from Britannia was a woollen cloth that was particularly efficient in the rain. Human cargo was also regularly transported from the Londinium docks: the quayside would have been the last sight a Celtic slave would have glimpsed of his homeland before embarking on a long and treacherous voyage to the far reaches of the empire.

Back inside the dock complex, a small market area lay close to the warehouses, used to sell perishable goods as quickly as possible.

Housewives and slaves would crowd around the stalls stacked with fresh fish, shellfish, fruit and vegetables, keeping their eye out for a bargain. Further along the riverbank, merchants and ship owners occupied smart detached houses or 'macellae' that had views over the river to the small cluster of workshops, taverns and slaughterhouses on the opposite bank. Behind them lay the lowlier homes of the dock employees. These were probably built of timber as today no archaeological evidence of them exists. Later, the dock workers became the inhabitants of London's first loft apartments when some of the old and disused warehouses were converted into domestic accommodation.

The docks were visited by a wide variety of ships with a huge selection of cargo. Although very little is known about the Roman ships that visited the port of Londinium, studies of three wrecks under the waters of the Thames at County Hall, Bermondsey and Blackfriars suggest that the largest overseas craft to dock at the port were sea-going merchant ships with wooden hulls and square sails, steered using two wooden side rudders. Larger craft weighed anchor at the mouth of the estuary where their cargo was loaded onto flat-bottomed lighters that were then steered up the Thames to the dock. Goods from other parts of Britain arrived on small sailing ships that could navigate both the coastal waters and the inland waterways. Once the ships and lighters arrived at the dock, the goods were cleared by customs officials and then unloaded.

Dockers responsible for unloading the ships had a particularly arduous job. Most goods arrived at the port in either barrels or amphorae – large storage vessels with two carrying handles either side of the neck. The barrels were fairly easy to handle as they could be rolled off the ship straight into one of the nearby warehouses, but the amphorae were a different matter altogether. On average they weighed around 100lb (50kg), although some of the larger varieties could weigh up to 220lb (100kg) – the weight of a well-built man. The dock workers no doubt dreaded the arrival of a consignment of large amphorae and cursed their weight as they lugged them into the warehouses one by one.

Due to the unpredictable nature of shipping, it is highly likely that a good proportion of Roman dock labourers were employed on a casual basis. At the time, it was impossible to tell when a ship was going to arrive at the port. During winter months, bad weather could delay vessels for days or even weeks, making a complete mockery of the schedules. Often, several ships would arrive at the same time but once they were unloaded, the dock would once again be deserted. Thus began a tradition that was to continue for nearly 2,000 years, of men queuing at the London docks to be selected for work.

A typical dock employee's family in Londinium lived unavoidably close to the breadwinner's place of work due to the fact that no point in the city was more than two miles away from the harbour. As is still the case today, their homes reflected their status in terms of size and decoration, but while the wealthy families oversaw the goings-on at the docks from their opulent 'macellae' on the waterfront, attended to by numerous slaves, the workers within the complex (who represented the majority of Londinium residents) lived a more lowly existence. Couples tended to marry very young, at the age of 15 or 16, and would immediately set about starting a family that would often grow to include five or more children. Infant mortality was a big problem in Roman Britain and despite the fact that many residents lived into their 60s and early 70s, the sheer volume of infant deaths brought the mean life expectancy of a new-born down to just 25 years. If a child survived its infancy, he or she would be educated to a greater or lesser extent depending on the amount of money the family had at their disposal. State schooling was not provided so children were either sent to private establishments or were taught at home, the basic subjects being reading and writing in both Latin and Greek and simple arithmetic. Most people seem to have been literate and wealthy Romans on secondment to Londinium regularly corresponded with friends and business associates in other provinces of the empire. A writing tablet addressed to a Londinium resident was rescued from the Walbrook in 1927. On the reverse it begins, 'Greetings to Epillicus and all his fellows' and after dealing with some mundane business affairs intriguingly requests that, 'the girl be turned into cash.' Even ordinary citizens seem to have been able to read and write as evidenced in some Latin found scratched on a Roman tile by an aggrieved worker who complained that, 'Austalis has been going off by himself every day for these 13 days.'

If the head of the family had a trade, he would in all likelihood pass his knowledge and skills onto his sons who began employment in their early teens. There was little prospect of a career for women, who had to occupy themselves with domestic chores and raising children. If a family was sufficiently wealthy, they would purchase slaves from the local market to assist them in both commercial and domestic work. In Londinium, most slaves were either Celts who had been captured as prisoners of war or children abandoned by parents who could not afford to keep them. Once sold into slavery, these people became the property of their owner and were doomed to a life of servitude with little chance of freedom. The only ways a slave could extricate himself from his situation was either by escaping, being freed by a kindly master or buying his freedom, the value of which was generally the price for which the slave had been bought.

Very few specifics are known about the families that lived in and around the Londinium docks during Roman times, although from time to time archaeologists uncover tantalising references to the city's first inhabitants. In 1806, excavations at Ludgate Hill revealed a tombstone commemorating an inhabitant named Anencletus, 'a slave of the province' who worked for the council. Another resident by the name of Turpillus engraved his name on a jar of wine and wished the drinker 'good luck', suggesting that he was perhaps a victualler or even a vineyard owner. On a gravestone found in 1980, a grieving father named Aurelius laments the death of his 10-year-old daughter, Marciana.

Another area that has revealed fascinating details of these ancient Londoners is religion. The Romans believed that their lives were quite literally in the lap of the gods. These fickle deities controlled every aspect of Roman Londoners' lives. If bad luck befell them, they reasoned that it was because they had offended one of the gods. On a more positive note, the divinities could be appeased with offerings and would look favourably on the provider of the gifts. There were many Roman gods, each with a specific area of control but subordinate to their master, the great Jupiter. The major deities included Jupiter's wife Juno, who was goddess of women; Mars, the god of war; Venus, the goddess of love and beauty; Minerva, the goddess of wisdom; and Diana, the goddess of hunting. Popular gods in Londinium included Bacchus, the god of wine, who watched over the vineyards and taverns; Vesta, the goddess of the home; and of course Neptune, god of the sea, who protected the island from invaders and ensured that ships bearing supplies or carrying passengers from the Continent had a safe passage.

As the Roman Empire expanded, new gods from other cultures were added to the Roman pantheon. For example, the Romans adopted the Egyptian goddess Isis and the Persian deity Mithras to whom a temple was erected in Londinium in the mid-third century. Following centuries underground, its rediscovery was rather ironically due to Adolf Hitler. It has since become arguably the most famous Roman ruin in the capital. In 1896, a stone slab was found in the subterranean River Walbrook depicting the god Mithras. Unfortunately its exact location was never recorded and as no other Roman artefacts were found with it, the carving was largely forgotten about. Nearly 60 years later, builders working on a bombed-out site on what had once been the east bank of the Walbrook discovered the ruins of what appeared to be an early Christian church. A team of archaeologists led by W. F. Grimes of the Museum of London were brought in to excavate the site further and to the dismay of the impatient developers, found that the remains were in fact a Roman temple to the god Mithras.

The Mithraic cult was a popular religion in third-century Roman London, with an all-male congregation comprising soldiers, government officials and wealthy merchants to whom the integral tenets of courage, honesty and purity appealed. They built an impressive temple to their god on the banks of the Walbrook, which at that time flowed at ground level. As Grimes and his team began excavating, they gradually revealed the remains of a building that was 60ft long by around 25ft wide, with a rounded triple-apse at one end within which stood a raised platform that would once have held the altar. Stretching away from the apse lay a large central nave in which the priests would have performed now obscure rites and rituals watched by the congregation who stood in long aisles either side, partially obscured by rows of classical columns. Intriguingly, excavations under the floor of the temple also revealed several small marble sculptures depicting various Roman gods including Minerva, Mercury and Serapis, who, like Isis, had roots in ancient Egyptian culture. It appeared that these figures had been deliberately hidden, suggesting that the priests had spirited them away during the reign of Constantine (AD306-337) when Christianity began to take hold in Londinium. Quite naturally, the followers of Mithras no doubt assumed that the new monotheistic religion would be a flash in the pan and their deities would eventually be retrieved from their hiding place and reinstated within the temple.

In addition to the hidden treasures, the archaeologists found an expertly carved head of Mithras amongst the ancient rubble and instantly recalled the stone relief carving that had been found in roughly the same place in 1896. Suddenly, when viewed in this context, the Victorian find took on a far greater significance and so was brought out to be studied. On close inspection, it was found that the main image on the slab depicted Mithras slaying a sacred bull, flanked by his attendants Cautes and Cautopates, the representatives of sunrise and sunset. Known as the Tauroctony, this image was central to the Mithraic faith in the same way as the crucifixion is to Christianity, making it very likely that the carving originally hung over the temple altar.

The steady stream of finds at the Walbrook dig quickly caught Londoners' imagination and the archaeological team were forced to open up the site to the general public, who were keen to see the temple ruins first hand. It quickly became one of the major tourist attractions in the city, with up to 7,000 people visiting in one afternoon and an onlooker describing the scene as 'like sales in Oxford Street'. The interest generated by the temple made it clear to all concerned that it was going to be extremely difficult to resume the building works. Once the excavators moved back in, the entire temple site would be destroyed for ever but the government refused to purchase the site. For some time it seemed that the Temple of Mithras would vanish under the bulldozers, but sustained public pressure eventually resulted in the developers offering to move the remains to a new site a short distance away in Queen Victoria Street at their own expense. This generous but probably wise move, given the mood of the public, meant that the temple was saved for posterity and the developers could sleep with a clear conscience. It can still be visited today in its new location, while the original site is now occupied by a Brutalist-inspired office block that betrays little of the mystical heritage of its location.

The Walbrook river held religious status long before the temple to Mithras was built. It had been used as a source of fresh water since the area was first developed and there is evidence that it was regularly used in rites and rituals. In the early decades of Londinium, the newly Romanised Celts continued their macabre tradition of ritually decapitating human sacrifices and depositing their heads in the Walbrook as an offering to the gods. However, the most fascinating ritual was the mystical culture of curses. Religion and superstition in Roman Londinium were so closely linked that they at times overlapped. If bad luck befell a family it was perceived that the gods were responsible; it was also possible to ask deities to exact revenge on enemies. In order to do this, a note was written and dropped into a water source such as the Walbrook, which acted as a conduit between man and divinities. One such note was discovered in the former riverbed of the Walbrook in the form of a small square piece of metal onto which the name Martia, otherwise known as Martina, had been hammered backwards – a sure sign that the writer meant Martina harm. Another curse, found in the Thames in the 1980s, asked Neptune to exact revenge within nine days on several wrongdoers including Silvicola, Sattavillus his son, Avitus and Varasius, although quite what these men had done to deserve such treatment is unclear. The most intriguing curse found to date was directed at a woman named Tretia (or Tertia) Maria who may have been blackmailing the author as the message reads, 'I curse Tretia Maria and her life and mind and memory and liver and lungs mixed up together and her words, thoughts and memory. Thus may she be unable to speak what things are concealed…'

Life for Roman Londoners, especially those labouring in and around the dock, was hard and uncertain. The absence of modern medicines meant that death could come unexpectedly and quickly, and prior to the introduction of Christianity to the capital in the fourth century there was no prospect of a heavenly afterlife. Roman Londoners could gain immortality only through the status achieved during their lifetime – the higher the status, the more likely that their name would be recorded for posterity. Most of the thousands of labourers, warehousemen and clerks that undertook the essential work at the Roman dock vanished into obscurity almost as soon as they passed away, although some such as Martina and Austalis gained immortality through curses or the graffiti of a disgruntled co-worker. However, those higher up the social ladder achieved immortality in the form of gravestones.

Roman Londoners could be buried in one of two cemeteries situated a short distance outside the city boundary. The northern burial ground was on the site now occupied by St Bartholomew's Hospital in Smithfield, while the southern graveyard lay across the river in Southwark. In the same way as we do today, Roman Londoners had a choice of being buried or cremated. To date, it is uncertain where Londinium's crematoria lay but evidence found in graveyards shows that once cremated, the deceased's ashes were placed in a large urn and buried in one of the crematoria. The actual burial of a body included a certain amount of ritual; often family and friends accompanied the coffin to the graveyard and sometimes placed items in the grave that had some significance to the person that had died. These items could range from personal possessions such as jewellery, toys or favourite drinking flagons to the downright obscure. Excavations of the Roman cemetery at Smithfield revealed bodies buried with a bell, a comb and a chicken.

After death, the Romans believed that the deceased became quite literally a shadow or 'shade' of his former self and it was important for those still living to ensure that the shades had an easy and uninterrupted descent into the underworld. If the bodies of the dead were disturbed, their shadows could come back and haunt the living so consequently Roman graveyards were always outside the city boundaries and often behind a high wall or bordered by a river to ensure peace and quiet. The tombs of the dead reflected the occupants' status. Wealthy members of society could have entire mausoleums constructed in their honour, often surrounded by tranquil gardens in which mourners could sit and contemplate their loss. The majority of Romans, including the men and women who lived and worked in Londinium's dock, would not have been able to afford the elaborate excesses of a mausoleum and so were usually buried in large communal underground chambers known as 'columbaria'. Social societies and trades guilds often purchased columbaria and sold the spaces therein to their members by subscription, which usually also included the cost of the funeral. Poorer members of society were buried with little ritual in common graves located in the furthest reaches of the cemetery. Following interment, a stone was usually erected to the deceased and dedicated to either the gods of the underworld or the shades of the dead. The names of those who erected the gravestone were also often recorded and sometimes, if finances permitted, a likeness of the deceased was carved in relief.

Although there are no existing reports of Londinium coming under any major attack after the Boudiccan revolt, the governors were obviously concerned for the city's safety. At the end of the second century, they decided that the fort in the north-western corner of the city was insufficient defence and so began construction of a huge wall which, when completed, ran right around the edge of the capital. Nearly 100,000 tons of ragstone were hauled up the Thames on barges from Kent and bonded together with mortar to make an impenetrable barricade for the city that measured a massive 20ft high by 8ft wide and ran for nearly two miles to the banks of the Thames. Once complete, the London Wall became one of the most impressive Roman building projects in the British Isles, rivalled only perhaps by Hadrian's Wall in the north of England. The wall was an incredibly imposing sight, from both within the city and from the countryside that stretched beyond it. The inner walls were reinforced by huge banks of earth from which sentries could climb on top of the wall and survey the countryside for miles around. On the outer side lay a huge ditch, which served as an almost insurmountable obstacle for any hostile invaders intending to breach the wall. For Roman Londoners, particularly those who remembered how the city looked before construction, the London Wall must have added a claustrophobic air to the streets as it loomed above the shops and houses, shading the queues of pedestrians, traders, horses, carts and livestock that crowded around its gates waiting to get in and out of the city.

The city gates boasted round-the-clock security and were protected by drawbridges that could be lifted at short notice to cut off the most obvious points of entry. There were various routes into Londinium. Watling Street ran from the sea port at Dover, over the bridge into the city and out again through Newgate towards the West Country. Goods from Camulodunum (Colchester) in the east arrived through Aldgate, while Bishopsgate provided access to the road running north to York. The thoroughfare leading out through the fort at Ludgate followed the line of today's Strand, while Stane Street led into the city across the Thames from Chichester. On busy market days, the streets in the capital, especially those on the trade routes above, must have been noisy, dirty and frenetic. Tacitus noted that Londinium 'thronged with great numbers of merchants and merchandise' as the traders brought in their goods from across the empire. Consequently, the properties in and around the docks, with panoramic views across the Thames to the south bank and beyond, became the most picturesque places in the capital and no doubt the most sought after.

By the advent of the third century AD, Londinium was a successful and busy outpost of the Roman Empire. The docks thronged with ships and the warehouses were packed so full of goods that, on occasion, more storage space had to be sought in the nearby forum. However, divisions were gradually beginning to appear across the Roman Empire and, very slowly, Londinium's fortunes began to decline.

The trouble began in the late second century when the Governor of Britain, Clodius Albinus, challenged the Emperor Septimus Severus for control of the empire. In the event, his rebellion failed and in response Britain was divided into two parts – Superior and Inferior – with Londinium becoming the capital of the former. Shortly after it was annexed, the trade routes to and from the capital from other parts of the empire began to be attacked by Saxon pirates keen to get their hands on the luxury goods destined for the wealthy inhabitants of Londinium. Ship owners began to dread voyages to Britain. In addition to the constant threat of attack whilst at sea, the levels of the Thames were beginning to fall, making it increasingly difficult to get larger ships into the dock.

In the meantime, the Saxon pirates were becoming increasingly daring in their raids and were now venturing up the Thames to plunder the city itself. The Saxon raids forced Londinium's officials to address the sticky problem of how to defend the dock and its surrounds. The huge wall that ran round the landward perimeter was extremely difficult to breach, but it was relatively easy for any invading force to enter the city via the north bank of the Thames. In an attempt to protect the rest of the capital, the officials decided to build another wall, this time around the perimeter of the docks in an attempt to stop the Saxons from venturing further into the city. This move proved to be disastrous for Londinium's dockland community as the wall effectively cut them off from the rest of the metropolis. The once easy routes out of the dock became ridiculously congested as carts laden with goods jostled to get through the narrow gate. The wall created a geographical divide between the dockland families and the rest of the citizens and, most worryingly, left them (and their businesses) at the mercy of any invaders. Once the gate to the city was closed, there was no escape. There is no surviving record of how many dock residents and workers died after being trapped behind the wall, but with little means of escape it is likely that during a raid, casualties would have been extremely high. The very reason that had made the riverfront a popular place to live – the open panorama that stretched before it – now made it the most dangerous address in Londinium. Those that could afford it no doubt relocated as quickly as possible to the safer streets behind the dock wall and a good number of businesses operating along the foreshore relocated to a new site beyond the city boundary at Shadwell that not only provided an open escape route from marauding pirates but also was able to accommodate larger vessels.

As if the Saxon raids were not enough, the increasingly beleaguered residents of Londinium were about to find themselves at the centre of a power struggle that was to further weaken the empire. In AD286, the British Governor, Carausias, decided to follow Clodius Albinus' example and declared himself Emperor of Britain. However, his reign was not destined to last and by AD293 he had been assassinated and was succeeded by his erstwhile colleague Allectus, who quickly set about acquiring as much wealth as possible by force. Realising that this rebellion needed to be nipped in the bud before it spread to other parts of the empire, Emperor Constantius Chlorus sent troops to Britain to wrest control from the usurper, a task in which they were resolutely successful. The panegyrist Eumenius wrote to Constantius of how, on reaching Londinium, his troops found Allectus' soldiers plundering the city but soon restored order, noting that 'not only did they bring safety to your subjects by the timely destruction of the enemy, but also induced a sentiment of gratitude and pleasure at the sight.' The recovery of Londinium was seen as a major victory for Rome and a medallion was struck commemorating the event on which Londinium is shown welcoming Constantius, its rightful leader, into the city. Following the removal of Allectus, the province was once again annexed and this time divided into four provinces: Britannia Prima, Britannia Secunda, Flavia Caesariensis and Maxima Caesariensis, with Londinium being the capital of the latter.

Following Constantius' retaking of the city, Londinium's fortunes appear to have been mixed. Estates surrounding the capital were enlarged and redeveloped, suggesting that their owners were experiencing a period of great prosperity. However, by the late third century the northern European markets that supplied Londinium were at the point of collapse and the province was once again under attack, this time from Saxons, Picts and Scots. Londinium's defences were improved, including the addition of at least 20 new bastions along the defensive wall, but this proved insufficient and the city came under threat on numerous occasions. The regular breaches of the wall and the subsequent destruction of the residents' homes and businesses was largely ignored by Rome until AD367 when a 'great conspiracy' by the combined hostile forces threatened to wrest control of the province away from the Romans for good. Realising that drastic measures were called for if he was to maintain control of this far-off territory, the emperor sent forth a full-scale invading army to drive the northern invaders out of the city. According to Ammianus Marcellinus, who recorded the events, Caesar's men marched to Londinium and once there 'attacked the predatory and straggling bands of the enemy who were loaded with the weight of their plunder, and having speedily routed them while driving prisoners in chains and cattle before them, he deprived them of their booty which they had carried off from these miserable tributaries of Rome.'

Despite the success of the troops, Marcellinus' description of the province as a 'miserable tributary' vividly illustrates that Rome was becoming tired of troublesome Londinium and the much-disputed lands beyond. In an attempt to deter the Saxon raiders, defences were built along the eastern coastline of Britain from Sussex to Norfolk and reconnaissance craft called 'pictae' were employed to patrol the area. Although these measures met with some success, elsewhere in the empire barbarians had managed to take control of large areas of Gaul and Spain, which seriously disrupted the trade routes between Rome and Britain. London, and indeed the rest of the country, was becoming increasingly cut off from the Roman Empire, which itself continued to become more and more fractured.

In AD407, a common soldier named Constantine declared himself emperor of the Western Empire and promptly took most of the British troops across the Channel to mainland Europe in an attempt to stop the constant invasions of the area by Germanic tribes. Left with virtually no military protection, the British people waited patiently for Constantine's return but gradually came to realise that neither he nor any of his troops were going to materialise. Fearing more devastating raids from the Picts, Scots and Saxons, the British appealed for help to the Roman Emperor Honorius but he refused to send any military support. So it was that in AD410, the Roman occupation of Britain officially ended.

2

A NEW ERA

Although Londinium ceased to be a Roman port city in the early fifth century, it would be foolish to assume that over 400 years of Roman influence was erased overnight. The people continued to live their lives in a very similar way to before and it is highly likely that some Roman merchants and businessmen stayed on in the city. However, down at the docks the departure of the Roman army, the change of government and the collapse of trade routes were catastrophic. The tall ships that once vied for space along the dock, laden with luxury goods from faraway provinces in the Mediterranean and North Africa, vanished. The vast warehouses that once held supplies waiting to be distributed among the great Roman towns across the south of England stood empty and the hauliers that had traversed the great trade routes wondered where the next job was coming from. Although there is little extant evidence from this period, it is extremely likely that, given the external factors in play, the decades following the departure of Constantine and his army saw the docks, the city beyond and indeed the whole of the South-East go into steep decline.

The almost total absence of well-organised armed forces meant that many towns in the former province of Maxima Caesariensis were susceptible to attack from hostile tribes. Fearful that Londinium and the surrounding settlements would be invaded by Picts from the north and realising that support from the Romans would no longer be forthcoming, the authorities turned in desperation to fierce warlords from Germanic tribes in northern Europe and asked for their help in return for land on which they could settle. They could not have made a worse move. Several warlords took the Britons up on their offer but soon reneged on the deal and began raiding the very areas they were supposed to be protecting. Kent suffered particularly badly at the hands of the Germanic warriors. In about AD455, an army under the command of a Danish general named Hengest attacked Aylesford. A bloody and violent conflict ensued during which Hengest's brother, Horsa, was killed, but the tribesmen finally succeeded in taking the town. With Aylesford successfully captured, Hengest turned his attentions to a nearby settlement named Crecganford (probably modern-day Crayford) and assembled his army on the town's outskirts in preparation for attack. The residents of Crecganford had no doubt heard of the horrors endured by their neighbours at Aylesford and desperately searched for a means of escape. The proximity of the town to Londinium meant that many of Crecganford's residents were familiar with the old Roman capital and knew about its high walls surrounded by impenetrable ditches and it was to here that they fled and barricaded themselves in the city.

Following the Crecganfordians' flight to Londinium, the Germanic tribes continued to terrorise and capture towns throughout the province. The victorious Hengest joined forces with another commander named Aesc and together they launched a brutal attack on a Kentish settlement known as Wippedesfloet. During the particularly ferocious battle that followed, no fewer than 12 tribal leaders of the defending armies were slain. By AD470, the warlords had developed such a fearsome reputation that townsfolk under threat would flee their homes with very little resistance, leaving the invading tribes to plunder as much bounty as they could lay their hands on, thus increasing their wealth and influence further. However, the old Roman city of Londinium stood firm. Perhaps because of its formidable fortifications, there are no contemporary reports of it coming under attack during these violent and turbulent times.

By the end of the fifth century, much of South-East England and the Midlands had been colonised by Germanic tribes. Collectively known as the Anglo-Saxons, they were comprised of three principal groups. The Jutes (including the fearsome Hengest) originated from northern Germany and Denmark, while the Saxons travelled to Britain from the Lower Saxony region of Germany. The third and probably the largest tribe originated from Angeln in Germany and were known as the Angles. In the eighth century, the Venerable Bede noted in his *Historia Ecclesiastica* that the entire Anglian nation emigrated to Britain during the preceding centuries. Whether this is true or not, certainly by AD500 much of the South-East was populated by the Angles and it seems reasonable to suppose that this warrior tribe were responsible for naming their new lands Aenglaland – the land of the Angles – which corrupted over time to England.

Following the arrival of the terrified Crecganfordians, the city of Londinium disappeared from all surviving documents for 150 years and there is no evidence that the newly arrived Saxons settled within its walls. Of course, it is possible that all trace of the Anglo-Saxons' settlement has either been lost in the mists of time or, more enticingly, has yet to be found. Archaeologists and historians have darkly suggested that perhaps the city was used as a centre for the slave trade, its high perimeter walls keeping the unfortunate captives imprisoned until they were loaded onto ships bound for the Continent. There is no doubt that the Saxons dealt in slaves and their human cargo would have left little trace. However, it is more likely that they eschewed the Roman city because its infrastructure simply did not suit their way of life. The Germanic tribes were predominantly farmers and thus required large areas of open land in which to graze their livestock and grow produce. Although Londinium could accommodate small farmsteads within its walls, they would have been insufficient for the Saxons' needs. Indeed, the Roman chronicler Ammanius noted that the Saxons avoided walled cities 'as if they were the tombs of their ancestors'.

Another reason why the Saxons disliked the Roman city was the position and layout of its dock. Unlike the Romans, who favoured sailing vessels, the early Anglo-Saxons used long, low boats powered by lines of oars, which were operated by a crew. The construction of these boats was completely different to that of Roman sailing ships. Their reduced height would have made them extremely difficult to unload at the high Roman harbour as goods would have to be lifted up on to the dock rather than lowered down to the landing stage. Consequently, the Anglo-Saxons moved their harbour further west, away from the city walls to an area of the riverbank that had an open foreshore and a shelved beach that was far more suited to their craft. A settlement soon developed around the new harbour and quickly grew into a town that stretched from the Aldwych to Whitehall, with the dock once again at its centre.

But what of Londinium? Although the Anglo-Saxons had little use for it, they seem to have respected and appreciated the building expertise of their predecessors. In the mid-ninth century, Bishop Helmstan of Winchester described the city as 'the illustrious place built by the skill of the ancient Romans.' Their appreciation of the fine way in which the city had been built prompted them to find a new use for it: in the late 500s, a Christian church was constructed in the city. Dedicated to St Paul, it was destined to enjoy a centuries-long reputation as both the centre of Christian worship for Londoners and an iconic building in its own right. The church quickly established itself as an important headquarters for the fledgling religion – as early as AD604, Ethelbert, king of Kent, used St Paul's as the venue for the consecration of Mellitus, Bishop of the East Saxons. Later, the old abandoned Roman fort in the north-west corner of the city was redeveloped into a royal palace frequented by kings of the region. Thus, 'London' divided into two settlements – the economic centre lying to the west became known as Lundenwic ('wic' meaning farm) and the walled city of Londinium was renamed Lundenburh ('burh' meaning fortified town). The idea of a city with two centres survives of course to this day in the Cities of London and Westminster.

As the years unfolded, the new Anglo-Saxon dock proved to be as successful as its Roman predecessor. By the 600s, trade was brisk, with ships journeying across the North Sea loaded with all manner of goods and by the 730s, Bede described the port as an 'emporium of many people coming by land and sea.' After centuries of obscurity, the Port of London was once again a major player in international trade. For 200 years, the Lundenwic dock remained at the foreshore that ran in front of today's Strand, backed by timber warehouses, shops and the homes of dock workers, ship owners and merchants.

Sadly, little is known about how the dock complex looked during this period as most archaeological evidence of the mainly wooden structures has long since disintegrated, but the dock's longevity combined with favourable contemporary descriptions suggest that it was highly successful. So successful in fact that by the ninth century, it had begun to attract the attention of Danish raiders who, in events that mirrored those at the end of the Roman occupation, made regular sorties down the Thames to plunder the city. The Danish attacks gradually increased in both frequency and ferocity as the attackers realised that the wealthy settlement had little means of defence. In 851, a massive army occupying a huge number of longboats rowed down the river and launched their most brutal raid to date. Fearing for their lives, the townsfolk fled to Lundenburh, whose high walls once again provided an imposing defence, and watched helplessly as the marauding Danes burned their settlement to the ground. Now homeless and fearful of reprisals, the people of Lundenwic had little choice but to retreat behind the city walls and redevelop the ruinous Roman harbour. The old city was about to experience a renaissance.

Twenty years after the disastrous Danish raid on Lundenwic, the great King Alfred came to power as ruler of the West Saxons. By 886, Alfred had moved his headquarters to Lundenburh and immediately embarked on a huge regeneration project. Using rubble from the ruins of the Roman city as foundations, he reinforced the crumbling fortifications, developed new housing and built a 'suth weorc' or 'southern fort' opposite the harbour that could protect ferries crossing the Thames from attack by hostile tribes. Over the centuries, Alfred's 'suth weorc' corrupted into Southwark, the name by which it is known today. The old Roman city's infrastructure was also reused to good effect, in particular the roads that led out of the city. In the late 19th century, the archaeologist T. W. Shore suggested that Ermine Street – the great road that led out through Bishopsgate to Lincoln and York – was named by the Anglo-Saxons after a pagan god called Irmin who drove over the night sky in a chariot, using the stars as his guide.

With the redevelopment of the city under way, Alfred handed control to his son-in-law, Ethelred, who in turn drew up yet more plans for improvement. Keen to encourage international trade, Ethelred identified the need for an efficient, modern harbour and chose a site west of the old, defunct Roman dock. Once completed, the new complex was named Ethelredshithe ('hithe' being the Old English word for 'landing place'). However, in the 12th century, the name was changed to Queenhithe in honour of Matilda, the heir of Henry I. Although the Saxon dock has long since disappeared, the area retains the name to this day.

By the 900s, Lundenburh was the largest city in Britain, populated by wealthy farmers, merchants and ship owners. The city's main export was wool, which was used to make blankets and various items of clothing and sent to numerous Saxon kingdoms across the North Sea. Unfortunately, trade did not always go smoothly. In the late eighth century, King Offa was dismayed to receive a letter of complaint from his Continental ally Charlemagne registering his dissatisfaction with the length of a consignment of woollen cloaks. Highly offended at Charlemagne's audacity, Offa responded by firing back a protest about the poor quality of grinding stones that had recently been received at the docks. It is not known whether either the cloaks or the grinding stones were replaced.

In addition to the grinding stones, the Lundenburh docks received imported goods from a variety of kingdoms. From the ninth to the 11th centuries, large amounts of pottery in the form of storage jars, bowls and cooking vessels for the home were imported from France and by the late 800s, the city's financial success was reflected in the fine fabrics that arrived at the harbour. Although much of the Anglo-Saxons' clothing was made from wool, more sophisticated garments made from silk were imported from Byzantium and the Levant, which covered parts of modern-day Palestine, Syria, Israel, Jordan and Lebanon.

Anglo-Saxon clothing comprised a loose-fitting tunic made from either linen or wool, which was belted at the waist or hip. Women's tunics were ankle length, while the men's version reached the knees and was worn with woollen leggings that were often wrapped tight against the leg with strips of linen (presumably for ease of movement). During colder times of year, wraps and cloaks were worn over the tunics in layers. Footwear consisted of sandals in summer and ankle boots in winter, both of which were fashioned from leather and fastened with laces.

Although the basic shape of clothing did not alter between rich and poor, the way clothes were embellished could distinguish the wealthier members of society from the average man on the street. In the absence of buttons, clothing was fastened using pins or brooches and the most expensive of these could be extremely ornamental, often being crafted from gold or silver and inlaid with precious stones. In addition to these, women often adorned themselves with strings of beads made from metal, glass or stones. The colour of clothing was also indicative of one's station in life. Poorer members of society wore clothes woven from wool and linen in its natural state, while their richer neighbours chose more colourful items that had been dyed using a variety of plant extracts. The most popular colour appears to have been woad, a blue dye taken from the plant *isatis tinctoria* that had been used since time immemorial for colouring fabrics, tattoos and even as a medicinal treatment for open wounds.

Much Anglo-Saxon trade was conducted with the Frisians, a tribe of people living along the coast of Holland and Germany, and tribes living along the Scandinavian coastline. Numerous coins minted in Lundenburh have been found at Saxon sites in these areas and the rules and regulations of the ports were extremely similar, thus making trading easier.

In addition to international trade, the Anglo-Saxon docks were also used for home-grown produce and materials. Wood for building or fuel was brought into the city on barges from the forests that surrounded Lundenburh. Not surprisingly, timber was a sought-after commodity that was so susceptible to theft that King Alfred was forced to rule that 'if any man burn or hew another's wood without leave, let him pay for every great tree with five shillings.' The forests around the city also provided a natural habitat for pigs, cattle and deer – wealthy merchants often rode out there to hunt. The sheer magnitude of woodland and forests surrounding Lundenburh are reflected in many modern place names. For example, areas as geographically diverse as St John's Wood, Norwood and Waltham Forest all derive their names from the time when these areas were covered with trees and bushes. In addition to timber and livestock, the Anglo-Saxons grew a wide variety of produce that was brought into the docks along the Thames and the River Lea. There were also vineyards close to the city where highly alcoholic wines were produced.

As has always been the case, Anglo-Saxon London was a very cosmopolitan place. The buoyant West Saxon economy meant that the city was a lucrative trading centre and merchants from the coastal settlements across the North Sea arrived in their hundreds. In order to encourage the newcomers to stay, local laws were passed allowing Scandinavians to live wherever they pleased in the city all year round. Even the troublesome Danes were permitted to enter Lundenburh for business purposes. Saxon London dealt in three currencies: Wessex pounds consisted of 45 shillings and each shilling was comprised of five pence, while Mercian pounds were made up of 60 shillings, each of which was worth four pence. The Mercian traders also had a coin called the 'thrymsa', which was worth three pence and survived until relatively recently in the form of the old three-penny bit. The Danes dealt in 'ora', which was valued at between 16 and 20 pence; the 'mark', which was worth 100 pence; and the 'mancus', which was comprised of 30 pence.

Apart from coinage, very little from Lundenburh has survived. The Anglo-Saxons were strongly connected to the land and used natural materials in their homes and at their places of work. The biodegradable nature of these materials means that precious little has survived the test of time. However, excavations of Saxon burial sites outside the city walls have revealed clues to their way of life in the form of objects buried with the deceased. A selection of spears and knives in male graves show that the men were required to be both hunters and warriors in addition to farming the land. Weaving and sewing implements in female tombs suggest that the womenfolk were employed in the hugely important wool industry and were responsible for turning the raw material into the highly prized cloths that became the city's main export.

Life in and around the port of Lundenburh was largely conducted out of doors. Saxon houses were primitive affairs roughly constructed from wood with a thatched roof. The interior consisted of just one open room, the only feature of which was a large hearth used for cooking, light and heat. These hearths were extremely hazardous and could quickly blaze out of control if they were not closely watched, so houses, streets and occasionally entire neighbourhoods were destroyed by fire. Even with the hearth under control, the interior of a typical Lundenburh house was smoky, dirty and dark. Consequently, the residents stayed out as much as they possibly could and tended to use the house purely for sleeping and sheltering from the elements, which made for a very social community.

Although life in Lundenburh was sociable, the average resident had little time for hobbies or pastimes and even special occasions were often linked to work. For example, races held on Plough Monday (the first Monday after 12th Night) guaranteed that the fields got tilled in record time and competitive equestrian events ensured that Lundenburh had enough skilled horsemen to defend its walls should the city come under attack. One such event is described in the epic tale *Beowulf*:

> *The warriors let their bay horses go*
> *A contest for the best horse*
> *Galloping through whatever path looked fair.*

Lundenburh's horses were also extensively used in hunting – a hugely fashionable pastime among the middle classes. Once the working day was done, the huntsmen would ride out to one of the forests of Middlesex in pursuit of quarry. Deer were a popular target as virtually all the animal could be used – the meat for food, the hide for warmth and the bones and antlers for tools and weapons – but wolves were also regularly hunted, to the extent that by the end of the 10th century they were almost extinct. Wealthier members of city society, who could afford the luxury of indulging in pastimes purely for their own sake, often rode out to the heaths to practise falconry, using birds brought to the city by Scandinavian traders who captured and trained them before selling them to the highest bidder.

In addition to sporting activities, socialising was a big part of Anglo-Saxon culture. Games were a particularly popular diversion, with dice and marbles being played regularly along with an obscure board game known as Taefl, which seems to have been similar to chess inasmuch that two opposing 'armies' embarked on a complex game of strategy. The *Codex Exoniensis*, a book of Anglo-Saxon verse, says of Taefl: 'The two shall sit round at Taefl, until their troubles glide off them, they forget their cruel fortunes, and have joy on the board.'

Storytelling and music (sometimes combined) were also a popular community pastime. Like the ancient Greeks, the Anglo-Saxons employed professional storytellers called 'scops' who would tour around relating bloody tales of ancient battles and moralistic parables, often accompanied by musical instruments. These storytelling sessions were well attended and seem to have been similar to today's recitals and concerts. The telling of stories was also popular within the home, with riddles being particular favourites. Some of these riddles were unexpectedly poignant, such as this example about a shield:

> I am all on my own,
> Wounded by iron weapons and scarred by swords.
> I often see battle.
> I am tired of fighting.
> I do not expect to be allowed to retire from warfare
> Before I am completely done for.
> At the wall of the city, I am knocked about

And bitten again and again.
Hard-edged things made by the blacksmith's hammer attack me.
Each time I wait for something worse.
I have never been able to find a doctor who could make me better
Or give me medicine made from herbs.
Instead the sword gashes all over me grow bigger day and night.

Others were very similar to modern nursery rhymes, such as this riddle describing a cow. The first line refers to its udder, the second its legs, the third its horns, the fourth its eyes and the last its tail:

Four dilly-dandies
Four stick standies
Two crookers
Two lookers
And a wig wag.

The Anglo-Saxon residents of Lundenburh lived rich, social, hard lives that were constantly overshadowed by the threat of attack. The city was very different to its Roman predecessor Londinium, which had developed into an advanced culture that was very urban in nature. By contrast, the city's first Anglo-Saxon residents led a rural, unindustrialised existence and, as such, had no need for the luxuries so coveted by the Romans. Their household goods were roughly made and carried little decoration, their clothing was less sophisticated and their homes were little more than huts. Although local government existed in Saxon London, it was not the well-oiled municipal machine of Roman times. Most importantly, the Anglo-Saxons were the last Londoners to have a true connection to the land. Almost everything they did was inextricably linked to their surroundings and their daily lives were largely controlled by Mother Nature. The elements were feared and respected and although Christianity had firmly taken hold in the city by the time of King Alfred, the ghosts of the old pagan gods still haunted its streets, especially during times of hardship.

However, by the time Ethelred died in 911, Lundenburh had evolved and its port had grown into an international trading centre that rivalled its Roman predecessor in terms of productivity and diversity. Goods arrived from as far afield as the Middle East to satisfy the demands of a prosperous population. Following Ethelred's demise, the city fell under the direct control of a succession of Anglo-Saxon monarchs who continued to increase its commercial status by introducing new industries such as metalworking. By the mid-900s, the city had become so densely populated that King Athelstan saw fit to divide it into 20 separate wards. An alderman was appointed to each of these areas to oversee the trades and commerce that operated therein and to ensure that taxes were paid to the newly appointed Portreeve, a predecessor of sorts to today's Revenue and Customs.

Unsurprisingly, the wealth within the city attracted the attention of the criminally minded and soon after the division of the wards a Peace Guild was established to apprehend felons. Although the Peace Guild met with some success, it was unable to control the numerous counterfeiters that operated in the narrow alleyways that ran through the crowded city. In an attempt to remedy the situation, King Ethelred II issued the 'Laws of London', which reduced the number of mints allowed to operate within the city and instructed officials to 'take care to see to those who make false money and transport it through the country.' Ethelred's reign was not only plagued with troubles concerning the control of the economy. During his time in power, Danish fleets appeared in the Thames and threatened the city on several occasions. In 994, ships under the command of the descriptively titled Sweyn Forkbeard launched a blistering attack on the city's docks and although his men 'suffered worse harm than they ever thought any citizens would do to them', the battle prompted the King to relocate the entire dock complex. The harbour was moved east to Billingsgate and a new, very low bridge was built just beyond it in an attempt to stop hostile ships from docking close to the centre of the city. While this new layout effectively shielded much of Lundenburh from attack, it once again put the dock workers and the surrounding community in great peril as they were now potentially the front line of any future attacks. No doubt those that could, swiftly relocated to homes that lay behind the newly constructed bridge. At first, the bridge did a good job of deterring hostile ships. Forkbeard returned in 1010, but failed to gain control of the city after the feisty residents 'resisted with full battle.' However, three years later, another Danish attack met with greater success and, after a bloody conflict, Forkbeard entered the walled city victorious, forcing Ethelred to flee to the Continent.

Sweyn Forkbeard did not enjoy his newly acquired city for long. Just a year after his victory, the Danish warlord died, leaving Lundenburh under the control of his son, the great King Cnut. After learning of Forkbeard's death, Ethelred hastily assembled an army and set sail for England. Having overseen the relocation of the docks himself, the King was fully aware of the problems associated with navigating ships under the bridge but succeeded in thinking up a devious plan. Under his command, the Anglo-Saxon ships rowed across the Channel and made their way up the Thames but stopped a short distance downstream from the heavily defended bridge. Here Ethelred sent men ashore with the instruction to rip as many roofs from the local houses as possible and bring them on board. Once this mission had been accomplished, the ships rowed towards the bridge. As had been expected, it was heavily manned by Danish troops who lost no time in bombarding the Anglo-Saxons with arrows, spears and any other missile they could lay their hands on. However, Ethelred's men simply raised the plundered roofs above their heads and using them as giant shields, managed to steer their ships under the bridge and throw ropes around the structure's supporting posts. They then began to row back down the river with all the force they could muster, pulling the bridge and the Danish garrison into the swirling waters of the Thames. With the river now free from obstruction, the Anglo-Saxons docked their ships at the old landing stage and marched up the bank to reclaim the city. This heroic victory became a popular tale over the ensuing centuries and legend has it that it was the inspiration for the nursery rhyme 'London Bridge Is Falling Down'.

Although it was strategically brilliant, Ethelred's victory was destined to be short-lived. Like his nemesis Sweyn Forkbeard, he died shortly after reclaiming his city in 1016. Cnut, who had been holed up in the Danish territories since his humiliating defeat, decided to launch another attack on the coveted city and once again sailed up the Thames ready for battle. Perhaps unbeknownst to him, Ethelred had swiftly rebuilt the obstructive bridge, which was now defended so heavily that it proved quite impenetrable. Cnut and his men were forced to spend some considerable time digging a channel around the foot of the bridge on the south bank while under almost constant bombardment from the Anglo-Saxons, so they could manoeuvre their ships to a feasible point from which to launch an attack. Once the Danish fleet had been dragged round to the west side of the bridge, the exhausted men camped out in the old city of Lundenwic and waited for an opportune moment to attack which, in the event, never came. On hearing of the Danes' arrival at the 'Ald Wych', Ethelred's cowardly son King Edmund fled the city and sent representatives to negotiate with Cnut over territory. Not surprisingly, Cnut did not treat the delegation at all seriously and proclaimed himself King of the West Saxons without hesitation.

Once back on the throne, the Danish king wasted no time in rewarding himself for his efforts on the battlefield. He levied a redemption tax on his new kingdom that succeeded in filling his coffers with 80,000 pounds, of which 10,500 pounds came from the wealthy but troublesome capital of Lundenburh. Although King Cnut had taken control of his new kingdom by force, he emerged as one of the era's greatest monarchs. Lundenburh thrived during his reign, mainly because he persuaded thousands of successful Danish merchants to set up businesses in the city. The docks thrived and were expanded to include sizeable shipyards where all manner of craft, from small lighters to large seagoing ships, were built. By the time Cnut died in 1035, Lundenburh's docks and the city beyond were experiencing a period of unprecedented prosperity. However, the King's death brought with it a new threat that would change the face of the docks, the city and indeed the whole kingdom forever.

Cnut was first succeeded by his eldest son, Harold Harefoot, but Harold died in 1040. Power was passed to his brother Hardacnut, but he too died just two years later and the crown passed to Cnut's stepson, Edward the Confessor. Edward was a serious-minded and pious individual who, having spent much of his life in Normandy, brought Norman influence and trade into the city. He was also responsible for reviving the old 'twin city' set-up when he founded his palace and adjoining abbey on an island in the Thames a few miles upstream from Lundenburh. His palace and grounds have long since been replaced by the Houses of Parliament (which retain the ancient name of the Palace of Westminster) but Westminster Abbey still remains on the site Edward chose for it nearly 1,000 years ago.

In 1066, just a year after his beloved abbey was completed, Edward the Confessor died leaving no obvious heir. His old ally William, Duke of Normandy came forward claiming that Edward had promised him the kingdom, but the Royal Council made the decision that the crown should be passed to Edward's brother-in-law, Harold Godwinson. This pronouncement proved to be pivotal in the history of Britain. No sooner had Harold been crowned king in Westminster Abbey than an incensed William of Normandy mustered his troops and set sail for the English coast. Lundenburh and its docks would never be quite the same again.

3

THE REBIRTH OF LONDON

On learning that Harold had been crowned king, William of Normandy assembled a huge army comprising over 8,000 men and, on 28 September 1066, a vast fleet of 700 ships set sail for England. Hearing of William's arrival, King Harold hastily recalled his men, who were exhausted having only just repelled an attempted invasion of Norwegian Vikings near York, and headed for the Kent coast. The result of the ensuing conflict is well documented, not least by the exquisite Bayeux Tapestry. However, what is not so well understood is that William did not conquer the entire kingdom in one fell swoop. Back in London, news of King Harold's death on the battlefield threw the city into chaos. Those who had enjoyed land and power under Harold were extremely reluctant to jeopardise their positions by surrendering to the Norman Duke and crisis meetings were held to discuss who might be put forward as heir to the throne. After much discussion, Edgar the Aethling – a teenage grandson of the late King Edmund – was deemed most worthy successor and the boy was swiftly proclaimed monarch.

The wealthy landowners had good reason to oppose the Norman invaders, but the ordinary citizens of Lundenburh were reluctant to engage in battle to defend a young boy's dubious right to the throne. Their hesitancy increased when the Norman army arrived at Southwark and proceeded to set light to the settlement, creating a macabre spectacle for those watching from the north bank of the Thames. The destruction of Southwark proved decisive. The people of Lundenburh agreed to submit to the Normans, William entered the city triumphant and was crowned king at Westminster Abbey on Christmas Day. Edgar, the young pretender to the throne, was initially taken into custody but eventually gained his freedom and went on to play a crucial role in several Anglo-Saxon uprisings in the north of England, all of which were suppressed. He eventually settled in Scotland and is thought to have died there *circa* 1126.

By the time of Edgar's death, the old Saxon capital of Lundenburh had been reborn as the Norman city of London and the foundations for the metropolis we know today had been laid. William regarded it as separate to the rest of the kingdom – London is not mentioned in the Domesday Book. The inhabitants' peaceful surrender to the King was rewarded through the granting of a charter in which the new monarch stated: 'I give you to know that I will that ye be all those laws worthy that ye were in King Edward's day. And I will that every child be his father's heir after his father's day, and I will not suffer that any man offer you any wrong.'

So it was that the residents of London were permitted to continue running their city in exactly the same way as they had before. From William's point of view, the wording of the charter shows that he was fully aware of the wealth being created in the city and wisely adhered to the modern adage, 'If it's not broken, don't fix it.' However, his attitude is remarkably generous when viewed in historical context. Following the Norman invasion, a huge number of Saxon landowners saw their property confiscated and redistributed among William's allies. Everyone who lived on these lands automatically became the servant of the new landowner. The fact that Londoners remained answerable only to the King gave them the incentive to develop and expand their businesses without fearing that all the profit from their labour would line a French baron's pocket.

William's recognition of the economic importance of London and its docks is underlined by the commencement of a major building project close to the harbour at Billingsgate in 1078. Keen to create an imposing building that would simultaneously symbolise Norman power while also serving as a protective fortress for his beloved London, he commissioned the construction of a huge tower behind the south-east corner of the old Roman wall. The result was the White Tower, now the central building in the Tower of London complex and one of London's premier landmarks. The White Tower was designed by Gundulf, a Norman bishop who was also responsible for the castle at Colchester in Essex. It is 90ft high by over

100ft wide, with walls that measure 15ft thick at their base. Tall turrets, which at the time afforded 360-degree views across the open countryside that surrounded the city, made any approaching hostile force very easy to spot. This masterpiece of Norman construction took nine years to complete and continued to be developed into the 13th century when Henry III constructed its first effective moat and whitewashed the exterior walls, giving it the name 'the White Tower'.

Upstream from the Tower, against the eastern edge of the city wall on land now occupied by numbers 12 & 13 Upper Thames Street, stood Baynard's Castle and its moated keep, Montfitchet Tower. Built by Ralph Baynard, one of William's most trusted commanders, it had a dual use as fortress and family home. Following Ralph's death it passed to William Baynard (probably his son), and then to the Fitz Walters, a Norman family with familial links to the Baynards. The castle remained in the possession of the Fitz Walter family for over 100 years until 1275, when Robert Fitz Walter sold the building and all its surrounding land to the church. Three years later, the old castle was demolished to make way for a church and cloisters for the Friar's Preachers, but this was not the end for Castle Baynard. Just over 60 years later, the name cropped up again, this time referring to a building further east along the riverfront. Whether or not this new castle had been constructed by the Fitz Walters is unknown, but it was certainly held in high regard by London's dignitaries. By the 1450s, the new Castle Baynard had passed into the hands of the Earls of Richmond and in 1461 it gained royal status when it was granted to Cecily, Duchess of York, the mother of Edward IV. By now, the 'castle' had become more of a small estate with a series of outbuildings, servants' quarters and impressive gardens leading down to the banks of the Thames. Its location in the heart of the city made it a prime piece of real estate and an ideal present for a royal bride-to-be. In 1540, it was bequeathed to Anne of Cleves just before her doomed marriage to Henry VIII. Despite its central situation, there is no evidence that Anne ever lived in Castle Baynard and after her death in 1557, it gradually sank into relative obscurity as a city pied-à-terre for the Earl of Pembroke. It was eventually burnt down in 1666 during the devastating Great Fire of London, but its original owner's name lived on when the site was redeveloped as Baynard's Castle Wharf.

The third major building project embarked on by the Normans along the north bank of the Thames was the first incarnation of the notorious Fleet Prison. It stood on an eyot in the mouth of the Fleet River on what today is Farringdon Street and was an imposing and sobering site to Londoners going about their business at the adjacent docks. Built of stone, the prison measured over 40ft long by 35ft wide, with walls measuring over 6ft thick. Probably intentionally mirroring the architecture of the White Tower, it had turrets on each corner from which sentries could keep an eye on the inmates below. In later centuries, the Fleet Prison became a debtors' prison where sometimes entire families were incarcerated until they could somehow find the means to pay back their creditors. During their stay, the inmates were forced to pay for their food and lodging thus adding to their debts. Somewhat understandably, the Fleet Prison was loathed by Londoners and was burnt down by angry mobs during the Peasants' Revolt in 1381 and the Gordon Riots of 1780. It was finally demolished in 1846.

As the imposing edifices of the White Tower, Baynard's Castle and the Fleet Prison rose along the banks of the Thames, the old Saxon dock underwent a complete transformation. Prior to the arrival of the Normans, the London docks had dealt with relatively small ships carrying limited cargoes. The size and low construction of these vessels meant that the easiest way to offload the goods was to pull the ship up on the riverbank and sell direct from the boat. However, developments in shipbuilding during the 11th century meant that by the time the Normans arrived, larger ships capable of carrying up to 100 tons of cargo were beginning to ply their trade across the Channel. These comparatively huge vessels were far too large to pull up on the foreshore and their cargoes too vast to be sold from the hold. The old beach market system had to change.

The Norman redevelopment of the docks brought with it a feeling of confidence and optimism among the city's merchants and landowners. It seemed to them that the Norman monarchs were committed to creating a buoyant economy and the arrival of many hundreds of families, staff and servants from across the Channel had increased the city's population significantly, thus increasing demand for consumer goods, fuels and building materials. This new-found optimism prompted the owners of the land at the old Saxon harbour to embark on an unprecedented expansion programme. From the mouth of the Fleet River in the west to William's White Tower in the east, new quays were built out into the Thames covering the old beach markets on the riverbank below. Much of the work was privately funded by consortiums of landowners, merchants, ship owners and fishermen, all of whom had a vested interest in the efficient running of the port. With the new quays in place, London was now capable of receiving even the largest ships.

However, there was another problem to surmount before the city could forge ahead as a truly international port. The Saxon method of trading direct from the ships meant that there had been virtually no need for any form of warehousing close to the quays. In addition, the dock was still confined behind the old defensive wall thus seriously limiting any prospect of expansion. It soon became clear that the ancient wall had to go and so the structure that had led to the demise of the Roman docks was finally demolished, leaving the way clear for the Port of London to expand with very little hindrance. New masonry warehouses were built over the wall's foundations providing a functional backdrop to spacious timber quays that stretched out over the river. On the western bank of the Walbrook, wine merchants built a dock and warehousing for the sturdy wooden kegs sent by their monastic suppliers in the Rouen region of France. Their speculative redevelopment project paid great dividends in 1152 when King Stephen acquired the profitable wine-growing lands of Gascony that lay in a temperate region close to the Spanish border. On the opposite bank of the Walbrook lay the dock for the German wine ships, which jostled for position with their French competitors as they picked their way down the shallow waters of the Thames. The Port of London was now world class, capable of handling virtually every type of cargo and its merchants, ship owners and warehouse proprietors prospered. In the mid-1170s, William Fitz Stephen wrote:

> Amongst the noblest and celebrated cities of the world, London, the capital of the kingdom of England, is one of the most renowned, possessing above all others abundant wealth, extensive commerce, great grandeur and magnificence ... There is also in London, on the bank of the river, amongst the wineshops which

are kept in ships and cellars, a public eating house: there every day, according to the season, may be found viands of all kinds, fish large and small, coarser meat for the poor, more delicate for the rich ... To this city, from every nation under heaven, merchants bring their commodities by sea.

As trade in London flourished, many hundreds of miles away on the chilly Baltic coast events were taking place that would result in the arrival of the docks' first major immigrant community. During the 12th century, the German town of Luebeck was at the centre of the northern European fishing industry. Demand for catches brought in from the Baltic Sea (especially herring) regularly outstripped supply and the Luebeck merchants realised that their potential sales territory was almost limitless if they could just solve a major problem. In the absence of any refrigeration methods, the storage of fish was problematic to say the least, especially during the warm summer months when catches could become inedible within a matter of hours, rendering transportation across any great distance an impossibility. However, a solution lay close at hand. The town of Hamburg, on the opposite side of the Jutland peninsula, had access to salt mines, the product of which could be used to preserve the fish. Talks opened between the two groups of merchants, a trading alliance was formed and before long, Luebeck's fish exports were going through the roof. The success of the towns' alliance caught the attention of other cities along the Baltic shore: by 1150, the coalition had grown to incorporate not only the Baltic ports but also inland cities such as Cologne and began to trade under the collective name of the Hanseatic League. League members soon found that their trading alliance afforded them much more than the ability to share goods and services. The sheer number of businesses now involved enabled them to control the markets within which they traded, which by now included timber, furs and wine as well as salt and fish. The alliance also protected the merchants' investments. Medieval ships were constantly under threat from the elements and piracy. Pirate ships lurked in the waters surrounding the European coastline waiting to attack vessels laden with valuable cargoes. Luckier victims of the pirates only had their goods stolen. Others watched helplessly as the sea bandits made off with their entire vessel. The

Hanseatic League realised that they could protect themselves against wholesale loss by spreading their cargoes over several ships which would then travel in a convoy to their destination, giving additional protection. Members of the League took shares in these vessels so no single merchant would have to bear the cost of the sinking or theft of a ship. This co-operative business practice combined with a range of goods that were in constant demand meant that the Hanseatic League quickly became the most powerful commercial alliance in Europe. With this power came the ability to negotiate special privileges with the countries to which their goods were exported.

In England, wine merchants from the Cologne branch of the League held talks with the new monarch, Henry II, and managed to negotiate a deal that would result in a manyfold increase in their collective wealth. Naïvely unaware of the potentially catastrophic damage such a deal might inflict on his own merchants, the King agreed to allow the members of the League to trade freely throughout the country and waived any import duty on the goods they brought through the docks. No doubt keen to reserve the best shipments for himself at bargain prices, he also gave the German merchants their own dock and warehouses close to the site of the original German wine quay on the Walbrook's east bank.

The Hanseatic League's new English headquarters were situated in the heart of the medieval dock complex. On its northern border lay Roperestrate, or Ropemakers Street, the home of the men and women who made one of the docks' most essential commodities. Rope played a vital part in virtually every stage of the import or export process. It was used to secure goods on the carts that arrived from the makers' yards, on the cranes and winches that lifted goods onto ships and, of course, on the rigging of the ships themselves. A map of any dock area from the 13th century right through to the 1700s would include numerous structures called 'rope walks' surrounding the quays and wharfs. These were long, thin buildings in which the raw materials were laid out and then twisted together to form the rope. As ships got bigger, the ropes got longer and consequently so did the rope walks. It was impossible to splice rope for ships' rigging as the double width of the spliced portion would not fit through the numerous buckles and pulleys. By the time the Hanseatic League arrived at their new premises in London, Roperestrate would have been a busy thoroughfare heaving with carts delivering hemp to the manufactories and loading up with long, heavy coils of rope destined for the ships that lay waiting in the docks.

The Hanseatic League's property was separated from the noisy Roperestrate by a high wall, immediately behind which they constructed their guild hall. The League were keen to make their mark in the Port of London and consequently created a building the like of which Londoners had never before seen. Using the finest Caen stone from Normandy, they built the largest mercantile structure in the entire kingdom. The finished building was up to 100ft long by 33ft wide and was set over two floors. The ground floor was used as a massive stock room where wine and other commodities were stored in bays separated by a series of columns that supported a fine vaulted ceiling. Upstairs, the floor space was divided into a large hall in which the merchants dined and socialised, some offices and living quarters for the resident traders and even a row of latrines, the contents of which were disgorged into the alleyway below. Outside, the guild hall led onto a private quay at which the League's ships docked and offloaded their cargo.

By the time the Hanseatic League moved into their new headquarters, the old timber bridge was virtually all that remained of the riverfront's Saxon heritage. Compared with the impressive royal fortresses that surrounded it, the bridge must have looked ramshackle, outmoded and a little embarrassing to the owners of the smart new quays and warehouses. Consequently, the decision was made to replace it with a modern masonry version. Peter, Chaplain of Colechurch, was employed as architect and, in 1176, building work commenced. Peter's design was an architectural masterpiece befitting the industrious and optimistic environment in which it would stand. The new bridge was over 800ft long and was supported by 20 arches erected on man-made islands built at shallow sites across the river. A drawbridge was built into the structure. This not only allowed larger ships to pass through to the quays that lay on the bridge's west side but also acted as a defence that could be raised to prevent any hostile forces entering the city. Near the centre of the bridge lay a chapel dedicated to St Thomas à Becket, the newly acquired patron saint of London, flanked by rows of terraced houses that teetered precipitously on the bridge's edge.

Building of the new bridge was slow and laborious. It took 13 years for the construction team to reach the south bank and work was not fully complete until 1209. Even after building work had ceased, it quickly became apparent that the bridge would require almost constant maintenance. Fires regularly broke out in the tightly packed houses and the drawbridge was in almost constant use so needed regular repairs. Medieval winters were significantly colder than today and the Thames sometimes froze over for weeks at a time, damaging the bridge masonry in the process. The bridgehouse account rolls show that stone was shipped from as far afield as Normandy to make the necessary repairs. In addition to this, the mid-stream islands on which the bridge was supported had to be constantly shored up to stop them from washing away as the fast-flowing waters of the Thames rushed past. 'Tidemen' were employed to maintain the bridge supports and theirs was one of the most treacherous jobs in London. Large wooden piles known as starlings were driven into the islands to protect the infrastructure, but they often either washed away or were damaged by passing vessels. The tidemen kept a close eye on the starlings and at low tide would row out to replace and repair them, taking great care to evacuate as soon as the tide began to rise for fear of capsizing and being sucked under by the whirling currents that ran around the islands.

At first it appears that funds for the maintenance of the bridge came out of the city coffers but, in 1281, the works became so costly that tolls were introduced. Pedestrians were charged one farthing to cross the bridge, while those on horseback were levied one penny plus an additional halfpenny for each pack of goods being carried. Later, considerable damage caused by carts with iron-clad wheels resulted in the vehicles being banned from the bridge altogether for fear that they might cause a total collapse. Down below in the murky Thames, tolls were also introduced for ships wishing to pass through to the western quays. The bridgehouse accounts reveal that by the late 14th century, ships had to pay one penny to have the drawbridge raised. Over 2,000 tolls were paid for this service every year, showing just how much traffic was entering the western quays at this time.

During the medieval period, work at the docks was erratic and seasonal. In spring and early summer, around 250 vessels would enter the port every month; however, in January the figure dropped to around 80. The owners of the quays would not know when a ship was arriving until it was spotted in the Thames. As soon as they received word that it was on its way, they called for labour by sending heralds out into the streets blowing long trumpets. Although this method of calling men to work seems archaic and almost comical, the sound would have been met with great relief by the casual dock workers, especially during the lean winter months.

4

MERCHANTS AND MONOPOLIES

By the beginning of the 13th century, London's rejuvenated docks were experiencing a period of great affluence. The archaeologist Gustav Milne described the city as a 'magnet for the medieval elite' and the numerous quays that now stretched along the Thames from the Tower to Baynard's Castle were interspersed with impressive residential properties providing homes for highly successful merchants, members of the clergy and prominent landowners. The Earl of Norfolk had a city residence called Bigod House at Broken Wharf, Arundel House was occupied by the Bishop of Bath, while close by, the Bishop of York stayed in the aptly named York House.

By 1203, an eighth of the total tax collected throughout England came from London, and a good proportion of that would have originated from the docks. The arrival of the Hanseatic League encouraged more international trade and country folk flocked to the capital looking for work. The narrow semi-rural lanes of Saxon Lundenburh became crammed with houses, shops, inns and offices. In between the waterfront quays, thin thoroughfares overshadowed by sturdy stone warehouses led down to the water's edge. These tiny pathways were all that remained of the common causeways that had existed since time immemorial, providing a much-needed place for Londoners to irrigate their livestock and obtain water for their own consumption. As an increasing number of these common causeways became enclosed by the quay owners, the few remaining access points to the river on the north bank became overcrowded and extremely dirty. Those with properties abutting the river built private stairs down to the water so they would not have to mix with the riff-raff who crowded onto the common waterfront, surrounded by industrial waste and effluent from the numerous latrines that emptied their malodorous contents into the Thames.

As London's population grew, the government decided to divide the city into wards in an attempt to bring greater order. The docks comprised seven of these new divisions, each of which specialised in handling specific commodities and had its own particular civic duties. The quays in Baynard Castle Ward handled mainly wood and building supplies; Queenhithe's main commodity was fish, closely followed by salt, much of which was used as a preservative. Vintry Ward rather obviously took delivery of wine, while further east, Dowgate's main cargo was hay. Oysters were brought to Bridge Ward (which also took responsibility for the bridge itself) and the ancient landing stage at Billingsgate handled all manner of goods from coal to corn. Finally, the Tower Ward retained its traditional role as the quay that dealt with the export of wool and its byproducts.

The officials of each ward were also responsible for maintaining law and order and ensuring that their quays remained in a presentable state. Men from Billingsgate and Dowgate were responsible for the area of the port that lay east of the bridge while the western portion was patrolled by sergeants from Vintry, Queenhithe and Castle Baynard. These men were a combination of modern policeman and council inspector and were not terribly popular with the ward residents, especially those with dishonest inclinations. Particularly in busy seasons, the docks were a relatively easy place from which to thieve or indulge in business practices that were not strictly legal. Many a dock labourer was tempted to leave the quay after a busy day unloading ships with some of the cargo secreted about his person and during the hard winter months it would be fair to surmise that this temptation became too great to be resisted.

In addition to theft, the local market traders constantly tried to gain the upper hand on their competitors by indulging in dodgy deals, the most popular of which was 'regrating.' This nefarious business transaction was usually conducted with goods such as food, wine or ale and comprised two stages. Step one was known as 'forestalling' and involved the market trader offering to buy up an entire consignment of goods direct from a recently docked ship. Obviously this proposition was very attractive to the vendor as it meant they could get rid of their cargo in one fell swoop rather than having to go to the expense of taking it to market. Consequently, the goods were sold at an extremely competitive price and the market trader could move on to step two. Once the deal was secured, the purchaser took the goods to market himself. Confident in the knowledge that he now had a temporary monopoly on the commodity in question, he could sell or 'regrate' his stock at an inflated price, thus making himself a quick and tidy profit. Regrating was justifiably frowned on. The church considered regraters to be 'manifest oppressors of the poor' and a royal statute from 1274 described a typical regrater as a man who 'hurries out before other men, sometimes by land and sometimes by water, to meet grain, fish, herring or other kinds of goods coming for sale by land or water, thirsting for evil profit (and contriving) to carry off these goods unjustly and sell them much more dearly.' Keen to maintain a fair and open trade on cargoes brought into the docks, the ward officials shared the church and crown's dim view of regrating and had the power to seize any goods they suspected were being traded in this way. If found guilty, the trader would be fined and repeat offenders were banished.

Overall governing of the city fell to the Common Council, which was presided over by the elected Mayor aided by aldermen and councillors from each ward. By and large the Common Council was left to run the city as it saw fit. However, by the mid-1200s, some of its members were becoming increasingly frustrated with the King, who took every opportunity to meddle with their affairs and remove those from office who disagreed with him. Crucially, the monarch also had the power to raise their taxes whenever he needed extra funds and force traders to give preferential treatment (and prices) to his supporters. By the middle of the 13th century, Henry III was exercising this power regularly and enthusiastically with little regard for the consequences. Divisions began to emerge within the Common Council that quickly spread and exploded onto the streets, severely threatening the stability of the entire country. Leading the cause for those who wanted Henry's power to be curtailed was Simon de Montfort, Earl of Leicester, while London's royalist perspective was defended with equal passion by one of the docks' most prominent merchants – John de Gisors.

The de Gisors family had originally arrived in London with William I and over the intervening years had set up a very successful business importing wine from Gascony. By the time John was born in about 1220, the family held high status as one of the docks' major employers, who in addition to their import business owned a fleet of ships. John reinforced the family's status by marrying the sister of Arnold Fitzthedmar, the alderman of the Hanseatic League, and by 1240 his social networking skills were rewarded when he was elected alderman of Vintry Ward.

Like many of the city's wealthiest merchants, the de Gisors lived in a splendid house on the banks of the Thames, close to their wine wharf and adjacent warehouses in the parish of St Martin. John evidently selected his Gascony wines well and the consistent quality of his product soon attracted the attention of the royal household, to whom he was appointed butler – a position that virtually guaranteed the future profits of his business. In his royal capacity, de Gisors became a trusted friend and adviser to Henry III, who rewarded his loyalty by granting him custody of the city in 1254. The resulting political status made him one of the most powerful men in London, but not all of de Gisor's peers had cause to share his devotion to the King. Their frustration with high taxes and unreasonable demands prompted them to question the need for a monarch. Their doubts were shared by Simon de Montfort, Henry III's brother-in-law and a highly respected military commander. Although originally a trusted ally of the King, de Montfort had gradually arrived at the conclusion that his brother-in-law's leadership skills were seriously flawed. In addition, he felt it was crucial to the realm's stability that the owners of its lands should have a much greater say in how the country was run. In May 1258, a deputation of barons led by de Montfort delivered an ultimatum to Henry in the form of a constitution known as 'The Provisions of Oxford', which demanded that they play a more active role in the governing of the country. Realising that the barons' demands reflected the mood of much of the nation, Henry reluctantly accepted their plans for reform and appointed an advisory council of 15 men, including Simon de Montfort.

Back at the docks, the barons' victory provoked mixed reactions. Those merchants not favoured by the King were ecstatic over this unprecedented edge towards democracy, but those employed by the royal household were full of trepidation over how the reforms would ultimately affect their status. For three long years, John de Gisors and his royalist colleagues feared for their future, but to their intense relief Henry soon tired of consulting his barons and took to bribing any member of the council who showed signs of disagreeing with him. As his plan began unravelling before him, Simon de Montfort stood firm. He appealed to the people of the kingdom to support him and Londoners, who had grown tired of high taxation, spiralling housing costs and inflated food prices took his cause to their hearts and rioted. Seizing the moment, de Montfort rode into the city and took the Tower, proclaiming himself London's new leader to rapturous cheers from the mob outside

By now, de Montfort and de Gisors were sworn enemies. During the riots, a group of royalists led by de Gisors himself had almost succeeded in capturing de Montfort before he reached the safety of the Tower. On learning of his narrow escape, the self-proclaimed leader of London drew up a list of rebels he planned to execute as soon as he got the chance, taking care to place de Gisors' name at the very top. However, before the executions could begin, he had to seize control of the rest of the country.

Realising that a victory for de Montfort would mean certain death not only for him but for many of his supporters, King Henry rallied his troops and went in pursuit of the usurper, finally catching up with him at Lewes in Sussex. A vicious and bloody battle ensued, but despite being severely outnumbered, de Montfort's men were victorious. Euphoric with this unexpected triumph, they wasted no time in setting up a new parliament with de Montfort, his general Gilbert the Red and the Bishop of Chichester at the helm. However, just months after its formation, the new government was in disarray. Disgusted and disappointed that de Montfort was treating his position as though he were the new king, Gilbert left the parliament and began talks with Henry's son Edward with a view to reinstating the monarchy. A huge army of royalist sympathisers were mustered and they marched on Gloucester, which was promptly recaptured. On hearing the news and learning of the vast size of the King's army, de Montfort is said to have lamented, 'Let us commend our souls to God, because our bodies are theirs.' His prediction turned out to be horribly accurate. On 3 August 1265, the royalists caught up with de Montfort and his men at Evesham. Tired and severely outnumbered, the would-be reformers were no match for the King's men and mass slaughter took place amid the green fields of Worcestershire. Simon de Montfort was slain and his lifeless body decapitated. His head was mounted on a pole and paraded around the towns of the kingdom as a warning to others who may have fostered notions of questioning the King's authority. At the London docks, news of de Montfort's demise was met with great jubilation by John de Gisors who ultimately outlived his arch enemy by nearly 20 years, dying in 1282.

By the end of the 13th century, the old Saxon docks had been transformed from simple beach markets into a busy centre for international trade. The merchants of the Hanseatic League had been joined by a number of Danes who enjoyed shared use of their guild hall. A small Spanish community had sprung up at the docks, importing textiles, pottery and olive oil, Italian merchants were in the throes of establishing a banking centre around Lombard Street and there may even have been a handful of Chinese resident in the city who traded in silks shipped from the Orient. These international traders worked side by side with the English merchants, many of whom specialised in cloth.

Since Roman times, wool had been the country's main export, but during the early medieval period sales of this commodity rocketed, making fortunes for the merchants involved. From the 1100s, wool tended to be exported in its raw state to Italy and the Low Countries where it was spun and woven into cloth. Rather than barter in the markets at the docks, the English wool merchants preferred to buy straight from the supplier. The best quality wool was farmed in the Cotswolds, often by monks whose monastic lands afforded them ample space to tend large flocks. Once the sheep had been shorn, the wool was packed into large sacks which were loaded onto the merchants' carts and taken to towns along the banks of the Thames such as Henley, where they were loaded onto barges bound for the Wool Quay next to the Tower. Once at their destination, the woolsacks were packed into the holds of ships and transported across the Channel where they were sold at Continental markets such as Calais.

By the late 1200s, over 30,000 sacks of wool were being exported every year. Seeing that this highly successful trade could significantly swell the royal coffers, the King levied a high export duty on the commodity. This duty was gradually raised and by the 1400s, the wool merchants were so heavily taxed that they only earned between £1 and £2 profit from each sack they sold, the purchase price of which had been around £8. In a bid to increase profitability, the canny merchants began to set up their own spinning and weaving businesses in premises behind the docks. Keen to benefit from the new industry, cloth cutters and dyers also moved into the city and settled around their guild hall, which stood to the west of the bridge in between the ancient quay at Queenhithe and the headquarters of the Hanseatic League. Across the Thames in Southwark, skilled 'Doche' weavers from Holland, Belgium and Germany also began to set up looms to service the flourishing trade. By the 1330s, the cloth industry was manufacturing not only woolen textiles but also fine fabrics made from imported silk that was sold to two main markets – the wealthy merchants and the even wealthier church. Amazingly, remnants of clothes made from this luxury product have been found in archaeological digs throughout the city and in some cases the items look barely worn, suggesting that the apparel was by no means a rare commodity. That said, wool continued to dominate the textile market throughout the medieval period and it was during this time that England gained the reputation for producing high-quality woollen cloth that it retains to this day. The impact of the wool trade on the medieval economy can still be seen today in the House of Lords where the Lord Chancellor speaks from the Woolsack, introduced into the House by Edward III to remind his government of the financial importance of this commodity.

If wool was medieval London's most successful export, then wine from France and Germany was its most popular if not its most profitable import. Although the labourers at the docks preferred to drink ale (mainly because it was cheaper), no middle or upper class dinner table was complete without a jug of Bordeaux, Burgundy or Riesling. In addition, the consumption of wine was an integral part of the Catholic mass, so every church in London needed to have access to a constant supply.

Like the English wool, much medieval wine came from monasteries. Both the Benedictine and Cistercian orders owned massive vineyards stretching across both France and Germany. Their wine was produced in barrels and sent in ships across to the Port of London when it was ready for consumption (vintage wines were unheard of during this period). Sailors handling the wine cargoes took on their job with wholehearted enthusiasm and numerous vessels arrived at the wine quay in Vintry Ward with half-empty barrels and a very jolly crew. The crews' bad behaviour, coupled with the fact that the quality of wine varied greatly depending on the consignment, prompted the dock authorities to impose strict regulations on wine imports from the 12th century. All traders were required to adhere to these regulations with the notable exception of the Hanseatic League, who continued to negotiate with the crown independently. Wine barrels on non-League vessels were required to reach the docks fully intact otherwise they could not be sold. On arrival at the port, the wine ships were required to dock at Billingsgate where the first barrel was opened and the contents sold to the English merchants at a cost of one penny per stoop as a sample of the quality. Once the quality had been tested, the ship had to moor in the Thames for 36 hours to give the King's sommeliers time to select the best barrels for the royal cellars. During this time, no other prospective buyers were allowed to board the ship for fear of being fined up to 40 shillings. Only after the monarch had taken his selection (and the 36 hours had elapsed) were the wine merchants permitted to board the ship and make their purchases.

Ships carrying other imported goods were also subject to tight restrictions on the way they traded, largely to protect the English merchants. For example, foreign traders wishing to disembark from their ship and sell their goods without the involvement of an English 'middle-man' had to abide by stringent rules that made their task almost impossible. The port authorities had to be informed if they intended to leave the vessel and no cargo could be brought with them for at least three days. Once ashore, no goods could be either sold or purchased at retail prices and even some wholesale purchases were limited in terms of quantity. Other than the Hanseatic League, the only foreign merchants who could trade with fewer restrictions were the Danes and Norwegians who, under the old Saxon right of 'Bosat' could operate retail businesses in the capital for up to one year.

By the 14th century, the wards containing the London docks were the wealthiest in the city. A subsidy roll from 1332 shows that the largest merchant groups dealt in either fish or wine and lived close to their precious cargoes on the thoroughfares that bounded the port. By contrast, the dock labourers tended to live a fair distance away from their employers on the northern and eastern edges of the city where property was significantly cheaper. In an age where few people could read or write, transactions at the docks were often recorded on 'tally sticks', which were an early form of credit card. Once a transaction had been agreed, the vendor would cut notches into both ends of a stick to record how much money was owed. Wider notches represented larger denominations and gradually decreased in width, with pence being represented by thin nicks. Once the amount due had been cut, the stick was sawn obliquely in half. One half was given to the purchaser and the other retained by the vendor. On settlement of the debt, the two halves were matched up and thrown away.

The branding of goods was also in its infancy during this period as many manufacturers and merchants put their stamp on products using metal seals. Over time, these seals were either lost or discarded and many lay undiscovered on the foreshore of the Thames for centuries. Over the past 100 years, some of these seals have been unearthed by archaeologists working on various riverside sites and these finds give tantalising clues to long-forgotten medieval traders including Pautonerius of Podio, Walter of Reigate, and Beatricis, daughter of Hugh. Sadly, the seals do not divulge what goods these men and women dealt in, but passages in the *Liber Albus*, a medieval compilation of the city's laws and customs, do reveal how and where they were sold. By 1280, there were two grain markets at the docks: one at Billingsgate and the other at Queenhithe. They took place on Mondays, Wednesdays and Fridays and opened as the church bells chimed 'half prime.' The grain was transported to the market in sacks and each one was carefully weighed before being sold, the process overseen by representatives from the bakers' and brewers' guilds, who of course had a vested interest in seeing that the grain was being weighed and sold fairly. The same process applied to salt, which was also sold at the market at Queenhithe.

One of the most profitable 'home-grown' commodities to arrive at the dock markets was fish. This foodstuff formed an integral part of medieval Londoners' diets, not least because the church dictated that no meat should be eaten on Fridays. The community at the London docks had a wide variety of fish to choose from, much of which had travelled a considerable distance to market. A rhyme dating from the 13th century lists 'eels from Cambridge, herring of Yarmouth, plaice of Winchelsea, merling of Rye, dace of Kingston, loches of Weybridge, barbels of St Ives, salmon of Berwick, cod of Grimsby and mullet of Dengie.' The most popular fish in London was herring, which was caught between September and November each year in nets off the coast of Great Yarmouth in Norfolk.

The Thames also provided Londoners with salmon and eels which were often sold by independent fishermen direct from the boat or caught by the residents using underwater traps known as kiddles. These submerged devices regularly caused havoc for smaller boats and lighters transporting goods to the dockside and the boatmen constantly petitioned to get the kiddles removed. In 1215, the Magna Carta banned the use of fish traps in the Thames, but the prospect of free and tasty food proved too much for Londoners to resist and the kiddles soon came back. In about 1237, the City Corporation dispatched a sheriff and several armed men to destroy all kiddles in the Thames and the Medway and numerous cottage industries in Kent had their livelihoods destroyed as the sheriff burnt their nets in front of them. However, as soon as one set of traps had been destroyed, numerous others appeared in a different location. By the end of the 14th century, the council had admitted defeat and thenceforth tried to regulate the use of kiddles rather than ban them altogether.

The original trade market for fish lay slightly north of Fish Wharf at the western end of the harbour but was moved to the site of Fish Street Hill once the medieval bridge was completed. The new site boasted a huge tank into which the catches were deposited before being sold. A secondary market existed 'near the stocks' at St Mary Woolnoth. Anyone could purchase the fish at these markets and lowly traders from the poorer parts of town rubbed shoulders with the King's officials as they jostled to find the best catches. It certainly paid to buy at the trade markets as up to 10 herrings could be purchased for a penny. At the retail market on Stockfishmongers Row, the same amount would buy only six or seven. Consequently, when the fishmongers petitioned for their market to become exclusively wholesale in 1320, their request was energetically opposed by the city residents.

Commodities such as grain and salt were generally taken by the purchaser from the market but porters were used for heavier goods such as wine. The porters worked on a freelance basis and once the consignment had been sold, charged no more than two pence to roll a barrel into one of the nearby dock warehouses that lined the quay at the Vintry. However, if the wine had to be taken further into the city, the following charges were levied:

- To a property on one of the lanes between Thames Street and the river – 2½ pence
- To a destination in St Martin Vintry (north of Thames Street) – three pence
- To other destinations in the Ropery (north of the Hanseatic League's headquarters) – six pence
- Anywhere else in the city – 10 pence.

The charges above could be reduced if the purchaser provided a cart for the porters to use. Portering at the medieval docks could be a dangerous business. In 1236, the aptly named Robert le Portour fell into the Thames and drowned while carrying coal from a ship and the court sessions for 1273 record two fatal incidents involving ships moored at the docks. In the first, a man named John Coubley was on board a ship docked at Laurence Hardel's wharf in the Vintry when a quarrel broke out between him and another man named Stephen le Esert. Punches were thrown, Coubley lost his balance and fell into the water where he promptly drowned. Some weeks later, a ship loaded with millstones belonging to Simon de Montfort's arch-rival John de Gisors was the venue for a particularly nasty accident in which a porter named Simon Stanhard was crushed to death when a rope carrying one of the millstones snapped.

As we have seen, the opportunity to sell goods at the busy dock markets did not come free of charge and both seller and buyer were liable for various taxes. By the 13th century, vessels moored in the Thames were subject to the following charges payable to the crown:

- Great vessels and vessels with bulwarks [raised woodwork running around the deck] – 2 pence
- Coaster with bails [as bulwark] – 1 penny
- Vessel with oarports – 1 penny
- Boat – 1 penny
- Vessel with tholes [oar supports] – 1 halfpenny
- Scout [a flat-bottomed boat] – 1 penny.

An eclectic selection of imported goods (including such disparate commodities as whalebone and figs) were subject to an inspection by the King's officials before being sold and merchants had to pay a duty known as 'scavage' for the privilege. Bulk items were weighed on the King's beam and the purchaser was charged a duty known as 'pesage' that was calculated according to weight – for example, goods weighing 10 hundredweight were taxed at one penny. In order to restrict the amount of wool brought into the docks from abroad, a duty known as 'tronage' was levied. Consignments were weighed by the palace officials and merchants were liable for tronage of approximately 11 pence on the first sack and a further 10 pence per sack for the rest of the shipment. Foreign merchants also paid a landing tax and a further duty that allowed them to store their goods in the capital.

Foreign merchants who took up residence in the city were subject to special taxation depending on their ethnicity – all Jews, for example, were considered alien regardless of whether they had been born in London or not and because their rituals and beliefs differed from Christianity, they laid themselves open for yet more taxes from the crown. A tax of 3½ pence was levied on Jews buried in their own graveyards. However, the Jewish community also used their faith to their advantage, especially when it came to money-lending. Under Christian law, it was illegal to practise usury (loaning money and charging interest). Recognising a gap in the market, the sharp-witted Jews set up money-lending businesses a short distance away from the docks in the heart of their small community known as the 'Jewry' near the Guildhall. These businesses flourished and by the end of the 1200s there were an estimated 16,500 Jews living in London. However, their profession and very private lifestyle did not make them popular. In 1290, they lost the protection of the crown and were forced to leave the city. Their lucrative profession was taken up by Italian merchants from Lombardy who lived near today's Lombard Street and also quickly found that the profession of money-lending won them few friends.

By the dawn of the 14th century, the dock wards had become a tightly packed jumble of quays, warehouses, shops and domestic property separated by narrow alleyways intersected by teeming thoroughfares. The largest homes in the area belonged to the wealthiest merchants dealing in sought-after wine, fish and wool products. The best real estate in town tended to be built in a square around a private courtyard, thus giving the family a modicum of peace and seclusion away from the constant activity in the neighbouring dockyards. The entrance to these properties fronted directly onto the street and comprised a combination of shops where the merchant's wares could be viewed and purchased, workshops where raw materials were turned into goods and a covered arch or open alleyway that led into the courtyard beyond. Often, the workshops were leased to craftsmen who lived in small rooms above their place of work. Any remaining rooms in these buildings were often let out. The shops and workshops led into the courtyard on the far side of which was the merchant's private residence – by far the most impressive building in the complex – which combined a large hall for eating and socialising with a series of adjacent chambers that were used as sleeping quarters for the family and any guests. The other two sides of the courtyard were taken up with kitchens, stables, storage sheds and servants' rooms.

With land prices in the prosperous city at a premium, the type of property described above could be afforded only by the very wealthiest of merchants. Consequently, the most common residential property to be found at the docks had virtually the same components but was built on a much smaller scale, with a street frontage that was between 10 and 15ft wide (the largest properties sometimes had frontages up to 40ft wide) with the main residential hall running off at right-angles behind it. A lease dating from 1384 reveals plans for a terrace of properties with this layout that were to be built close to the docks. These structures were three storeys high, each individual floor measuring 12ft long by 10ft wide and 7ft high. Behind each shop, there was a hall measuring 40ft by 23ft, a parlour, kitchen and a larder known as a buttery. A cellar lay under the main hall providing a useful storage place for the merchant's goods and raw materials. It is highly likely that these properties were timber framed (oak being the preferred material) with a wattle and daub infill. In order to suggest great wealth, the halls may have been given a masonry façade as only the very richest men in the docks were able to afford a home made entirely of stone.

The sheer amount of property constructed in London during the early medieval period resulted in three major problems for the city residents, especially those residing in the overcrowded dock district. As more people crowded into the area, new buildings sprang up on virtually every available piece of land. Consequently, some paths and alleyways became virtually impassable, neighbours were driven to distraction by constant noise and, most worryingly, fires broke out on a regular basis and quickly spread through the tightly packed properties, leaving total destruction in their wake. In a bid to ease the noise and fire safety problems, the Common Council laid down a series of strict building regulations. The new rules stated that the walls of adjoining properties had to be at least 3ft thick to reduce noise levels. In order to stop fires burning out of control, all roofs had to be tiled rather than thatched and each storey had to be accessed by an exterior stairway or ladder, giving the occupants a fair chance of escape.

The problem of congested roads proved to be a far more difficult nut to crack. Many streets around the docks resembled tunnels as the sky was almost completely obscured from view by the overhanging upper storeys of buildings. Higher rooms in medieval dwellings were allowed to protrude above the ground floor as long as they began 9ft above street level (high enough for a man on horseback to pass underneath them). Of course, developers took full advantage of this and built upper floors that projected out so far that they almost touched the building on the opposite side of the street. This obscuration of daylight was made worse by the proliferation of shop signs that projected out into the thoroughfares on long poles sometimes up to 7ft long. In a period when only a very small proportion of the population could read, these signs were essential to traders as they not only identified the location of a shop but also often showed what was sold there. For example, a wine shop might be identified by a bunch of grapes. Today, the striped barber's pole and the three golden spheres that hang outside pawnbrokers' shops are all that is left of the medieval signage that once lined London's streets.

Even at ground level, medieval streets were not a place for the claustrophobic. Shops were not as we know them today. Many were more like stalls with shutters that folded down to make a counter on which the customers were served. It was rare to actually enter shops unless they were selling higher quality goods that had to be inspected before purchase, for example cloth or silverware.

Along medieval London's shopping streets, pedestrians' senses were bombarded by a cacophony of noise from the workshops and a barrage of odours emanating from the shops and elsewhere. Due to their unsavoury function, medieval privies were generally built on the outside walls of properties or in cellars. Consequently, most Londoners caught short in the night tended to either use chamber pots or the nearest window. In the morning, the contents of the chamber pots were simply tipped out into the street. As the notion that disease was caused by bad smells increased in popularity, the Common Council ordered that all privies should be lined with stone to trap any dangerous odours. In the interests of public health it was also decreed that the new, lined privies should be cleaned every two years. However, despite these reforms, the authorities failed to identify the real cause of the stench. Although the bowl was now lined, deposits into the privies finished up in a cesspit directly beneath it. Often these cesspits were built dangerously close to wells and the local residents ended up drinking their own effluent with fatal results. The privies themselves could be just as dangerous – an unfortunate gentleman named Richard le Rakiere drowned when the plank of wood covering his latrine cracked and caused him to fall into the cesspit below.

During his time in office, London's most famous medieval merchant, Richard (Dick) Whittington was so appalled with the state of the dockside latrines that he left money in his will to construct an impressive new edifice with 64 seats that was to be built in an area where the cesspits would be cleansed every day by the tide. It is impossible to calculate how many lives may have been saved by this venture.

While the merchants enjoyed a comfortable existence in their fine halls, the properties in the surrounding streets along the riverside played host to a diverse range of poorer communities to whom the sea provided a living. The yards that led down to the quays rang out with the sounds of anchorsmiths, carpenters and joiners plying their trade, while sailors, fishermen and sea pilots spent their hard-earned pay in the taverns and hostelries that lay close to the quaysides. Some of the quays had their own inns that took the form of private drinking clubs exclusively for the use of their own employees. At the Hanseatic League's headquarters there was a large cellar called 'Hell', which was most probably a tavern for thirsty crew recently disembarked from the German ships. These seafaring men and their contemporaries lived a hard and at times treacherous life. They were used to living on board ships in cramped and unsanitary conditions for sometimes months on end, enduring fierce storms or even capture by a hostile vessel. By the end of the 1330s, the mariners' work became even more dangerous when conflict broke out between England and France.

In 1337, the death of the King left the French throne with no obvious heir and resulted in two royal houses – the French House of Valois and the English House of Plantagenet – embarking on a long and bitter series of conflicts that has come to be known as the Hundred Years War. Following the outbreak of hostilities, the livelihoods of London's wool merchants were severely threatened as trade between them and the weaving centres at Ghent, Bruges and Ypres virtually ground to a halt. Realising that the breakdown of trade in this highly lucrative market could seriously damage the economy, Edward III invited the foreign weavers to set up business in England, granting them special privileges in return for rescuing the wool trade. To the wool merchants' relief, many of the weavers decided to take the King up on his generous offer and left their homeland to begin new businesses across the Channel.

As the conflict continued, several towns along the south coast fell prey to attacks from French forces and many feared that London would be their next target. In preparation, a military commander named Simon Turgys was given a retinue of six men by day and 12 by night to keep a close eye on the Thames from a vantage point in the Tower. The docks themselves were put on high alert and ward aldermen Henry Darcy, Richard de Pole, Sir John de Pulteneye and Reginald de Conduit were dispatched to ensure that watchmen were patrolling the quays at all times. Further along the river, aldermen Richard de Hackeneye and Richard de Rothyng oversaw pile-driving works that effectively stopped more than one ship passing down the river at any time. The merchants and warehouse owners prepared for attack by building temporary battlements on the quays to impede any marauding French forces that might reach the docks.

As with any conflict, Edward III's war with France came at a price. In November 1339, desperate for more money to fund his campaigns, the King decided to levy a war tax on London. The residents of each ward were assessed and the resulting calculations give an interesting insight into where the wealthiest merchants and quay owners resided. In total the following amounts were collected from the wards:

Tower Ward – £25 16s
Bridge Ward – £24
Vintry Ward – £23 14s
Billingsgate Ward – £21
Queenhithe Ward – £12
Castle Baynard Ward – £7

In addition to this tax, the King also raised the duty payable on commodities such as wool, wine and cloth throughout the kingdom and appointed officials to oversee its prompt collection. Most provincial ports were assigned two officers, but the sheer amount of cargo handled at the London docks resulted in 42 officials being appointed. Most of the tax collectors were wealthy merchants to whom the King owed money. Therefore it was in their best interests to see that the tax was collected quickly and efficiently. The system worked well and in 1382 the King's officials were provided with their own offices when a purpose-built custom house was erected at Wool Quay.

In addition to the new taxes, Edward also asked the merchants for the loan of ships. Seeing that they had little option, most of the merchants complied with his wishes and in 1340, the King's hastily assembled fleet defeated the French navy. Encouraged by this victory, the London merchants provided the King with more vessels and following the successful siege of Calais in 1347, Edward returned home with sufficient war loot to pay the merchants back in full.

The King's victorious return to the capital proved to be relatively short-lived. Following a period of uneasy peace, French-backed Spanish ships began attacking English wine fleets travelling to and from Bordeaux. The dock merchants once again bequeathed ships to police the route and managed to deter the Spanish from any further attacks. On the French mainland, the King's son Edward, known as the Black Prince, defeated the French at the Battle of Poitiers in 1357 and leaving the crippled French army in disarray, brought the captured French king back to London as a prisoner of war amid scenes of riotous celebration. The resulting Treaty of Bretigny in 1360 brought the conflict to a brief halt but by 1369, the wine ships once again came under attack. As Londoners reinforced their city's defences and prepared for war, one of the wine merchants – a man named John Philpot – decided to take matters into his own hands. Frustrated with the lack of protection his ships were receiving from the crown, Philpot organised his own fleet and with a makeshift army of 1,000 men on board, he sailed into the Channel and lay in wait. His daring plan could not have worked better. The Spanish ships were not expecting to meet the merchant's fleet and their surprise attack resulted in the capture of 50 ships laden with bounty.

However, despite this unexpected success, conflict between the English and French monarchs continued to flare up and in 1379, London braced itself for attack once again when a French and Spanish fleet launched a raid on Gravesend and Tilbury. Although the ships travelled no further along the Thames, the attack prompted a swift review of security on the river and Cooling Castle on the estuary in Kent was rebuilt with stronger defences. Although London was never directly attacked by the French, hostilities between the two countries continued, finally ending in 1453 when the Plantagenets were expelled from much of France. In the interim, despite John Philpot's best efforts, the seizing of rival vessels in the Channel became so rife that several English and French ports agreed set ransoms for captured crew. For example, mariners from Lydd and New Romney in Kent agreed with their French counterparts the following pay-offs: a captured shipmaster was to be ransomed for six nobles (a gold coin worth approximately 6s 8d) plus expenses for every week he was held; a sailor was worth three nobles plus expenses and one half-noble to ensure his safe conduct; a fishing boat was worth 40 shillings. The merchants ran the greatest risk if they were captured as no set ransom was agreed, the captors preferring to negotiate as much money as they could. The ship owners took the threat of kidnap extremely seriously and there are records of property being mortgaged prior to voyages to ensure that enough funds were available to free the crew should they be captured and held for ransom.

Once on board the ship, sailors' contracts were drawn up according to the maritime law that applied to their country. Mariners from the Mediterranean worked to 'Il Consolato del Mare' or 'Regulation of the Sea';

employees of the Hanseatic League observed the Laws of Wisby (a prosperous Scandinavian sea port); and English and French sailors' contracts were drawn up according to the Laws of Oleron, a revised version of the older Consolato del Mare that had been drawn up by Eleanor, Duchess of Guienne, the mother of Richard the Lionheart circa 1160. According to their contracts, all sailors were effectively freelance and were employed for the duration of the ship's voyage. Their pay was relatively poor (for example, mariners working on the wine ships sailing between London and Bordeaux in 1375 were paid just eight shillings per voyage) but their meagre wages were supplemented by free food and drink while on board, extra pay for loading or unloading the cargo plus free carriage on goods they wished to purchase themselves while at the trading port. There was also some opportunity for betterment and, in time, more ambitious members of the crew could work their way up the ranks to become shipmasters which, in addition to higher pay, often came with the added responsibility of buying and selling goods on behalf of the merchants.

The difficult and sometimes highly treacherous circumstances endured by medieval mariners meant that by the time they returned to London after completing a voyage, they were keen to relax in the company of women and plenty of alcoholic beverages. The ale houses and inns within the city walls were subject to restrictive rules and regulations, so the eager sailors gravitated towards an area where things were a little more relaxed. Prior to 1327, the old riverside settlement across the bridge at Southwark did not fall under the tight control of the City Corporation or its guilds and so it became a popular retreat for pleasure seekers keen to indulge in leisure pursuits that might be frowned upon by their more virtuous peers. Rather incongruously, many of the inns that lay along the south bank of the Thames formed part of religious residences owned by abbots and priors from the south of England. These men used the Southwark properties as London pieds-à-terre for occasions when they were called to Westminster on business. Rather like the wealthy merchants' homes, the buildings were a combination of living quarters and commercial real estate and many had brewhouses attached wherein the locals could sample the abbots' fine home-brewed ales. The Priors of St Swithin, Winchester and St Pancras, Lewes and the Abbots of Battle, Waverley and St Augustine's, Canterbury all had properties in the area.

However, the most famous of all was the Abbot of Hythe's Tabard Inn on Borough High Street from whence Chaucer's pilgrims commenced their journey to Canterbury. Chaucer wrote:

Bifel that in that season on a day,
In Southwerk at the Tabard as I lay
Redy to wenden on my pilgrimage
To Caunterbury with ful devout corage,
At nyght was come into that hostelrye
Wel nyne and twenty in a compaignye
Of sondry folk, by aventure yfalle
In felaweshipe, and pilgrimes were they alle,
That toward Caunterbury wolden ryde;
The chambres and the stables weren wyde,
And well we weren esed atte beste.

Southwark's medieval inns did not only attract pilgrims and sailors, however. The crowded and raucous south bank inns welcomed patrons from right across the social scale from the wealthiest merchant to the lowliest dock labourer. This largely male clientele were not always simply there for the beer either. Many, especially the sailors who had been locked up with a same-sex crew for weeks, yearned for some female company and thanks to a royal ordinance from 1161 that allowed the licensing of prostitutes, Southwark was the place to go. The south bank whores obtained their licence to trade from the Bishop of Winchester – who held jurisdiction over the area – and consequently became known colloquially as 'Winchester geese' ('goose' being a medieval euphemism for a prostitute). For nearly 500 years, their activities resulted in Southwark holding a dubious reputation as London's centre of vice.

Of course, not everyone was in favour of the south bank fleshpots and the women who chose or were forced to work in them were often ostracised by their neighbours, even in death. They were refused a Christian burial, as noted by John Stow in 1603: 'I have heard of ancient men, of good credit, report that these single women were forbidden the rites of the church, so long as they continued that sinful life, and were excluded from Christian burial, if they were not reconciled before their death. And therefore there was a plot of ground called the Single Woman's churchyard, appointed for them far from the parish church.'

The final resting place of the medieval Winchester geese was lost for centuries until building excavations at the junction of Redcross Way and Union Street in the 1990s uncovered hundreds of female skeletons, many of which showed signs of syphilis, a common occupational hazard for prostitutes in this era. Since then, the people of Southwark have taken the final resting place of the prostitutes to their hearts and have energetically opposed any development of the site, preferring that the area be transformed into a public park.

Today's sympathetic attitude towards the Winchester geese and the inns in which they plied their trade was certainly not shared by the medieval employers at the docks, who no doubt quickly tired of employees turning up to work late with a monstrous hangover. Some even placed stern restrictions on their staff in a bid to keep them on a righteous path. During the first half of the 14th century, the Hanseatic League expanded their dock complex onto rented land surrounding its perimeter. They built more warehouses and shops on the new site and also constructed living accommodation for the resident merchants, most of whom were under 40 years old, single and no doubt greatly attracted to the pleasures to be found in Southwark. In a bid to curtail any unwholesome activities across the water, the League laid down new regulations for their inmates whereby they were forbidden to bring local women back to their quarters nor permitted to entertain anyone within the complex who was not connected with the League. Any merchant found guilty of flouting these rules was forced to pay a fine in the form of candlewax for All Hallows church, which stood next door to their premises. During the 14th century, this seamen's church on the banks of the river benefited greatly from its proximity to the Hanseatic League's headquarters as in addition to the candlewax, the wealthy German merchants endowed it with a chapel, altars and a magnificent stained glass window depicting the German two-headed imperial eagle. They also used the church for worship on religious occasions specific to their homeland. For example, at the feast of St Barbara on 4 December the League held a particularly impressive mass, which must have been a curiosity to any English in the congregation.

By the mid-14th century, the London docks had established themselves as the kingdom's premier port and the city merchants enjoyed a virtual monopoly on luxury items destined for the south of England. By the 1340s, for example, an average of 3,500 tuns of wine were handled at the Vintry quays compared with just 972 tuns at Hull, which at the time was the wine trade's second choice of port. But as the merchants enjoyed this period of great prosperity, little did they realise that Mother Nature was about to unleash a global epidemic that would threaten their very existence.

5

PLAGUE AND POLITICS

In 1347, Genoese workers at the port of Kaffa in the Black Sea began to be struck down with a strain of bubonic plague thought to have originated in Asia. This deadly disease was carried by fleas that lived on the rats on board ships. Once a ship had docked at port, the rats swarmed into the town looking for food and the disease-ridden fleas began transferring to humans. The plague spread throughout the Black Sea region with alarming speed, leaving utter devastation in its wake by wiping out on average ⅓ of the population of any town it visited. The flea-carrying rats transferred to ships bound for England and by November 1348, residents of London were beginning to fall prey to the deadly epidemic. Symptoms of the plague included painfully swollen lymph nodes accompanied by a high fever, vomiting, severe muscular pain, bleeding lungs and an overwhelming desire to sleep which if succumbed to proved fatal. Once contracted, the disease developed frighteningly quickly and most victims died within four days of falling ill.

The ferocity of the plague, which later became known as the Black Death, threw the residents of the docks into a state of blind panic. No one had any idea how to treat the symptoms and although physicians desperately tried all manner of methods, from herbal bouquets to leeches, none had any effect. Families watched helplessly as their loved ones slipped away from them and soon the daily death toll was so large that victims were buried in large communal pits hastily dug outside the city wall. As more clergy succumbed to the disease, the church granted permission for anyone to administer the last rites to the dying.

Over the following 12 months, the Black Death decimated London. Before its arrival, the city's population was estimated at between 40,000 and 60,000. By the time the disease had run its deadly course, approximately

20,000 Londoners had died. Many of its victims were poor dock labourers who lived in overpopulated tenements where there was little chance of escape but even wealthy merchants fled the stricken capital to towns and villages in search of uncontaminated air only to find that the countryside was also in the grip of the epidemic. By the end of 1350, between 30 and 40% of the population of England had been wiped out and entire communities were destroyed. This shocking aftermath was to have a profound effect on both the country's economy and the attitude of its people.

Back in the docks, the quay owners and merchants had lost up to 30% of their workforce and were faced with a chronic labour shortage. Capitalising on the situation, the surviving workers demanded higher wages and their employers had no choice but to oblige. As a result, the greater cost of bringing goods to market resulted in a long period of inflation. The structure of the dock community also underwent an unprecedented change as families from the devastated villages and towns around the city's perimeter moved into homes that had previously been occupied by plague victims. For these survivors, things were never to be the same again. In an era largely bereft of science, people placed their faith in religion, but the horrors of the plague had severely tested their faith to the point where the population began to question the idea that the Catholic Church held all the answers. This new cynicism combined with the fact that many clergy had died in the epidemic, thus considerably decreasing the numbers of churchmen within society, resulted in the church sliding into a steady and unstoppable decline that ended with Henry VIII's dissolution of the monasteries in the 16th century.

The decimation and loss caused by the Black Death combined with the paranoia and suspicion engendered by the prolonged conflict with the French brought fear and distrust to London and transformed areas of the dockside landscape. A lengthy programme of redevelopment was embarked upon at the Tower Wharf, which centred around the enlargement of the quayside so it could cope with the export of munitions to France. Completion of the final stage of this enlargement was overseen by none other than Geoffrey Chaucer, author of *The Canterbury Tales*, who at the time held the post of Clerk of the King's Works. Defences at the Tower itself were also redeveloped. A new outer wall was constructed and the moat substantially enlarged, costing a massive £4,150.

Many residents believed that the plague epidemic had been spread by sailors and merchants arriving at the port from infected areas. Consequently, foreigners were made to feel increasingly unwelcome as misinformed Londoners tried to isolate themselves. For some time, the London merchants had been unhappy with the wealth created in the city by their Italian counterparts, many of whom supplemented their mercantile endeavours with the lucrative but unpopular activity of money-lending. In 1357, simmering tensions between the two factions reached boiling point when two Italian merchants named Francisco Bochel and Raynard Flanny were viciously assaulted by Henry Forester, Thomas de Waldon and Thomas Meleward in Old Jewry. The attack was witnessed by several bystanders and the perpetrators were swiftly caught and imprisoned in the Tower. At the subsequent trial, the judge was determined to ensure that attacks on the city's foreign inhabitants were not allowed to get out of hand. After the jury concluded that they could find no 'just cause for such outrage', the trio were promptly issued with gaol sentences. However, their business connections afforded them a swift release once the furore surrounding the case had died down.

Following the imprisonment of Forester, de Waldon and Meleward, an uneasy peace prevailed between the English merchants and their foreign peers. However, beneath the surface, tensions were still close to breaking point, especially where the Italian usuries were concerned. Instead of using outright violence, the English took to spreading rumours about the powerful money-lenders and in 1376, their malicious lies had whipped public feeling into such a frenzy that the House of Commons called for the expulsion of all Italian money-lenders on the grounds that their numbers included 'Juys and Sarazins, and privees Espies'.

The English merchants' venom did not stop there. They soon turned their attention to foreign merchants from any country. In 1377, the mayor, aldermen and citizens of London petitioned King Edward III to address the situation. The resulting pressure forced the monarch to hastily issue a decree stating that no foreign merchants could engage in retail trade (with the exception of the all-powerful Hanseatic League). However, this rash edict was destined to be short-lived. While the merchants simply saw the foreigners as a threat to their businesses, the King and government found the foreign traders very useful as they supplied high-quality goods, paid high taxes and could be regularly tapped for loans. Somewhat unsurprisingly, the King's decree was overturned by Parliament just a year later and the foreign merchants resumed their retail activities. Four years on, however, the continuing friction between England and France prompted the King to pass the Navigation Act, which commanded that exported English merchandise could only be carried on 'ships of the King's allegiance' and that any alien who continued to export English goods would forfeit them to the crown.

Competition from foreign merchants combined with the labour shortages precipitated by the outbreak of the Black Death forced the English merchants to become more organised and cohesive. In 1370, a royal decree declared that all staple goods (for example, wool and cloth), should be exported via controlled channels so the tax due on them could be more easily assessed. A 'staple town' was established at the English outpost of Calais and all exported goods had to pass through it *en route* to their final destination. At the same time, a company of merchants specialising in export was formed under the name of the Merchant Staplers. Using the Hanseatic League as their model, the Staplers joined together in their business ventures and had soon monopolised the wool trade in much of Europe. The success of the Merchant Staplers was such that the company soon evolved from dealing specifically with raw materials to also exporting finished cloth. Two decades after the Merchant Staplers Company had been established the wonderfully titled 'Wardens and Company of the Mystery of the Mercers of the City of London' was incorporated. In addition to selling cloth like the members of the Merchant Staplers Company, the Mercers also dealt in any commodity sold by 'little balance' (i.e. relatively light) such as haberdashery. The company held their meetings in the Hospital of St Thomas of Acon on Cheapside, the thoroughfare along which they also sold their wares from stalls and shops. John Stow observed in his *Survey of London*, '... divers[e] sheds, from Sopars lane to the Standard' all let by mercers and by the mid-15th century the area was so renowned for mercers' shops that it was immortalised in the words of a song published by the *London Lickpenny*:

> Then to the Chepe I began me drawn
> Where mutch people I sawe for to stand;

One ofred me velvet, silke, and lawne
An other he taketh me by the haunde
Here is Parys thread, the finest in the launde.

Spurred on by their initial success and keen to develop new markets, the Mercers and Merchant Staplers began to seek new areas in which to trade. Their combined activities resulted in them being superseded by a new organisation that utterly embodied the spirit of the age – the Merchant Adventurers.

The market at the top of the Merchant Adventurers' list was Germany. Supplying cloth to this large and wealthy region promised potentially huge rewards for the merchants, but it was dominated by the Hanseatic League. Much to the irritation of the English merchants, the League had gradually expanded their original wine import business to include the export of British cloth to Germany and the Baltic ports. By the 1380s, trade in this commodity was so important to their operation that their headquarters on the Thames riverbank had become known as 'The Steelyard', a corruption of the German verb 'stalen' meaning to verify the quality or origin of cloth by applying a lead seal. The dominance of the Hanseatic League in Germany meant that the Merchant Adventurers were forced to concentrate their efforts in the Low Countries. In 1407, they set up headquarters at Antwerp for this very purpose but began to watch the activities of their arch-rivals very closely, waiting for an opportune time to challenge the League's monopoly.

The remaining years of the 14th century saw London's docks enter a new phase of improved organisation and increased cooperation between the previously autonomous groups of English merchants as the port struggled to regain momentum after the devastation caused by the Black Death. By 1450, the city was beginning to find its feet again, but the people of the docks found themselves at the centre of a series of violent events that once again threatened London's stability.

The first sign of trouble came when the people of Kent rose up against rampant taxation, high-level corruption and weak leadership from King Henry VI. At their helm was a shady character known as Jack Cade, a self-styled people's champion with great ambitions. Following several successful rallies in Kentish towns, Cade marched his now

5,000-strong army of rebels to London, crossing the bridge to the city virtually unchallenged on 3 July 1450. Once inside the city wall, Cade proclaimed himself mayor and declared war on the existing government, Common Council and monarch, all of whom he considered to be utterly immoral and dishonest. At first, Cade's rebellion was relatively peaceful. The people of London agreed wholeheartedly with his populist agenda of lower taxes and the creation of a democratically elected government and so had allowed his men to enter their city unchallenged. However, once there, Cade's army (many of whom were poor farmers or exhausted soldiers recently returned from fighting in France) caught sight of the great riches displayed in the shops and homes and began to loot the city. Realising that Cade's troops were little more than dishonest thugs, the people of London appealed to the King and council to expel the rebels and plans were swiftly hatched.

Under cover of night, the garrison from the Tower of London were dispatched to seek out and surprise the rebels as they slept and the men of Bridge Ward were called to arms and sent by the Common Council to defend the river crossing, which by now had no drawbridge as Cade had cut the ropes. The Tower garrison routed the rebels and succeeded in driving them back towards the bridge where the ward's men lay in wait. As daylight broke, a vicious battle broke out. London's men fought bravely, throwing the increasingly desperate Kentish rebels into the swirling waters of the Thames, where many were sucked into the fierce current and were drowned. By morning, they had succeeded in taking the northern half of the bridge and their commander, Lord Scales, was keen to resume the assault on the southern half. However, his plans were foiled by the arrival of the Bishop of Winchester with a hastily prepared bundle of forms offering a full pardon to any rebels who cared to sign them and make a swift departure. Still reeling from the previous night's hostilities, many of Cade's men lost no time in signing up and beat a hasty retreat, leaving their leader with very little support. Realising that his ambition to wrest power from the King and government was now hopeless, Cade managed to escape Southwark and fled to Rochester. He was eventually captured and killed near Heathfield in Sussex.

The people of the docks had barely recovered from the battle with Jack Cade and his men when prejudice against the foreign merchants boiled over into violence once again. During the riots that ensued, many foreign businesses were looted, burned and ransacked and the targeted families hid from the mob in fear of their lives. Although the riots were quickly brought under control, they proved to be the last straw for the majority of Italian merchants. Sick and tired of the prejudice they had suffered at the hands of Londoners for generations, they decided to move south, relocating their businesses to the coastal towns of Southampton and Sandwich and transporting their goods to the capital by horse and cart. This signalled the end of the Italian merchants' association with the docks, but their presence is often revealed today through the unearthing of 'galley halfpennies' at old dock sites along the banks of the Thames. Despite their modern name, these coins are actually Italian 'soldini' dating from the 14th and 15th centuries. They were originally brought to the docks by merchants and sailors principally from Venice, who docked their ships in Galley Quay, hence the coin's nickname. During this period, there was a great shortage of coins in England due to many being taken abroad, melted down and turned into more lucrative currency by unscrupulous merchants. This posed real problems for the poor who dealt almost exclusively in small change. They petitioned the King, requesting that more farthings and halfpennies be minted but nothing was done. Consequently, the poor took to using the Italian soldini in their place. Realising that the use of foreign currency could only spell bad news for the economy, the government tried to ban them several times but they continued to be used by Londoners until the mid-1500s, a forgotten legacy of the much-persecuted Italian merchants.

Now rid of the troublesome Italians, the English merchants turned their animosity towards the Hanseatic League who were in some ways much more deserving recipients of their wrath. In the mid-1400s, the League began to put pressure on the German and Scandinavian monarchs to restrict trading by English merchants in Hanseatic towns. Back in their Steelyard headquarters at the docks, this move caused a great deal of friction. The members of the League that hailed from Cologne (and who were the original settlers of the Steelyard) placed a great deal of value on their good relationship with the English and were horrified that the rash actions of their countrymen might jeopardise the *status quo*. In a bid to distance themselves from any conflict resulting from the League's actions, the Cologne merchants made it very clear that they would rather leave the League than wreck their trading alliance with England. This reckless decision vividly illustrates just how important the English market was to the Cologners at the time. However, despite their threats, the rest of the League continued to lobby successfully for wholesale restrictions on English trade in the Baltic.

As town after town banned the English merchants from trading, they understandably became extremely upset at the injustice of the situation. The Hanseatic League had enjoyed the right to trade without restrictions throughout England for centuries, but the same privileges were no longer being reciprocated by the Baltic towns. The English banded together and led by an aggrieved fishmonger named William Overey, who had recently had his lucrative trade in Prussia and Germany curtailed by the League, petitioned Henry VI to retaliate. The King sympathised with the merchants and would have acceded to their request had it not been for some desperate negotiating by the Cologne merchants who eventually managed to broker an uneasy and ultimately short-lived truce.

Despite the Cologners' best efforts, the relationship between the English merchants and the Hanseatic League gradually deteriorated and a series of altercations between English and Danish traders (who had Hanseatic ships from Danzig in their service) in the winter of 1467/68 prompted Henry to finally lose his patience with the squabbling merchants. He sent troops to the Steelyard, arrested all the merchants there (with the exception of the Cologners), seized their property and withdrew all privileges. That the King's action was assertive is to be admired, but unfortunately it was also hasty and badly thought through. As soon as the Continental branches of the League heard what had happened to their colleagues in London, they dispatched mediators who rightly argued that the League could not be blamed for the actions of the Danes. Realising they had a point, Henry was forced to release the prisoners and let them back into the Steelyard but shrewdly decided to withhold their trading privileges until the English merchants were granted the same treatment in the Hanseatic towns.

The League merchants returned from their period of incarceration in a furious state of mind. Laying blame for their imprisonment firmly at the feet of the Cologners, they promptly expelled them from the League and threw them out of the Steelyard as punishment for what they viewed as seriously misplaced loyalties. However, they soon realised that the expulsion of the only League members on good terms with the English had been a little foolish as they now had no one to negotiate the reinstatement of their trading privileges. Desperate to make amends, they grudgingly began to curry favour with the King by providing him with ships for his navy and opened up talks with the English merchants. After several years of negotiations, their efforts were finally rewarded in 1474 when the Treaty of Utrecht reinstated their privileges on the proviso that the English merchants would enjoy reciprocal rights in the Hanseatic territories. Relieved that the League's lucrative English operation was finally back in business, the King showed his wholehearted support by allowing them to formally acquire the land that they had previously rented to allow for expansion of the Steelyard. In grateful response, the League constructed an impressive new guild hall on the site to replace the building that had been the centre of so much conflict and invited the Cologne merchants to rejoin them. The new hall quickly became one of the four main 'kontors', or counting houses, of the Hanseatic League (the others being Bruges, Bergen and Novgorod) thus underlining the overwhelming importance of their trading operation in England.

6

VOYAGES OF DISCOVERY

The resolution of the problems between the Hanseatic League and the English merchants heralded an era of expansion for the docks as London reinforced its position as the country's premier port. By the end of the 1400s, the city was handling over 60% of the kingdom's overseas trade, but the dock complex stretched no further along the Thames than it had in the early 1200s when London was handling just 17% of shipping. The central portion of the riverside was now crowded with quays that handled the ever-increasing number of merchant ships arriving in the port, leaving virtually no space for repair yards or docks for the King's growing fleet of naval vessels.

When Henry VIII came to the throne in 1509, he immediately began to hatch plans to claim the much-coveted French crown. Realising that his kingdom would require protection during the resulting hostilities, he set about developing the embryonic Royal Navy into the finest fleet in the world and began to look for suitable locations in which to build his ships. The Port of London was an obvious choice as it was sufficiently close to Henry's palace at Greenwich for the King to keep a close eye on proceedings. The riverside at Westminster was quickly deemed too inaccessible for a major shipyard and so locations further east were sought. The first to be selected was a small dock in the Kentish riverside village of Woolwich, which Henry chose as the location to build the *Henri Grâce à Dieu* (Henry Thanks be to God), known colloquially as *Great Harry*. Construction began in 1512 and took two years to complete but resulted in a finished vessel that was the most impressive and formidable ship in Europe. Weighing over 1,000 tons, its forecastle (front end) was four decks high, lowering to two decks at the stern. The gun deck was furnished with 20 state-of-the-art bronze cannon that could be fired simultaneously, plus 43 heavy and 141 light guns. However, although she had been built as a warship, the King preferred to use the *Great Harry* for ambassadorial purposes. Instead of leading the royal fleet into battle, she became more of a symbol of the King's wealth, even sporting sails made from golden cloth on occasion.

While the *Great Harry* was being completed at Woolwich, the King's attentions turned to the small fishing village of Deptford which stood on the south bank of the Thames a short distance downriver from Southwark. Small shipbuilding businesses had occupied the area for some generations and by the end of the 15th century, Henry VII used the Deptford dock to anchor and repair his small royal fleet. Henry VIII decided to expand and improve the dock and the subsequent redevelopment quickly transformed Deptford from a simple Kentish fishing village into a hive of industry densely populated with families involved in the creation of the King's ships. It took almost 30 years to create the finished complex which stretched across 30 acres of riverside land. Known locally as the King's Yard, the Deptford dockyard comprised two wet docks (one double, one single), three slips for warships and an expansive basin enclosed by a quadrangle of buildings comprising numerous workshops and stores, a huge smith's shop, several forges for making anchors, rope walks containing state-of-the-art rope-making machinery, copious warehousing and domestic property for the officers who oversaw the works.

From the outset, the facilities at the King's Yard meant that existing ships could be repaired there at the same time as others were being built. Additional shipbuilding centres at coastal sites further afield sometimes undertook the basic construction of a new royal vessel, which was then sailed into Deptford to be finished. One of the first ships to be built in this way was also destined to be the most famous vessel of the period.

At the same time as he commissioned the *Great Harry*, Henry VIII also authorised £700 for the construction of two additional warships – the *Peter Pomegranate* and the *Mary Rose*. The latter was built in Portsmouth and then sailed to London where she was fitted with huge bronze and iron guns at the Deptford yard. The finished vessel was a masterpiece of Tudor engineering and although half the size of the *Great Harry*, she too contained the latest technology such as watertight gun ports that allowed more guns to be carried low in her hull without the fear of water getting in and destabilising her. The King was delighted with his latest naval addition, designated it a flagship of his navy and named the ship *Mary* after his sister and *Rose* to commemorate the Tudor symbol.

In 1512, Henry's military plans came to fruition when he declared war on France. Commanded by Sir Edward Howard, the *Mary Rose* took part in a major sea battle off the coast of Brest during which she succeeded in crippling the French flagship and drowning most of the crew. The victorious fleet sailed back to Greenwich where they were reviewed by the King who promptly organised a race in order to establish which vessels should lead any further hostilities. The *Mary Rose* out-sailed all others in the fleet and Captain Howard declared her 'the flower ... of all ships that ever sailed.' The conflict with the French continued for a further two years until a peace treaty was uneasily agreed after Henry reluctantly consented to the betrothal of his beloved sister Mary to the aged French king, Louis XII. However, despite this forced marriage, hostility between the two nations continued on and off for the next 29 years until 1543, when Henry once again declared war on the French, capturing the port town of Boulogne some months later. In response, a huge French fleet set sail for Portsmouth. Although the French ships vastly outnumbered the English vessels, their attempts at destroying Henry's navy initially met with little success due to good strategic command from the King himself. However, they refused to give up and on 19 July 1545, the English fleet once again came under fire from the French and set sail towards the hostile ships, with the *Mary Rose* at their head. As the battle commenced, Henry and his commanders watched helplessly from Southsea Castle as the King's favourite flagship capsized and sank, losing virtually her entire crew. The remaining ships fought on and eventually forced the French to withdraw. Horrified at the loss of the *Mary Rose*, the King tried to have her salvaged from the seabed but, despite his best efforts, all attempts proved unsuccessful.

The true cause of the catastrophic sinking of the *Mary Rose* was not recorded by either the English or the French and for centuries she was simply regarded as one of many casualties of war. However, the discovery and subsequent exploration of the wreck in 1982 suggested that the ship's state-of-the-art equipment may have been to blame for her demise. Experts theorised that in the heat of the battle, the *Mary Rose*'s crew began firing the guns on one side of the ship and then as she abruptly turned to avoid another vessel, they rushed over to use the artillery on the opposite side, forgetting to close the gun ports. As the ship turned, water rushed through these low-level apertures causing the ship to become dangerously unstable and then sink below the waves in a matter of minutes.

By the time of the *Mary Rose*'s sad demise, the King's Yard at Deptford had long since established itself as a major dockyard. A list from 1521 reveals that on 18 September, the complex contained the fated '*Mary Rose* ... lying in the pond ... beside the storehouse there' alongside the *Great Barke*, the *Less Barke*, the 'twayne *Row Barges*' and the *Great Galley*. These vessels, which had a combined portage of over 3,000 tons, had obviously taken up all the available space in the dockyard proper as nearby, the '*John Baptist* and *Barbara* ... do ryde together in a creke of Deptford Parish' and the '*Great Nicholas* ... lyeth in the east end of Deptford Strond.'

The sheer number of ships and the resulting industry that prevailed throughout the King's Yard made it a popular destination for visiting dignitaries and even royalty. Keen to impress their visitors, the dock officials went to great lengths to make official visits as memorable as possible and no expense was spared in impressing their most illustrious guests. When Edward VI visited the dockyard on 19 June 1549, he was treated to a mock battle that left such an impression on him that he was moved to record the event. He later wrote:

> I went to Deptford, being bedden to supper by the Lord Clinton ... After supper was ober, a fort [was] made upon a great lighter on the Temps [Thames] which had three walles and a Watch Towre, in the meddes [midst] of wich Mr Winter was Captain with 40 or 50 other soldiours in yellow and blake. To the fort also appertained a gallery of yellow color with men and municion in it for defence of the castel; wherfor there cam four pinesses [small sailing vessels] with other men in wight ansomely dressed, wich entending to give assault to the castil, first droue away the yellow piness and aftir with clods, scuibs, canes of fire, darts made for the nonce [purpose made], and bombardes assaulted

the castill ... and droue away the pinesses, sinking one of them, out of which all the men in it being more than 20 leaped out and swam in the Temps. Then came th' Admiral of the navy with three other pinesses, and wanne the castel by assault, and burst the top of it doune, and toke the captain and under captain. Then the Admiral went forth to take the yelow ship, and at length clasped with her, toke her, and assaulted also her toppe and wanne it by compulcion, and so returned home.

Edward's account of the staged battle at Deptford gives the impression that a life on the ocean wave in the 1500s was full of excitement and heroic deeds. However, the reality for the hundreds of men employed by both the King's navy and the dock merchants was very different. Although beautifully crafted and finished, Tudor ships were wide, slow and difficult to manoeuvre. Voyages could sometimes take years to complete and the crew had to endure cramped and filthy conditions on vessels infested with rodents. Attacks by pirates or other hostile forces were not uncommon and diseases such as scurvy caused by poor nutrition were rife due to a poor diet that consisted mainly of pickled, salted or smoked fish or meat with very little in the way of fruit or vegetables.

The crew of a large ocean-going ship numbered around 400, the majority of whom were simple sailors who would undertake the general running of the vessel under the orders of the officers. The senior members of the crew were afforded better conditions than the sailors. They undertook a series of highly important jobs and thus were much sought after by merchants and navy alike. Skilled carpenters and cooks experienced in catering for large numbers of men using very basic provisions were constantly in demand and another specialist member of the crew was the barber surgeon. Like their land-based counterparts, these men combined the pleasurable and sociable profession of hairdressing with the skill to treat disease, dress wounds and even amputate limbs if necessary. Back in the 1500s, it was generally believed that disease was caused by bad smells and so the barber surgeons often gave out pomanders to sickly members of the crew in an attempt to relieve their symptoms. Needless to say, the pomanders were not in any way effective, especially when the patient was suffering from a serious illness such as scurvy or typhus. While the former was caused by a lack of vitamin C, typhus was spread by lice and fleas and was frighteningly virulent, sometimes killing entire crews within weeks.

The fact that crews were almost wholly comprised of men meant that once the ship docked in port, the mariners immediately sought out female company and regularly contracted syphilis as a result. Syphilis is a disease that progresses slowly in stages, the first two being so mild that most sailors probably ignored them. However, up to 40% of those infected with the disease went on to the tertiary stage in which bacteria attacked the brain, heart and nervous system. Sailors suffering from tertiary syphilis on board a Tudor ship found to their horror that very little could be done to ease their pain and many endured the terrifying effects of mental collapse, blindness and repeated heart attacks before finally succumbing. In desperation, the barber surgeons inexplicably took to administering mercury to their frightened patients, which served only to make them lose their minds faster.

While the mercury treatment was downright dangerous, other remedies prescribed by the barber surgeons were simply unpleasant and/ or entirely useless. Most ships had a large supply of spiders on board so these were caught and administered to patients suffering from a high fever. Infected wounds were burnt with irons and all manner of ailments were treated using blood letting. The most dreadful procedure for a barber surgeon, however, was amputation. Although their medical knowledge was rudimentary to say the least, the barber surgeons did realise that if damaged or diseased limbs were removed without too much loss of blood, the patient could make a full recovery. They also knew that during an amputation, speed was of the essence. Prior to the surgery, the patient would be given alcohol to get him so drunk that he was almost senseless and was then restrained on a table. Rope was tied around the infected limb to restrict the blood supply and then the surgeon would select his spot and saw as fast as he could. Once the limb had been removed, what remained was dowsed in wine to keep it clean, the arteries were tied off and the wound stitched up and bandaged. There are no contemporary figures to show how many patients survived this most brutal of treatments, but the fact that amputations were performed at all suggests that at least a few were successful.

While much of the barber surgeons' work boiled down to trial and error, the men who possessed the most tried and tested expertise on board a ship were the pilots, whose skills and knowledge ensured that the vessel steered a safe course through sometimes very hazardous waters. Pilots tended to work in specific locations that they had often spent years studying and, rather like today's black cab drivers, their knowledge was impressive. In addition to recognising all the major landmarks, the pilots became familiar with tidal streams, the contents of the sea bed and even the smell of an area and used this wisdom to foresee any hazards. In 1514, John Wodlas, the pilot of the *Mary Rose*, wrote to the King's Council to claim expenses for bringing the ship through 'a danger in the sea called the Nase', taking her back to the port at Harwich and then meeting the King on his way back from Calais before navigating his way through the ominously named 'Blake Depes' and sailing the ship down the Thames to the dock at Deptford.

The piloting of Tudor ships was a complicated business involving plotting a course using a compass and dividers on sea charts called 'portulans', which marked coastlines and ports. Potential dangers were avoided by consulting 'rutters' – books that listed major landmarks, danger zones, tide tables and shallows in which a ship could weigh anchor. Of course, in order to plot an accurate course, the speed of the ship had to be measured and this was done using a log reel – a large barrel-shaped construction with a long length of knotted rope wound around it. To measure the ship's speed, a lump of wood called a chip was attached to the end of the rope and thrown overboard. Each knot on the rope was tied at seven-fathom (42ft) intervals and as the rope unravelled, the knots were timed as they passed over the side of the ship. The rate at which the knots went over was then used to calculate the velocity of the ship and although this method has long since fallen out of use, the speed of ships is still measured in knots today.

Pilots also had to keep a close eye on the depth of the water as it was easy for ships to run aground in unfamiliar waters. This was done using a similar method to the log reel. A lead weight was attached to a length of rope along which strips of cloth were tied at regular intervals so that the depth could be measured. The hollow bottom of the lead was filled with tallow, which picked up the contents of the sea bed when the lead hit the bottom, thus giving the pilot an idea of the terrain that lay beneath them.

The night sky was also an invaluable navigational aid to Tudor pilots. The age of the moon helped determine high and low tide, latitude was calculated by measuring the altitude of the Pole Star using a device known as an astrolabe and longitude was ascertained using 'dead reckoning' – an estimate of distance and direction over a given period of time. The information provided by all the pilot's navigational aids was combined and plotted onto a 'traverse board' – a wooden block with peg holes that was set onto a compass rose – every half hour for a four-hour period. The results would then be interpreted and transferred onto the pilot's portulan chart using the dividers to plot the course. Although the pilot's job was highly skilled, its accuracy was dependent on a number of factors. Several nights of thick cloud could ruin the calculations and if a ship was caught in a severe storm or attacked by a hostile vessel she could easily lose her course and end up totally lost. Consequently, for Tudor pilots, knowledge was power and those who had the most experience of traversing the seas commanded the highest fees.

One of the Tudor period's most famous pilots, Sir Thomas Spert, was also responsible for establishing a corporation that still survives today – Trinity House, the authority responsible for the safety of British waters. Spert was born in Stepney and came from seafaring stock. His cousin Margaret was married to a shady character named John Lok, a merchant at the docks with connections to the slave trade. Spert worked his way up through the ranks of the Royal Navy and by 1514 had captained both the *Mary Rose* and the King's most impressive vessel, the *Great Harry*. As master of these prominent ships, he had responsibility for their upkeep which meant navigating them down the Thames for maintenance works at Deptford and Woolwich. At the time, the Thames presented a tricky route for large ships as the riverbed was by no means flat. Only the most experienced mariners could negotiate the waters successfully and ships often ran aground. Navigable routes down the Thames were closely guarded secrets, the knowledge of which would ensure a handsome reward. An indication of how coveted these secret routes were is revealed by the fact that in November 1514, Thomas Spert was paid £20 a year for keeping the secret of the newly discovered Black Deep channel in the Thames (a confidence he evidently shared with the *Mary Rose*'s pilot, John Wodlas).

Although their confidential routes brought them financial reward, Spert and his contemporaries were becoming increasingly concerned about the number of ships running aground in the Thames. They blamed these accidents on inexperienced or dishonest pilots who were sometimes bribed to wreck a ship on purpose by rival merchants. Spert and his allies decided that the situation was rapidly spiralling out of control and wrote to the King with their concerns, suggesting that all Thames traffic should be controlled by a governing body that in turn would ensure that the river pilots were properly trained and vetted. Cannily appealing to the monarch's paranoia, they also mentioned that if English seamen were not properly trained, the Thames might fall under the control of the Scots, Flemish or, heaven forbid, the French. Their shrewd tactics worked and in 1514, Henry agreed to the foundation of a corporation dedicated to the efficient management of shipping on the Thames. On 19 March, 'The Master, Wardens and Assistants of the Guild or Fraternitie of the most glorious and blessed Trinitie and Saint Clement in the parish Church of Deptford Stronde in the County of Kent' were granted a royal charter. Spert was elected Master of the new corporation and held the position until his death in 1541. During his time in office, his commitment to the welfare of corporation members was demonstrated in the introduction of free education for all their children. However, philanthropic acts such as this had to be funded and it fell to Spert to initiate exactly how the corporation would acquire the necessary finance to continue its work. From its inception, it had been agreed that Trinity House (as it swiftly became known) would take responsibility for providing experienced pilots to navigate overseas ships down the Thames to the docks and also ensure that all beacons and buoys in the river were properly maintained. In return, the ship owners would pay a fee to the pilots and every ship that entered the Port of London would pay the corporation for the use of the navigation aids. It was agreed that two-mast ships would be charged six pence, one-mast ships would pay four pence and all other craft would pay two pence. The dues were paid to the officials at Customs House who then forwarded them on to Trinity House.

In order to maintain standards and to ensure that the corporation was run efficiently, members of Trinity House were organised in a strict hierarchy. At its head was the Master, who was responsible for the general running of the corporation and was assisted by a deputy. The Master was supported by a committee of 31 Elder Brethren who met at a monthly court to discuss pressing issues. These men were all highly experienced mariners, ship owners and merchants who were easily identified while at their headquarters by their distinctive uniform of a smart navy blue tail coat with brass buttons and red cuffs decorated with fine, gold brocade and topped with a cocked hat. The remaining members of the corporation made up the Younger Brethren and were largely master mariners, pilots and merchants.

Although Sir Thomas Spert held the position of Master at Trinity House for 17 years, after his death the Elder Brethren decided that a new Master should be elected every three years and over the ensuing centuries many illustrious names held the office including Samuel Pepys (from 1685) and the Duke of Wellington (from 1837). The work done by Trinity House was recognised by Elizabeth I who extended their remit to include responsibility for all navigational aids (including lighthouses) along the coastline of the kingdom and in 1796, the corporation moved to grand new premises in Trinity Square, close to the Tower of London. Still there today, it is the official General Lighthouse Authority for England, Wales, the Channel Islands and Gibraltar and holds responsibility for all lighthouses, lightvessels, buoys and electronic communication systems. It also acts as the Deep Sea Pilotage Authority and still provides navigators for ships in North European waters.

At the time of its foundation, the only foreign merchants not obliged to use the services of Trinity House were the Hanseatic League. Despite the Merchant Adventurers' best efforts to loosen their stranglehold on the Baltic and German markets, the League continued to be the most influential and wealthy corporation in the London docks.

In 1526, the great German renaissance artist Hans Holbein the Younger arrived in England at the invitation of Sir Thomas More. While staying in the capital, his host's influence generated commissions for several society portraits including members of More's family, the Archbishop of Canterbury and the mathematician and astronomer, Nicholas Kratzer. On completion of this work in 1528, Holbein journeyed to Basel where he used the money earned in England to purchase property, but he returned to London in 1532 in the hope that the reputation he had established there would result in some more lucrative commissions. However, on arriving in the capital, Holbein quickly realised that the political atmosphere had radically changed since his last visit. In 1530, Henry VIII had strained relations between the crown and the Vatican to breaking point by declaring himself Supreme Head of the Church of England. Holbein's former host Thomas More was vehemently opposed to the King's radical actions and on discovering this, the artist quickly aligned himself with families who retained favour with the monarch, no doubt hoping that this allegiance would result in a royal commission. For many months, Holbein did his utmost to impress members of Henry's inner circle such as the Boleyn family and Thomas Cromwell and in order to support himself during this period, he turned to his fellow countrymen at the Steelyard.

The merchants at the Hanseatic League's headquarters welcomed Holbein with open arms and several of their members commissioned portraits. The resulting works of art served two purposes: firstly, work by such a well-respected artist enhanced their social standing immensely; and secondly, the resulting portraits could be sent to their families many hundreds of miles away as a visual record of a relative who many would not have seen for some years. Holbein's portraits of the League merchants meant that, for the first time, an integral part of the dock community was immortalised on canvas. The results not only show what the young and successful merchants looked like but the artist's prowess at composition also provides a fascinating insight into the personalities of some of the most powerful men to live and work in the Port of London during the Tudor period.

At first glance, Holbein's pictures of the men from the Steelyard seem to be simple portraits of successful and perhaps slightly arrogant young men, but closer study reveals a wealth of clues to their true character. For example, in the portrait of Dirk Tybis (a member of the Cologne branch of the League that had worked so diligently to protect their trading relationship with England during troubled times) the sitter is shown wearing a restrained but fashionable and costly fur-lined doublet. In his hands he holds a letter addressed to him at the Steelyard, while a piece of paper lying on the desk beside him is headed 'Jesus', under which is written the sitter's name and his age – 33. In medieval Germany, reaching this age was considered highly significant as it was the age at which Christ was crucified, hence the reference to Jesus at the top of the paper. Although Dirk Tybis was keen to make his financial success very evident, he was also keen to show his piety and commitment to business.

Another Cologne merchant to be immortalised by Holbein was Hermann von Wedigh, a young member of a German merchant dynasty. Like his colleague Dirk Tybis, the expensively dressed von Wedigh is pictured sitting at a desk or table on which is placed a book – possibly a reference to the Lutheran texts imported by the League into England. A sheet of paper is inserted into the book bearing the words 'truth breeds hatred', which is generally agreed to be a reference to the controversy surrounding Protestantism at the time.

By far the most elaborate portrait to be painted by Holbein of the Steelyard employees is that of a young merchant from Danzig named George Gisze. While most of the sitters are portrayed in simple surroundings with few props, the setting in which Gisze is depicted is positively awash with symbolic items. In direct contrast to his soberly attired colleagues, Gisze is pictured wearing a lively pink silk doublet surrounded by the tools of his trade including pens, money, scales and a medieval clock. His desk is covered by an opulent Turkey-work rug on which a vase of flowers stands precariously. Plants held much symbolism during the Tudor period and those depicted in the vase were deliberately chosen. Carnations were often connected with marriage and were also thought to ward off disease, while rosemary represented remembrance, suggesting that the sitter was eager that his relatives back in Danzig should not forget him. The words 'no joy without sorrow' are deliberately inscribed on the wall next to tipped scales, suggesting that balance is the key to a happy and successful life.

During his time in the Steelyard, Holbein painted at least seven of the incumbent merchants. In addition, his countrymen also commissioned him to paint a magnificent two-panelled wall hanging entitled *The Triumphs of Riches and Poverty*, which hung in their dining room in the guild hall. Painted with watercolour on linen, the panels depicted two processions above which were inscriptions warning that money (whether too much or too little) is at the root of all things evil. This salutary moral offers a very interesting insight into the merchants' attitude to wealth and suggests a surprisingly sagacious point of view that some of today's city merchants might do well to heed.

On 31 May 1533, a huge pageant stretching from Fenchurch Street to Fleet Street was organised to welcome Henry VIII's queen-to-be, Anne

Boleyn, into the city. As Holbein had spent the last 12 months ingratiating himself with the Boleyn family, he was no doubt keen to be involved in the festivities and soon found an opening. The pageantry surrounding Anne's procession was made the responsibility of various guilds and companies, each of which were given a themed tableau to create – for example, *The Three Graces or the Judgement of Paris*. The Hanseatic League was given responsibility for the second display, the subject of which was Apollo and the Muses. As the League were known for their mercantile skills rather than any artistic prowess, they asked Hans Holbein to design it and the resulting tableau was a sight to behold. Anne's procession was welcomed with verses specially written for the occasion by the antiquarian John Leland and playwright Nicholas Udall in which Henry's already pregnant bride's beauty and fertility were praised. A surviving sketch by Holbein shows the tableau was set at the peak of Mount Helicon. Here Apollo sat in an elaborate throne topped with the symbol of the League, the eagle. The Muses sat around the throne playing musical instruments while beside them a white marble fountain ran with wine. While this scene may seem a little quaint for modern tastes, at the time it was hugely admired and even controversial. One of the visiting ambassadors interpreted the eagle as the symbol of Emperor Charles V, nephew of Henry's first wife, Catherine of Aragon, and thus took it as an insult to Anne Boleyn.

While the Hanseatic League discussed the royal pageant under Holbein's marvellous panels in their guild hall dining room, the English company of Merchant Adventurers were going through a difficult period. In 1528, their major market in the Netherlands ground to an almost complete halt when the Dutch went to war with Spain following increasingly bitter disputes with their rulers, the Spanish Habsburgs. Demand for English cloth from this lucrative market diminished to such an extent that the government was forced to order the English merchants to keep buying it for fear the industry would collapse, resulting in mass unemployment. Prior to the problems in the Netherlands, the cities controlled by the Hanseatic League had once again begun to impose restrictions on the English merchants. At first the Merchant Adventurers battled on and tried to make the best of a difficult situation but as trade became increasingly difficult, their members decided enough was enough. In 1552, they petitioned Edward VI to resolve their problems by playing the League at their own game. In a bold move, the King temporarily rescinded the Hanseatic merchants' privileges but soon lost his nerve and restored them after the League assured him that the Merchant Adventurers would be treated fairly. The temporary withdrawal of trading benefits was of course nothing new to the merchants at the Steelyard and no doubt many of them took the King's action with a pinch of imported salt. However, unbeknownst to them, the Hanseatic League's monopoly on Anglo-German trade was on borrowed time.

Outside the walls of the Steelyard, the beleaguered Merchant Adventurers continued to be gravely concerned about their future. Caught in a commercial rut that forced them to focus their concentration on the European markets, they were in desperate need of fresh blood that could help them break out of their restrictive trading pattern. In 1553, the answer to their prayers came along in the form of Sebastian Cabot, son of the great explorer, John Cabot.

Sebastian Cabot was born *circa* 1481, the second son of John and his wife, Mattea. Brought up close to the bustling docks at Bristol, the young Sebastian gained his first experience of seafaring when he accompanied his father on several crown-funded expeditions to the New World. In 1505, the receipt of a royal grant enabled him to temporarily concentrate on the study of cartography and navigation and by 1512 his knowledge and seafaring experience had earned him a solid reputation as a skilled mariner and talented map-maker. Around this time, he moved to Spain where he remained for many years in the employment of the crown but took care to retain contact with his colleagues and patrons in England and in 1547, he returned, taking up advisory posts in both Bristol and London. By this time Sebastian Cabot was over 65 years old, but it appears that his energy and enthusiasm were undiminished as he immediately set about persuading members of the Merchant Adventurers Company that the discovery of a new passage to the Far East would bring with it untold wealth. At first, Cabot was concerned that the Merchant Adventurers would see the potential Far Eastern market as a threat to their existing businesses, but the growing problems in Europe prompted them not only to welcome his idea but also invest in it. In 1553, the China Company was formed and immediately attracted interest from the dock-based merchants who were keen to explore new opportunities. At a cost of £25 each, 240 shares in the new company were sold, Cabot was made governor and a charter was swiftly applied for. In May 1553, two expeditions headed by Sir Hugh Willoughby and Richard Chancellor set sail in search of a new 'north-west passage'.

This first exploration turned out to be both arduous and treacherous. Willoughby and his crew made slow progress and that winter became stranded on the inhospitable northern coast of Russia. Exhausted, bereft of supplies and miles away from civilisation, all hands were lost in the Arctic blizzards that ceaselessly battered their stricken ship. Thankfully, Chancellor and his men were more fortunate. Although they too endured almost overwhelming conditions along the freezing coastline, they somehow managed to make landfall and find their way through the frozen wastes to Moscow where Chancellor managed to rescue the doomed voyage by persuading Tsar Ivan IV to grant exclusive trading privileges to the Merchant Adventurers.

Although they failed to realise their ultimate ambition of discovering a new passage to China, Chancellor and his men received a heroes' welcome on their return to the London docks. Queen Mary hastily granted the company charter and changed its name from the now inappropriate China Company to the more apt but unwieldy 'Merchant Adventurers of England for the Discovery of Lands, Territories, Iles, Dominions and Seignories unknowen, and not before that late adventure or enterprise by sea or navigation commonly frequented'. Somewhat understandably, the company quickly became known by the catchier title of the Muscovy or Russia Company and Sebastian Cabot was named governor for life. Alas, the great explorer had little time to enjoy his new position and England lost one of its most energetic and creative mariners in 1557. However, Cabot's legacy lived on. The Russia Company continued to explore new markets across the huge Russian Empire and this new and lucrative trade brought with it fresh vigour and hope for the Merchant Adventurers who now realised that the expansion of their business had few frontiers.

Sebastian Cabot's ambitious plans brought the docks to the attention of Queen Mary and ever keen to extract money for the royal coffers, she ordered that all import businesses at the port be scrutinised by her officials with a view to increasing the amount of tax obtained from this lucrative source. When Elizabeth I succeeded Mary in 1558, she immediately reviewed the reports and appointed her Lord Treasurer, the Marquis of Winchester, to draw up a wholly revised Book of Rates, which listed the amount of tax due on commodities arriving at the London docks. The marquis was diligent in his duties and added 300 goods to the list of taxable merchandise as well as increasing the duty liable on existing items.

This huge increase in taxation tempted many merchants to consider smuggling their cargoes into the city but unfortunately for them, the Marquis of Winchester was one step ahead and drew up plans that would revolutionise the way the docks operated. In order to effectively monitor every consignment that arrived in the Port of London, he ruled that with the exception of beer, coal and corn, all overseas shipments had to dock at one of the quays on the north side of the Thames, between the Tower and Queenhithe. These landing stages became known as 'legal quays'.

In preparation for the effective execution of this mammoth task, Winchester purchased the two wool quays located close to the Tower on behalf of the crown and constructed a new Custom House there which was to become the headquarters of the officers employed to inspect the ships as they arrived in port. These inspectors were known as 'waiters' and were assigned specific quays in which they would carry out their unpopular work. As soon as a ship had docked, the waiters boarded the vessels to obtain an official certificate drawn up by the owner that stated the ship's name, its home port, its size, the master's name and nationality, the port of departure and a bill of landing for its cargo. The information on these certificates was entered into a book and taken to the Custom House by the officials who then calculated the exact amount of tax due on the shipment using the Marquis of Winchester's new rate book. Sometimes, the amount of cargo on board was unknown and so the entire contents of the hold had to be carried by lighters to the Custom House quay where it was unloaded and counted by the waiting officials.

In order to effectively instigate the new system of tax assessment, surveys were conducted at the majority of the quays on the north bank of the Thames to record the types of goods accepted therein. One of these surveys was published in 1584 and gives a fascinating snapshot of the docks during the Elizabethan period. In typical Tudor fashion, the description of the Port of London was excessively verbose and appeared on the document thus:

> The names of all the kays and wharfs in the Porte of London used for landinge of wares and merchandizes before the making of the statute in anno primo that doth appoint landinge and landinge places together with a declaracon with what kyndes of wares they were most occupied before that tyme begynninge att the kaye next to the Tower and naming them in order as they lye towards the Three Cranes in the Vyntrew.

The ensuing descriptions of the various quays reveal just how much the area had evolved since the beginning of the medieval period when the Port of London had comprised just 10 small landing stages dotted along the waterfront:

Galley Quay – greatly occupied with all kynde of merchandizes bothe inward and outward.

Olde Wollkaye – used only for shippinge of wolle and felts and when the Staplers had ended there shippinge then cost men occupyed it for woode and other cost wares.

Custom Howse Kaye – well occupied with all kyndes of merchandizes both inward and outwarde.

Greenberys Kaye – well occupied with wares inward and outward for Fraunce and with cost mens goodes.

Crowne Kaye – occupied but with cost men.

Beare Kaye – with Portingall commodities by reason the merchants of that contree did lye and had ther ware howses there and with some cost men.

Thrustans Kaye – well occupied with all kynde of merchaundizes inward and outward.

Sabbes Kaye – with pitche tar and sope ashes and such like.

Gibsons Kaye – with lead and tynne and other cost wares.

Yongs Kaye – with wares belonginge to merchants of Portingale by reason they did lye there and was vsed for shippinge of straungers of clothes.

Raffs Kaye – with all kynde of merchandizes inward and outwarde.

Dyse Kaye – altogether with cost wares.

Old Thrustons Kaye – with goodes of certan Flemyngs lyeinge there and with cost wares.

Smarts Kaye – altogether with fyshe.

Sommers Kaye – wholly inhabited by Flemyngs and used for there merchandizes.

Buttolphe Wharff – with straungers goodes that ley and had ware howses there and with wynes and by cost men.

Cocks Kaye – altogether for straungers goodes who had merchandizes and lodgings.

Gaunts Kaye – for landinge of barrell fyshe and suche like havinge no crane.

Freshe Wharff – for fyshe and eele shippers.

The Stillyard – for all theire owne merchandizes only.

Three Cranes – for wynes and waynscotts onely.

Three additional quays that formed part of the Elizabethan port are not listed in the survey. Billingsgate, which lay between Smarts and Sommers Quay, was, like the quay at the Tower, not included in the legal quay legislation. Busshers Wharf and Thomas Johnsons Quay, which lay either side of the Steelyard, also do not appear but perhaps were considered part of the Hanseatic League's complex.

Most of the 'straungers' mentioned in the survey were not permanently resident in London. Most merchants would travel over to the city on board their ships and stay in small lodgings within their respective quays until their cargo had been sold and the ship was loaded and ready to travel to its next port of call. However, as the survey notes, a small community of Portuguese merchants resided in properties that formed part of the dock complex at Yong's and Bear Quay. England and Portugal had benefited from a trading relationship since 1386 and by the 1500s the Portuguese traders were importing goods such as Indian cotton, sugar, figs and oranges into the capital. However, despite the two countries' long trading relationship, it appears from the survey that by the middle of the 16th century the Portuguese merchants in London were experiencing hard times as the gibbet (small crane) at their Bear Quay headquarters is described as being 'very unfit for merchaundize'.

Despite the vast increase in duty payable on imported goods following the Marquis of Winchester's introduction of the legal quay system, London still provided the merchants with such riches that the port continued to attract vessels carrying goods from across the known world. The Merchant Adventurers and their colleagues numbered some of the wealthiest and most powerful men in London but unlike their opposite numbers in the Continental ports, they had no central headquarters in which they could discuss and conduct business. In 1565, this situation changed thanks to the generosity of a Merchant Adventurer named Thomas Gresham, one of the docks' most successful incumbents.

Thomas Gresham was born *circa* 1518 in Milk Lane, the second son of Richard Gresham, a successful merchant who would rise through the ranks of the Corporation of London to become mayor in 1537, and his wife Audrey. By the time Thomas was born, his father was well established in business but was keen to engender in his sons the drive to make their own way in life rather than rely on family money. To this end, Thomas was apprenticed at the age of 17 to his uncle and over the following eight years he learned the merchants' trade and gained, in his own words, 'experience and knowledge of all kinds of merchandise'.

As the young Thomas grew more experienced, his father and uncle introduced him to their operations in the Netherlands, which centred round the trading of fine fabrics such as velvet and satin in addition to high-quality woollen cloth, tapestries, armour and weaponry. During this time, he learned to speak both Flemish and French – languages that would help him considerably in his future business dealings.

By 1543, Thomas had completed his apprenticeship and gained the freedom of the Mercers' Company. Over the following years, he gradually took charge of the Gresham family's business in the Netherlands and also gained favour with Henry VIII by acting as a diplomat and arranging several commercial 'favours' for the King. Thomas protected his financial wellbeing in his private as well as his commercial life. In 1544, he married Anne Ferneley, the wealthy widow of a mercer named William Read who had inherited valuable estates and a prosperous business from her deceased husband. Thomas wasted no time in merging Read's business with his own and took on the management of two large estates that had been left in trust for Anne's two young sons. Following their betrothal, the couple lived in a rented house in Basinghall Street and the extensive records that survive from this period show what life was like for a successful merchant's family in the 16th century. Thomas's business in the Netherlands often took him away from home for long periods of time, but his wife had little opportunity for solitude or loneliness. While her elder son Richard boarded with a tutor for much of the time, Anne's younger child, William, remained with her and they shared their home with her husband's apprentice, Thomas Bradshaw, his factor or agent, John Elliot, and a number of domestic staff. When Anne fell pregnant with her and Thomas's only son, her father also moved in to keep his daughter company during her confinement. Mr Ferneley was a generous house guest and when the expectant couple bought a new home in Cheapside to accommodate their growing family, he was responsible for purchasing much of the furniture.

The new house became the base from which Thomas conducted his business affairs in the Netherlands, managed the estates of Anne's sons and made regular visits to his father's properties – Ringshall in Suffolk and Intwood Hall in Norfolk – which he inherited after his father's death in 1549. The Greshams treated their employees well. Records show that Thomas took cloth from his stores and had it made into garments for his staff and also provided them with shoes. The family enjoyed entertaining and at Christmas 1547 even hired some minstrels to entertain their guests. Like many other men of his class, Thomas was also fond of gambling, regularly playing dice and a long-forgotten game known as 'bank notes', while Anne enjoyed spending time with friends and their children – christening gifts often appear in the couple's accounts.

In addition to their London property, the Greshams also owned a home in the Lange Nieustrate in Antwerp. In July 1553, considerable inconvenience was caused when Thomas recorded that 'my plate, household stuff and apparel of myself and my wife (which I sent and prepared unto Antwerp to serve me during my service there) … were all lost' during a storm at sea. Since the death of Thomas's father, the Greshams had also taken on Intwood Hall where they were expected to receive any dignitaries who happened to be visiting the area. However, although the entertaining of the sometimes rather dull worthies that arrived on their Norfolk doorstep was no doubt a little tiresome, Thomas appears to have had a fondness for the area. In 1553, he bought two more properties in the county and three years later enlarged his East Anglia portfolio further with the acquisition of Austin Canons priory at Massingham, the manor and rectory at Langham and the manors of Walsingham, Narford, Merston and Combes.

By this time, Thomas had been made royal agent in the Netherlands, a post he would hold until 1564 and would lead to a knighthood in 1559. His enhanced status prompted another foray into property acquisition and by the mid-1560s his already impressive portfolio included real estate at Mayfield in Sussex and Osterley in Middlesex. The Mayfield property was a particularly lavish affair, with furnishings valued at over £7,500. Thomas also upgraded his main London residence, building Gresham House on Bishopsgate in 1566.

By the 1560s, it seemed to all intents and purposes that Thomas Gresham was living a charmed life. However, in 1564 tragedy struck when Richard, his only son, died. The death of his child had a profound effect on him and as his biographer Ian Blanchard succinctly notes, 'with this link to immortality through his son suddenly severed, he soon set about recreating it – in stone'.

The following year, Thomas offered to build London a 'comely bourse' or meeting place for merchants, with his own money if the City Corporation would provide the land. Plans were drawn up, modelling the new building on the existing bourse in Antwerp, which of course had been visited by Gresham on many occasions. The design included a trading floor, offices and shops set around an open courtyard where merchants could meet and conduct business – a set-up similar in format to the long-forgotten Roman forum. Planning permission was granted on a site on Cornhill and the current occupants were handsomely rewarded for quietly finding accommodation elsewhere. Three years later, Gresham's bourse was complete and in 1571 it acquired the title of the Royal Exchange when Elizabeth I visited the building.

Following the construction of the Royal Exchange, Gresham continued with his philanthropic endeavours by building eight almshouses behind his mansion in Bishopsgate and providing the funding for the foundation of Gresham College in London. He eventually died at Gresham House on 21 November 1579.

The Royal Exchange flourished as a centre for mercantile trade until it was destroyed in the Great Fire of 1666. By this time, it had become such an important part of London commerce that a second exchange was built on the site in 1669. This building too was destroyed by fire in 1838 and was replaced with the current structure, which continued as a vital component of London-based trade until 1939. Today, the Royal Exchange is but a shadow of its former self, operating as an upmarket shopping centre offering overpriced giftware to wealthy city traders.

While Thomas Gresham and his fellow merchants were discussing the pressing business of the day in the newly opened Royal Exchange, many thousands of miles away one of the kingdom's most notorious knights was busy conducting an altogether more unsavoury kind of business which would eventually result in one of the most prestigious events ever witnessed by the community at the Deptford shipyard.

Francis Drake was born in 1540 in the village of Crowndale, near Tavistock in Devon. His father Edmund had originally been a priest but following the Dissolution of the Monasteries he gave up his life of piety, found work as a shearman and married a local girl. The young Francis began his seafaring career at an early age when his mariner uncle William Hawkins invited him to join his crew on a series of voyages to the coasts of Africa and Brazil. Francis proved to be an eager and efficient crew member and by his early teens he had moved out of his family home and joined his uncle and cousins at their house in Plymouth. The Hawkins family were high-profile members of society in this nautical town. William was a respected member of the council and educated his sons and nephew to mix easily with the town's great and good. From an early age, all three boys could articulately discuss all manner of subjects, from politics to religion, and to all who met them the Hawkins family seemed eminently respectable. However, what the good people of Plymouth did not realise was that once at sea, the Hawkins family supplemented their reputable maritime business by indulging in both piracy and slave trading.

In his early twenties, Francis began sailing on Hawkins' slave ships as they plied their despicable trade between Sierra Leone and the West Indies and was dazzled by the amount of money that could be made through selling human cargo. He also learned that fortunes could be acquired by capturing foreign merchant ships which themselves were indulging in shady trade. Many of these ships carried undeclared cargo. While transporting contraband offered the potential to make a lot more money, it also meant that if their vessel was attacked or sank, the loss of their illegal shipments could never be reported. Consequently, the pirate ships could get away with murder.

As Drake made his way up through the ranks of Hawkins' fleet, he began to embark on daring mainland raids in addition to taking ships. These raids concentrated on small Spanish settlements in the Americas and brought the crew untold riches. In 1571, Drake and his crew joined forces with French pirates and raided several Spanish outposts at Panama, claiming booty worth over £100,000 – a fabulously large amount of money in Tudor times. By 1576, Drake had grown so rich through his nefarious activities that he was able to purchase a fine house in Plymouth with staff and even a personal page. Around this time, he increased his social status immeasurably when he found favour with the Earl of Essex after providing him with money and ships for a campaign in Ireland. Drake's generosity paid dividends as his new acquaintance introduced him to many powerful people and resulted in him being selected to command an English fleet of ships on a crown-funded mission to raid the Spanish settlements in the Pacific. Captaining a ship first known as the *Pelican* but later renamed the *Golden Hind*, Drake led the fleet on a lengthy and treacherous voyage that lasted three long years but resulted in unimaginable riches.

The fleet set sail in November 1577 and began their campaign of terror by taking six Spanish and Portuguese ships off the coast of Morocco. The ships were plundered for their cargo and one, a large fishing smack, was commandeered by Drake and subsequently renamed the *Christopher*. Following a brief stop in Maio in the Cape Verde islands (where they were disappointed to find that other pirates had beaten them to any booty that might have been there) the fleet sailed to Sao Tiago where they captured a Portuguese merchant ship with a hold full of wine. Drake took the pilot – Nuno de Silva – hostage and forced him to navigate the fleet around the unfamiliar South American coast. De Silva's ship was also taken and renamed the *Mary*.

Thus far, Drake's voyage had met with considerable success but by the middle of 1578, divisions within the fleet were beginning to reveal themselves. In June they weighed anchor in Port St Julian on the southern coast of Argentina in a state of turmoil. Following the capture of de Silva's wine ship, Drake had fallen out with one of the fleet's other captains – Thomas Doughty, a colleague of his old friend the Earl of Essex – after Doughty had begun to spread rumours that Drake's brother Thomas had been stealing cargo. The resulting argument came to a head when Doughty challenged Drake's leadership and, in response, was put on trial for mutiny. At the resulting trial, Drake claimed that Doughty had jeopardised the success of the voyage by trying to discredit him and even insinuated that he had plotted to kill him. The jury of mariners were too scared to disagree with Drake's wild accusations. Doughty was found guilty, unceremoniously beheaded and his erstwhile allies were ordered to stay on the ship *Elizabeth* where they would have no access to the ears of other crew members. Some weeks later, the disgruntled crew of the *Elizabeth* were separated from the rest of the fleet during a storm and the ship's captain, John Wynter, took the opportunity to give Drake the slip and sailed quietly back to England.

Although it was probably the last thing on his mind at the time, Wynter's ship was possibly the first to circumnavigate the globe. On her return home, the government began to disseminate tales of the *Elizabeth*'s round-the-world voyage, but as soon as Drake appeared laden with vast riches, the earlier story was quickly abandoned and the honour given to Drake.

Following the desertion of the *Elizabeth*, another ship – the *Marigold* – disappeared and de Silva's ship was abandoned. Drake's reduced fleet continued on the voyage and on 25 November 1578, docked at the island of Mocha with the intention of plundering the mines known to exist there. However, the mariners' plans were thwarted by fierce resistance from the islanders who fought a ferocious battle in which four of the sailors were killed and Drake himself narrowly escaped being blinded when an arrow pierced his skull just below his right eye. The fleet beat a hasty retreat from Mocha and sailed to Valparaiso where the recuperating Drake oversaw the capture of a ship carrying 200,000 gold pesos and directed the plunder of several buildings, where the crew were delighted to find a collection of charts and navigation instructions for all the Pacific coastal ports.

By now, word of Drake's raids in the Pacific had spread throughout Europe and his booty-laden ships were now prime targets for pirates. In preparation for attack, Drake armed his ship with heavy guns and sailed for the north coast of Chile, arriving at Arica on 5 February 1579. Here, the fleet captured a merchant vessel with a significant amount of silver on board and would have got themselves a second ship had a drunken member of the crew not dropped a lamp into its hold, resulting in the vessel being burned. From Chile, the fleet continued up the coast towards Mexico, attacking and plundering any vessel that got in their way.

At this stage of the voyage, the fleet's unrivalled success resulted in Drake becoming rather too big for his boots. His practical mariners' clothing was discarded in favour of fine silks and velvets. He organised lavish dinners at which he bragged to his captive audience that he could sail anywhere he pleased and he even took over the duties of the fleet's chaplain. Whilst holding court, Drake was often very free with his words and soon everyone on board the ships, including Spanish and Portuguese prisoners, were aware of how he intended to travel back to England. Eventually it dawned on Drake that he had perhaps said too much. His prisoners, including the pilot de Silva, were abandoned at Guatalco in modern Mexico and the charts for the journey home were redrawn.

Following essential repairs to his ship, Drake then sailed for the Moluccas where the fleet loaded up with provisions and a cargo of spices provided by the islands' friendly king and set sail for home. The journey, however, proved treacherous. After leaving the Moluccas, Drake's newly repaired ship ran aground and all the provisions were thrown overboard in an attempt to free her. The chaplain dared to pronounce that this was divine retribution for the execution of Captain Doughty and after the ship was freed, an infuriated Drake forced him to spend the rest of the voyage with the crew as punishment for daring to question his judgement.

The fleet finally arrived back in Plymouth on 26 September 1580 to a rapturous reception. Drake wasted no time in securing his huge hoard of booty, which by now included gold, silver, wines, luxury fabrics and fine jewellery, and caught the next coach to London. Once arrived in the capital, he had a private audience with Queen Elizabeth where the two decided that the amount of treasure brought home from the voyage should not be disclosed. It remains unknown just how much wealth Drake brought back on his ships, but it was sufficient to pay the crew and himself, give generous gifts to the Queen and her retinue and pay back investors, who received an excellent return on their money.

In return for his generosity, Elizabeth bestowed a knighthood on Drake and decided to put his ship, the newly renamed *Golden Hind*, on permanent display at the royal dockyard in Deptford. A lavish ceremony was organised to commemorate this auspicious occasion. The *Golden Hind* was decked out in royal regalia and an impressive banquet was laid out in Drake's cabin. Queen Elizabeth arrived at Deptford welcomed by a huge crowd who craned out of windows, climbed onto roofs and crowded into the dock complex itself to see the arrival of the monarch. As the Queen approached, a bridge carrying nearly 100 people collapsed, sending the shocked well-wishers into the murky depths of the Deptford Basin. Once inside the *Golden Hind*, the Queen, Drake and the accompanying worthies dined on a fabulous meal after which the great pirate's status was finally granted when Elizabeth confirmed the knighthood.

The Queen's actions proved to be well timed. Just six years after she bestowed a knighthood on Francis Drake at Deptford, King Philip II of Spain gathered a fleet in Cadiz harbour in preparation to invade England. On the orders of Elizabeth, Sir Francis Drake gathered a fleet of warships and sailed to the Spanish coast. On reaching the harbour he used the skills he had honed during his three-year voyage to the Pacific to destroy 20 of the Spanish ships, famously describing this daring feat as 'singeing the King of Spain's beard'.

Undeterred by this setback, King Philip amassed a huge armada of 130 ships and drew up plans for them to sail to the Spanish-ruled Netherlands, where they would collect an army of 30,000 men before sailing for the English coast. In May 1588, the armada set sail from Lisbon but quickly ran into a storm during which they lost a great quantity of supplies and ammunition. Word was leaked to Drake about the Spanish ships' imminent arrival and he prepared his fleet for battle. Under the command of Drake and Lord Howard, the English fleet ambushed the Spanish armada on 21 July off the coast of Drake's home town of Plymouth. Realising they were trapped, the Spanish ships quickly retreated to the harbour at Calais, hotly pursued by eight English fireships. In the resulting battle, Drake and Howard's fleet managed to totally destroy four of the Spanish warships and severely damage many more. The defeated armada was forced to retreat but found the passage through the Channel too dangerous and so were forced to sail around the treacherous coast of Scotland in order to return home. In the event, just 60 of the original 130 ships made it back to Spain.

Back at the docks, the sustained hostilities between the English and Spanish had caused serious problems for the merchants. Trade between England and the Spanish-ruled Netherlands had been strained to breaking point and, to make matters worse, the Hanseatic League had capitalised on the situation and tried to block English grain imports to the Low Countries. This proved to be the last straw for the English merchants and they begged the Queen to retaliate. In previous times, the monarchy had considered the Steelyard much too lucrative to dispose of, but the activities of the Russia Company prompted Elizabeth I to view things differently. Realising that the Hanseatic League's presence was no longer integral to the economy, she complied with the English merchants' wishes and gave the League just two weeks to leave the Steelyard.

Elizabeth's expulsion of the Hanseatic League effectively ended a unique trading relationship that had lasted for over 400 years. Following the succession of James I in 1603, the German merchants renegotiated trading terms with their English counterparts and consequently were let back into the Steelyard, but by then this ancient commercial enclave on the banks of the Thames had changed irrevocably. During the League's absence, the shops, warehouses and quay had been taken over by English merchants who had no intention of relinquishing their prime trading site. Thus, the German merchants were forced to share their premises with their hosts and the Steelyard lost its strong Teutonic identity forever. The site continued to function as the headquarters of the Hanseatic League and following its destruction during the Great Fire of 1666 it was considered sufficiently important to be rebuilt. Incumbent German merchant Jacob Jacobson oversaw the redevelopment and commissioned the sculptor Caius Gabriel Cibber of Holstein to carve a magnificent crest depicting the League's symbol of the double-headed eagle to hang over the Steelyard entrance on Thames Street. In addition, the League also presented their church of All Hallows with an exquisitely carved oak screen which ran the full length of the building. This screen was later moved to St Margaret, Lothbury, where it can still be seen today. Jacobson ran the Steelyard until 1745, when it passed into the joint ownership of the cities of Bremen, Hamburg and Luebeck. It continued to be jointly owned by these three cities until 1853, when the site was sold to the Victoria Dock Company for warehousing. What remains of the once-glorious headquarters of the Hanseatic League now lies buried under Cannon Street Station, a forgotten relic of a centuries-long German presence in London.

The gradual but unstoppable demise of the Hanseatic League's trading activities in London coincided with the rise of a company that was to have a huge influence on the economic and social history of not only the London docks but the entire kingdom.

In 1581, Elizabeth I granted a royal charter to a group of Merchant Adventurers with a view to creating an overland trading relationship with the East Indies and China. Several excursions into the region were made and the merchants returned with enthusiastic tales of the riches that could be acquired if sea trade could be established between England and Asia. A fact-finding voyage set sail in 1591 with three ships under the command of George Raymond, but unfortunately this first foray quickly turned into a financial disaster. One of the ships was lost with all hands in a storm, another was forced to return to England after being badly damaged and the third was seized by the Spanish. However, on returning to London, Raymond spoke with the Queen and assured her that with better organisation, the opening up of trade routes was eminently possible.

Inspired by the prospect of trading with profitable new markets, Elizabeth actively sought to open up dialogue with the countries in question. In 1596, she dispatched two London merchants – Richard Adam and Thomas Bromfield – to China armed with letters to the emperor that waxed lyrical on how trade between the two countries could be mutually beneficial. However, while Good Queen Bess was busy courting the Chinese Emperor, the Dutch were busy establishing a trade route to her other main target, the East Indies. By the end of the 16th century, the Dutch merchants were threatening to monopolise trade in the region and the English merchants realised that they could spend no more time prevaricating. A group of Merchant Adventurers agreed to embark on a voyage to the East Indies and on 23 September 1600, a meeting of the company recorded that 'they have undertaken to sett forth a voiage for the discovery of the trade of the East-Indyes' after receiving royal assent. Two days later, the newly formed East India Company purchased its first ship – the *Susan* – for

£1,600 and less than a month later they bought three more ships – the *Malice Scourge* (subsequently renamed the *Red Dragon*), the *Hector* and the *Ascension* – along with a pinnace. In total, these ships required a crew of 500 men (the *Malice Scourge* alone held 180) and men were sought from the communities at the docks to embark on this exciting and dangerous sortie into unknown territories.

The committee of the East India Company also drew up a list of provisions required for the long voyage and an inventory of goods to be traded, which included such diverse commodities as iron, tin and lead, coloured fabrics and lace. Presents for officials at the foreign ports were also wisely included as was a large consignment of bullion, which could be used as currency. The *Red Dragon*'s captain, James Lancaster, was made Admiral of the Fleet, a responsible position that required excellent negotiating skills in addition to strong leadership and an expert maritime knowledge.

On New Year's Eve 1600, Elizabeth signed a charter that officially endorsed the 'Company of Merchants of London Trading to the East Indies' and granted it a monopoly on all trade east of the Cape of Good Hope. Shares in the company were floated and were quickly snapped up by subscribers keen to profit from this potentially lucrative market. Captain Lancaster's fleet set sail from Woolwich on 13 February 1601 to much celebration, but unfortunately the voyage had an inauspicious start. The journey was delayed for weeks due to the ships being becalmed in the doldrums and by 9 September, with their destination still some distance away, 105 members of the crew had succumbed to scurvy. Undaunted, the merchants persisted and by the spring of 1602 the fleet reached the port of Achin in Sumatra where, to Captain Lancaster's delight, the sultan permitted them to trade without paying any custom. The merchants wasted no time in establishing a small trading settlement on this large Indonesian island and flushed with success, sent the *Susan* to the neighbouring city of Priaman to obtain one of the region's most prized commodities – pepper.

Once the *Susan* had returned with her sought-after purchase, Lancaster sent her and the *Ascension* home while the *Hector* and *Red Dragon* set sail for Bantam in Java where once again he succeeded in agreeing terms and established a small trading post. The pinnace that had accompanied the ships on the voyage was dispatched to the Moluccas to purchase cloves and nutmegs. The voyage now complete, the jubilant crews set sail for England, arriving at the south coast in September.

Captain Lancaster's exemplary leadership during the expedition earned him the respect of the East India Company and he was elected director on more than one occasion. However, little is known of the personal life of one of the dock's most influential inhabitants. When he died in 1618, Captain Lancaster was buried in the grounds of All Hallows, which for centuries had been known as the sailors' church. His will does not mention a wife or children, although it does reveal that he had two brothers named Peter and John and a sister who married a man named Hopgood. With no immediate family to provide for, Captain Lancaster left the bulk of his not inconsiderable wealth to the poor of the city, many of whom were later to have their lives transformed by the influence and unparalleled success of the captain's employers. By the time Lancaster died, the East India Company was fast growing into one of the country's most powerful organisations. As it headed towards its 18th-century zenith, it controlled a turnover so vast that it would dwarf even the largest modern companies, such as Microsoft. Unsurprisingly, the company was to play a central role in the future of the Port of London and its people, particularly those living near the sleepy village of Blackwall.

When the East India Company was first founded, it acquired the ships it needed by either purchasing 'second-hand' vessels (usually warships) and altering them to suit its requirements, or by commissioning new ships from shipbuilders based at the yards in East Anglia. However, as its trade increased, the company decided that the vessels that made up its fleet were too small. The shipyards in Suffolk and Essex simply did not possess the facilities to make craft to the new specifications and so the ambitious decision was made to create its own dockyard, which could not only build huge new ships but also carry out repairs and load cargo.

Responsibility for finding a location for this new dockyard fell to the company's shipwright John Burrell. After surveying several potential sites along the banks of the Thames, Burrell found a private dockyard in Deptford which seemed suitable and the company hurriedly secured the lease. Work began at the Deptford site but it soon became apparent that even more space was needed. Once again, Burrell was dispatched on a search for suitable locations. The new site had to be large enough to accommodate the construction of ships of up to 1,000 tons and also needed to have enough adjoining land to house workshops and offices. All the sites close to the legal quays were too small so Burrell travelled further east where he became interested in an area of marshland that lay beside a tiny village called Blackwall, on the north bank of the Thames, some distance away from the city.

Although little more than a fishing hamlet, Blackwall did possess a maritime history as during the Tudor period long-disappeared workshops in the area had taken the overflow from the royal shipyards, undertaking small repairs and maintenance. Although the village had no actual dock, a long natural reef in the Thames provided a safe harbour for ships. Consequently, Blackwall had been a popular stop-off point for travellers, who disembarked there and made their way into London by road instead of waiting on board the ship while it slowly made its way around the Isle of Dogs. However, despite the regular arrival of ships, Blackwall remained largely undeveloped save for a flight of steps leading to the water's edge, a small slip for fishing boats, a cluster of inns to serve the passengers and a crumbling causeway that led to the road into London. That said, the undeveloped land that surrounded the village prompted Burrell to deem it the ideal location for the East India Company's new premises. He assessed the amount of land required and staked out a large site on the eastern side of the old causeway. The owners of the land were approached, a lease on their land was obtained and by May 1614, work began on the new dock complex. Just three months later, the new dry dock had been excavated and the new Blackwall Dock received its first ship – the *Dragon* – for a series of repairs.

The arrival of the East India Company's new dockyard completely transformed Blackwall. Construction of the complex was completed by 1619 and the fully operational dock employed up to 400 people during its busiest periods. Consequently, tradesmen and labourers flocked to the area to find work and the once desolate causeway became lined with hastily constructed dwellings for the newly arrived workforce.

The Blackwall dock complex was a massive development, larger than any of its competitors, and was constructed along similar lines to the Hanseatic League's Steelyard. The site was surrounded by a high wall, behind which lay a series of buildings that housed virtually everything the dock required to function. There was a smithy and forge where everything from nails to ships' anchors was crafted, a rope walk for rigging, a tar house for waterproofing the ships and huge storehouses where supplies were kept. In the north-west corner of the site, a large house, later known as the Mansion House, provided accommodation for East India Company employees and next to the causeway a gatehouse was built into the perimeter wall, within which lay the porter's rooms and the offices of the Clerk of the Yard. As an added security precaution, large water-filled ditches surrounded the site and these doubled as a useful storage place for newly sawn masts before they were fitted onto the waiting ships. Keen to keep its employees on site during the working day, the company even built a 'victualling house' for the workers, insisting that they should 'bring their meat and drink with them in the morning, or take it in the yard.' Anyone who ignored this instruction and stole out to the nearby taverns during his lunch break risked instant dismissal.

Its huge size and equally large workforce meant that the Blackwall Dock proved to be extremely expensive to run and it soon became apparent that the East India Company's hubristic decision to build and maintain a fleet of monster-ships might prove to be a commercial folly. During the halcyon days of the 1620s the company's profits proved sufficient to sustain its costly yard, but when the business hit financial difficulties in the 1630s, the directors were forced to admit to their shareholders that the Blackwall Dock 'doth daily exhaust [the company's] treasure in a very great proportion'. As trade decreased, the need for huge ships receded and it became clear that the company could easily revert to using independent dockyards. In addition to this, security concerns had meant that valuable imported goods had never been stored at Deptford. Shareholders began to question the value of retaining such a drain on the company's resources and by June 1650 the pressure to dispose of the dockyard had become so intense that the directors reluctantly announced that the lease was up for sale. The Blackwall Dock was initially offered to the Admiralty who rejected it, so private buyers were sought. Eventually it was purchased by a shipwright named Henry Johnson in 1653 for £4,350 – considerably less than the East India Company had hoped for.

7

BLACK GOLD

While the East India Company was busy squandering its profits in Blackwall, an altogether more sinister trade was growing around the West African coast as slave ships loaded their holds with an ever-growing quantity of human cargo. British involvement in African slave trading was by no means a new activity. In fact the viability of such an enterprise had first been investigated in the 16th century by a mariner named John Hawkins who traded from his headquarters at Deptford, close to the royal shipyard.

Hawkins had been born in Plymouth in 1532, the son of Francis Drake's seafaring uncle. When John had finished his education, he entered the family firm along with his brother William. After gaining several years' experience of undertaking voyages and overseeing the company's financial concerns, John decided to expand the operation to London and opened the new premises at Deptford. This move proved to be profitable and soon after his arrival in the capital he had amassed sufficient funds to acquire a smart city residence in the parish of St Dunstan in the East and the hand in marriage of Katherine, daughter of Benjamin Gonson, treasurer of the navy. His social status now assured, Hawkins decided to part company with his brother, sold his share of the company for several thousand pounds and used this money to set up his own venture, trading with the Canary Islands.

While on one of his regular trips to the Canaries, Hawkins heard tales of the fortunes that could be made by trading slaves from the coast of Guinea in West Africa with the Spanish colonies in the Caribbean, who were desperate for labour to work on their plantations. Inspired by greed, he returned to London and successfully persuaded several of his wealthy associates, including his father-in-law, to finance an exploratory voyage.

In October 1562, Hawkins set sail for the West African coast with a small fleet of three ships and around 100 crew. After collecting an experienced pilot at the port of Tenerife, the fleet continued to their destination, docking at Sierra Leone where, according to Hawkins, they managed to capture around 300 Africans. After acquiring another ship from Portuguese traders to accommodate their unexpectedly large 'cargo', Hawkins and his crew sailed to Hispaniola (Haiti) where he exchanged his prisoners for cash and a variety of luxury goods including hides, sugar, ginger and pearls. Now laden with their valuable merchandise, the fleet set sail for London with a joyous crew, keen to lay their hands on their share of the profits. However, Hawkins' ships attracted the covetous attention of foreign customs officials during the journey home and the contents of two of the vessels were seized at ports by the Spanish and Portuguese authorities as punishment for trading without a licence. That said, such were the riches on board that once safely returned to Deptford, there was more than enough to satisfy the crew and give Hawkins' financiers a healthy return on their investment.

News of Hawkins' voyage and the potential riches that lay between Africa and the Caribbean reached Queen Elizabeth and eager to claim a share for herself, she encouraged a second foray to the African coast. Hawkins was granted permission to charter one of the largest ships in the Royal Navy – the *Jesus of Luebeck*, which had been purchased some years before from the Hanseatic League – and also prepared three of his own ships for the next voyage, which set sail on 18 October 1564. This trip proved to be even more lucrative than the first and the fleet returned home with holds full of fine merchandise, yielding a profit of 60% for the delighted investors.

After the unparalleled success of the first two voyages, it seemed as though Hawkins' venture could not go wrong. However, the next expedition quickly turned into a complete disaster. After setting sail on 2 October 1567, the fleet was quickly dispersed during a severe gale off the Spanish coast of Finisterre. The ships managed to rendezvous at Tenerife but their stay on the island was marred by disagreements between the crew. Once at the African coast, Hawkins found few slaves at the markets there and was forced to venture elsewhere to capture more. He docked at Cape Verde and made a sortie into the island where his men launched an attack on a village. However, the villagers (who may have received advance warning of the ships' arrival), bravely fought back and despite having vastly inferior weaponry, managed to badly wound both Hawkins and several of his crew with poison arrows. Undeterred, the British sailors hurriedly departed from the island and sailed to Sierra Leone, where Hawkins joined forces with a local king and launched a vicious attack on a nearby town. This time, the local population was overpowered and the ships' holds quickly became full of prisoners.

Following a few weeks of successful trading at a succession of island ports, Hawkins and his men once again set sail for England, anxious to get out of the area before the hurricane season set in. Before they commenced their Atlantic crossing, however, the fleet docked at San Juan d'Uloa on the Mexican coast to make some necessary repairs, weighing anchor at a small island some 500 yards from the shore. The local townsfolk were expecting a Spanish fleet to arrive any day carrying the new viceroy of Mexico, so when Hawkins' ships arrived, they naturally assumed that their new governor had arrived and left the fleet to its own devices. However, the next day, the real Spanish fleet appeared and the viceroy, one Don Martin Enriquez, took great exception to the presence of the English in his midst. Battle commenced and the Spanish succeeded in sinking several of Hawkins' ships including the Queen's *Jesus of Luebeck*, leaving just the *Minion* (commanded by Francis Drake) and the *Judith* unscathed. On realising that the *Jesus* was sinking, Hawkins hurriedly transferred the treasures that lay in her hold to the *Judith* and with this ship struggling under the weight of the sudden increase in cargo, he hastily departed the scene of devastation.

Soon after the ships had sailed a safe distance away from the irate viceroy, Francis Drake and the crew of the *Minion* decided that they had endured enough of Hawkins and his disastrous decisions. They turned and set sail for England, leaving the heavy *Judith* lumbering after them in desperation as they had taken most of the supplies. As the *Minion* disappeared over the horizon, Hawkins and his crew were forced to stew some of their cargo of hides along with rats and parrots in order to survive until a safe port could be found. By now, Hawkins had lost approximately 90 men and after the *Judith* docked in the Gulf of Mexico in a frantic search for supplies, even more crew members were lost when they were captured by the Spanish. Hawkins finally returned home on 16 October 1568 with just a handful of survivors. Amazingly, the riches on board the two remaining ships were sufficient to make the voyage a financial success. However, the loss of life and the tremendous hardships endured by the crew prompted both financiers and sailors to conclude that any future slave trading voyages were simply not worth the risk.

Although 16th-century attempts at organising a slave trade with the Americas ended with John Hawkins' disastrous voyage of 1568, the prospect of colonising North America remained an idea worthy of consideration. Several attempts were made to establish townships on its eastern shores during the remaining years of Elizabeth's reign but none met with success due to the alien and inhospitable surroundings in which the settlers found themselves. However, as the 17th century dawned, continued attempts by the British to colonise the vast and potentially valuable lands across the Atlantic began to reap rewards as tireless exploration of North America's east coast began to reveal less inhospitable regions.

Three years after Queen Elizabeth's death in 1603, King James I granted a charter to the Virginia Company – a joint stock corporation that had been formed by a group of London merchants and financiers with the express intention of profiting from the exploration and settlement of the east coast of North America. At this time, 'Virginia' applied to all the lands along the coast from present-day Maine to South Carolina and also included the island of Bermuda – an area that had first been brought to the attention of the British when Sir Walter Raleigh dispatched an expeditionary force to the region while attempting to establish a colony in today's state of Florida.

On 20 December 1606, the Virginia Company sent a fleet of three ships under the command of Captains John Smith and Christopher Newport across the Atlantic and after an arduous five-month voyage the vessels finally landed on the southern edge of Chesapeake Bay. After exploring the surrounding area, the settlers established a camp in a secure area close to a natural harbour, which they named Jamestown in honour of their king. This little encampment was destined to become the first permanent British settlement in North America but life there proved challenging from the outset. The pioneers initially managed to maintain peaceful relations with the native population of Algonquian Indians by providing them with metal tools and weaponry. However, disputes over land and property regularly brought tensions to boiling point, bringing periods of fierce conflict between the settlers and the Algonquian. Although many of the Native Americans were aggrieved about the British occupation of their land, not all were in favour of war, reasoning that a lucrative trading arrangement could be negotiated that would be of mutual benefit. Indeed, if Captain John Smith is to be believed, it was the daughter of a powerful Algonquian chief who eventually restored peace to the area.

According to Captain Smith, a brutal battle broke out between the warring factions during which he was captured and taken to an Algonquian camp where he was sentenced by the chief to execution. Smith was secured to a rock and preparing to meet his maker when, as the chief approached with a large club, his daughter threw herself across Smith's prostrate body in a valiant attempt to save him. Impressed by his daughter's dramatic action, the chief promptly reprieved Smith and allowed him to return to Jamestown.

Understandably grateful that the Indian princess had saved his life, Captain Smith struck up a close friendship with the woman whom he came to know by her nickname, Pocahontas. Through her relationship with Smith, Pocahontas met and befriended many of the other settlers, including the owner of a tobacco plantation named John Rolfe, whom she subsequently married, thus ensuring peaceful relations between her people and the English for many years. It is worth mentioning at this point that, contrary to the events depicted by animated filmmakers, there is no evidence that Pocahontas and Captain Smith were ever romantically involved.

In 1616, Rolfe and his Indian bride journeyed to London, where the Algonquian lady became the toast of society, even being presented to King James. However, the damp and smoky atmosphere of the city combined with exposure to illnesses to which she had no immunity took its toll on her health. Soon after she and Rolfe set sail for the return trip to Virginia in March 1617, Pocahontas was taken ill. The ship quickly returned to the English coast, docking in Gravesend, but it soon became clear that nothing could be done to save her. She was buried in the little churchyard of St George in Gravesend on 21 March.

Although Pocahontas' marriage to Rolfe was brief, she left a legacy which continues to this day. Prior to embarking on the fatal voyage to

England the couple had a son and it is through him that many Americans claim to trace their roots back to the first settlers and the 16th century Algonquian Indians. These claimants include such notables as Edith, wife of President Woodrow Wilson, and Nancy Reagan, but although they are undoubtedly descendants of Virginia's founding fathers, a direct link to Pocahontas is, at best, debatable.

Following Pocahontas' death, relations between the colonists and the Algonquian once again deteriorated, resulting in attacks on several plantations on 22 March 1622, when over 300 English settlers were slaughtered. However, although nearly ⅓ of the colonists were wiped out in the massacre, the remaining plantation owners felt that the riches gained by the trade in tobacco and an equally addictive substance – sugar – made their settlement well worth persevering with. European demand for these two commodities regularly outstripped supply and it rapidly became clear that the plantations required considerably more labour. Keen to keep production costs to a minimum and faced with reluctance from British workers to emigrate to this dangerous land, the plantation owners and merchants began to discuss the previously unthinkable possibility of resurrecting the trade in slaves from the African coast.

In an attempt to organise this shameful and disreputable trade, a group of London investors formed the Company of Adventurers to Guinea and Benin and in 1632 Charles I granted a licence to a second merchant group who planned to revive the transatlantic slave trade. Slowly, markets on the West African coast were established as the London merchants opened up dialogue with Portuguese slave traders and unscrupulous African tribal leaders who viewed the European slave ships as a convenient way to dispose of their enemies.

As the first ships arrived back in the London docks with their holds full of riches, the financial potential of the sordid business became glaringly evident. By 1660, a third chartered company, known as the Royal Adventurers Into Africa, was operating out of the city using funds provided by several members of the royal family and other London notables such as Samuel Pepys. Their investment quickly paid off. By 1665, the Royal Adventurers were making nearly £100,000 per annum from their trade.

In 1672, the Royal Adventurers Into Africa were superseded by a new chartered organisation known as the Royal Africa Company. By this time, the transatlantic slave trade was a major force in London's financial markets and a huge number of city investors held shares in the lucrative enterprise. In addition to the slave trade, the Royal Africa Company also traded in gold and a new coin was introduced to Britain struck from this most precious of metals. The treasury named it the 'guinea', should anyone need reminding of the origin of the material from which it was struck.

The dubious occupation of the slave trade combined with the vast wealth that could be made from it attracted the attention of numerous privateers who went into direct competition with the Royal Africa Company and their competitors. The African agents cared little about who they sold their captives to and the plantation owners were willing to purchase slaves from anyone who was selling at a reasonable price. The activities of the privateers constantly affected the profits of the chartered companies but the ungovernable nature of business along the West African coast made it impossible to curtail. Investors in London constantly grumbled about the privateers, but in 1713 their worries were eased when – as part of the Treaty of Utrecht, which temporarily ended the hostilities with Spain – Britain was given 'asiento' to supply slaves to the Spanish colonies in the Americas. Realising the potential value of the exclusive trading privilege and desperate to increase the funds in their dwindling coffers, the government effectively sold most of the national debt to a consortium of merchants known collectively as the South Sea Company. In return, the company was given the right to charge 5% interest on the loan annually and, more importantly, was granted the exclusive contract to trade with the Spanish settlements across the Atlantic. Believing that they could create a monopoly in the transatlantic slave trade, the South Sea Company began to feverishly issue shares, which investors were promised would bring them unprecedented wealth.

The South Sea Company did sterling work in ensuring that its trading proposal excited potential backers. The first share issue was snapped up and consequently the value of the company went through the roof. Over the following months, the South Sea Company and any business connected with it had investors clamouring at its doors. In an atmosphere very similar to that which sparked the dot com boom, shares in an increasingly ludicrous array of businesses (most of which had little connection to the South Sea Company) were sold to an avaricious public.

The most ridiculous share offering was rumoured to be from a company formed 'For carrying on an undertaking of great advantage but no one to know what it is.' Not surprisingly, the lunacy that surrounded the South Sea Company's trade in slaves was destined to end as abruptly as it started. Gradually, investors realised that trade with the Spanish Americas was not going to single-handedly revive the British economy and that many of the associated companies were nothing more than white elephants. What became known as the South Sea Bubble quickly burst, leaving foolish investors who had been seduced by the hysteria with nothing. The effect of the crash reached across the British Isles and affected all classes. Servants who had invested their life savings in this financial mirage lost everything while their equally imprudent employers found themselves in severely straitened circumstances. Even the King was affected when it transpired that two of his mistresses – the Duchesses of Kendal and Darlington – were exposed as major shareholders. Despite the dramatic aftermath of the South Sea Bubble, the company at its core survived and continued to profit from slavery until the 1730s, when the centre of the trade finally shifted from London to Bristol.

The rise of the transatlantic slave trade of the 18th century is a horrifying example of greed triumphing over humanity. While the merchants were busy lining their pockets with the proceeds of their transactions with the plantation owners, their 'cargo' was enduring almost unbearable suffering. Determined to keep the horrors of the infamous 'middle passage' to themselves for fear it would affect their profits, the slave merchants forbade crews to speak publicly about the scenes they witnessed on Atlantic crossings. For the slaves themselves, it was impossible to disseminate the truth about the inhuman existence that awaited them once aboard a slave ship. Virtually no one managed to escape and return to their birthplace where they could warn others and once at the plantations, the prison-like conditions made it impossible to organise any kind of cohesive campaign against their captors. That said, as trade continued, a few Africans made their way to England (usually as servants to merchants) and once there, discovered more opportunity to publicise the plight of their countrymen in the Americas. One such slave was a young man named Olaudah Equiano, who went on to play an integral role in the abolition of slavery in Britain. Through his tireless campaigning and the publication of his own biography, Olaudah brought the plight of the slaves to the masses and also gave a vivid account of the life of an enslaved African. The story of his capture and subsequent incarceration is typical of what many thousands of others endured but never found the opportunity to speak about. It represents the darkest and wickedest trade ever to emanate from the London docks.

Olaudah Equiano was born in 1745 in Benin, West Africa. Brought up in a small village, the young Olaudah watched how his elders worked a living from the landscape that surrounded them, farming the land and hunting the local wildlife for food and clothing. No doubt he expected that he would eventually join them in their labours. Much of the community's trade involved barter and a market existed not far from the village where goods were exchanged. Olaudah visited the market on numerous occasions and it was here that he became aware of the existence of slaves, most of whom had been brought there to be sold or were *en route* to larger markets. At the time, it was quite usual for the people of Benin to commit prisoners of war and criminals to a life of servitude and impoverished families sometimes resorted to selling their youngest children in order to survive. Thus, the Benin villagers were familiar with the concept of slavery but associated it with either punishment or extreme poverty.

By the time Olaudah was born, African slave traders working in cahoots with the Europeans had begun to resort to kidnapping in order to provide more captives for the transatlantic slave ships. Shortly after the boy's 10th birthday, he and his sister were alone in the family home when three such kidnappers stole into the village and spirited the two youngsters away. Over the following three days, he and his sister were taken deep into the vast jungle. Then, much to Olaudah's horror, his sister was taken away with no explanation and he found himself the property of an African goldsmith. During his brief stay with the goldsmith and his family, Olaudah was treated kindly and the time allowed him to recover from the arduous and frightening journey from his village. However, he was quickly resold to another group of slave traders who promptly took him to the market town of Tinmah – a popular stop-off point on the slave trade route. Here, he was taken to the home of a wealthy widow who provided accommodation for several boys of similar age. Olaudah enjoyed his time at the widow's house. He was well fed and treated so well that he hoped he might be taken on as a permanent servant. But the good treatment he received had a dark purpose which suddenly became clear when a group of slave traders arrived at the widow's house and took Olaudah away. Too late he realised that, like livestock, he had been fattened up for market.

Following several days' journey along an unidentified river (possibly the Niger), Olaudah and his captors arrived at the coast where European ships were waiting. Before this point, Olaudah had never seen a white man and was terrified by the sailors' rough behaviour and strange appearance, particularly their red faces and long hair. As he was taken on board one of the ships, the enormity of the situation he was in fell on his conscious like a ton of bricks. Unable to cope with the horror of what was happening, Olaudah passed out on the deck of the ship. Once he awoke, he found himself on the lower deck of the slave ship in conditions he could not have imagined in his worst nightmares. The sole purpose of a slave ship was to transport as many slaves as possible in the smallest amount of space. Consequently, captives were confined in woefully inadequate conditions. In 1789, the abolitionist Thomas Clarkson published a plan of the interior of the slave ship *The Brooks* to vividly illustrate the conditions endured by its prisoners. The lower deck resembled a modern-day sardine tin, with slaves laid out in rows with virtually no space between them. More slaves were accommodated on a gallery platform which was situated just 2ft 2in above the lower deck, making it difficult for those beneath it to sit upright, let alone stand. *The Brooks* was designed to carry a maximum of 482 slaves, but in the absence of any regulatory inspections it often took far more.

The horrendous conditions below deck resulted in Olaudah finding it impossible to keep food down as he struggled to keep his sanity amid the foul stench and atmosphere of dread that hung over the ship. Lavatory facilities consisted of a few buckets that were shared between the Africans, so disease rapidly became rife. As Olaudah watched his fellow captives die around him, his own sickness was treated by being taken up on deck and flogged. However, although the sadistic captain and crew subjected the Africans to barely tolerable conditions, they were loath to allow them to die as this would affect their profits. When some of the slaves decided to take their own lives by jumping overboard, the captain ordered his crew to do whatever it took to rescue them. Once the desperate men were safely back on board, they were flogged for having the temerity to choose death over their current situation.

After several weeks at sea, Olaudah's ship finally docked at an island which he later discovered was Barbados. Desperate to get off their floating prison, the slaves willingly followed their captors to market where most were sold to plantation owners working close to the port of Bridgetown. However, the hellish voyage had taken a serious toll on Olaudah and he failed to sell due to his obviously failing health and undernourished physique. To his dismay, he was loaded onto another, smaller boat named the *African Snow*, which promptly set sail for the North American mainland. The ship docked in Virginia and Olaudah was purchased by a plantation owner named Ian Campbell for whom he was to work as a casual labourer. Once at the plantation, he quickly realised that although conditions were better than on board the slave ship, the place functioned in the same way as a gaol. The work was tedious and laborious and communication between the slaves was discouraged whenever possible. On one occasion, Olaudah was summoned to Campbell's house and was shocked to see his black cook wearing an iron muzzle, which he surmised not only prevented her from speaking but also must have seriously restricted eating and drinking.

Olaudah's stay at Campbell's plantation turned out to be mercifully brief as he was purchased by a captain named Michael Pascal who had visited the plantation and obviously liked the look of him. He was taken to Captain Pascal's ship, which promptly set sail for England, landing at Falmouth in the spring of 1757. This journey across the Atlantic turned out to be infinitely more enjoyable than the voyage on the slave ship. The crew were friendly to Olaudah and even took the time to teach him a little English. Possibly in an attempt to cover up Olaudah's recent past, Captain Pascal changed his slave name from Jacob to the altogether more impressive Gustavus Vassa. His status, however, remained the same.

Following their arrival in Falmouth, Olaudah was employed on a series of ships before being taken to London where he divided his time between working as a servant for Captain Pascal's spinster cousins, the Guerin sisters, and assisting his owner with the recruitment of crews in and around the docks. During this period, he became well acquainted with the area and spent much time in the company of the watermen who operated the wherry boats used to transport both people and goods to the ocean-going ships moored in the Thames. The relationships that Olaudah formed during his early days at the docks were to serve him well as he would be employed on vessels from the Port of London on many occasions over the next 25 years of his life. His travails enabled him to save a little money of his own and by 1766 he had accumulated over £40 – enough to finally buy his freedom.

Olaudah continued to work on board a wide variety of ships as a free man until he reached his mid-40s, when he returned to London. Despite his relative success in recent years, he had never forgotten the men and women he had left behind on Campbell's plantation and almost immediately became involved with the abolition movement, which had been steadily gaining momentum during the 1780s. He proved to be an impassioned speaker and a persuasive writer on the subject of slavery and he quickly gained the support of several wealthy sympathisers who were keen to sponsor a lecture tour of the British Isles. The tour proved to be a huge success and while travelling the country, Olaudah was urged to write his autobiography in order to help the case for the abolition of slavery. This he ably did, publishing the first edition in 1789. *The Interesting Narrative of Olaudah Equiano, or Gustavus Vassa, the African*, as it was known, subsequently ran to nine editions with each print run rapidly selling out.

The success of the lecture tour and *The Interesting Narrative* made Olaudah sufficiently wealthy to settle in England without the need to go back into the service of sea captains. In 1792, he married a young English woman named Susannah Cullen in Soham, Cambridgeshire. The couple had two daughters – Anna Maria in 1793 and Joanna in 1795. Following Susannah's death in 1796, Olaudah left his daughters in the care of their extended family in Cambridgeshire and moved back to London, eventually taking lodgings with a Mrs Edwards in Paddington Street, Marylebone. He died there on 31 March 1797 at the age of 52. An obituary in the *Gentleman's Magazine* announced his demise thus, 'In London, Mr Gustavus Vasa [sic], the African, well known to the publick by the interesting narrative of his life, supposed to be written by himself.' It appears that despite Olaudah's tireless efforts to prove otherwise, some quarters of the British press still had great difficulty believing that an African possessed sufficient intellectual prowess to write a book.

Sadly, Olaudah did not live to see the abolition of slavery. Just 10 years after his death, the Slave Trade Act was passed, which outlawed the trafficking of slaves throughout the British Empire and on 1 August 1834, all slaves in British territories were emancipated. However, the slaves on the plantations across the Atlantic had to wait another 31 years until they gained their freedom in 1865.

8

FIRE

As the 17th-century predecessors of Olaudah Equiano were enduring the horrors of the Virginian plantations, the people of the London docks watched ignorantly as the slave ships sailed out of the busy port, blissfully unaware that their world was about to be turned upside down. By the mid-1600s, the area that lay immediately behind the docks had grown into a centre for all manner of noxious industries including dyeing, rope making, soap making, brewing and salt boiling. Most of these workplaces used coal extensively and this resulted in the streets and quays along the north bank of the Thames becoming black with soot and the air polluted with thick, choking smoke which constantly permeated the lungs of the residents bringing with it an array of respiratory problems.

By 1661, the air quality in this area of the city had become so awful that it prompted the writer John Evelyn, who lived across the water in Deptford, to pen an essay entitled *Fumifigium: The Inconvenience of the Aer and Smoak of London Dissipated*. In it, Evelyn lamented, 'columns and clouds of smoak ... are belched forth from the sooty Throates [of workshops] ... rendring [the city] like the approaches of Mount-Hecla [an Icelandic volcano]. That hellish and dismal cloud of sea-coal [means] that the inhabitants breathe nothing but an impure and thick mist, accompanied by a fuliginous and filthy vapour ... corrupting the lungs and disordering the entire habit of their bodies, so that cattarhs, phthisicks, coughs and consumption rage more in that one city than the whole earth besides.'

The poor air quality was only one problem encountered by dock residents. Despite the best efforts of men such as Richard Whittington to improve the health and safety of Londoners, the cheaper areas of the city, including the streets adjacent to the quays, were still a labyrinth of narrow alleys and crowded unsanitary thoroughfares packed with families living on the breadline. In 1665, a particularly virulent strain of bubonic plague broke out in London, killing up to 100,000 residents. The only positive effect of this devastating outbreak was the easing of overcrowding in some areas. However, the plague hit the suburbs of London that lay outside the city wall far worse than the areas within it. The death toll from plague for parishes within the walls was recorded as 15,200 – although it is likely that the actual figure was higher as many families never officially declared deaths for fear of being ostracised. Despite the docks escaping the worst of the plague outbreak, population numbers did fall significantly in its wake. However, this temporary ease of overcrowding did little to protect the residents from an equally devastating threat – fire.

Over the previous decades, London's prosperity had resulted in thousands of impoverished families from the shires arriving in the city looking for work. In order to accommodate them, cheap housing had been hurriedly thrown up and existing properties had been divided into tiny units in an attempt to cram in as many people as possible. For example, the Three Crowns Inn in the parish of Christ Church was reported to have rooms that were 'intermixed with other houses', giving a confusing and potentially dangerous layout. Outside the houses, any additional space such as stables or warehousing was converted into living accommodation and back gardens acquired rows of squalid tenements where trees and shrubs had once stood. The residential streets around the docks became a popular place for this type of development. By 1638, 857 buildings in the city were classified as tenements and nearly 25% of these mean dwellings were situated in the dockside parish of St Michael, Queenhithe.

As parishes became increasingly overcrowded, fires became an almost constant threat. Households used naked flame to cook, give light and to heat their homes and unattended fires could very quickly burn out of control, sometimes destroying entire streets. By 1643, outbreaks of fire had become so rife that the mayor issued a pamphlet entitled *Seasonable Advice for Preventing the Mischief of Fire*. It was advised that this useful tome should be displayed in every household and noted numerous fire hazards including 'bad hearths' and 'chimnies', 'clothes hanged against the fire' and 'drunkards, as many houses were burnt [by the carelessness of the inebriated] in Southwark.' *Seasonable Advice for Preventing the Mischief of Fire* also gave counsel on how fires could be prevented. In addition to instructing the reader to be ever vigilant for signs of smoke or the smell of burning, it also gave more specific guidance, such as 'If you will use candle all night, let your candlestick be a pot of water brim-full, and set it where it shall stand, and then light a candle, and stick a great pin in the bottom of the candle, and let it slowly into the water, and it will burn all night without danger.' If, despite all precautions, fire did break out, instruction was given on how to tackle a variety of blazes including, 'if chimnies be on fire, either wet hay or straw, or a wet blanket, or a kettle of water hung over, or bay-salt cast into the fire, or a piece shot up the chimney, will help it.'

In addition to distributing the mayor's pamphlet, the city wards employed fire officers to ensure that residents were not contravening fire regulations by throwing out glowing embers or keeping a sooty chimney. Night-watchmen were also instructed to keep an eye out for smoke or fire and householders were requested to keep a bucket of water outside their front doors in the warm, dry summer months in case they were required. For more major fires, each parish was required by law to have a selection of fire-fighting equipment at their disposal. These tools included ladders, fire hooks (a large metal hook mounted on a long pole, used to pull down buildings) and axes (which were useful for breaking into nearby water pipes). Some of the wealthier parishes also had rudimentary fire engines, which had first been imported into London by a merchant named John Jones in 1625. Made in Germany, these contraptions comprised a large barrel of water on wheels, from which water could be manually pumped through a hose attached to the side. Although the fire engines were more effective than buckets of water, they were very slow and cumbersome to move, meaning that many fires were out of control before they arrived at the scene. This, however, did not dent their popularity and by the mid-1600s several manufacturers had set up business in London and approximately 100 engines were operating throughout the metropolis.

Water for fighting the fires was primarily drawn from the rivers that ran through the city. As far back as 1580, a Dutchman named Pieter Morice had engineered a conduit that could convey water from the

Thames at the foot of London Bridge right up to Leadenhall and in 1595 another conduit was constructed by Bevis Bulmar at Broken Wharf. These water channels proved to be effective except during dry spells when the level of the Thames decreased, making it very difficult to create enough pressure to convey the water all the way along them.

Although each parish had the equipment to tackle conflagrations, there were no designated fire-fighters. Consequently, when fire broke out, it was literally a case of 'all hands to the pump', which unsurprisingly often resulted in chaos. In the mid-1670s, a Londoner named Andrew Yarranton described watching a row of buildings burn while 'all the Rable runs crying Fire, Fire, to the great affrightment and amazement of most people near where the fire is…Then one cries Pull down, and another cries, Blow up this house, another cries, Blow up that house. So grows a confusion not to be parallel'd.'

As the devastating plague year of 1665 gave way to 1666, many Londoners saw in the New Year with trepidation. The events of the previous months had left them in an apprehensive state of mind and the connection of the numbers 666 with the doom-laden 'Book of Revelation' only served to increase their anxiety. Down at the docks, many merchants were experiencing severe disruption caused by outbreaks of plague in supply towns and foreign markets, which was threatening to jeopardise their already beleaguered overseas trade. In 1652, disputes over shipping had caused a two-year sea war to break out between the English and Dutch and in 1665, the two countries clashed once again. English merchants trading with the Hanseatic ports were severely affected when the Dutch successfully blocked their passage into the Baltic. Between 1660 and 1664 an average of 100 English vessels docked at the Baltic ports every year. In 1666 not a single ship managed to get past the blockade. In January 1666, matters deteriorated further when France joined the conflict, making voyages out of London even more difficult for the merchant ships. The navy fought back and had some success in taking several Dutch-occupied islands in the West Indies as well as the settlement of New Amsterdam on the North American mainland. Nonetheless, the battles took their toll and the already disheartened people at the London docks had to deal with the depressing sight of war-weary sailors disembarking from their battle-scarred ships only to find that their loved ones and friends had been taken by the plague.

By the end of August 1666, London was a city tired of war and disease. The summer had been long and dry, however, and the sunny climate no doubt cheered the spirits of its inhabitants a little. But these temperate conditions turned out to be harbingers of a catastrophe far greater than anything the Dutch or French could unleash on the city and its docks.

At 10pm on Saturday 1 September, in a biscuit bakery on Pudding Lane (a narrow thoroughfare that led down to Fresh Wharf), Thomas Farriner extinguished the fire in his ovens and retired for the night. Approximately three hours later, he was awoken by smoke emanating from the bakehouse and, on investigation, was horrified to discover a fire that was already dangerously out of control. Wasting no time, Farriner gathered his family on the upper floors of their home and, realising that escape at street level was impossible, instructed them to climb out of the window and edge their way along a narrow gutter to the safety of a neighbouring property. The family managed to negotiate this treacherous escape route successfully, but their maid was too scared to climb along the outside of the building and remained in the burning house, eventually becoming overcome by smoke.

By 3am, all attempts to put out the fire had failed and the conflagration had spread to such an extent that it was noticed by a servant named Jane who lived in Seething Lane, about a quarter of a mile away. Realising that this was no minor fire, Jane woke her master, the celebrated diarist Samuel Pepys, who went to the window to see what all the fuss was about. On viewing the fire for several minutes, the weary Pepys decided that it was too far off to be a danger and went back to bed. His conclusion was shared by the mayor who reckoned it was not necessary to pull down the surrounding properties in a bid to halt the advance of the flames. Had he been advised of what lay on Pudding Lane, he may have made a very different decision. At the time of the fire, the street ran through the middle of an area full of narrow alleys, tenements and 'close built' wooden houses. Most of the shops along the thoroughfare were occupied by ships' chandlers and other maritime suppliers whose yards were often full of combustible materials such as tar, hemp, coal and timber. As a brisk wind blew the flames westwards, these goods quickly caught alight, causing the fire to become an inferno.

At 7am, Samuel Pepys once again rose from his slumbers and went to his window to check on the progress of the conflagration and came to the conclusion that it had begun to die down. This opinion was shared by many Londoners, especially those living east of Pudding Lane (like Pepys) as the fire was being blown westwards, away from their properties. However, to the west of the bridge, the scene was very different. Having watched the advancing flames throughout the night, many of the families living in and around the docks began to fear the worst and started to load their possessions onto lighters, then rowed out to the relative safety of the south bank. By the time dawn broke, the steady stream of people taking goods to the water's edge had become a torrent and the tiny medieval lanes became clogged with a teeming mass of bodies, all fighting to get their treasured goods onto the next boat.

As the people of the docks were desperately loading their possessions onto the lighters, the fire became so bad that the King was informed. He quickly made his way to Queenhithe and once there, took charge of the so far fruitless attempts at fighting the advance of the flames. His efforts met with little success. During Sunday 2 September, the fire raged through the riverside streets and beyond consuming everything in its path. Half a mile of the docks were destroyed along with an area to the north that stretched in an arc from Queenhithe to the top of St Michael's Lane and down to Fish Street Hill at the Cannon Street junction. Worryingly, the flames also began to creep eastwards along the waterfront towards Billingsgate, destroying several quays in the process. Merchants and labourers alike watched helplessly as their homes and places of work fell victim to the blaze. By the time the sun began to set on this most dreadful day, the fire had destroyed the ancient waterside guild halls of the Dyers', Fishmongers' and Watermen's Companies along with the magnificent Steelyard of the Hanseatic League. Many of the dockside churches were also destroyed including St Magnus the Martyr at the foot of the bridge and St Margaret in New Fish Street. An increasingly desperate King Charles ordered that any house that lay in the path of the conflagration should be pulled down to create a fire break. However, by now fires were breaking out in so many places that it was difficult to tell where to start the demolition. In a bid to speed up the process, sailors watching the events from their ships moored in the Thames suggested using gunpowder, but the fire officers reasoned that this volatile substance was too dangerous to transport through the fiery streets.

By Monday morning virtually the whole of the city was preparing to evacuate. John Evelyn travelled up the Thames from his Deptford home and noted that the river was 'cover'd with goods floating, all the barges and boates laden with what some had time and courage to save.' Inland, it soon became clear that there was much money to be made from hiring out carts. Hauliers began to quote obscene amounts of money to convey householders' goods away from danger. Contemporary reports suggest that carts could not be had for less than £4 and porters were charging 10 shillings per journey. Consequently, the hire of transport became the preserve of the wealthy and everyone else had to fend for themselves. Pepys described the streets on Monday morning as being 'crowded with people, running and riding and getting of carts at any rate to fetch away things.' In a frantic bid to better organise the fighting of the fire and limit any further damage to the city, King Charles put the Duke of York in overall control of the situation. The duke quickly established eight fire posts around the perimeter of the fire at Temple Bar, Cliffords Inn Gardens, Fetter Lane, Shoe Lane, Cow Lane in Smithfield, Aldersgate, Coleman Street and Cripplegate. A privy councillor took command of each post aided by three justices of the peace, parish constables, a team of local residents and 30 foot-soldiers. The duke also organised armed guards to protect the belongings of evacuated families, as much looting had been reported during the previous day.

While the duke and his men battled to halt the flames, the stunned residents of the city began, unfairly, to vent their frustrations on foreigners residing in the city as they searched for a scapegoat for their misery and loss. Due to the ongoing hostilities with the Dutch and French and the uneasy peace with the Spanish and Portuguese, families from these countries were treated with the utmost suspicion. A citizen's arrest was made on a servant of the Portuguese ambassador after his captors claimed to have seen him throwing an incendiary device into a house. On investigation, it turned out to be a piece of bread he had found on the street. In another incident, tennis balls found in the chest belonging to a Frenchman were also taken to be cunningly disguised fire bombs. These unfortunate individuals were taken to the fire posts, where they were kept under armed guard for their own protection.

By sunset on Monday 3 September, the fire had spread along the docks, destroying the quays at Queenhithe and Broken Wharf before reaching Baynard's Castle. Residents vainly hoped that this tall, solidly built structure would withstand the flames and create a fire break, but in the event it too was completely destroyed. So far, most damage had been done to the west of the bridge, but by Monday evening the flames that had been slowly creeping eastwards set Billingsgate alight, creating fears that the Tower of London would be destroyed. The Tower garrison hurriedly dispatched a message to the shipyards at Deptford and Woolwich, asking them to send any available fire-fighting equipment without delay. It was essential that the Tower was saved. Not only was it a potent symbol of the strength of the city, it now was also the temporary store for a massive amount of cash and valuable goods hastily deposited within its sturdy walls by fleeing merchants from the docks. Some of these merchants were already facing financial ruin. As it spread northwards, the fire had claimed Thomas Gresham's Royal Exchange, destroying a great quantity of fine fabrics and other luxury goods stored there, including the East India Company's entire supply of pepper. By the time the flames were finally extinguished, all that was left of London's bourse was the smouldering statue of its founder.

Almost in despair but refusing to be beaten, the Duke of York attempted to create another fire break on Tuesday morning by ordering that all property along the banks of the Fleet River should be pulled down. A massive effort was made by the now exhausted demolition crews, but by the time the fire reached the river it was so fierce that the firebreak had virtually no effect and it continued on its destructive journey westwards, threatening palatial homes such as Somerset House, which lay beyond the docks towards Westminster. Further north, people stood and watched helplessly as another of their city's iconic buildings – St Paul's – caught alight. Like the Tower, this great church had been used to store the possessions of hundreds of Londoners and as the flames licked around its walls, vast amounts of valuable goods were lost.

Over to the east, the fire had now raged through Billingsgate and had reached the King's Custom House, which was totally ruined. Renewed efforts were made to protect the Tower which by now was under serious threat. Samuel Pepys viewed the fiery scene from the tower of All Hallows church and was dismayed to find 'the saddest sight of desolation that I ever saw.' He was not alone in his despair, but as most Londoners were giving up hope of saving even the smallest portion of their city, the wind began first to change direction and then drop, allowing many of the fires to finally be extinguished. The fire-fighters continued to douse the flames throughout Wednesday and the next day the King wisely ordered militia from the northern Home Counties to come and relieve the exhausted crews and begin a massive clean-up operation. He also ensured that supplies were brought into the city to feed the remaining population, many of whom had sought temporary accommodation in outlying villages such as Islington and Hampstead or had camped out on the open spaces at Moorfields, Hatton Garden and Covent Garden piazza. By Thursday evening the fire was finally extinguished, but now the people of London were faced with the challenge of rebuilding their devastated city.

The Great Fire of 1666 completely changed the city's landscape. So many landmark buildings were destroyed that people who had been resident in the city all their lives found it difficult to find their way around. On 10 September, King Charles commissioned map-makers Wenceslas Hollar and Francis Sandford to create 'an exact plan and survey of the city, as it now stands after the calamity of the late fire.' Hollar and Sandford worked quickly and their first plan of the city was completed by the end of 1666. It still survives today and vividly illustrates the destruction: over 436 acres of land were affected by the fire. Within the city wall, only 75 acres had remained untouched by the flames. Landmarks destroyed included St Paul's, the Guildhall, the Royal Exchange, Baynard's Castle, Newgate Prison, the gates at Newgate, Ludgate and Aldersgate and 87 churches, six chapels and 52 livery company halls. Following the commission of a survey, the Corporation of London assessed that in addition to these buildings, 13,200 houses had been destroyed, making up to 65,000 Londoners homeless.

Down at the docks, the only quay to survive the fire was Tower Wharf. Westwards from this point, the entire dock complex was destroyed. Close to the Tower, Custom House and its quay stood in total ruins alongside the smouldering remnants of several of Queen Elizabeth's legal quays including Galley, Dice and Smart's Quays. Next to Smart's lay the ancient dock of Billingsgate, temporarily abandoned until the debris and burnt out buildings that once surrounded it could be cleared away. A little further west lay what remained of St Botolph's church, which faced out onto devastated Thames Street, the once bustling thoroughfare reduced to wreckage.

At the foot of the bridge, the old church of St Magnus the Martyr lay in ruins and the properties to its west fared no better. In between the charred remains of Fleur de Lis and Blackraven Alleys lay what was left of Fishmongers' Hall. A short way off stood the smoking ruins of the guild hall of another trade that had contributed much to the success and prosperity of the Port of London – the dyers. A little further along Thames Street, the Hanseatic League's favoured church, All Hallows, was now nothing but an empty shell, its fine interior almost completely erased. Next door, the League's magnificent guild hall, apartments and stores were also irreparably damaged. Even further west, the Walbrook had done little to provide a natural fire break and amid the burnt out alleyways that led to the waterside stood the ruined remains of another four guild halls including that of the vintners, who had been trading at the neighbouring docks at Vintry for centuries. Along the timber wharves, Woodmongers' Hall was completely destroyed, as was Baynard's Castle, which was never rebuilt. Beyond this point, the fire had continued along the bank of the river, across the mouth of the Fleet and over the city wall before finally dying out just before it reached the stairs that led down to the Thames at Temple.

News of the catastrophic fire quickly spread across England and collections were held to aid London's recovery. The first wave of fundraising produced nearly £13,000 with a further £1,077 worth of gifts, while a second collection brought in another £2,306. In total, the disaster relief fund raised just over £16,000, which although appreciated was nowhere near enough to rebuilt the city. It quickly became apparent that the restoration of London would have to be paid for by the Londoners themselves.

Of course, not everyone was in a position to help with the rebuilding of the city. The loss of property had seriously affected many people's incomes as in addition to being made homeless, they no longer had property to let out. Older members of the community fared the worst. An elderly lady named Frances Aske was left destitute when her only source of income – a house in Fetter Lane – was destroyed. Blind and infirm, Frances was forced to ask for charity in order to survive.

Merchants at the docks also faced serious financial problems. Daniel Berry lost an estimated £500 worth of stock when his dye house and wharf on Cousin Lane were destroyed and tobacco merchant John Jeffreys claimed £20,000 for stock that had literally gone up in smoke. At Blackwell Hall, merchants dealing in the country's lucrative clothmaking industry lost goods estimated at £25,000. Coal stores at the docks were also decimated, making it virtually impossible for the workshops so loathed by John Evelyn to operate. The situation was made worse by the fact that coal ships travelling down the coast from Newcastle were constantly harried by hostile Dutch vessels. Consequently, the price of coal shot up, making small fortunes for those merchants lucky enough to have stock.

Coal was not the only thing that increased in price. Due to the sudden property shortage, both commercial and residential rents increased exponentially. The poor were forced to live in shanty towns on the outskirts of the city until cheaper housing had been erected and their landlords complained that it was impossible to find a builder. However, this potentially desperate situation was tackled creatively by those affected. While camping out in the suburbs of the city, the poor used canvas from the Deptford and Woolwich dockyards to build shelters and, amazingly, within a week of the fire being extinguished, most of the temporary campsites had gone after the residents either found new accommodation back in the city or took up lodgings in the outlying villages. Traders were just as enterprising and soon got back to business, setting up stalls on burnt out sites across the capital.

As the city began to rebuild itself, the crown ordered an inquiry into the cause of the fire, primarily to stop conspiracy theories from getting out of hand. At the ensuing sessions, all evidence pointed to the fact that, despite his continued denial, the fire had started at Thomas Farriner's bakehouse. The cause, however, remained a mystery, until a young Frenchman named Robert Hubert came forward to give evidence. Hubert claimed that he and a colleague named Stephen Peidloe had arrived in London shortly before the fire broke out. At first he admitted only to having thrown a fireball near Whitehall Palace after the fire in the city had taken hold, but after further questioning he changed his story, stating that he and Peidloe had actually started the fire by pushing fireballs through a window of Farriner's bakehouse on the Saturday night. Farriner was asked if a window existed in the location described by Hubert and he said that it did not. However, when the Frenchman was asked to show the jury where Farriner's property had once stood, he surprised them by going straight to it. This was enough to confirm his guilt and he was hanged on 29 October. London had found its scapegoat.

One positive result of the fire was that it helped to end the hostilities with the Dutch. After the conflagration, the people of London were far more concerned with rebuilding the city than planning sea campaigns and called for peace in early 1667. This prompted talks to open between the two countries but unfortunately did not stop the Dutch raiding the Medway, burning three of the King's warships and capturing the flagship *The Royal Charles*. Following the raid, they blockaded the Thames and no ships were able to enter or leave the Port of London for over a month. The blockade ended when the Treaty of Breda was signed in July 1667. Finally, the docks were back in business.

Almost as soon as the fire ended, Londoners began to make plans to rebuild their city. However, the Corporation of London and the government were adamant that there should be an organised plan for the redevelopment and householders should not be allowed to simply throw up buildings where and how they pleased. Plans for a totally new street layout were discussed and some MPs even spoke of moving the capital to a new location. However, the docks proved a deciding factor in keeping the centre of the city within the area surrounded by the old Roman wall, which although by now only partially standing, still provided an invisible boundary. No one was in favour of moving the docks, partly because their location was so long established and partly because, during the Civil War, the Royalists had attempted to move the country's main port to Exeter and Bristol with limited success.

On 13 September 1666, the King ended the debate by ordering that no rebuilding could take place until the government had finalised the new building regulations. These new guidelines were drawn up to ensure that such a devastating fire could never happen again. All 'eminent' streets would be built wide enough to act as fire breaks. At the docks, the construction of narrow alleyways would be prohibited wherever possible, no houses were to be built on the quaysides and the smoky industrial sites that had previously lain directly behind the docks were to be moved to a less enclosed location. Plans for a more organised layout for the capital were also talked about at length. Everyone agreed that congestion should be kept to a minimum. Before the fire, much of the city had been a warren of medieval streets along which lay, in the words of Evelyn, 'a Congestion of misshapen and extravagant Houses.' Architects suggested that the inclusion of some parks and piazzas within the new layout would afford Londoners some much-needed open spaces. Down at the riverside, an eminent diplomat named Sir William Temple suggested that a quay should be built along the entire stretch of the Thames between the Tower and the Temple to replace the individual wharves. This idea was met with a great deal of enthusiasm as it would serve as an impressive entrance to the city and give the authorities the opportunity to organise the docks in a far more effective manner.

Ideas for the rebuilding of London were so many and various that the King decided to invite plans to be formally submitted by anyone who cared to spend time drawing them up. The response was enthusiastic as entries arrived from a diverse selection of people including the renowned architect Sir Christopher Wren, John Evelyn, the scientist Robert Hooke, cartographer Richard Newcourt and a sea captain named Valentine Knight, who understandably had great ambitions for the docks. Captain Knight's scheme centred around the construction of a great canal, which would run in a semi-circle across the city from the Fleet River in the west to Billingsgate in the east. The canal would be used to convey goods to and from the docks and a charge would be levied on all those using it for commercial purposes. He calculated that the canal would prove so popular that it would pay for itself within just a few years and would then provide more long-term revenue for the crown. Although this idea seemed reasonably sound, Knight had seriously misjudged the monarch's mood. Appalled at the revenue-creating scheme, the King promptly arrested the unfortunate mariner for daring to suggest that he 'would draw benefit to himself, from so publick a calamity of his people.'

Although they avoided gaol, Captain Knight's competitors were no more successful in bringing their plans to fruition. It soon became apparent that the ownership of land within the city was so complex that redesigning its layout would present all manner of problems. The only answer lay in compulsory purchase by the crown, but the recent wars had left insufficient funds in the royal coffers to enable this to happen. In the end, it was decided that the street pattern would remain barely unchanged but stringent building parameters would be agreed in order to make the city appear more uniform. In October, King Charles organised a commission to set and enforce the new regulations. Following several meetings, the commission decided that the new 'high streets' should be 70ft wide, secondary streets at least 42ft wide and 'least' streets a minimum of 25ft wide. It also recommended that the large, open drains that ran down the centre of many main streets should be made thinner, thus increasing the amount of space available for traffic. All streets should be paved and downpipes should be fitted to all houses to prevent water cascading off the roofs onto the heads of passers-by. The bow windows and overhanging upper storeys that had enveloped so many of the medieval streets were banned on all but the widest thoroughfares. The buildings themselves were to be built of brick or stone and wooden exteriors were prohibited except for doors, window frames and shop-fronts. Houses were divided into categories and each type had to adhere to strict guidelines. Small dwellings in 'by-streets or lanes' could have just two storeys and a garret. Homes that fronted 'streets or lanes of note' or the Thames could be built with an additional storey. Houses on the main thoroughfares could be four storeys high (plus a garret) and 'mansion houses for citizens and other persons of extraordinary quality' could be as large as the owner wished but could not contain more than four storeys.

Now that all the regulations were in place, rebuilding of private property could finally begin but the problem remained of how to fund public buildings such as churches. Many parishes, particularly those at the docks, were poor and would never raise enough money for the construction of an elaborate place of worship. Consequently, it was decided that the duty on coal should be raised and ¾ of the extra revenue be used to build new churches. This plan worked well and a total of 51 new churches were built, many of which were designed by Sir Christopher Wren.

As the commissioners staked out the charred land in preparation for rebuilding, the landowners themselves began work. Most of the redevelopment was self-financed as although the fire brought financial ruin to some, many had sufficient funds to bear the cost. Before the fire,

London had been an extremely wealthy city. In his book *The Making of the English Middle Class*, Peter Earle noted that in late-Stuart London, the average tradesman had £255 in cash at the time of his death; merchants had average savings of £671. The former's money was sufficient to construct a modest house and workshop on one of the side streets; the latter's would fund an altogether more impressive property – for example, after the fire, it was calculated that a corner house on fashionable Lombard Street would cost £700 to rebuild. In addition to this, wealthy Londoners were happy to lend money for redevelopment projects as, despite the fire, they regarded property as a relatively safe investment. Samuel Pepys noted in his diary that he had loaned money for this very purpose.

As the new houses were built, demand for building supplies soared. Brick kilns struggled to keep up with demand and extra timber had to be sourced from Scandinavia and the Baltic, much to the merchants' delight. Progress was fast and 85% of the properties destroyed in the fire had been rebuilt by 1671. Plans for a new Royal Exchange were drawn up, the King himself laying the foundation stone amid much ceremony on 23 October 1667. The new building had much the same layout as Thomas Gresham's original, but at the monarch's insistence it was enlarged and decorated more elaborately. The resulting bourse cost a massive £62,000 to complete, paid for by the Mercers' Company and the Corporation of London. Like the Royal Exchange, the Custom House was also swiftly rebuilt. A royal warrant authorising construction was issued on 23 June 1669 and building work commenced to a design by Wren. Eighteen months later, the building was finished and the final bill ran to £10,272 – almost double the estimate.

Although King Charles had angrily rejected Captain Knight's proposal for a canal linking the docks with the city centre, part of his plan did eventually get utilised. The Fleet River had been collecting dirt and detritus from the workshops on its banks for decades and as a result had become insanitary, dirty and smelly. The commission decided to rectify this state of affairs and, under the direction of Wren, straightened and canalised the Fleet from Holborn Bridge to the Thames. The project cost over £50,000 to complete but it improved the environment considerably. The river became easily navigable for barges and lighters and the warehouses that lined its banks began to be used by various merchants and manufacturers. That said, the project ultimately proved to be a commercial failure. Much less traffic used the canal than was expected and the warehouses failed to achieve the rents anticipated by the commission. By 1730, this potential valuable satellite of the docks had fallen into disrepair and was described as 'ruinous'. In 1733, the portion of canal between Holborn Bridge and Fleet Bridge was enclosed and just over 30 years later, the remaining section was also covered over, effectively taking the Fleet River underground, where it remains to this day.

East of the Fleet, it was initially agreed that the construction of a huge quay running the length of the docks would significantly improve the efficiency of the port and the introduction of an expansive wharf along the river frontage would also stop any future fires from reaching the ships docked there. Plans were drawn up for an 'open, gracefull key', which would sweep away the maze of individual wharves and narrow alleyways that ran down to the water. Behind it would be built a fine complex of offices and warehouses. There is no doubt that this project would have greatly improved the docks but in the event the commission found it was fraught with difficulty. A proposed rear line of the quay was marked out beyond which the only building allowed would be Fishmongers' Hall. However, the quay owners had other ideas. The docks were split into numerous sections, all owned by different individuals dealing with diverse commodities brought to the quays on a wide variety of vessels and as such, each quay had very different requirements. Compulsory purchase of the entire dock area by the Corporation of London was financially unviable, so the grand plans for a huge 'Thames Quay' never came to fruition and although the fire enabled landowners to generally tidy up their quays, the London docks remained a jumble of privately owned sites, each with its own distinct character.

The docks were not the only places that were tidied up as a result of the fire. Out of the devastation there emerged a more commodious and spacious city than its medieval predecessor and its residents were keen to keep it that way. One of the most positive results of the conflagration was the introduction of fire insurance, which ensured that the hardships suffered from future fires were greatly eased. The first insurance scheme was set up by a speculative property developer named Nicholas Barbon and by the 1720s there were six fire insurance companies operating in

London. Subscribers displayed their insurance by fixing plaques bearing the insurer's logo onto the front of their houses, many of which can still be seen today. In addition to covering losses sustained in a fire, the insurance companies also provided their own fire fighters to supplement the facilities provided by the parishes thus further reducing the devastation fire could cause.

Six years after the Great Fire, the city was almost totally redeveloped and King Charles proudly noted that the 'handsomest part' had been 'rebuilt with greater magnificence'. However, the future of the new London was not entirely bright. Trouble was once again on the horizon, especially for the people of the docks.

In 1672, war broke out with the Dutch once again, severely affecting deliveries of Newcastle coal and timber from the Baltic. Shipping travelling to and from the Baltic ports fell dramatically from an average of 125 vessels in 1671 to just eight in 1673. In addition to this, the London merchants lost at least 700 ships during the conflict, many of which were taken by Dutch pirates. The merchants started to become seriously concerned about the state of their trade, especially as they had spent much of their savings rebuilding the quays at the docks. The dangers of working on the shipping lanes through northern Europe, combined with myriad work opportunities in the building trade, meant that it was now difficult to attract enough crew for voyages. Some merchants became so desperate that they took to employing press gangs who prowled the taverns and brothels of Southwark looking for drunk and unwary victims to trick onto the boats.

9

MR LLOYD'S COFFEE HOUSE

As the merchants and ship owners at the docks desperately tried to keep their businesses afloat during the difficult final quarter of the 17th century, the dangers encountered by their ships whilst at sea made them search for a way to protect themselves from the loss of a vessel and its valuable cargo. Traditionally, a certain amount of protection had been obtained by distributing cargo over several ships and purchasing shares in vessels rather than putting all the proverbial eggs in one basket. However, when Nicholas Barbon set up his fire insurance office after the fire of 1666, the businessmen at the docks began to wonder whether the same method could be applied to the insurance of ships and their cargoes.

While the merchants and ship owners were discussing the possibility of marine insurance, London was in the grip of a mania for a new drink – coffee. The coffee bean had been boiled to make a popular beverage in Arabia since the 1400s and European merchants trading there had quickly developed a taste for it. In 1583, a German physician named Leonhard Rauwolf returned from a lengthy stay in the region, describing coffee as 'a beverage as black as ink; useful against numerous illnesses, particularly those of the stomach. Its consumers take it in the morning ... in a porcelain cup that is passed around and from which each one drinks a cupful.'

Coffee found its way to Europe via Venetian merchants trading with the Near East and by 1600 its popularity in Italy was such that it had even received approval from the Vatican. At first it was generally drunk at home by the few families wealthy enough to purchase it. However, it soon became clear to the importers that they might create a much larger market by encouraging the opening of coffee houses where the end product could be sold at affordable prices.

The first coffee house in England arrived in 1650 when, according to the chronicles of Antony à Wood, 'Jacob, a Jew, opened a Coffey House at the Angel, in the Parish of S. Peter in the East, Oxon, and there it was by some, who delighted in Noveltie, drank.' Jacob's coffee shop was imitated two years later in London when a merchant in oriental goods named Mr Hodges set his coachman, Christopher Bowman, up as a 'coffeeman' at a house named Pasqua Rosee in St Michael's Alley, Cornhill. The premises were large, incorporating no fewer than eight rooms with expensive hearths, suggesting that the Pasqua Rosee also operated as an inn. Bowman made a success of the new venture but following his death from consumption in 1663, his wife decided not to continue with the business and sold it to an acquaintance named George Backler. However, by this time, the popularity of the Pasqua Rosee had not escaped the notice of other entrepreneurs and coffee shops began springing up across London. Their arrival was not welcomed by the vintners and brewers, who viewed them as direct competition. In 1673, a group of irate brewers raised a petition calling for the prohibition of coffee, claiming it could cause their industry to collapse. Rumours also circulated that drinking coffee had a detrimental effect on one's health; in 1674, the 'Women's Petition Against Coffee' complained that, in the words of Bryant Lillywhite, 'it made men as unfruitful as the deserts whence the unhappy berry is said to be brought.'

Despite this alarming claim, the consumption of coffee was unaffected and as the century progressed, London acquired even more coffee houses. At a time before the existence of an organised postal service and little in the way of newspapers, the coffee houses became places where the news of the day could be discussed and businessmen could conduct their affairs. The merchants and ship owners from the docks gravitated to the establishments that now surrounded the Royal Exchange and the Custom House to chew the fat with their associates while they supped the steaming beverage from elaborate china cups. They and others like them found coffee to be a most agreeable alternative to gin or port, not least as they could conduct their business affairs at length without the fear of a colossal hangover the following day.

As the coffee houses increased in number, they began to attract clientele from specific trades. Those with business down at the docks favoured two particular houses: John's in Birchin Lane, just off Lombard

Street, and Garraway's on Cornhill. The former was established in 1683 and according to H. B. Wheatley, in his encyclopaedia of *London Past and Present*, was 'the principal place of resort for merchants, ship brokers and ships' captains for the transaction of shipping business'. In addition to providing convenient meeting facilities, John's was also the venue for ship auctions, known as '*vente à la bougie*' or 'sale by candle'. Unlike the fast-paced sales of today, the vente à la bougie allowed plenty of time for bids to be submitted. Before the sale began, a candle was marked up into 1in sections. The auction began when the candle was lit and continued so long as at least one bid was submitted before the candle burned down to the next inch mark. If an entire section of the candle burnt down without any bid being submitted, the auction finished. In May 1690, the *London Gazette* published the following advertisement: 'On Thursday 5th June at three of the clock in the afternoon, will be exposed to Sale by the Candle, at John's Coffee House, in Birching Lane, the Ship *Revenge*, Portuguese built, Burthen 300 Tuns, 26 iron guns, 12 brass Patereroes (guns): and the Ship *Delight*, English built, square stern'd, 130 Tuns, 10 guns and two Patereroes, etc.'

In addition to attending auctions and business meetings, many Londoners used the coffee houses as places in which to recover from a hangover. John's responded to this by selling a powder called 'Jatropoton', which when added to wine or beer was said to correct all 'noxious aigre'. The entrepreneurial nature of its owners kept John's Coffee House in business for nearly 40 years. The last known mention of it appears in an advertisement in the *Daily Courant* from January 1722.

Twelve years prior to John's opening in Birchin Lane, Thomas Garraway opened a coffee shop in nearby Exchange Alley, close to the merchants' bourse on Cornhill. Mr Garraway was an experienced landlord, having previously run a house called The Sultanes in Sweetings Rents and, almost immediately, auctions and sales were taking place at his premises. Garraway's Coffee House was used extensively by shipbuilders and owners. In 1674, the *London Gazette* carried an advertisement for a 'new invention for sheathing ships against the Worms etc with Lead and Lacker' and invited interested parties to visit 'Mr Thomas Rastel, or Mr Francis Dracot, every Tuesday and Thursday, from Twelve to One a clock at Mr Garraway's Coffee House.'

Thomas Garraway either died or sold his eponymous business in 1692 and the coffee house was taken over by Jeremy Stoakes, who continued to cater for those in the shipping sector. As late as 1798, commercial directories describe Garraway's as 'frequented by merchants, exchange, policy and ship brokers in general.' Fifty years later, it was mentioned by Charles Dickens in several of his works. In *The Uncommercial Traveller* he noted, 'There is an old monastery-cript under Garraway's [I have been in it among the port wine], and perhaps Garraway's, taking pity on the mouldy men who wait in its public room, all their lives, gives them cool house room down there on Sundays.' Dickens' vivid description of the place suggests that by the mid-1800s the old coffee house had become a tavern selling the very commodities from which its 18th century patrons were trying to escape. By then its reputation as a lively meeting place for merchants had long since disappeared and the building was eventually pulled down *circa* 1873 to make way for bank offices.

Approximately five years after the opening of John's near the Royal Exchange, a new coffee house opened near the Tower of London. Its owner Edward Lloyd and his wife Abigail worked hard to make a success of their new venture and Lloyd's Coffee House quickly attracted a regular clientele. As early as 1688, patrons were using Lloyd's as informal offices – the *London Gazette* ran a notice concerning the theft of property from one Edward Bransby in February of that year. It read: 'Whoever gives Notice of them at Mr Edward Lloyd's Coffee House … shall have a Guinea Reward.'

The coffee house proved to be a financial success and by 1691, Edward Lloyd had raised sufficient capital to acquire the lease on a larger property formerly known as the Puntack's Head in busy Lombard Street, close to the General Post Office. On opening his new venture, Lloyd quickly began to attract custom from the docks by arranging marine-related auctions. The first advertisement for these sales appeared in the *London Gazette* in October 1692 and stated that: 'On Tuesday the 8th November next, Bennet's Coffee-house in Plimouth, will be exposed to sale by Inch of Candle, three Ships with all their furniture; the names whereof are the *Teresa*, the *St Thomas*, and the *Palmo*, two of 400 Tuns and the other 100. The Inventories thereof to be seen at Lloyd's Coffee-house in Lombard Street, London. The said Ships are enter'd out for Barbados or Virginia.'

Through his work, Edward Lloyd made many contacts with ship owners and merchants with businesses at the docks and he soon became very knowledgeable about the comings and goings of the vessels operating out of the Port of London. He was among the first to learn of successful expeditions, the acquisition of new ships, the emergence of new markets overseas and the capture or destruction of vessels. Regulars at his coffee shop soon realised that important maritime information could be gathered at Lloyd's and the premises quickly became an informal shipping information centre. However, after the Hudson's Bay Company paid Lloyd £3 for supplying intelligence on their ships, he realised that he could use his knowledge to financial advantage.

Lloyd decided that the information he obtained while serving coffee could be published on a weekly basis in a news sheet. Thus, in 1692, the first copies of *Ships Arrived at, and Departed from several Ports of England, as I have account of them in London [and] An Account of what English Shipping and Foreign Ships for England, I hear of in Foreign Ports* was published. It proved to be a huge success and Lloyd's Coffee House rapidly evolved into a vital centre for shipping intelligence – an essential port of call for anyone involved in the trade.

Edward Lloyd continued running his coffee shop until his death in 1712. By then a wealthy and influential man, he was buried under the centre aisle of St Mary Woolnoth. The coffee house was taken over by his son-in-law, William Newton, and following his death just two years after Lloyd, it passed to Samuel Sheppard, whom Newton's widow married in 1715. The house was then passed to Sheppard's brother-in-law, Thomas Jemson, and under his enlightened leadership, the *Ships Arrived* news sheet evolved into *Lloyd's List* – an indispensable provider of marine intelligence, which is still used today.

By the time *Lloyd's List* made its first appearance in 1734, the coffee house with which it shared its name had established itself at the heart of London's shipping business. Merchants used the premises as their headquarters and as they learned of the week's losses in *Lloyd's List*, they began to evolve ways to protect their investments down at the docks. Many of Lloyd's clientele became self-styled brokers and underwriters as they saw the potential riches of a marine insurance scheme. The brokers worked closely with the business owners at the docks and learned of any ship or cargo for which the owner required financial protection. They would then bring the proposal to the underwriters at Lloyd's who would write up a policy for the vessel detailing all the possible risks. This policy was then touted around a number of wealthy financiers, who were invited to help fund the insurance of the ship. Once sufficient funding had been raised, the underwriter informed the broker that insurance was now in place and the ship could set sail with its owners reassured that should the worst happen, they were protected. Thus, Lloyd's involvement in the business of insurance began.

The underwriting business at Lloyd's Coffee House proved to be extremely successful, but with that success came a number of investors who were more concerned with the gambling element of the business rather than the effective protection of shipping. In 1768, the *London Chronicle* published an article by 'Mercator', which complained that 'the introduction and amazing progress of illicit gaming at Lloyd's Coffee-house is, among others, a powerful and very melancholy proof of the degeneracy of the times.' Appalled at the direction in which the business was heading, Lloyd's more reputable underwriters persuaded one of the waiters, Thomas Fielding, to help them set up a rival establishment. The lease on a building at 5 Pope's Head Alley was secured and Fielding distributed cards to patrons of his erstwhile place of employment stating that the 'New Lloyd's Coffee House' was open for business and would, most importantly, be the place to which shipping intelligence from the General Post Office would be brought. The underwriters at the original Lloyd's protested loudly at this blatant untruth and assured their customers that business would continue as usual. After a lengthy war of words, the original Lloyd's Coffee House lost out to the new operation as most of its customers transferred their allegiance to the underwriters at Pope's Head Alley. It finally closed its doors in 1788. In contrast, New Lloyd's went from strength to strength. The business soon outgrew its premises and in 1774, rooms at the Royal Exchange were leased. With the coffee house connection finally severed, the business evolved into the Lloyd's we know today, gradually expanding to underwrite many different forms of insurance. Marine insurance, however, continues to form the backbone of the underwriters' work there.

10

FUR, WHALES AND NEW DEVELOPMENTS

While the coffee houses surrounding the Royal Exchange were busy
building up their prestigious clientele, the demand for fur from the fashion
and furnishing industries reached an unprecedented peak. Fur was used to
trim and line garments worn by both sexes and pelts were also extensively
used to keep the inhabitants of draughty, badly heated homes warm during
the cold winter months. By the late 17th century, demand was so great that
it prompted a rare moment of co-operation between the French and
English. In a bid to find new sources of this lucrative commodity, two
French traders – Médard des Groseilliers and Pierre-Esprit Radisson
(namesake of today's hotel chain) – joined forces with two English captains
named Zachariah Gillam and William Stannard and planned an exploratory
voyage to the frozen waters of Hudson's Bay in modern Canada, where it
was rumoured that an unlimited supply of beaver pelts could be found.
Funding was secured from several fur merchants at the Royal Exchange
and on 5 June 1668 the quartet set sail from Deptford on two ships – the
Nonsuch and the *Eaglet* – bound for the frozen wastes across the Atlantic.
The voyage had an unfavourable start when the *Eaglet* got into serious
difficulties shortly after reaching the ocean and was forced to turn back.
However, the *Nonsuch* continued with the journey undeterred, reaching
the southern end of Hudson's Bay in early 1669. On exploring the area, the
crew realised to their delight that the rumours of plentiful beaver pelts were
true and lost no time in setting up a trading post at what is known today as
James Bay. After a successful winter acquiring their cargo, the *Nonsuch*
returned victorious to Deptford, its hold packed with pelts.

Following this successful exploratory voyage, the London fur
merchants, along with a number of their counterparts in the North

American settlements, formed the 'Company of Adventurers of England Trading into Hudson's Bay.' Realising that the company's activities could bring a great deal of revenue to his coffers, King Charles hastily granted a charter and made his favoured cousin Prince Rupert of the Rhine the organisation's first governor. As the century progressed, the company set up a hugely successful trading operation between London and Hudson's Bay. They claimed 1.5 million square miles of the vast and largely unoccupied North American territory as their own, naming it 'Prince Rupert's Land' to honour their esteemed governor. This valuable land went on to form nearly 40% of modern Canada.

Following the establishment of the trading post at James Bay, the adventurers slowly expanded their operations and evolved from a company dealing exclusively with furs to a massive corporation with commercial interests in places as diverse as Siberia and Hawaii, trading in all manner of goods. The company still exists today and is now known simply as the Hudson's Bay Company. Now the oldest commercial corporation in North America, it operates several major retail outlets including a number of department stores from its headquarters in Toronto.

The activities of the Hudson's Bay Company and the new confidence in shipping created by the insurance underwriters at Lloyd's Coffee House resulted in a steady but significant increase in traffic on the Thames, especially along the stretch of riverbank occupied by the legal quays. As trade escalated, the river became packed with vessels waiting to come into the docks to be unloaded or repaired. Sometimes the congestion was so great that the area around the bridge became impassable. Captains complained of having to constantly move their waiting craft as they jostled for position at the entrances to the quays and many took to mooring their ships further east in order to avoid getting caught in the mêlée.

This brought its own set of problems. Ships moored outside the city perimeter were surrounded by open countryside that in winter was ravaged by galeforce winds, fierce storms and sub-zero temperatures that made the Thames freeze over. These inclement conditions often caused considerable damage to the ships and in extreme cases ruined their cargo. The construction of the Blackwall Dock in the early 1600s had served to ease some of the congestion further up the Thames, but by the end of the century even more dock space was required, especially for ships arriving at the port for repairs.

In 1695, a wealthy landowner from Streatham named John Howland put together a dowry for his teenage daughter Elizabeth who was betrothed to Wrothesley Russell, the Marquis of Tavistock. The dowry contained a large parcel of land in the village of Redderiffe (modern-day Rotherhithe) which lay on the south bank of the Thames, east of Southwark. Although it did not possess a dock, Redderiffe had long since been an overflow site for the shipyard at Deptford and consequently a number of shipbuilding businesses had premises there. In the late 17th century, it was described in a gazetteer as 'a hamlet where there is and long hath been a dock and arsenal where ships are laid up, built and repaired.'

On receiving John Howland's generous gift, the Russell family set about putting their newly acquired land to profitable use. Realising the current demand for more moorings on the Thames, they conceived the idea of building a dock at Redderiffe. At first, the Russells commissioned plans for a dry dock that would be used solely for building or repairing vessels. However, it soon became clear that more money could be made by creating a wet dock which in addition to carrying out repairs could also be used as a safe waiting place for ships bound for the legal quays. The family petitioned Parliament for the revision of their plans, stating that 'the Petitioners are well advised that the making of a wet Dock there, will not only be a great Improvement of the said Estate, but of Use to the Publick.' The revised plan was quickly approved and the Russells leased their land to two shipwrights – John and Richard Wells – who, with an advance of £12,000 from their landlords, began work on the first commercial wet dock on the south side of the Thames in 1696.

John and Richard Wells began by excavating a massive area covering 12½ acres and within this space they created a huge rectangular basin that measured approximately 1,000ft long by 500ft wide, with a depth of 17ft, enabling it to accommodate even the largest craft. Following the laying out of the dock, a Stepney carpenter named William Ogbourne was brought in to line the basin's sides with wood and create a lock at the river's edge through which the ships would gain access. Aware of the bad weather that sometimes wreaked havoc in the area, the Russell family cleverly oversaw the planting of dense lines of tall trees along the perimeter of the dock, which they hoped would act as an effective wind-break.

The finished dock was a triumph. Its area was vast, capable of accommodating up to 120 ships protected from the elements. The Russell family proudly named it the Howland Great Dock after the land's previous owner and commissioned John and Richard Wells to build them an impressive mansion at its head from which they could survey their creation. However, once the mansion was built, the Russells soon realised that living next door to a dock did not make for a peaceful existence and quickly decamped elsewhere. Their fine house gradually fell into disrepair and was eventually demolished in the early 19th century. Thankfully, the mansion was the only part of the Howland Great Dock that was not a success. Soon after the project was completed, the protective wall of trees was tested when a fierce storm ravaged Redderiffe and the surrounding area during the winter of 1703. Many ships were badly damaged as the wind whipped down the Thames, but the vessels moored at the Howland emerged unscathed. Twenty years after it opened, the Howland's relatively remote location away from the fine houses of London gave rise to the introduction of a malodorous industry on its quayside – the extraction of oil from whale blubber.

Whaling was by no means a new trade at the London docks. A small whaling fleet had existed since the late 1500s when Queen Elizabeth granted a charter to the Muscovy Company to hunt baleen whales off the coast of Norway. The successful capture of one of these majestic creatures yielded a wealth of products: the oil extracted from its blubber was used for both municipal and domestic lighting, its meat for food, and its baleen (rows of keratin resembling combs attached to this particular species of whale's upper jaw, through which food was filtered) was used in the manufacture of corsets, upholstery and fishing rods.

The whaling ships working out of the London docks averaged around 350 tons and generally held six whale boats and 50 crew or so. They departed on their voyages to the popular whaling territories off the coast of Norway and Greenland in April each year, arriving at their destination in early May. Their quarry was the right whale, so-called because it was literally the 'right' kind of whale to catch, for a variety of reasons. Firstly, whaling had been shore-based in the past and right whales habitually frequented the shallower waters around the coastline, making them easy to spot and reach using rowing boats. Secondly, they

ENGLAND — EAST COAST
RIVER THAMES
LONDON BRIDGE TO WOOLWICH

PREVIOUS PAGE: Map of the Thames showing the enclosed docks. *National Maritime Museum*

RIGHT: Hanseatic League member George Gisze, by Hans Holbein the Younger (1532). *Getty Images*

BELOW: Gresham's Royal Exchange. *Mary Evans Picture Library*

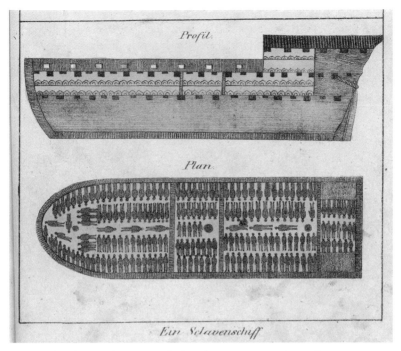

Profil.

Plan.

Ein Sclavenschiff

ABOVE: Plan showing the interior of a slave ship. *Mary Evans Picture Library*

BELOW: Waiting for the 'call-on' at the London Docks (March 1931). *Getty Images*

ABOVE: Dock workers unloading bananas from the SS Jamaica Producer at the West India Docks (1946). *Getty Images*

BELOW: Docker resting at the Surrey Commercial Docks (*c.*1950). *National Maritime Museum*

ABOVE: HMS *Penans* at the Millwall Docks (1932). *Getty Images*

ABOVE: The *Dominion Monarch* in the Royal Docks (1950). *Getty Images*

BELOW: The Royal Albert and George V Docks (*c.*1935). *Getty Images*

ABOVE: Routemaster bus at the Millwall Docks (1966). *Getty Images*

ABOVE: Canary Wharf prior to development (1952). *Getty Images*

BELOW: Container ships at Tilbury (1970). *National Maritime Museum*

were relatively slow swimmers, which made them easier to catch. Thirdly, they tended to float to the surface when dead, enabling the whalers to flay them with the minimum of effort.

Once the whaling ships had reached their hunting area, the wait was on while the lookout searched for prey. Once a whale had been spotted, stealth was the key to success. The ship moored some distance away and the whale boats were quickly launched as silently as possible. The crews then gently rowed up to the creature and, once close enough, threw harpoons attached to ropes at the unlucky animal until one became embedded in its flesh. Thence followed the most dangerous part of the hunt. Obviously alarmed by the sudden attack, the whale usually began to thrash about in the water in a bid to loosen the harpoon. The crew on the boat had to desperately try to maintain a hold on the rope while avoiding being capsized amid the squall. The whale's best chance of escape at this point was to dive deeply, forcing the hunters to cut the rope or risk being pulled under. However, many were so badly wounded by the harpoons that they simply did not have the strength to do this. Once the exhausted whale had been successfully captured, the crew would finish it off by directing harpoons at its vital organs and on believing the creature to be dead would raise a flag signalling for the ship to come and pick them up.

The whale was towed to the side of the ship and the crew set about cutting the flesh into manageable 'blanket pieces', which were then hoisted onto the deck with block and tackle. The blanket pieces were then cut down into smaller strips, the meat was cut away and the remaining blubber was placed in iron pots and boiled down to extract the oil. This oil was then poured into casks which were stored in the hull of the ship. The whole process was very labour intensive and took hours to complete. Captain W. J. Brookes, commander of the whaling ship *Active*, kept a journal which vividly recounts how his crew tackled the procedure on three captured whales: 'Tuesday November 27th. 3pm began to cut in the two small whale. 3.30 secured the large whale alongside. 5.30 finished cuting [sic] the two small whale, cleared the deck up – commenced mincing blubber, cutting up the junks and boiling oil … 6am [the following day] began to cut in the large whale and boiling oil at the same time. At noon finished taking in the body.'

Once the whale had been stripped of all its usefulness, the whale ships would cut the mutilated carcass free and leave it to descend to the murky depths as they continued with their hunt.

Back at the Howland Great Dock, the shrewd management realised that they could make whaling voyages significantly more productive by removing the need for the ships to extract the oil while at sea. They installed huge boilers and tanks on the dock's perimeter which were capable of handling the oil extraction process in bulk quantities. Now, the whaling ships needed only to load their hull with blubber and baleen before moving on. Not surprisingly, the Howland's new facilities proved exceptionally popular and in the early summer months the dock became crammed with whaling ships unloading their cargo. In recognition of this lucrative new revenue stream, the dock was renamed 'Greenland Dock' after the country along whose coastline the whaling fleet most successfully plied their trade.

Although the construction of the Howland Great Dock helped to ease the traffic on the Thames a little, Londoners affected by the congestion sought additional ways to deal with the problem. As merchants and ship owners discussed the possibility of enlarging the Port of London further, the ship brokers (who had traditionally been concerned with the buying and selling of vessels) saw an opportunity to increase their business. One of the primary necessities at the docks was to keep traffic moving. Just one ship forced to wait for cargo could create massive problems as it took up valuable space. The brokers realised that they could use their contacts at the coffee shops and the bourse to match up vessels with cargoes. Thus, while a ship was unloading at the legal quays, the broker would be busy arranging merchandise for its return journey.

The ship brokers' new service proved to be popular, especially with the Baltic traders who dealt extensively in oil, flax, hemp, seeds and tallow for candles and soap. Many of the Baltic ships' captains and merchants met in the Virginia Coffee House, which was located behind the Royal Exchange in Threadneedle Street. As its name suggests, the coffee house had traditionally dealt with traders in North American goods and had in the past thought up some novel ways to attract custom. In January 1734, the *Daily Journal* reported that 'At the Virginia Coffee House ... is to be seen the largest rattlesnake ever seen in England. Just arrived from Virginia in the Fortune.' The captive snake proved to be a popular curiosity. It remained at the coffee shop for over 18 months and in 1735 was joined by 'a very large scorpion near a foot long from the coast of Angola.'

As trade continued, the Virginia Coffee House began to attract increasing numbers of Baltic merchants and in 1744 it recognised the importance of its newest group of customers by renaming itself the Virginia and Baltick Coffee House. An advertisement in the *Daily Post* on 24 May announced the name change and went on to state that it was the place where 'all Foreign and Domestick News are taken in; and all Letters or Parcels, directed to Merchants or Captains in the Virginia or Baltick Trade will be carefully delivr'd according as directed, and the best Attendance given by Reynailds and Winboult [the proprietors].'

Reynailds' and Winboult's advertising campaign and special arrangements with the Post Office paid dividends as their coffee house became the centre for discussing Baltic trade and the ship brokers who worked within it saw their new service take off as they skilfully distributed cargoes among the ships in port. The service continued in a very informal way, with deals being done over a bowl of stew, for nearly 100 years until 1823, when a sudden rise in dangerously speculative stock dealing prompted the Baltic brokers to introduce a tightly regulated membership system in an attempt to protect themselves from any negative fallout. A committee of 23 brokers, merchants, tallow chandlers and soap makers was formed and it was decided that the brokers' services would thenceforth only be available to subscribers, the number of which was limited to 300. This new, private enterprise set up headquarters known as The Subscription Room, which opened on 1 May 1823 and the foundations for what was to become the Baltic Exchange were laid.

In 1857, subscribers formed the Baltic Company and moved to larger premises at South Sea House on Threadneedle Street. Over the next 50 years, membership steadily grew and in 1903 the Exchange moved again, this time to purpose-built premises in St Mary Axe (then known as Jeffrey Square). The new Baltic Exchange featured a magnificent trading floor with domed ceilings, elegant plasterwork and tall supporting columns encased in fine Italian marble. The trading floor became a vibrant part of London's commercial district; in the early 20th century up to 250,000 tons of grain were traded there every day. However, in 1929 the economic crisis that followed the Wall Street Crash signalled the end of the Baltic's commodity market and the organisation began to concentrate its efforts on establishing a foothold in the embryonic air-borne freight trade.

In 1949, the Baltic Exchange's endeavours paid off when it became the first airfreight exchange in the world and in 1985 it expanded into the lucrative but risky international freight futures market. It was not the only organisation to see the riches that could be gained by dealing in this new facet of commerce. In 1988, it was forced to merge with other organisations trading futures in Baltic goods in order to streamline what was becoming a dangerously complicated system. The merged companies became known as the Baltic Futures Exchange and moved into new premises at the London Commodity Exchange. The move from the premises at St Mary Axe proved timely as on 10 April 1992, an IRA bomb containing 100lb of Semtex detonated outside the old Baltic Exchange building, killing three people and destroying the trading floor.

The Baltic Exchange was never rebuilt. Those still working at the site prior to the bombing moved to offices nearby and the old property was sold to developers Trafalgar House in 1995, who decided that the site was perfect for the construction of a landmark building. They employed the services of the architect Norman Foster and the resulting building, formally known as 30 St Mary Axe, is today known and loved by most Londoners as 'The Gherkin'.

11

THE PROS AND CONS OF PROSPERITY

During the 18th century, the population of London doubled from 400,000 to 800,000 as the city experienced a long period of unparalleled success brought about by the mechanisation of agriculture and industry. In 1708, the agricultural pioneer Jethro Tull invented the seed drill – a mechanical sowing device that transformed the previously slow, labour-intensive and back-breaking task of planting seeds. This allowed farmers to begin producing large quantities of crops without the expense of a huge workforce. A year later, one of the key developments of the Industrial Revolution arrived when a Staffordshire-born Quaker named Abraham Darby discovered a way of smelting iron ore using coke (which was in abundant supply) rather than the traditional charcoal (which wasn't). Iron could now be produced in much greater quantities and became the Industrial Revolution's chosen material in the construction of structures, such as bridges, and machines – for example, Thomas Newcomen's revolutionary steam engine in 1712. Later in the century, cottage industries such as weaving were also transformed by mechanisation with the introduction of John Kay's 'flying shuttle' in 1733 and James Hargreaves' 'spinning jenny' – a mechanised spinning wheel – in the 1760s.

Commercial transport was also revolutionised with the introduction of canals. The first to open was the Bridgewater Canal in 1761, which ran from Worsley to Manchester. The new industrialists realised that they could now transport raw materials and finished products across the country in bulk rather than relying solely on horse-drawn carts. Eleven years after it opened, the success of the Bridgewater Canal prompted it to be extended to the Mersey and in 1777 a canal network was dug connecting the Mersey to the Trent, and the Midlands to ports at Bristol, Liverpool and Hull.

The construction of the new canals in the North and the Midlands proved to be hugely beneficial for London's rival ports. Soon, concern about the effect they might have on trade at the docks induced the government to pass an act for the construction of a new canal linking London to the port of Bristol. The Kennet and Avon Canal opened in 1789 and, for the first time, bulk transportation between the two ports was possible.

The effect that these wholesale changes had on London was mixed. The increase in the number of people now inhabiting the city resulted in business and recreational facilities becoming so numerous and diverse that they provoked Dr Johnson to famously remark, 'When a man is tired of London, he is tired of life, for there is in London all that life can afford.'

Jonathan Swift was equally complimentary when he described the city as an optimistic, frenetic and irreverent place in his poem 'Description of the Morning' in 1709:

> Now hardly here and there a Hackney coach
> Appearing, showed the ruddy morn's approach.
> Now Betty from her master's bed had flown,
> And softly stole to discompose her own;
> The slip-shod 'prentice from his master's door
> Had pared the dirt and sprinkled round the floor.
> Now Moll had whirled her mop with dext'rous airs,
> Prepar'd to scrub the entry and the stairs.
> The youth with broomy stumps began to trace
> The kennel-edge, where wheels had worn the place,
> The small-coal man was heard with cadence deep,
> Till drown'd in shriller notes of chimney sweep:
> Duns at his lordship's gate began to meet;
> And brickdust Moll had screamed through half the street.
> The turnkey now his flock returning sees,
> Duly let out a-nights to steal for fees:
> The watchful bailiffs take their silent stands,
> And schoolboys lag with satchels in their hands.

However, not everywhere in London was able to cope with the challenges that the Industrial Revolution brought. Down at the docks, the already crowded river and quays were at bursting point. The rise in international trade resulted in a shipbuilding boom, the yards at Deptford, Woolwich and Blackwall becoming the national centre for this industry. But instead of ordering small fleets of huge craft capable of carrying a massive amount of cargo, the merchants tended to commission large fleets of smaller vessels which ultimately took up far more space on the river. In addition to this, the inadequate facilities at the legal quays meant that ships often had to drop anchor in the middle of the river and offload their cargo onto small rowing boats known as lighters which then transported the goods to the docks. The London-based writer Daniel Defoe surveyed the early 18th-century docks one afternoon and came to the conclusion that there were 'about two thousand sail of all sorts, not reckoning barges, lighters or pleasure boats, or yachts using the wharves and quays.'

In order to relieve the strain on the legal quays, a series of wharves had been built along the banks of the Thames, the most famous of which was Hay's Wharf (now Hay's Galleria) on the south bank. The wharf had experienced an illustrious past as the city residence of the Abbot of Battle. During the medieval period, it was known as the Inn of Bataille and after the abbot's departure it continued the centuries-old tradition of brewing beer and selling it to the local populace. In 1651, the lease on the old inn was purchased by Alexander Hay, who immediately set about remodelling the premises into warehousing for goods handled at the legal quays. Hay's warehouses were in a convenient location and soon the buildings were full of stock, but this did little to ease congestion on the Thames.

Despite the best efforts of the management at the Greenland Dock, many ships still lay moored in the river, sometimes remaining for over a week while they waited for space at the quayside. This attracted the attention of river pirates and other criminally minded individuals who would board the vessel and plunder its contents while the crew enjoyed themselves in the taverns of Southwark. The river pirates were a motley bunch of opportunist thieves who, although disorganised, caused no end of problems for the merchants at the docks. In his book *The Mysteries of London*, George W. M. Reynolds explained:

These river pirates are of several kinds ... there's the light-horsemen, or men who board the unprotected vessels in the night. Then there's the heavy-horsemen who wear an under-dress called a jemmy, which is covered by their smocks: the fellows obtain employment as Lumpers – that is to load or discharge ships in the pool [of London], during which they contrive to stow away anything portable in the large pouches or pockets of their underdress.

Afterwards, the heavy-horsemen give information to their pals, and put them on the scent of which ships to rob at night. Next there are the mud-larks, who get on board stranded lighters at low water, and carry off what they can when the vessels are unprotected, or ask some questions to lull suspicion if they find anyone on board. This mode of river-piracy is very profitable, because numbers of lighters and barges are often left for hours alongside the banks, without a soul on board. Game lightermen are those pirates that are in league with dishonest mates and sailors belonging to vessels that come up the river to discharge: and they receive at night from their pals on board, through port-holes or over the quarter, any thing that's easy to move away in this manner. Last of all there's the scuffle-hunters, who put on smocks, and obtain work as porters on the wharves where a ship is loading: then, if they can't contrive to steal any thing by those means, they can at all events carry some useful information to their pals – so that the ship is generally robbed in one way or another.

In order to deter the activities described by George Reynolds, punishment of those caught committing crimes at the docks was harsh. In May 1719, Edward Whippy was indicted at the Old Bailey for stealing 20 iron shots, an iron crowbar and 250lb of rope from Captain Harrison's ship while it was moored at Shadwell. After taking the items, Whippy had wasted no time in selling the rope to a Mr Beason who, on discovering he was in the possession of stolen property, shopped Whippy to the authorities. At the ensuing trial, the prisoner put up an improbable defence, stating that the items had mysteriously found their way on to his boat and he capitalised on this good fortune by selling them. Unsurprisingly, the jury did not believe his story and reasoned that even if it were true, he should not have been so quick to sell them. Whippy was sentenced to transportation for his misdemeanour.

John Mann, a waterman from Billingsgate, suffered the same fate after he was tempted to steal some clothes from a vessel. The Old Bailey proceedings of 13 October 1723 report that he was indicted for stealing 'three jackets value 12s the goods of John Loan, Oct. 12. It appear'd that as the Prosecutor's ship lay in Billingsgate Dock, the prisoner ... got into the cabbin [sic] about midnight, and took away the goods. He was perceived just as he went off; and being pursued, he dropt the jackets, and was taken to Thames Street.'

Unfortunately some maritime crimes tried at the Old Bailey were more serious than theft. In November 1738, a sailor named James Buchanan was indicted for murder at the court. The story that emerged from the resulting trial gives a vivid account of how men came to work on ships that plied their trade from the London docks and also how the testing conditions on board an 18th century vessel could prove to be the undoing of some men.

James Buchanan was born in 1706 in Stirlingshire, Scotland. His early years seem to have been happy, but when his father suddenly died he was put into the care of an uncle who packed him off to a boarding school to improve his education. Buchanan hated his new school and decided to run away to Newcastle, where he found work on a series of ships. After voyaging to Virginia and several other destinations he returned to Britain and married 'a young woman with a good portion'. However, not long after his marriage, his (presumably childless) uncle died, leaving him with considerable debts amounting to about £1,200. Unable to pay off this vast sum, Buchanan found he had no choice but to leave his wife and take to the seas once again.

He first travelled to North America and tried to set up his own shipping business with two colleagues. The men purchased a sloop and began to trade along the east coast. However, after docking at an unidentified port belonging to the French, the trio found themselves accused of illicit trade and their ship was seized, forcing Buchanan once again to return to Britain. He decided to try his luck at the London docks and secured work with the East India Company. In the autumn of 1737, he set sail as a mate on the *Royal Guardian* under the command of Captain Henry Hoadley. The vessel docked at Canton and shortly after its arrival at the port some boats carrying goods bound for London arrived unexpectedly. Most of the crew, including the captain, had disembarked and wandered into the port looking for entertainment, so it fell to the fourth mate – a man named Michael Smith – to try to find enough labour to load the ship.

While searching for help, Smith found Buchanan in the forecastle 'carousing with two of his countryfolk' over a large bowl of punch. Smith forced the inebriated Buchanan up on to the deck so he could help with the loading, but the Scot took great exception to being manhandled and a fight broke out during which Smith was fatally stabbed. Captain Hoadley arrived back to find his ship in uproar and after hearing from witnesses that Buchanan had been seen lunging at Smith and then throwing something over the side of the ship, he reluctantly clamped him in irons until the *Royal Guardian* returned to London.

At the ensuing trial Buchanan pleaded not guilty, claiming that although he had fought with Smith, he had not stabbed him. However, the jury found him guilty as charged. It was only after the judge handed down the sentence of death by hanging that Buchanan thought it best to come clean. He admitted his guilt and, according to the Ordinary, 'seem'd to be in the greatest Consternation and Confusion, scarce avoiding tears.'

The date of execution was set for 20 December. In preparation for his end, Buchanan immersed himself in religion, taking the sacrament and constantly repenting for his sins. On the day of his execution, he was taken to the waiting gallows by horse and cart from his cell at Newgate Prison and took his mind off the grim purpose of the journey by reading religious literature. Once at the scaffold, he warned his fellow sailors to 'beware of Passion' and confessed his sins once more before singing the 23rd psalm – 'The Lord Is My Shepherd'. The Ordinary then recorded, 'After I had done my duty, and left him for about five minutes, some Sailors got on the Scaffold, and endeavour'd to cut him down; on which a scuffle ensu'd between them and the Officers; but many other Sailors coming to the Assistance of those who first made the Attempt, he was cut down (as I was inform'd) in less than six minutes after I parted from him, and his Body carry'd off in a Boat, with loud Acclamations of Joy, accompanied by a great many Sailors.'

The place at which James Buchanan met his end was the notorious Execution Dock in Wapping. The dock had a macabre significance for sailors as it was traditionally the place at which condemned mariners were hanged. Historically, serious crimes committed at sea had generally been tried by the Admiralty courts and the place of execution in London was situated within their jurisdiction, just beyond the point of low tide in the river Thames. The open situation of the dock meant that executions could be watched by members of the public and many Londoners regarded the hangings as a fine piece of entertainment.

All those who found themselves with an appointment at Execution Dock were hanged, but special treatment was meted out to pirates. The illegal seizing of vessels was a constant and expensive problem that seriously affected the economy and, consequently, any wayward sailors who had the audacity to capture their homeland's ships were punished in the most shocking manner possible as a warning to others. Convicted pirates executed at the dock were hanged on a shortened rope, which ensured that they were not granted a quick end by having their neck broken by the drop. Instead, the rope would slowly asphyxiate them. As the jeering spectators watched their laboured death throes, some convicts were seen to perform the ghoulish 'marshal's dance' as their limbs flailed about in a desperate but ultimately hopeless attempt to get air into their lungs. When death finally came, the body was left hanging on a gibbet until three tides had washed over it as a final act of disrespect. After this, particularly notorious offenders were sometimes tarred and suspended on a gibbet on the banks of the Thames estuary in Kent where they could be seen by all ships entering or exiting the river.

The most notorious mariner to be hanged at Execution Dock was Captain Kidd, a Scottish privateer and pirate whose exploits on the high seas have since passed into legend. William (sometimes referred to as John) Kidd was born *circa* 1645 in Greenock, Renfrewshire, the son of a Church of Scotland minister. Virtually nothing is known of Kidd's early life. His name first crops up in records in 1689, when the governor of the Leeward Islands in the West Indies employed him as a privateer to help capture hostile French ships that had been harrying English vessels in the Caribbean Sea. Kidd was given control of a ship called the *Blessed William* and a motley crew comprised mainly of pirates. After participating in two sea battles but acquiring little from the French ships to reward their efforts, Kidd's men tired of working for the governor and stole the *Blessed William*, taking it up the Atlantic coast to New York.

Incensed that he had been duped by his own men, Kidd followed the ship to New York hell bent on revenge, but on arrival was frustrated to find that his erstwhile crew had vanished along with the ship. However, instead of retreating into the service of the Leeward Islands' governor, he decided to stay in New York and used his considerable charm to win the support and financial backing of a group of influential Whig politicians who put his skills as a privateer to good use to protect their port. While working on the politicians' ships, Kidd fell in with a prominent businessman and fellow Scot named Robert Livingstone and soon the two men were busy devising money-making schemes.

Kidd came up with a plan that he believed would make his fortune. Whilst working on the privateer ships, he had heard stories of a pirate settlement on the island of Madagascar to which much plundered treasure was taken. If he could use Livingstone's contacts to raise enough money to acquire a ship, they could sail to the island, arrest any pirates found there and seize their vessels. The pirates would then be taken either to Britain or North America for trial, where it was certain they would be found guilty and either transported or executed, leaving their ships and treasure to be divided between Kidd, Livingstone and their investors.

Livingstone was seduced by Kidd's ambitious plan and soon managed to attract some eminent investors in the scheme, including Lord Bellomont, the governor of New York. Enough finance was raised to obtain a ship – the *Adventure Galley* – and on 6 September 1696, Kidd set sail for Madagascar with a crew of 90 experienced pirates.

At first, the voyage went according to plan but when Kidd spotted a pilgrim fleet on their way home to India from the Islamic holy city of Mecca, his avaricious nature got the better of him. He rapidly launched an attack on the ships, but was taken by surprise when the Sceptre – an East India Company ship that was travelling with the pilgrim fleet – retaliated, forcing the *Adventure Galley* to retreat. Frustrated with this narrow escape, Kidd went on to attack several merchant ships and by the time they reached Madagascar, he and his pirate crew had completely forgotten about their original plan. Instead of capturing the pirates on the island, they socialised with them and Kidd decided to return to New York claiming that they had been unable to make any arrests.

Meanwhile, the East India Company had become enraged over Kidd's unprovoked attack on the pilgrim fleet and appealed to the British government who sent orders to Lord Bellomont to arrest him as soon as he arrived in New York. However, Kidd learnt of the warrant for his arrest while on the return voyage and quickly set about disposing of the stolen treasure on board the *Adventure Galley* by selling it at various ports, carefully keeping some prize items back with which he would attempt to bribe Lord Bellomont. Once back at New York, he anchored some distance off the coast, waited there until Bellomont could be found and then brought him to the ship to show him the bribe. It is not known exactly what treasure the lord was offered, but whatever it was, it proved insufficient for him to give Kidd his freedom. He was duly arrested and sent for trial in England.

As he prepared for trial, Kidd was offered one last means of escaping the hangman's noose. The Liberal government (of which Bellomont was part) had been succeeded by the Tories and party members visited Kidd in gaol in an attempt to persuade him to testify that his Whig contacts in New York had been plotting against their homeland. For reasons that he kept to himself, Kidd refused to betray his former financiers and effectively sealed his fate. At the ensuing trial, evidence for the defence mysteriously went missing and it soon became clear that there was to be only one outcome. Captain Kidd was sentenced to be hanged at Execution Dock at low tide on 23 May 1701.

On the day of the hanging, Kidd was taken to his place of execution in a horse and cart but as he ascended the scaffold, the proceedings descended into chaos. The first noose broke and as Kidd fell to the floor, he must have though that fate was on his side. However, he was hastily grabbed by guards and held while a second rope was secured. This time, the noose did its job and Kidd's luck finally ran out.

Following his death, the tale of Captain Kidd passed into folklore. His story was regularly used as a cautionary tale against greed and deceit, the *Newgate Calendar* commenting that, 'The story of this wretched malefactor will effectually impress on the mind of the reader the truth of the old observation that Honesty is the best Policy.' Stories also abounded of the wealth acquired by Kidd on his voyage to Madagascar. Soon tales emerged of vast treasure hidden away by the captain on his journey back to New York. However, although many have tried to find Kidd's alleged hoard, all attempts to date have proved unsuccessful and there is doubt as to whether any such treasure ever existed.

Although the gruesome sights at Execution Dock discouraged some Londoners from indulging in piracy, the ships waiting in the Thames still proved too much of a temptation for many and robberies from these vessels continued on an all too regular basis. This crime, coupled with the chronic congestion on the river, finally forced the government to act. In 1796, a Select Committee for the Improvement of the Port of London was formed with the express intention of establishing 'the best mode of providing sufficient accommodation for the increased trade and shipping of the Port.' In the same way as they had tackled the rebuilding of London after the Great Fire, Parliament invited architects and engineers to submit plans designed to solve the problems at the docks. One, submitted by a Mr Ogle, creatively utilised the stretch of the Thames from the Tower to Greenland Dock. It was proposed that a 250ft-wide channel running down the middle of the river would be reserved for ships to move in and out of the port while either side, new quays would be constructed, each one serving a different market. For example, the land immediately east of the Tower would be used by ships trading with Germany, while opposite in Southwark, ships from Oporto and Lisbon would be moored. Further east, the area surrounding Execution Dock at Wapping would deal with Dutch and Mediterranean goods, while both banks of the river along a large stretch beyond would accommodate ships carrying sugar and spices from the West Indies. The riverside at Limehouse would serve the Russia Company's fleet, the approach to Greenland Dock being reserved for coal and timber supplies.

Mr Ogle planned to arrange the ships in tiers running parallel with the riverbank and secured with a series of mooring chains. There would be space for six ships in each tier and an estimated 1,199 vessels could be accommodated using this method – according to Ogle, 'a greater number by 450 than was in that part of the river at any one time in the Year 1795'. Although Ogle's plan certainly made the most of a limited amount of space, it required the government to compulsorily purchase all the land from the current owners, which was deemed prohibitively expensive.

Another plan, drawn up by London-based architect Samuel Wyatt, seemed more financially viable. Wyatt planned to remove the notoriously slow passage round the Isle of Dogs by building a canal leading from Blackwall through Limehouse, Ratcliff and Shadwell to Wapping. He also proposed the construction of huge docks at the northern boundary of the Isle of Dogs, along with another smaller dock complex at Wapping.

Samuel Wyatt's scheme was scrutinised by the committee and time passed as they considered its viability. In the end, Wyatt was never commissioned to realise his vision of the new docks, but the locations identified on his plan caught the attention of men with a vested interest in solving the Port of London's problems. One such individual was a West Indies merchant named Robert Milligan who had arrived in the capital some years previously, having spent much of his adult life managing his family's sugar plantation in Jamaica. On setting up business at the docks, Milligan had been horrified at the amount of time lost by ships waiting to enter the legal quays and had been equally concerned about the reports of river piracy. On discovering that the government was finally prepared to do whatever it took to remedy the parlous state of affairs, Milligan saw his chance and took it. Using contacts at the Royal Exchange, he proposed the formation of the West India Dock Company – a corporation with the specific remit to develop suitable moorings, dock facilities and warehousing for ships involved in trade with the West Indian plantations. Milligan and his associates held sufficient financial clout for Parliament to take note of their intentions and in 1799 the West India Dock Act was passed. Construction could now commence.

Taking note of Samuel Wyatt's proposal, the West India Dock Company (under the deputy-chairmanship of Milligan) commissioned an engineer named William Jessop to design its new dock on land acquired on the Isle of Dogs, near the High Street at Poplar. Jessop created two vast docks which stretched across over half the isle's width. The northernmost dock was designed for imports and covered an expanse of 30 acres, while below it lay the export dock covering a slightly smaller 24 acres of land. Vessels entered the docks through massive locks leading to holding basins, which in turn led to the docks themselves. The entire complex was surrounded by a high wall surmounted by iron railings and bordered by a water-filled ditch, making illicit entry virtually impossible.

Once ships had made their way to the docks, security reached almost paranoid levels. The crew had to leave the vessel immediately and not even the captain was allowed back on until it was ready to be unloaded. The ships were dealt with on a first come, first served basis. Unloaded cargo was taken to the Custom House officials, who had offices at each dock, and once it had been weighed and counted it was loaded onto carts and lighters that had been queuing up outside the docks since the ship's arrival. The lighters that transported the cargo were not owned by the West India Dock Company. These hardworking little craft were generally privately owned by individuals, continuing a long tradition of independent transportation of goods from ship to quayside. The lightermen and their craft were so highly valued at the port that the government had written a clause into the 1799 Act that allowed wharfingers (wharf owners) and lightermen to enter the West India Docks to collect goods without paying a fee to the owners. This became known as the 'free water clause' and would serve the lightermen well in years to come.

Commodities that did not require immediate dispatch from the docks were taken to a series of tall warehouses surrounding the basin. These structures were five storeys high and designed to withstand a great weight of merchandise. The upper floors were loaded through large wooden exterior doors by iron cranes mounted at the top of the building, thus making the dock labourers' work considerably easier than it might have been if they had been required to carry goods to the upper floors themselves. Transportation of these items to other parts of the country was carried out mostly by road and an important part of the new dock scheme was the construction of a new route leading from the West India Docks to Whitechapel, where it connected with roads leading into the city and beyond. Named the Grand Commercial Road, this thoroughfare inevitably ran through the eastern suburbs of London and the problems caused by existing infrastructure resulted in its construction being long and laborious. At one point, the new road converged with an older track and the resulting congestion earned this stretch the nickname 'Cumbersome Street'. At Limehouse, part of the old churchyard had to be dug up, prompting the controversial removal of several bodies. These problems mean that it took far longer to build the road than had been initially anticipated. In 1804, two years after the docks had opened for trade, the road was still not finished and a visiting journalist concluded that 'it will be a considerable time before the business is completed.' That said, the construction of the road proved to be very beneficial for property owners in the area, who saw the value of their estates rise to five times their previous worth. The finished thoroughfare also became a valuable part of London's road network and still exists today, although the 'Grand' in its title has long been dispensed with.

The foundation stone for the West India Dock complex was laid on 12 July 1800 amid much pomp and ceremony. According to *The Times*, 'The stone had been previously prepared to receive two glass bottles, one of which contained the several coins (gold, silver and copper) of his present majesty's reign, and in the other, the following inscription and translation thereof in Latin, were placed:

Of this range of BUILDINGS
Constructed, together with the Adjacent DOCKS,
At the Expense of public spirited Individuals,
Under the Sanction of a provident Legislature,
And with the liberal Co-operation of the Corporate Body of the
CITY OF LONDON
For the distinct Purpose
Of complete SECURITY and ample ACCOMMODATION
(hitherto not afforded)
To the SHIPPING and PRODUCE of the WEST INDIES at this
Wealthy PORT
THE FIRST STONE WAS LAID

After the stone-laying ceremony, the company and its guests were taken on a tour of the site before retiring to the London Tavern where, according to the *Times* journalist, 'the remainder of the day was passed with great conviviality'. The West India Docks opened for trade two years later.

12

THE CANAL BOOM

By the late 18th century, the Port of London was experiencing a period of unprecedented growth. As the number of docks along the Thames increased and demand grew for the industrial goods being produced in the north of England, it soon became clear that a new distribution network was urgently required. The horse-drawn carts that had traditionally carried merchandise to and from the docks were no longer able to cope with the massive increase in trade. Merchants dealing with suppliers from the Midlands and the North were aware of how beneficial their canal network was to the distribution of goods and it soon became clear that the construction of man-made waterways through London might provide a solution.

At the time, London already had one canal of sorts, which had originally been a tributary of the Thames. The River Lea flowed from its source near Luton through Bedfordshire and along the Hertfordshire/ Essex border before joining the Thames at Bow Creek, just east of the Isle of Dogs. The Lea was navigable up to Hertford and had been used to convey vessels to and from London since time immemorial. The earliest record of its use dated from the ninth century when Vikings sailed up the river to build an encampment at Ware in Hertfordshire. By the Middle Ages, the river was being used to transport grain to Thames-side mills and in 1577, traffic on the Lea was so busy that an act was passed granting permission to make navigational improvements, including a lock at Waltham Abbey in Essex. The people living along the banks of the river in Hertfordshire were indispensable during the plague years of the 17th century, particularly during the great outbreak in 1665, when they continued to bring grain into the city despite being at great risk of catching the disease. Local legend has it that bodies of plague victims were taken back to Hertfordshire on the boats' return journeys and buried in the marshland between Ware and Hertford when the London churchyards could not cope with the amount of burials.

Canalisation of the Lea began in 1766 when 15 short cuts were excavated along its course to form what is now known as the River Lea Navigation. At the mouth of the Thames, the Limehouse Cut was dug to create a more accessible entrance for vessels and additional locks were also added. Locks had traditionally been used on rivers to bypass rapids and weirs but by the 18th century, engineers realised that they could also be used to convey man-made waterways across undulating countryside, thus creating the most direct route possible. The principle of an 18th-century lock was (and still is) very simple. The construction comprised a watertight chamber – large enough to accommodate a vessel – with gates at either end. The chamber acted as a lift that either raised or lowered craft to the water level on the other side of the gate, thus removing the need for it to be laboriously towed uphill or dangerously shoot the rapids. For example, on reaching a lock, the boatman on a craft travelling upstream would check to see if the chamber was empty. If it was, they would open the lock gates using gear located on the waterside and move into the chamber, closing the gates behind them. Once inside, the lock gear for the opposite doors was turned to open a valve which sent water gushing into the central chamber, raising the craft up to the water level beyond. Once the chamber was full – a process that generally took around 10 minutes – the second gates were opened and the craft continued its journey.

The canalisation of the Lea proved to be extremely successful, but it was to be nearly 30 years before engineers embarked on an entirely man-made canal for London. In 1793, pressure from London merchants finally paid off when the government passed an act authorising construction of the Grand Junction Canal, a waterway that would at last link the city with the northern canal network. William Jessop – who, as we have seen, was later to be involved in the building of the West India Docks – was employed in the role of chief engineer and William Praed, after whom Praed Street in Paddington is named, was elected chairman.

Initially plans were drawn to connect the canal to the Port of London by joining it to the Thames at Brentford. However, once work was under way, the company decided it would be financially prudent to also create a spur running from Bull's Bridge (in modern Southall) to Paddington, which was then a village on the outskirts of west London. Not only was Paddington much closer to the city than Brentford but it also had an excellent transport link in the form of the New Road which connected the village to the metropolis.

After lengthy negotiations with local landowners, the Paddington branch of the Grand Junction Canal opened on 10 July 1801. This new waterway terminated at a basin measuring 400 yards long by 30 yards wide, flanked by wharves and warehouses, a hay market and pens for livestock and its arrival must have come as quite a shock to the residents of this rural backwater. The opening of the canal was celebrated across London, the Sadler's Wells Company even putting together a musical extravaganza in its honour. Titled *The Grand Junction Canal or A Trip to Paddington*, the performance featured several scenic backdrops of the waterway including 'an accurate view of the first bridge, with the Aquatic Procession of Barges, Passage and Pleasure Boats coming through it into the Basin.' These ambitious sets were accompanied by a variety of songs including a homage to the grape called 'Virtues of Brandy' and the excitingly titled 'War and the Watermen'.

The Paddington branch of the Grand Junction Canal proved to be an instant success and continued to play an important part in London's network of waterways until the rise of the railways in the mid-19th century. To this day, the basin remains a focal point of the area and now forms a very attractive although virtually redundant centre to the upmarket area of Little Venice.

Almost as soon as the Grand Junction Canal at Paddington opened, the merchants at the docks began to press for an extension of the waterway which would lead directly to the Port of London. They reasoned that this new branch of the canal would remove the need for goods bound for the docks to be shipped down the busy Thames from Brentford or taken by horse and cart along the increasingly congested New Road. Parliament was petitioned and in 1812, an act authorised the construction of a canal linking Paddington with Limehouse. In charge of the project was an architect named John Nash, the man largely responsible for Londoners' mid-19th century obsession with stucco-fronted villas, who was on very good terms with the Prince Regent. In a coup guaranteed to attract investors, Nash announced that he was to name the canal after his great friend and thus the regally titled Regent's Canal came into being.

However, despite an auspicious start, construction of the waterway proved to be slow and fraught with difficulty. A state-of-the-art hydro-pneumatic lock was installed at the junction with the road to Hampstead but failed to operate correctly and had to be completely scrapped. Soon after this disaster, on 21 March 1815, three navigation men working for the company found themselves in the dock at Bow Street Magistrates' Court charged with riot and assault. The prosecutor was one Mr Agar, a barrister who lived in a house in Camden Town, the grounds of which led down to the canal construction site. Mr Agar claimed that on the previous Monday, the three prisoners along with around 20 other 'navvies' had trespassed onto his land, knocking down a fence in the process. When they were confronted by Mr Agar's gardeners, a fight had ensued during which the gardeners were 'knocked down and violently assaulted.' As the case unfolded, it transpired that far from being simply an aggrieved householder, Mr Agar was strongly opposed to the construction of the canal through his back garden and had refused to sell the company his land on several occasions. The navvies pleaded complete ignorance to the fact that they were trespassing and were eventually found not guilty. The resulting coverage of the story in the press did, however, give the Regent's Canal Company some unwelcome negative publicity which it could have well done without, but, more importantly, the dispute was not resolved. Works ground to a halt while Mr Agar stood firm and the company was forced to ask subscribers to contribute more funds in order to tide them over. Eventually, after two years of wrangling, Mr Agar agreed to relinquish his land for an undisclosed (but no doubt handsome) sum of money and the beleaguered canal company was forced to obtain a government loan so that works could continue.

By 1820, the Regent's Canal was finally completed and the docks were at last connected to the Midlands and beyond by an uninterrupted canal network. At the stretch that lay close to the boundaries of Ratcliff and Limehouse, loading facilities for lighters and other small craft were provided in the form of the Regent's Canal Dock, otherwise known as the Limehouse Basin. Numerous goods were distributed via this little dock including ice, salt and timber, but the most regular cargo proved to be coal shipped down from the northern mining towns to fuel the workshops and households of the metropolis. The dock was so popular with colliers that it was almost immediately enlarged to accommodate larger craft and it quickly became an important distribution centre for both the coal and timber industries. Some years later, 'J.M.C.', writing for the *Manchester Guardian*, visited the dock and wrote about the scene he found there. Although there had been significant changes to the Port of London by the time he wrote his article, it seems that the Limehouse Basin had altered little from when it first opened: 'A cluster of little wooden barques, timber laden from the Baltic lie (within the dock). White-hulled and copper-bottomed, apple-bowed like the ships of 100 years ago, they are brave little craft, which well know the weight of a North Sea gale, and have struggled into the estuary with clean-swept decks and the arms of their windmill pumps revolving for dear life. Now moored in safety after the perils of the sea, their trimly curtained cabin windows and the homely picture of the cook peeling potatoes at the galley door lend an air of quiet domesticity to the Limehouse Basin.'

Along with the barques and other small sailing craft that used the Regent's Canal were literally hundreds of narrowboats. These long, thin vessels were made of wood and were specifically designed for use on the canals. Until the 20th century, they were drawn slowly and silently along the waterways of Britain by sturdy horses that walked steadily along the towpath, pulling the rope behind them. Evidence of this now almost extinct practice can still be seen on the corners of canal bridges where the impressions of thousands of narrowboat ropes can be seen carved deep into the brickwork.

Although progress was slow, the amount of cargo transported on a narrowboat was around 10 times that which could be carried by a horse and cart. The boatmen themselves lived transient lives travelling up and down the waterways of Britain, sometimes for months on end. It was a lonely profession. In the early days, families could not accompany the boatman as all available space was reserved for cargo and to pass the time, the boatmen often decorated their craft with beautifully painted murals and motifs – a tradition that continues to this day. The docks along the journey provided welcome breaks for the boatmen; rather like modern truck stops, they were used as meeting places for colleagues keen for a chat and a smoke in one of the local taverns before continuing on their journey.

Like the boatmen who travelled along them, the men who dug the canals also lived transient lives – working wherever a canal was being dug. They were originally known as navigators but this quickly corrupted into the shorter 'navvies'. Our modern perception of navvies is that they were often of Irish heritage, but the original navigators were overwhelmingly English. Ireland's countrymen had not yet been forced to leave their homeland by the devastating famine of the 1840s and preferred to tend the fields rather than embark on exhausting excavations.

A navvy's work was exceptionally hard and required huge physical strength and stamina. Each man was expected to be able to shift up to 20 tons of London clay per day without the benefit of any machinery. The arduous and transient nature of the work meant that the canal navvies were usually young, single and very well built. They certainly captured the attention of the artist Ford Madox Brown, who described his masterpiece *Work* thus: 'Here is presented the young navvy in the pride of manly health and beauty; the strong fully developed navvy who does his work and loves his beer.'

The canal navvies tended to live together in cheap lodgings close to their place of work. Consequently, trips to the pub were common and their arduous lives were interspersed with occasional opportunities for mischief. In 1842, *The Times* reported, 'A party of navvies being at work at one side of the Thames, and lodging on the other, hit upon an ingenious plan for reducing the bridge toll. They deputed one of their party to inquire of the collector how much weight a man was allowed to carry, and whether any sort of weight was allowed. The collector answered "carry what you choose, and as much as you can." They took him at his word, and assembled the whole force on the bridge, they divided the party into two sections, and one carried two through the gate, more to the merriment of the lookers on, than to the amusement or profit of the collector.'

The navvies' fondness for a pint also landed them in trouble on occasion. In September 1813, John M'Ritchie, a navigator working on the Regent's Canal, had £50 stolen from him after the consumption of a few drinks left him less careful than perhaps he should have been. The Old Bailey sessions recorded that Mr M'Ritchie had been invited to a dockside pub by a former colleague named Thomas Oakley. At the trial, M'Ritchie stated, 'I sat down and drank with him, and I [eventually] fell asleep alongside of him. I stopped all day with Oakley at the public house; at night my wife and a friend fetched me home. The next morning I missed my bundle of notes.' M'Ritchie's supposed friend was found guilty of theft and transported for seven years. Inebriated navvies seem to have been a target for their dishonest colleagues. In July 1832, a navvy named Michael Stanley was also robbed by his workmate William Garson after falling asleep in a pub.

Although the navvies' hard work on the Grand Junction and Regent's Canals reaped dividends for their employers, not all canal projects in London were as successful. In fact, several areas of the city still hold the unrecognisable remnants of failed waterways, one of which was the Grand Surrey Canal.

The government authorised construction of this canal in 1801, hoping that it would turn out to be the south London equivalent of the Grand Junction spur in Paddington. Sadly, the venture was beset by problems from the beginning, mainly because the company responsible for its construction allowed itself to become distracted by other schemes. The Grand Surrey was originally planned to run from the Thames at Rotherhithe to Epsom, but constant diversion of funds to other developments meant that it never got further than today's Camberwell Road, where a large wharf-lined basin was created. This short stretch of waterway opened in 1809 and, luckily, traffic was sufficient for a branch to Peckham to be opened in 1826. However, despite limited success, the canal's original path through Surrey to the rural fields of Epsom never appeared. Eventually, the little canal fell into disuse and was drained and built over. The basin at Camberwell now lies buried beneath Burgess Park.

In the same year as the curtailed Grand Surrey Canal opened, another south London canal was also completed. The Croydon Canal joined the Grand Surrey at its basin before travelling across the countryside via Forest Hill, Sydenham and Penge to a spacious basin at Croydon. Although this long canal was at least completed, it quickly proved to be under-used and the managing company struggled to survive. By the 1830s, plans for a railway linking Croydon to the city were being discussed and the Croydon Canal Company's directors saw a way to minimise their losses. They sold their land to the London & Croydon Railway Company and the canal closed on 22 August 1836. Following the sale, the railway company drained the canal and used it as part of the trackbed between Croydon and London Bridge. The basin was also emptied and formed the foundation for West Croydon railway station.

The Croydon Canal was not the only waterway to succumb to the superior service offered by the railways. The Kensington Canal ran from the Thames at Chelsea to a basin near today's Warwick Road at Earls Court. The waterway had originally been a tributary of the Thames known as Counter's Creek and had been used as a common sewer for many years. The owner of the land on which it stood – William Edwardes, Lord Kensington – had seen the success of the Grand Junction Canal and resolved to put his stinking sewer to more profitable and commodious use. A Kensington Canal Company was formed and plans were drawn up to construct a 'Canal for the Navigation of Boats, Barges and other Vessels.' The prevailing situation during the initial stages of construction did not bode well. The original contractors went bankrupt and when their estimate was looked over by new contractors, it quickly became apparent that the canal was going to cost four times the amount originally quoted. The fated canal eventually opened in 1828, with Lord Kensington and his cronies arriving at its Earls Court basin on a ceremonial barge amid much flag waving from the assembled crowd. However, more trouble was afoot. The canal regularly silted up and in places became impossible to navigate. Because of this, traffic was limited and the projected income of £2,500 per annum (raised through tolls) was never achieved. Like the Croydon Canal, Lord Kensington's failing enterprise was eventually sold to a railway company in 1836. The canal now forms part of the trackbed of the West London line, which runs between Willesden Junction and Clapham.

Not far from the blighted Kensington Canal lay the equally unlucky Grosvenor Canal. This waterway, which led from the Thames at Chelsea to modern Victoria via Pimlico, started life as ponds belonging to the Chelsea Waterworks Company which supplied drinking water to west London. The ponds were purchased by the Grosvenor Canal Company and extended to create a workable waterway. In 1823, the canal opened and was initially well used by builders' merchants carrying materials to new housing developments in the locality. Small wharves and warehousing sprang up along the canal and around its basin close to the grounds of Buckingham Palace, which had recently been remodelled by the Regent's Canal creator, John Nash. Ironically, the basin's excellent location contributed to the canal's inevitable demise when the railways arrived in London.

In 1858, the Victoria Station & Pimlico Railway Company was incorporated, its intention being to construct a railway from the Pimlico area across the Thames where it would connect with an existing railway that ran through to Sydenham – the site of the relocated Crystal Palace. While surveying the area in search of a suitable line for its track, the company looked at the northernmost part of the Grosvenor Canal, including the basin, which was in an ideal location for the railway terminus. After negotiating with the canal owners, it purchased both the basin and a small section of canal that ran directly from it. The site was drained and redeveloped as Victoria Railway Station. What was left of the Grosvenor Canal struggled on. In 1866, it found a new use as the route for refuse barges carrying away the detritus of west London, but in 1899 it was shortened once again when Victoria Station was enlarged. In 1927, the remaining part of the canal north of Ebury Bridge was filled in to form part of a new housing estate. The last surviving part of the Grosvenor Canal continued to serve as a dock for refuse barges until the mid-1990s when the land was purchased by property developers who planned a luxury housing complex around the edge of the waterway. Today, all that remains of the Grosvenor Canal is a short inlet lying just east of Chelsea Bridge.

13

THE GREAT 19TH CENTURY DOCKS

While navvies were busy excavating the Grand Junction Canal's great basin at Paddington, the government's Select Committee for the Improvement of the Port of London was carefully considering plans submitted by a consortium known as the London Docks Company for another dock complex on the north bank of the Thames at Wapping. In many ways, the area in which the proposed development would be situated was ideal as it was in close proximity to the legal quays and the city. However, its central position also meant that the area already had a well-established community who were not remotely interested in vacating their homes and business premises to make way for a new dock.

In addition to being the traditional venue for the execution of pirates and rogue mariners, Wapping had long since attracted a wide range of industries connected with the Port of London. By the late 18th century, the Thames was lined with small independent wharves, most of which served the timber trade. In between these wharves were ancient river stairs that led to narrow alleyways lined with yards and warehouses behind which lay a long road known variously as Wapping Dock or simply the High Street. Back in the 16th century, the historian John Stow had described this thoroughfare as 'a filthy strait passage, with alleys of small tenements ... inhabited by sailors' victuallers'. By the end of the 1700s, the area was little changed, although some of the establishments had been recently destroyed after a fierce fire broke out at a cork-cutter's workshop in March 1790.

While drawing up its proposal, the London Docks Company had surveyed the shabby streets of Wapping and concluded that the creation of the dock development would only serve to improve the area. Ambitious plans were drawn up covering a site that stretched from the boundary with Shadwell in the east to an old basin near the Tower known as Hermitage Dock. Ships would enter the new docks via one of two gates situated at the eastern perimeter and Wapping Old Stairs, which lay close to the middle of the development. These gates would open into large basins, which in turn would lead to three wet docks known as the Eastern, Tobacco and Western. In total, the three docks would be capable of holding up to 390 ships, thus significantly easing congestion on the river. Lighters used to unload the ships would gain access to the docks through a third gate at the western end. Around the perimeter of the docks, the company planned to construct spacious quays for landing the cargo, beyond which a series of warehouses would be built. These structures would be among the largest of their type in the whole of Europe. The proposed tobacco warehouse alone measured a mighty 752ft long by 160ft wide and had the capacity to store up to 24,000 hogsheads of the evil weed. Close by, the vintners' warehouses could hold over 65,000 pipes of wine.

Although most people agreed that the new London Docks would provide a much-needed resource for the port, the company's plans met with a great deal of opposition, especially from the residents of Wapping. Objectors calculated that up to 2,000 houses would have to be demolished to accommodate the development and long-established businesses along the river's edge would be forced to relocate or shut down completely. The construction of the docks would also inevitably affect the existing infrastructure, not only in Wapping but also in neighbouring parishes. Complaints were received from the Shadwell Waterworks (which supplied the area with drinking water), the Commissioners for Sewers in Tower Hamlets and even the 'scholars of King's Hall and Brazen-Nose College, Oxford' who were the patrons of the nearby rectory of St Dunstan in Stepney.

For five years, the Select Committee prevaricated as all objections were duly considered. In the end, however, the need to tackle the problems on the Thames proved so great that the plans were approved. The London Docks opened for trade in 1805, specialising in the handling of wine, brandy, tobacco and rice, for which they had been granted exclusive unloading and storage privileges for a period of 20 years. The previous inhabitants of Wapping grudgingly moved further east to the rapidly expanding districts of Limehouse, Poplar and Blackwall. East London was getting bigger and the docks were the catalyst.

While plans for the London Docks were being discussed by Parliament, unprecedented events in France brought a fresh set of problems for the merchants at the port. On 21 September 1792, King Louis XVI was deposed and his erstwhile kingdom was hastily declared a republic. There followed the dramatic 'reign of terror' during which up to 40,000 enemies of the revolution were executed in a bloody attempt to clear a path from which a new France could emerge. The events across the Channel caused a great deal of anxiety for the British aristocracy, who were justifiably terrified that there could be a revolution in Britain. The subsequent rise of the French army under Napoleon Bonaparte caused Parliament even greater concern and in 1793, Britain formed a coalition with Spain, Prussia, Austria, Sardinia and Naples in an attempt to halt the new republic's advances through Europe. War against France was declared but the coalition collapsed four years later after Austria was forced to hand over territory to Napoleon's forces. Lacking support on the Continent, Britain had no choice but to temporarily cease hostilities with the French but remained determined to limit Napoleon's advances through Europe and the Near East (which threatened several lucrative trading markets). A new coalition was quickly formed with what remained of Austria plus Sardinia, the Papal States of Italy, Russia, Portugal and the Ottoman Empire. Once again, war was declared but this time the coalition met with more success, mainly due to the fact that France's great general was otherwise occupied trying to win territory in Egypt. However, on 23 August 1799, his forces arrived back in France and Napoleon immediately set about destroying the hostile coalition once again.

Britain had so far failed in her attempts to halt the advance of the French Republic, but King George III and his generals refused to give up hope and kept good relations with countries not yet invaded by Napoleon in the hope that another coalition might be formed. Vexed by the constant intrusion of the small but extremely wealthy island across La Manche, Napoleon began to hatch plans to invade Britain but soon found that British sea power was vastly superior to his navy. Following the Battle of Trafalgar in October 1805, he decided to shelve his invasion plans and instead worked on a scheme that would have a disastrous effect on the Port of London.

As he continued his march across mainland Europe, Napoleon introduced a 'Continental System' of commerce which effectively forbade any conquered territories from trading with Britain. The merchants at the docks were horrified to learn about the implementation of the general's new system and pleaded with the government to respond with force. However, the politicians realised that the country's 200,000-strong army was no match for Napoleon's troops, which numbered up to 1.5 million men. Instead, they advised the merchants to tighten their belts and concentrate on developing other, non-European, markets. The merchants reluctantly agreed and soon their worries were somewhat relieved as they gradually realised that many of Napoleon's territories in Europe were not in favour of the Continental System either. Conspiratorial meetings were held to discuss ways of smuggling merchandise in and out of the Continent and soon illicit trade routes opened across Europe with the full knowledge (if not the public endorsement) of Napoleon's hand-picked governors of Spain and Germany.

The Continental System of trade was finally scrapped in 1814, when even Napoleon came to the conclusion that it was damaging commerce in his territories far more than British trade. By this time, his vision of a French Empire stretching across Europe was also proving impossible to control. Britain emerged from the hostilities victorious. Recent sea battles such as Trafalgar had proved that the country's navy was the best in the world and the international network of markets that had expanded and evolved during the enforcement of the Continental System made Britain economically invincible. The country's position at the centre of the Industrial Revolution reinforced this financial supremacy. Britain had become the world's first superpower.

Britain's commercial supremacy in international markets, combined with the successful development of the West India and London Docks, prompted the East India Company to revisit the possibility of re-creating its own dock in the Port of London. Although its previous attempt in the mid-1600s had almost ended in financial ruin, the company had undergone a transformation during the 1700s and no longer simply traded with Asia. Thanks to the mid-18th century military campaigns led by Robert Clive, the company now governed huge swathes of India and held lucrative trading associations with regions as far east as China. This unique and unparalleled position, combined with increased consumer demand for the merchandise it imported, meant that the creation of its own London docks was a much safer proposition than ever before.

For years, the East India Company's ships (which still tended to be larger than the average vessel in the Port of London) had found it necessary to unload some of their massive shipments of merchandise at Gravesend in Kent in order to safely travel down the shallower waters of the Thames to Brunswick Dock, a deep-water basin that had been built at its erstwhile yard at Blackwall in 1790. This system seemed to work well, so when the Select Committee invited plans to redevelop the port, the East India Company showed little interest. However, when the West India Docks proved to be an immediate success, the East India merchants trading in London petitioned their governing company to draw up plans for its own complex. Not wishing to lose out during a potential land grab as others sought to emulate the West India Docks' success, the East India Dock Company was duly formed to spearhead the development and government approval for the scheme was quickly granted.

Owing to the success of the West India Docks, the East India Dock Company had little problem attracting investors for its project. Within three months of securing government approval, nearly £200,000 had been raised from the sale of shares. With the initial funding in place, the company set about employing engineers and architects to oversee a massive redevelopment of the docks at Blackwall. The Brunswick Dock was purchased from its owners, John and William Wells, for £35,660, along with some 65 acres of Bromley marsh, on which an import dock would be constructed. In total, all land acquired cost more than £63,000 – over a quarter of the total available capital.

Once the land had been purchased, the construction of the docks could begin. Plans were drawn up by engineers John Rennie and Ralph Walker (who had worked on the West India Docks) in March 1803 and the total cost for the development was calculated at £198,740. Of course, this meant that more money would have to be raised than initially thought, but confidence in the project was high. The plans were approved and excavation began.

At first, Rennie and Walker envisaged the complex having just two basins – the existing Brunswick Dock for exports and a larger dock on the marshland to handle imports. However, after work got under way, it soon became clear that a third basin should be excavated to hold ships waiting to enter the docks at busy times without getting in the way of vessels already at the quayside. This unforeseen alteration resulted in the cost of the finished docks going through the roof. The final bill came to a massive £322,608 but, despite this, sufficient funds were raised, the East India Docks were completed almost to schedule and a grand opening ceremony was organised for 4 August 1806.

Although smaller than the West India Docks, the East India Company's new facilities were impressive. The 30-acre site was accessed through a huge entrance lock that, according to *The Times*, was 'capable of admitting the largest Indiamen [merchant ships], and his majesty's ships of war, of 74 guns.' Once inside the complex, the vessels either made their way to the nine-acre export dock to be loaded, or discharged their cargo at the new import dock, which was nearly double the size. In total, the two docks could handle up to 250 ships at any time. Like the West India and London Docks, the East India Company's site had spacious quays that stretched 240ft away from the waterside but unlike its rival docks, very little warehousing was built. The company's imports often comprised high-quality textiles, rare spices and other valuable commodities and so it was agreed that it should retain its tried and tested high-security warehouses at Cutler Street (in the City).

The grand opening of the East India Docks was a great success, provoking interest from the press and London worthies alike, all keen to see the ceremony put on by the docks' powerful owners, who did not disappoint. At 2pm on the day of the opening, the regimental guns of the company's volunteers fired the signal for a procession of ships festooned with a colourful array of flags and streamers to enter the docks to the strains of 'Rule Britannia' played by the company band on the deck of the *Admiral Gardner*. The crowd seated around the quay numbered up to 20,000 and *The Times* noted, 'as such exhibitions are always attractive of female curiosity, it is scarcely necessary to add, that the whole formed a lively coupe d'aile, richly studded with beauty and elegance.'

The development of the London and East and West India Docks completely transformed the previously semi-rural areas of Blackwall, Poplar and Limehouse. Before their arrival, the region had largely comprised small clusters of buildings either adjacent to the river or around the perimeter of the old Blackwall dockyard. Beyond these communities lay a patchwork of market gardens and orchards which led into open fields. The arrival of these leviathan docks changed the landscape for ever. New residential streets were hastily built to accommodate the massive influx of warehousemen, labourers, craftsmen and refugees from Wapping. By the 1830s, land north of the East India Docks, which had previously been covered with market gardens and grazing pasture for livestock, had been built over to create Poplar New Town. The maritime village of Blackwall opened up to accept a new community of dock workers who settled in homes close the entrance of their place of employment, which was also conveniently the site of the company tavern. By 1827, the Grand Commercial Road had been joined by the East India Dock Road, which forked away to the south shortly after passing St Ann's church in Limehouse. On either side of this road, new homes were built for dock workers, management and mariners' families. Gradually, the rope walks that once proliferated in Limehouse gave way to rows of tenements and the rural atmosphere was lost under builders' rubble and house bricks.

The rapid expansion of east London and indeed many other regions in Britain prompted a massive rise in demand for imported building materials such as timber and basic foodstuffs such as grain. In 1806, a wealthy London timber merchant named William Richie decided to capitalise on this unprecedented growth and purchased the old Greenland Dock in Rotherhithe, which had gradually fallen into disuse as the whaling trade declined. Once the site had been acquired, Richie formed the Commercial Docks Company and set about raising finance to transform the Greenland Dock into a centre for handling timber and corn imports. His venture quickly attracted investors and the monies raised were used in part to purchase additional land. In 1807, massive redevelopment of the old dock began. A row of large granaries was built alongside two new docks and ponds were dug close by in which the timber cargoes could be floated to stop the wood from drying out and splitting. The completed development covered an area of 49 acres and was capable of accommodating 350 ships. It was briefly named the Baltic Docks in deference to the region from whence much of the timber came, but was quickly renamed the Commercial Docks in a bid to attract trade from other countries.

At the same time as William Richie was expanding the Greenland Dock, a corporation known as the Surrey Docks Company purchased land to the west of the Rotherhithe peninsula and built two long docks designed to handle the same commodities as their neighbours. The finished docks were slightly smaller than the Commercial Docks but could still handle up to 300 ships at a time, thus taking even more pressure off the crowded Thames.

Such was the demand for timber and grain that both dock complexes were an immediate success. In 1811, Richie purchased more land immediately south of the old Greenland Dock and built a long, thin basin which he named the East Country Dock. This new addition could handle up to 28 ships and in addition to grain and timber shipments also took deliveries of hemp, flax and tallow to supply the local shipyards. Another dock, known as the Norway Dock, was simultaneously constructed to the north of the original basin to receive vessels from Scandinavia.

Over the following 65 years, both the Surrey and the Commercial Docks companies steadily expanded their operations until their premises covered around 85% of the Rotherhithe peninsula. In 1851, the East Country Dock was enlarged, improved and renamed the South Dock. Four years later, the Albion Dock was added, which stood on land to the west of the Surrey Docks. By this time, the two dock complexes had virtually combined geographically. In order to improve access and more effectively manage their bustling premises, the dock companies wisely decided to merge and in 1865 the Surrey Commercial Docks Company was formed.

The heavy nature of the merchandise handled at the Surrey Commercial Docks meant that the new railways being built on the Surrey side of the Thames provided a transportation service far more efficient than carts. In the same year as the two dock companies amalgamated, the East London Railway Company purchased the Thames Tunnel which ran under the river between Wapping and Rotherhithe. The tunnel had been constructed between 1825 and 1843 by the great engineers Marc and Isambard Kingdom Brunel and had originally been intended as a carriageway, although in the event it was only ever used by pedestrians.

When it first opened, this engineering masterpiece caused quite a stir and was featured in several newspapers and periodicals of the day. *Mogg's New Picture of London and Visitors' Guide to its Sights* described it thus: 'The tunnel consists of two brick archways, thus forming two paved roads, with paths for foot-passengers. In the centre, between these two roads, runs a line of archways, by which persons may pass from one side to the other, and in each of these arches is a gas light. The approach to the entrance of the tunnel is by a spacious flight of steps, of very gradual descent; and the general effect of these sub-aqueous roads, when viewed from the end, the whole being brilliantly lighted with gas, is imposing in the extreme. This vast work, now extended entirely across the river, excited the admiration of all visitors, and, regarded as an exhibition, is perhaps the most interesting of which the metropolis can boast.'

However, despite being widely admired, the tunnel was not well used and by the 1860s it had fallen into disrepair. The East London Railway Company spent four years renovating and laying tracks in the tunnel and in December 1869 the line opened, running from New Cross to Wapping, with a station at Deptford Road (now Surrey Quays) directly serving the Surrey Commercial Docks.

Close to the Rotherhithe entrance to the Thames Tunnel was a site known by the local dock workers as 'Cuckold's Point'. Some of the older workers at the Surrey Commercial Docks could remember when this oddly named spot was marked by a pair of horns mounted on a long pole and liked to relate the story of this strange sight to their younger colleagues. According to the dockers, back in the early 13th century, King John tired of hunting on Blackheath one day and searched for a place at which he could find refreshment and rest awhile. He soon came across the house of a miller and his wife and decided to knock at the door. The miller was out, but his wife, who was very beautiful, let him in and soon the King was receiving refreshment of a very different kind. At this point, the miller arrived home, catching his wife and the monarch in a compromising position. Furious, he drew his dagger and the King was forced to reveal his identity in order to avoid a premature death. As the miller calmed his wrath, the King offered to make amends for his indiscretion. He bestowed on the miller the right to hold an annual fair in Charlton (the proceeds of which he could keep) and also agreed to give him all the land that could be seen from his house to the Thames. The miller looked to the horizon and his eyes settled on the point at Rotherhithe. King John kept his word and granted him the land, but also issued the caveat that on the day of the fair each year (18 October) the miller must walk to the northernmost point of his land wearing a pair of horns on his head to remind him of how he had acquired his riches. The miller honoured the King's wishes and thus the fair became known as Horn Fair and the point to which the miller walked was christened, somewhat unkindly, by the locals 'Cuckold's Point.'

Although the horns at 'Cuckold's Point' disappeared some time in the early 19th century, the neighbouring docks went from strength to strength. In 1876, the complex was enlarged once again when the Canada Dock was opened directly south of the Albion, the writer Walter Thornbury, who visited the docks during this period, describing them as 'the most prosperous establishments of the metropolitan harbour.' However, the Surrey Commercial Docks' success was destined not to last. Although a further dock, the Quebec Dock, was opened in 1926, the complex eventually suffered the same fate as the rest of the Port of London. The docks closed in 1969 and today all evidence of these once bustling centres of trade lies buried beneath an ecological park, a housing estate and Surrey Quays shopping centre, while what remains of the Canada, Greenland and South Docks lies silent.

The final docks to be built in the first half of the 19th century were the St Katharine Docks, next to the Tower of London. Prior to their construction, the area was dominated by St Katharine's church and hospital, which was surrounded by some ancient rookeries that housed the poor of the parish. A dock had existed in the area for some time, but it was tiny and could be accessed only by small craft serving the coal and brewing industries that were a feature of the neighbourhood.

In 1825, the St Katharine Docks Act was passed by Parliament. The cost of building the new docks was estimated at £1.5 million – an extraordinary amount of money at the time. However, funds were quickly raised by selling shares in the company and through borrowing against projected profits once the site was up and running. Work began in 1827. In order to build the development, 1,250 houses had to be pulled down and up to 11,000 residents of forbiddingly named streets and alleys such as Hangman's Gains and Cat's Hole were forced to seek accommodation elsewhere. Most of these streets were classed as slums, so the general public did not mourn their loss that greatly. What they did take issue with was the removal of many ancient wharves and workshops along the banks of the Thames and, in particular, the destruction of the church and hospital, which had survived the dissolution of the monasteries and the Great Fire of 1666 only to be erased in the name of progress. Following a public outcry, the dock company was forced to pay not only £125,000 for the land on which the church stood but also a further £36,000 for it to be relocated near Regent's Park. There also came the sticky problem of what to do with the bodies in the churchyard. The company promised to disturb the graves as little as possible, but once works began it became clear that the churchyard would soon become submerged beneath the waters of the Eastern Dock. Realising this, some families reluctantly paid to have their loved ones removed to a drier resting place.

Despite these problems, the company forged ahead with the excavation of the site, taking the soil removed up the Thames to swampy land behind Millbank Gaol, where it formed the foundations for several smart residential streets. Its chief engineer was Thomas Telford, who had become well known for several of the Industrial Revolution's iconic developments such as the Ellesmere Canal (including the majestic Pontcysyllte Aqueduct over the River Dee) and the Menai Suspension Bridge. Over 2,500 workers were employed at the site and they worked at record speed. Walter Thornbury visited the docks shortly after their completion in 1828 and called the construction 'a Herculean bit of work, performed with a speed and vigour unusual even to English enterprise'.

The finished docks covered just under 25 acres of land, 11½ acres of which were taken up by two wet docks – the Eastern and the Western – which were connected via a central basin and were capable of holding up to 120 ships. The docks were surrounded by six warehouses designed by the architect Philip Hardwick. These six-storey buildings were the first to be built directly facing the street, thus removing the need to build a security wall around the perimeter of the complex. Their high ceilings were supported by elegant columns embellished with Doric capitals and made from the Industrial Revolution's favourite material – iron. Using cranes located on the quayside, ships' cargoes could be loaded directly into these warehouses, which substantially cut down the time a ship spent in the dock. At other docks, it took up to eight days in summer and 14 days in winter to unload a 350-ton ship. At St Katharine's the job could be done in two days. The warehouses were not the only innovation at the St Katharine Docks. Access from the Thames was provided via a canal 190ft long and deep enough for ships weighing up to 700 tons to enter at any time of tide. The water in the lock was controlled by steam engines designed by the great engineer James Watt.

The St Katharine Docks specialised in handling two valuable commodities – wool and tea. Along with the neighbouring London Docks, the site handled just under half the country's wool exports and up to 600,000 bales of wool could be stored in the warehouses. The docks also handled up to 700,000 chests of tea every year and had sorting and packaging facilities in one of the warehouses where the tea was boxed up before being distributed to wholesalers. In addition to these staples, the St Katharine Docks also became known for handling luxury items. Cargoes included ostrich feathers, ivory, marble, spices, carpets and perfume, for which there was an on-site workshop where the scent was extracted from the raw materials. However, the main luxury items brought into the docks were shells. An entire floor of one of the warehouses was dedicated to the storage of these items, sorted into lots in preparation for sales which took place six times a year. The warehousemen took care to display the shells to their best advantage. Mother-of-pearl was illuminated using overhead lighting to show off its peacock's tail colours while tortoiseshell was skilfully lit from the side to show the translucent pattern to its best effect. The shells were used by their purchasers for a variety of ornamental purposes, including buttons for clothing, mirror backs and inlays for furniture. During the docks' early years, they provided an important source of revenue for the heavily indebted company.

The development of the St Katharine, London, Surrey, Commercial and East and West India Docks in the first half of the 1800s certainly helped to ease the congestion on the River Thames as hundreds of ships retreated behind their high walls to have their vast cargoes discharged into the surrounding warehouses. However, developments in engineering meant that by the middle of the century, the Port of London was faced with another challenge – the arrival of steam-powered ships.

14

THE AGE OF STEAM

Back in 1698, Thomas Savery, a military engineer, patented 'A new invention for raiesing of water and occasioning motion to all sorts of mill work by the impellent force of fire, which will be of great use and advantage for drayning mines, serveing townes with water, and for the working of all sorts of mills where they have not the benefitt of water nor constants windes.' His innovative idea was noted by a French inventor named Denis Papin, who realised that steam might also be used to propel vessels through water. Papin developed a prototype vessel driven by large steam-powered paddle wheels similar to those used in mills and took his invention to London in the hope of obtaining funding to develop the prototype into a fully functioning craft. However, on his arrival in the capital, Papin soon realised that potential investors were unable to visualise the benefits his design could bring to shipping. He returned to France empty-handed and for the next 50 years the concept of a steam-propelled vessel was all but forgotten.

In the meantime, the potential of industrial steam power continued to be explored and during the first half of the 18th century several engineers grappled with how to harness the power of steam effectively. The major breakthrough came in 1765 when the Scottish engineer James Watt (who would later be responsible for the St Katharine Docks' steam-powered lock) created the first successful steam engine. Watt's invention was immediately modified by several marine engineers who tried to make the concept work on a vessel. Although the earliest models had a habit of sinking, by the 1780s, the design had been refined to the point where successful voyages on inland waterways were possible and in 1815 Pierre Andriel made the world's first steam-powered sea crossing when he took his ship, the *Elise*, across the Channel.

Following Andriel's successful voyage, the race was on to create a steam-powered ship capable of ocean-going voyages. In 1819, the North American vessel *SS Savannah* arrived in Liverpool having crossed the Atlantic using a combination of sail and steam and in 1838, the first purpose-built ocean-going steamship – the *Great Western* – was designed by Isambard Kingdom Brunel. Brunel's ship was built in Bristol to controversially large dimensions, measuring over 230ft long. Knowing that her predecessors were prone to sinking, many observers of her construction worried that she was too enormous to be seaworthy. However, Brunel remained convinced that her large size would ultimately make the *Great Western* more fuel efficient.

To the casual observer at the Bristol docks, the *Great Western* looked much the same as any other large ship apart from her tall steam funnel. She had a traditional oak hull and sported four masts for sails, which would help keep her on an even keel in rough seas in addition to aiding propulsion. However, after the main body of the ship had been finished, she was sailed around the coast to London, where she was fitted with the machinery that made her unique – two huge paddle wheels driven by steam engines concealed below deck, which were fitted by the engineering firm of Maudsley & Field. Work was quickly completed according to plan and on Saturday 31 March 1838, the *Great Western* began her journey back to Bristol, from whence she was due to set sail for New York the following Saturday.

The new steamship did not have a promising start. Shortly after stopping at Gravesend to allow passengers to alight, a fire was discovered in the boiler room and the attempts to put it out quickly descended into chaos. In order to access the engines, which were now engulfed in smoke, the captain ordered his crew to saw through the deck and douse the flames below with water from the fire pump. The resulting smoke and steam caused visibility to become so bad that when Brunel was called to take a closer look at the source of the fire, he lost his footing and fell nearly 40ft through the hole in the deck. Now with two emergencies on their hands, the harassed captain ordered some of his crew to row to nearby Southend and Leigh-on-Sea in search of medical assistance. No doctors could be found in either town and eventually the crew decided to go to Holyhaven, where they found a surgeon. It transpired that Brunel was badly injured by the fall, breaking his shoulder and one of his legs. In addition to this, three of the crew were hospitalised after suffering severe burns while fighting the fire.

Once the flames were extinguished and the casualties taken off the ship, engineers from Maudsley & Field desperately searched for the cause of the blaze. It turned out that the fire was caused by a dangerous but easily rectifiable design flaw. Christopher Claxton of Lloyd's (where the ship had been insured) was brought to inspect the vessel and reported that, 'The felt, which had been put on the boilers having injudiciously been placed too near the chimney, took fire.' Luckily, the engines themselves, although blackened by soot, were undamaged. Following the removal of any remaining felt and the completion of any necessary repairs to the boiler room and the deck, the *Great Western* completed her journey to Bristol and then voyaged, as planned, to New York.

On 23 May 1838, *The Times* reported that the *Great Western* had arrived back in Bristol, having departed from the North American port 'with 68 cabin passengers at 35 guineas each (the greatest number of cabin passengers which ever came across the Atlantic in one ship), upwards of 20,000 Post Office letters, and a cargo consisting of cotton ... indigo, silks, and miscellaneous articles. During her voyage home she encountered head-winds nine days out of the 14, and on one occasion a severe gale, yet she accomplished 7½ knots during its greatest severity, with the wind directly in her teeth and completed her voyage ... in 14 days and 17½ hours ... with a consumption of less than a ton of coal per hour.'

The main benefit that steamships had over wind-propelled vessels was speed. The *Great Western* had travelled from New York to Bristol in less than 15 days. A sailing ship could take more than a month to complete the same journey. This extraordinary reduction in travelling time was noted with interest by a ship owner from Halifax, Nova Scotia, named Samuel Cunard, who for some time had considered the possibility of setting up a transatlantic steam packet company. The *Great Western* had proved that a fast, efficient service was now eminently achievable and Cunard wasted no time in persuading business contacts to invest in his proposal. In May 1840, the British and North American Royal Mail Steam Packet Company was formed and, soon after, the steamship *Britannia* left Liverpool on the company's first voyage to Cunard's home town of Halifax. The steam packet service proved to be a huge success. The initial fleet of four ships was quickly enlarged to six and by 1848 demand was such that the British government agreed to subsidise the company so that the number of voyages made could be doubled. The steam packets rapidly developed a reputation for speed and safety and in 1878, eight years after the death of its founder, the company was reorganised and renamed the Cunard Steamship Company. The Cunard Line still operates today, although the steam packets have long since been replaced by luxury ocean liners.

While Samuel Cunard was busy establishing his shipping line, the now recovered Isambard Kingdom Brunel was busy refining the engineering technology used on the *Great Western* to create a faster and more cost effective steamship. The result was the *SS Great Britain*, a revolutionary vessel that transformed the shipping industry when it was launched in 1843. The ship was huge, measuring 322ft long, with a cargo capacity of 1,200 tons. However, its real advantage was that it uniquely combined an almost impenetrable and sturdy iron hull with a screw propeller instead of paddle wheels, which not only enabled the ship to travel at high speeds but was also more compact, efficient and less easily damaged than its predecessor. Unfortunately, the *Great Britain* had an even more troubled early career than the *Great Western*. Construction of the ship took far longer than had initially been projected and when the finished vessel became stranded off the coast of Ireland in November 1846, the expensive salvage operation forced her owners into bankruptcy. Following her rescue, the *Great Britain* spent several years ferrying convicts and settlers to Australia before serving as an army troop ship. In the 1850s, she was remodelled as a sailing ship and spent the rest of her working life transporting coal before being abandoned at the Falkland Islands following a devastating fire. In 1970, the remains of this once great ship were salvaged and brought back to Bristol where she was painstakingly restored and opened to the public. Brunel's most illustrious ship is now one of the city's most popular visitor attractions.

Although the SS *Great Britain*'s early years were financially disastrous, the bad fortune had little to do with her design. The speed at which she and Cunard's steam packets crossed the Atlantic forced the ship owners at the Port of London to keep up with the competition by purchasing their own steamships. Soon the British shipyards were inundated with orders. In

London, the construction of many new steam vessels was carried out by the Thames Ironworks and Shipbuilding Company from its yard at Leamouth, close to the East India Docks. The company had been founded in 1837 by engineer Charles Mare and shipwright Thomas J. Ditchburn, who were determined to profit from the new craze for steam. At first, the Thames Ironworks specialised in the building of small paddle-steamers of no more than 100 tons, but by the 1840s they had begun to construct significantly larger vessels including a 12-gun brig for the Royal Navy. As the size of its commissions increased, the company realised that more space was required. Following the retirement of his business partner in 1847, Charles Mare purchased an additional site close to the Leamouth yard, on the opposite side of Bow Creek, which could handle the construction of much larger ships. This move initially paid dividends. Several commissions were received for large vessels and in 1853 the SS Himalaya left Mare's shipyard with the distinction of being (albeit briefly) the world's largest passenger ship. However, all was not well at the Thames Ironworks. The company had been in financial crisis since the late 1840s and in 1855 Charles Mare finally admitted defeat and declared the company bankrupt. For a time it looked like the shipyards would be forced to close, putting over 3,000 employees out of work, but in 1857, Mare's father-in-law Peter Rolt took charge of the firm's assets and transferred them to a new, limited company named the Thames Ironworks & Shipbuilding & Engineering Company. There followed a long period of prosperity during which the shipyard gained an international reputation for quality work and orders from as far afield as Prussia and Greece were received at the company offices. While many London shipyards were forced to close by strong competition from their competitors in the north, the Thames Ironworks continued building steamships until 1912. Sadly, the shipyards are now long gone, but the company left an enduring, if unexpected, legacy through its football team.

In 1895, at the suggestion of company foreman, David Taylor, the Thames Ironworks' managing director Arnold Hills agreed to finance a football club for his staff. Thames Ironworks FC was duly set up and Taylor immediately began to search for a ground on which to train and play matches. He soon came across a good ground in Hermit Road, Canning Town, which had recently been made available due to the demise of a professional team called Old Castle Swifts. The ground was only a short distance away from the ironworks and so Taylor and his colleagues took it over and began trials for their team. Players from the defunct Swifts club heard about the new Ironworks team and four (goalkeeper George Furnell, full- and half-back Robert Stevenson, and forwards James Lindsay and George Sage) were eventually selected, the remainder of the team being made up of company employees and enthusiastic local players. The first match took place on 7 September 1895 against the Royal Ordnance FC, the final score being a disappointing 0-0.

Despite their inauspicious start, the Ironworks FC soon began winning matches and it became apparent that one of the Ironworks' own employees was rapidly becoming their star player. Charles Ernest Dove, known to his colleagues as Charlie, had been born in Poplar in 1877, the son of a Cornish shipwright named George Thomas Dove and his wife Clara Ann. Like thousands of other families that earned their living from the London docks and its associated industries, the Doves lived close to the Thames, so the journey to work could be undertaken on foot, thus saving money. By the time he was 16, Charlie Dove cut an imposing figure, standing nearly 6ft tall and weighing a muscular 12 stone, which was unusual for a teenager from a dock worker's family. By this time, he was employed as an apprentice riveter at the Thames Ironworks, but spent many evenings and Sundays playing with local football teams. When David Taylor began recruiting for the company team, Dove's innate talent for the game resulted in him being selected and over the following five seasons he proved to be a versatile and resourceful team member, eventually playing in every position, including that of goalkeeper. On 23 April 1898, the *East Ham Echo* wrote, 'Charlie Dove, if not absolutely the finest right half-back in Essex ... is undoubtedly one of the most brilliant men in the country in that position.'

Charlie was not the only talented player in the Ironworks' team. By 1900, the club's success prompted a committee decision to take it to the next level. The amateur club was duly closed and reopened as West Ham United. Just as the club was re-forming, its most talented player was making changes of his own. In the summer of 1900, Charlie Dove married a young woman called Eliza Crick whose family hailed from Canning Town, close to the football ground. Soon after, Charlie left the Thames Ironworks FC and, probably lured by money, joined their arch-rivals

Millwall. Sadly, his football career was cut short in 1902 when an injury prevented him from playing professionally again. However, his old team continued to go from strength to strength. West Ham United eventually went on to win the FA Cup three times and currently play in England's Premier Division. Although the club is much changed from its early days, its origins are still remembered in both its nicknames ('the Hammers' and 'the Irons') and its crest, which includes a crossed pair of rivet hammers – tools that Charlie Dove and his colleagues at the Thames Ironworks would have been very familiar with.

Meanwhile, at the Port of London the introduction of steam-powered shipping was presenting problems for the docks. Many of these new vessels were too large to reach the shallower waters beside the legal quays and with the existing deep-water docks working at full capacity during the busy summer and autumn periods, it soon became clear that the port needed custom-built basins to accommodate these huge vessels. In response, a consortium of interested parties formed the Victoria (London) Dock Company. It set about drawing up plans to create a vast new dock on Plaistow Marsh specifically engineered to receive steamships and connect with London's railway network which was stretching across the capital with extraordinary speed. Recognising the need for this type of dock, the government swiftly approved the proposal and building work commenced in 1853.

At the time of its construction the Victoria Dock was the largest man-made body of water in London. It was accessed from the Thames via enormous deep-water locks secured by hydraulically powered wrought-iron gates which were located on an area of the Thames known as Bugsby's Reach, a short distance away from the Thames Ironworks at Leamouth. These locks ran underneath a section of the East Counties & Thames Junction Railway which had been built in 1847 to connect North Woolwich with central London. In order to allow tall ships to pass through the locks, a swing bridge was incorporated into the railway line. A short distance north, a new station – known as Custom House – was built to directly serve the new dock.

Once they had passed through the locks, the ships entered a deep tidal basin, which in turn led into the main dock. This vast expanse of water was indented on its north side with four long piers interspersed with smaller jetties that extended out into the basin, allowing vessels of all sizes to moor alongside them. Railway tracks were laid along the length of these landing places so that goods could be unloaded directly onto trucks which were then conveyed either to the nearby station or long storage sheds that lay just beyond the quay. The company offices were built facing the centre of the north quay and were flanked by large tobacco warehouses, wine vaults and coal sidings; smaller warehouses lay on the south quay, storing commodities such as jute, salt and guano, which was extensively used in agriculture as manure.

The Victoria Dock Company was eager to attract shipments of valuable cargoes such as those handled at the St Katharine Docks but realised that the merchants dealing in these goods would be reluctant to store them on its relatively remote site. Consequently, it acquired the Hanseatic League's old Steelyard site in Upper Thames Street with the intention of building high-security warehousing. However, this project proved unprofitable and the site was subsequently sold to the South Eastern Railway Company in preparation for the construction of Cannon Street Station, which opened in 1866. However, by this time the Victoria Dock was handling up to 850,000 tons of shipping each year – double that of the London Docks – and was the busiest dock in London.

The instant success of the Victoria Dock prompted speculative developers to search for other locations suitable for the construction of similar facilities. The massive wave of dock building in the first half of the 19th century had finally solved the problem of large ships being forced to wait in the Thames for space to discharge their cargoes. Indeed, during the quieter winter season, the new docks often found themselves competing for trade. Nonetheless, there was still a need for shipbuilding and repair resources and new sites were sought to fulfil this requirement. The land south of the West India Docks had long since been considered a prospective location for a new dock as although the riverside perimeter of this tongue-shaped peninsula already incorporated the small maritime settlement of Millwall, the land between was largely undeveloped.

The land on which Millwall sat was known as the Isle of Dogs. The story behind this odd name had been long obscured by the 19th century, but the most popular and plausible theory was that the area was once used as kennels for hunting dogs when the monarch resided in Greenwich.

By the mid-18th century, the area had an altogether more gruesome reputation as a companion site to Execution Dock in Wapping. Roque's 1746 map of the locality shows gibbets standing along the riverbank and it was rumoured that the pensioners at Greenwich Hospital operated a profitable sideline, hiring out spyglasses to members of the public wishing to watch the hangings from the south bank of the Thames.

The windswept landscape of the Isle of Dogs also attracted millers, who from the late 1670s built several windmills close to a riverside wall on the west bank of the peninsula, where grain and oil seeds were ground. The river wall was originally known as Marsh Wall, but following the arrival of the windmills the name was changed to Mill Wall. By the early 19th century, the name applied to the entire district and the mills had been joined by a series of independent wharves owned by shipwrights and associated maritime traders.

In the centre of the Isle of Dogs the land was almost entirely rural save for a few farm buildings and an old medieval chapel dedicated to St Mary, surrounded by footpaths and fields. For centuries, cattle and sheep had been put out to graze in the meadows as it was thought that the pastureland was particularly nutritious and some even believed it had curative properties. However, this rural idyll was soon to be shattered.

In 1859, Nathaniel Fenner, an oil merchant who owned a wharf at Millwall, came up with the idea of constructing a series of non-tidal wharves behind his premises that connected with the Thames on both sides of the peninsula and led up to the West India Docks. Convinced that his idea would appeal to several local shipwrights keen to expand their operations, he consulted an engineer named Robert Fairlie and asked him to draw up a set of plans. Fairlie came up with a scheme that incorporated a wide canal-type waterway shaped like an inverted 'T', which was accessed by two locks on either side of the Isle and had a central branch that led up to the West India Docks. This waterway was bordered by space for quays and warehousing, but Fenner and Fairlie decided not to build any of the structures themselves. Instead they opted to let the land in plots to private businesses which could then develop them as they saw fit.

The two men's plan seemed to be workable but they had neither the finance to fund construction themselves nor the connections to go about obtaining the necessary approvals to commence work. Consequently, they contacted a well-known engineer named William Wilson who, after looking at their proposal, agreed to oversee the project. After making some minor alterations to Fenner and Fairlie's scheme, Wilson submitted the plans to Parliament under the title 'The Millwall Canal, Wharfs and Graving (Dry) Docks Bill' and promptly severed all contact with its originators, reasoning that they were now surplus to requirements. Now believing that he could move on with the project unencumbered by two naïve and inexperienced partners, Wilson began discussing the plans with wealthy engineers and contractors who had sufficient clout both financially and socially to push the Bill through Parliament and finance the initial stages of the scheme. His discussions attracted the interest of two developers – John Kelk and John Aird – who had previously worked together on the construction of the Metropolitan Railway and the development of Victoria Station. The two men agreed to offer financial assistance and with their monies in place, an influential engineer, Sir John Fowler, was retained to add weight to their proposal.

While Wilson recruited his eminent team of engineers and contractors, word got back to Nathaniel Fenner and Robert Fairlie that they were being sidelined in favour of wealthier and more prominent individuals. Understandably, the two men were infuriated by Wilson's duplicity. They energetically opposed the Bill and succeeded in causing sufficient problems for Wilson to reluctantly pay them off to the tune of £5,000 and offer Fenner a seat on the board of the company. It transpired that Fenner and Fairlie were the only opponents of the Bill and once a tentative cost of works had been agreed at just over £500,000, an Act was passed that incorporated the Millwall Canal, Wharfs and Graving Docks Company, and granted permission for the construction of 'Accommodation for Shipbuilding and other Businesses requiring Water Frontage.'

Although the company had now been given the green light to proceed, the raising of the necessary finance proved more difficult than initially expected. In December 1864, John Kelk approached the directors of the East and West India Docks, reasonably confident that they would be interested in investing in the scheme, but his proposal was rejected. By this stage, the company had agreed to purchase a large amount of land on the Isle of Dogs and the board were now faced with the monumental task of raising over half a million pounds purely through public subscription. Optimistically worded advertisements were placed in the press, but it soon became clear that the target was never going to be reached. Eventually the company was forced to employ the services of one Albert Grant, a financier of dubious reputation, who agreed to fund the scheme in return for a majority share in the company and an astronomical 'arrangement fee' of £100,000. The board were in no position to refuse his offer and new papers were drawn up, renaming the company the Millwall Freehold Land and Docks Company.

The payment of Albert Grant's fee combined with the costs incurred while the project was delayed meant that the projected construction sum of £500,000 was now woefully inadequate. Nevertheless, Grant used his creative skills to present his network of investors with an opportunity that seemed too good to pass by. However, as time went on, doubts about the financial viability of the project began to spread and several shareholders bailed out, forcing the company to apply for bank loans. To make matters worse, the banking firm of Overend Gurney and Co went bust in 1866, sparking a period of turmoil in the City as investors lost confidence in the markets and cut back on investments. The resulting recession inevitably affected all sectors of manufacturing, including shipbuilding. Realising that it would take years for confidence in the market to be fully restored, the Millwall Docks Company was forced to rethink its scheme and the plans for the wharf-lined canal with shipbuilding facilities mutated into the only type of development the company had a hope of succeeding with in the short term: deep-water docks that could accommodate both sailing vessels and steamships. The downside of this change of plan meant that the company would now be in direct competition with the Victoria Dock. Undeterred, the board pressed on with their revised scheme and, in a small coup, managed to lure the superintendent and clerk of works from the Victoria Dock to come and work for them.

Construction recommenced using the revised plans in late 1866. The original plan of a 'T'-shaped canal was shelved and only two channels were excavated. The new deep-water basins were drained using steam-powered pumping engines, which disgorged the marshy water into the Thames, and the soil removed was used to build up land on which the quays would stand. Determined not to waste any more time, the board employed up to 3,000 workers at the site and, consequently, work progressed quickly.

By the beginning of 1868, the development contained two long docks laid out in a reversed 'L'-shape, accessed from the Thames via a hydraulically operated double lock which at the time of its construction was the largest in London. In addition to the two wet docks, a huge dry dock was constructed on land once occupied by the ancient church of St Mary. The site was named the Millwall Docks and on 14 March 1868, they finally opened to shipping in a partially completed state.

The saga of the Millwall Docks proved to be a cautionary tale for speculative developers at the Port of London as it showed that not all schemes came with a guarantee of success. Had it not been for the tenacity of the board, the project might well have ended in financial ruin. In the event, the economic crisis that prevailed during the docks' construction eventually passed. Trade improved and thanks to the people that worked within it, the Millwall Docks developed a solid reputation, handling a range of cargoes, particularly wool, grain and timber. However, London's dock building boom was most definitely over for the time being.

While the board of the Millwall Docks Company were desperately trying to keep their troubled scheme alive, the ancient royal dockyards across the water at Woolwich and Deptford were struggling to build the huge ships now required by the Royal Navy. For centuries, the shipyards had been at the forefront of new shipbuilding techniques – in 1698, even the Russian Tsar, Peter the Great, had visited the Deptford yard to see at first-hand how the British Navy's enviable fleet was constructed. However, as the size of ships steadily increased, the relatively shallow waters surrounding the yards became very difficult for vessels to navigate. Realising that this was a problem destined only to get worse, the Admiralty began to open more accessible dockyards at Portsmouth, Plymouth and the Kentish town of Chatham.

The royal dockyards in London experienced a brief but glorious renaissance when the advent of the Napoleonic Wars prompted a surge in demand. Huge crowds lined the banks of the Thames to see the unveiling of great warships such as *HMS Nelson*, which was launched at Woolwich in 1814. However, once the wars with the French ended, the demand for new warships came to an abrupt halt. In an attempt to find an additional use for the two sites, the Admiralty expanded its victualling yards and over the following 40 years many of the old workshops were converted into breweries, bakeries and slaughterhouses serving the Royal Navy. Many of the resident shipwrights found that they either had to retrain in a completely different trade or seek employment elsewhere. The majority chose the latter option and the community living in and around the yards began a slow but inexorable change of identity.

The arrival of steamships finally signalled the end for the Woolwich and Deptford shipyards. At first, they attempted to update their facilities to cope with the new engineering techniques and for a few years it looked hopeful that the yards might survive by supplying small steamships to the navy. However, as Brunel had discovered, size was crucial to the cost-effectiveness of steam-powered vessels and the Admiralty began to favour its own yard at Chatham, which had more space and better resources. Despite this, the skilled workers at the London yards managed to produce some impressive vessels during their final years of existence, notably *HMS Royal Albert*, a 121-gun steam-powered warship launched at Woolwich on 13 May 1854 in a lavish ceremony presided over by Queen Victoria. Four years later, the monarch also visited the Deptford yard and the Admiralty wasted no time in renaming their converted workshops the Royal Victoria Victualling Yard, which brought a certain cachet but no new orders for ships.

By 1860, the yards' royal status could no longer disguise the fact that they were a constant drain on the Admiralty's resources. After much discussion over possible alternative uses, the decision was made to close the Deptford and Woolwich shipyards and their workers walked out of the gates for the last time on Saturday 18 September 1869. *The Times* reported, 'It was feared that there would be a disturbance of the men leaving the yard for the last time, a strong feeling showing itself, and it was said that an effigy of the First Lord of the Admiralty, after being paraded through the town, would be burnt; but the weather turning out wet frustrated this intention.'

The closure of the royal shipyards ended a shipbuilding tradition that had existed in Woolwich and Deptford for over 300 years. It also left 2,431 men and women jobless. The unemployment problem in Woolwich was exacerbated when job losses were also announced at the nearby arsenal. That said, the majority of redundant workers managed to avoid the workhouse. Figures published at the end of 1869 revealed that following the royal dockyards' closure, a total of 1,235 employees were transferred to other naval shipyards, 249 received pensions from the Admiralty valued at an average of 10 shillings a week, 171 people were given a lump sum of money on discharge and 42 were either sacked, died or were retained on a temporary contract. A 'Relief and Emigration Fund' was set up and this helped 342 workers to settle in either Canada or Queensland. Little is known of the fate of the remaining 392 workers who left with no form of support. Although some no doubt found work at private yards along the Thames, at least two men from the royal shipyards were driven to suicide after concluding that their situation was utterly hopeless.

The closure of the royal dockyards combined with the fraught construction of the Millwall Docks and the recession sparked by the collapse of bankers Overend Gurney & Co in 1866 resulted in a hiatus in dock construction for much of the 1870s. The Commercial Docks Company opened its Canada Dock in 1876, but this new facility was an alteration of its existing site rather than an exercise in speculative construction. However, across the river, a large tract of land east of the Victoria Dock lay ripe for development.

The struggle to survive the lean years of the late 1860s and early 1870s had prompted a merger between the St Katharine and London Docks Companies and the amalgamated firm had gone on to purchase the Victoria Dock and the adjoining undeveloped site. At first, the board of the new company were dismissive of any schemes to build a dock on the vacant land, but international events were soon to influence their mindset on this particular matter.

By the 1870s, the Industrial Revolution and a boom in world population had resulted in demand for consumer goods reaching unprecedented levels and quick international transportation methods were essential. In November 1869, the Suez Canal had opened, revolutionising trade between Europe and Asia and cutting travelling times for vessels trading between the two continents dramatically. Coupled with these two factors was the fact that advancements in steamship engineering meant that vessels were now only limited in size by the places at which they docked. British ports such as Liverpool saw the direction in which marine engineering was heading and developed their facilities accordingly, but the Port of London once again began to struggle to accommodate the largest vessels, which found it very difficult to navigate around the multitude of ships, lighters, barges and pleasure craft that were perpetually in and around the docks.

On 3 September 1878, matters came to a head when a paddle-steamer named the *Princess Alice* made her way up the Thames after collecting revellers from Rosherville Pleasure Gardens in Gravesend. As the ship crossed the river ready to dock at Woolwich Pier, her crew were horrified to see a 900-ton coal steamer, the *Bywell Castle*, heading straight for them. The crew of the two ships made desperate attempts to avoid one another and when collision seemed inevitable, the *Bywell Castle* threw her engines into reverse in a last-ditch attempt at damage limitation. Sadly, this was not enough to avert a disaster. The captain of the coal steamer recorded in his log, 'The two vessels came in collision, the *Bywell Castle* cutting into the other steamer with a dreadful crash. We took immediate measures for saving life by hauling up over our bows several passengers, throwing overboard ropes' ends, life buoys, a hold-ladder, and several planks, and getting out three boats, at the same time keeping the whistle blowing loudly for assistance, which was rendered by several boats from shore, and a boat from another steamer. The excursion steamer, which turned out to be the *Princess Alice*, turned over and sank under our bows.' The *Bywell Castle* and the rescue boats managed to save around 100 people from the *Princess Alice*, but up to 550 others were drowned. Many of the victims were never identified, their remains being buried in a mass grave in Woolwich cemetery.

Unfortunately, steamship collisions in the Thames were all too common, particularly in Woolwich Reach. While families were still grieving for loved ones lost in the *Princess Alice* disaster, the *SS Canada* ploughed into a pier just yards away, causing the whole structure to collapse into the Thames. On learning of these terrible events, George Chambers, the chairman of the London and St Katharine Docks Company, surmised that the safety of the Thames in this area could be significantly improved if large steamers like the *Bywell Castle* could moor east of the treacherous Woolwich stretch of the Thames. The redundant land next to the Victoria Dock could easily provide such a resource and there was sufficient space on the site to create a basin large enough to accommodate even the most immense steamships, some of which had already outgrown the Victoria Dock. Chambers put his idea to the board who, after considering the proposal at length, agreed that plans should be drawn up for the new dock complex. The resulting scheme combined vast size with the latest technology. The dock that formed its centrepiece was to be 490ft wide and 1¾ miles long, while the wood-planked quay surrounding it would be laid with railway lines along which steam engines would operate, conveying cargo-laden trucks to a series of warehouses clad in corrugated iron. As the tracks approached these warehouses, they would be sunk 3ft 3in below the floor, thus enabling unloading to be accomplished with the minimum of effort. On the western edge of the south quay, two dry docks were to be excavated in which ironclad steamships could be repaired and updated. Crucially, all vessels would enter the site via a lock on its eastern edge, thus removing the need for them to travel down Woolwich Reach. Even ships destined for the Victoria Dock would enter it via the new lock system and access their final destination through a connecting canal.

The company decided that its proposed dock would not only be used for cargo ships. The speed of steamship voyages – particularly after the opening of the Suez Canal – meant that international travel was becoming increasingly accessible to the general public and so the board decided to include a passenger terminal at the entrance basin, complete with a hotel and a railway station (to be named Manor Road), providing connections to central London. Two further stations – Central and Connaught Road – were to be built for the transportation of goods and workers. Two additional innovations were also included in the scheme that would be unique to the site. Firstly, drinking water would be available to all ships via 36 hydrants built along the quayside and the complex would be illuminated by electric lamps, each of '6,000 candle-power', mounted on tall poles up to 80ft above ground level. This artificial light would allow vessels to be loaded or unloaded at any time of day or night, thus dramatically reducing turnaround times.

The plans for the new dock were quickly approved by Parliament and, on 23 April 1879, the company received royal assent to name the development the Royal Albert Dock in memory of the Queen's beloved spouse, who had died in December 1861. Queen Victoria also gave her consent to rename the Albert's sister dock the Royal Victoria. On 24 June 1880, the Royal Albert Dock was opened by the Duke and Duchess of Connaught (after whom the station was named). By this time, the board were unanimous in agreeing that their initial reservations about creating another enclosed dock in the Port of London had been unfounded. By the time the duke and duchess arrived at the opening ceremony, all the quay and warehouse space on the north side of the basin had been let to private enterprise along with approximately ⅓ of the space on the south quay.

The immediate popularity of the Royal Albert Dock inevitably took trade away from other docks further along the Thames. In response, the East and West India Docks Company, which had been formed following the amalgamation of the two separate organisations some years previously, opened a site at Tilbury in Essex in the hope that shipping would be lured away from the central London docks altogether. However, the new development was not an immediate success and in fact was barely used for many years following its opening in 1886. The sight of the empty quays and barren warehouses prompted the writer Joseph Conrad to remark with great prescience, 'From the first the Tilbury Docks were very efficient and ready for their task, but they had come, perhaps, too soon into the field. A great future lies before the Tilbury Docks.'

15

THE RISE OF THE WHARVES

The initial failure of Tilbury to attract shipping was due in part to the remote site being snubbed by numerous merchants, watermen (who transferred the cargo from ship to shore) and wharfingers, who ran the smaller landing stages in the Port of London.

As the huge enclosed docks gradually took over from the old legal quays, the wharves which had existed along the Thames since medieval times were left to handle the unloading and storage of commodities rejected by their vast neighbours. During the first half of the 19th century many wharfingers struggled to survive as a huge amount of cargo was exclusively handled by the enclosed docks. However, these exclusive rights generally expired after 21 years and so by the middle of the century the wharves were experiencing a resurgence in trade as their rates were lower than those of the docks. In 1853, the Customs Consolidation Act brought more opportunity for the wharves as it stipulated that they could now handle dutiable cargoes in the same way as the enclosed docks. In addition, merchants took full advantage of the lightermen's and bargees' 'free water clause', which permitted them to collect cargoes inside the enclosed docks but did not compel them to store those same cargoes within the complex. Instead, many goods were taken to the cheaper wharves to be warehoused, much to the chagrin of the dock companies.

The 19th-century Thames wharves could be split into two general groups. The first group were privately owned by wharfingers, who unloaded a wide variety of cargoes and let their adjacent warehousing to many different merchants. The second were owned by industrial companies or services whose wharves formed an integral part of their business. Both types of wharf used the Thames watermen to convey cargoes and the vessels used were invariably barges or lighters. These craft took what was termed as 'overside delivery' of goods from ships moored either in the Thames or at one of the enclosed docks. Once the cargo had been passed over the bow of the ship onto the lighter or barge, it was conveyed to the relevant quay where it was unloaded by porters and taken either to waiting carts or the wharf's warehouse, where it was stored for the merchant until required.

The men who worked on the barges and lighters were required to obtain licences to operate on the Thames from the Company of Watermen and Lightermen, an ancient organisation that had been founded in 1555, initially to regulate carriage fees. The company was responsible for overseeing the training of Thames watermen who, strictly speaking, were expected to complete a seven-year apprenticeship before operating their own craft and to ensure that the set fees were adhered to. However, by the 19th century, competition from rival vessels had resulted in the watermen costing each job depending on how much work was available at the time. Work was notoriously erratic. In 1849, the writer Henry Mayhew spoke to watermen working for Trinity House, which employed 108 lightermen working on 52 60-ton craft, conveying gravel ballast from beds in the river to ships waiting at the docks. He later wrote, 'The men on board the carrying lighters are paid 5d a ton for bringing the ballast from the dredging-engines to the ships. This is divided equally between the four men (manning each lighter). The staffs-man, in addition to his fourth share, receives £10 a year for his extra duties, but out of this he has to buy oars for the boat and lighter locks, "fenders" and shovels. Upon average, the cost of these will be about 30 shillings a year. Each man's share of a 60 ton load is 6s 3d, and there are about seven loads brought up by each lighter in the fortnight. Some weeks the men can earn as much as 37s, but at others they cannot get more than 12s 6d.'

The lightermen employed by Trinity House were lucky that they had a regular employer. Many Thames watermen were forced to take whatever work they could find and some were forced to resort to alternative employment during particularly slow periods in order to make ends meet. The wharves to which the watermen delivered their cargoes lined both sides of the Thames from London Bridge to the Royal Albert Dock. Many such as Fresh Wharf and Custom Quay had originally formed part of the legal quays network, but had long since run out of space to moor the increasingly large ships that entered the port. The south bank of the Thames opposite the legal quays had been lined with wharves dealing with merchants' cargoes since the 17th century. One, which was first opened in the mid-1600s, went on to become the largest wharf in the Port of London.

In 1651, Alexander Hay took the lease on a brewhouse on the south bank of the Thames, next to a tidal creek on what is now known as Tooley Street. At the time, this area of Southwark was a busy part of the Port of London, providing refreshment and accommodation for mariners and merchants and the streets were lined with breweries, inns and taverns. Due to its location, the area also provided warehousing for ships' cargoes and Hay saw that the banks of the creek would provide an excellent landing stage for vessels. He set about converting the brewhouse into warehousing, updated its riverside perimeter and named the new development 'Hay's Wharf'.

The wharf proved to be an immediate success and by 1676, its warehouses were so full of valuable merchandise that Hay felt compelled to insure himself against fire breaking out at his wharf, which due to the prevalence of naked flames used for lighting and heat was an all too common occurrence. He joined forces with two neighbouring wharfingers and created 'Ye Amicable Contributors' insurance scheme, which in addition to paying out compensation for fire-damaged goods also provided the services of six watermen to fight any fires that broke out on the premises.

As the decades passed, the Hay's Wharf warehouses handled a wide variety of cargo, the most unusual of which took the form of German Protestant refugees who in the early 18th century had fled their homeland to escape religious persecution. The German families sheltered in granaries attached to the wharf for some time while a suitable final destination was sought. Naturally, these granaries were not built for human habitation and, consequently, conditions were dire. There was no access to drinkable water, very little food, no toilet facilities and the refugees soon became ill. They were eventually rescued from their plight by the local MP, Sir Charles Cox, who used his influence to secure them a passage on a ship bound for Carolina in North America, where they eventually settled.

By the 1790s, the majority of the warehouses at Hay's Wharf had been leased to W. Humphrey & Son, which used them for the storage of tea and other valuable cargoes. This merchant company remained at the wharf for over 60 years and when the last of the Hay family to have a financial interest in the wharf died in 1838, the Humphrey family took over the lease and set about drawing up plans for a more convenient, up-to-date complex, which included a spacious central dock. The resulting wharf (still known as Hay's) opened in 1857 but just four years later, disaster struck.

In the late afternoon of Saturday 22 June 1861, the men of Cotton's Wharf, a little further down Tooley Street, were packing up for the day when the foreman spotted smoke emanating from a hemp and jute store on the first floor of the wharf's warehouse. He quickly called some of his men back and set about trying to extinguish the fire with buckets of water, but was soon driven back by the choking smoke that had now filled the warehouse. Realising that the fire was rapidly getting out of control, the fire brigade were called and the first engines arrived quickly, accompanied by the brigade's director, James Braidwood. Under Braidwood's direction, two floating fire engines were positioned at the wharf's quayside, while several land engines were sent to Tooley Street. Unfortunately, a good number of these engines were unable to access any water for over an hour and had to stand idle as the crews watched the fire make steady progress across the remaining floors of the warehouse. By 6pm, the entire building was alight and flames were rapidly approaching Hay's Wharf and other neighbouring properties, igniting several highly combustible stores of tallow and saltpetre. The firemen struggled on, desperately trying to halt the advance of the flames, but their attempts were futile. By 9pm, a huge amount of property along the south bank of the Thames was aflame. A journalist from *The Times* was dispatched to the scene and reported, 'Although the sun had not set, and the evening was bright and clear, the whole of the public buildings in the city and along the waterside were tinged by the lurid glare of the conflagration, while the Pool and eastern part of the metropolis were darkened by the huge cloud of smoke which rose from the burning mass.'

Journalists were not the only people who journeyed to Southwark to watch the destructive progress of the fire. London Bridge, which provided the best vantage point, became packed with onlookers who craned over the railings to get a better view of the flames, causing one unfortunate man to be pushed into the river where he was drowned. The local public houses became so full with sightseers and evacuated residents that they decided to ignore the licensing laws and remain open all night. Their crowded rooms created an ideal environment for the local pickpockets, who worked their way through the hostelries, helping themselves to treasures from the pockets of unsuspecting visitors before disappearing into the smoke-filled streets.

The fire brigade finally managed to bring the blaze under control in the early hours of Sunday morning. As the sun rose, the full extant of the damage was revealed. The fire had claimed at least four victims, including the fire brigade's director, James Braidwood, whose remains lay buried beneath the charred rubble of a collapsed warehouse wall. Another fire-fighter, known only as Sullivan, had died when his neck was broken by the chains of one of the floating engines.

Before it was finally contained, the fire had destroyed over three acres of riverside property. The whole of Cotton's Wharf was gone, along with much of neighbouring Chamberlain's Wharf and the surrounding premises, many of which were let to potato merchants and victuallers. Significant water damage had also been inflicted on properties at the perimeter of the fire and many residents complained that their furniture and personal possessions had been broken and spoiled as they hurriedly tried to rescue what they could from the flames. Hay's Wharf, which had been at the centre of the conflagration, was virtually in ruins. Four of Humphrey & Son's new five-storey warehouses were totally destroyed, despite the fact that they were supposed to have been fitted with fire-proof iron doors. A further warehouse had been badly damaged by both fire and water from the firemen's hoses. The estimated cost for rebuilding the total area affected by the fire was estimated at £2 million and the leaseholders of Hay's Wharf were left with the prospect of an almost total rebuild, less than five years after the last wave of development. However, undeterred, they cleared the site and on its charred earth rose the complex that can still be seen today as Hay's Galleria. Keen to stay ahead of the local competition (who of course were also building brand-new wharves simultaneously), the directors of Hay's decided to install a pioneering refrigeration system into one of the warehouse floors. This innovation gave the wharf an edge over its neighbours and the first delivery – a consignment of butter from New Zealand – was received in 1867. The pioneering attitude of the Hay's Wharf management resulted in dramatic expansion of the site during the following decades. By the 1960s, all the wharves on the south bank between London Bridge and Tower Bridge (with the exception of the Gun & Shot Wharf) were taken over by Hay's. The complex was responsible for handling nearly ¾ of all foodstuffs imported into the city – an achievement that earned it the nickname 'the larder of London'.

While Hay's Wharf acquired a solid reputation for handling food and general merchant goods, other wharves were being developed to receive more specific cargoes. For example, the Truman Brewery's Black Eagle Wharf in Wapping was used to store barrels of beer destined for northern and overseas markets, while Irongate Wharf was used by the London, Leith, Edinburgh & Glasgow Steam Packet Company as its London mail depot. Probably the largest cargo delivered to any wharf was an actual ship destined for one of the Thames shipbreakers' yards. One of the most notable mid-19th century shipbreaking firms was Henry Castle & Sons which operated from two Thames wharves.

The company had originally been founded by Henry Castle in 1838 at a leased wharf in Rotherhithe. Business was good during the early years and in 1843 the company moved west to Baltic Wharf which was located close to Vauxhall Bridge, where it specialised in breaking old Royal Mail steam packets. By this time, Henry Castle had been joined by his two sons, Sidney and Abercrombie, and the family presided over their business from a large house overlooking the yard on Upper Grosvenor Road. In the 1850s, the Castle family decided to go into partnership with William Beech, who owned a shipyard at Bull's Head Dock in Rotherhithe and almost immediately managed to land themselves a profitable contract breaking up ships belonging to the Admiralty. This additional work prompted the company (which was now known as Castle & Beech) to open up another shipbreaking yard, this time in Charlton. The location of this new site meant that larger ships could be worked on without having to tow them down the Thames into the busiest part of the river. In the meantime, the company's original site at Vauxhall Bridge continued to break up smaller vessels, the timber from which was transferred to an adjacent yard where it could be purchased by builders and furniture makers. The conditions endured by ships' timbers resulted in the wood becoming weathered and extremely strong. Consequently it was popular for both garden furniture and the exterior of buildings – timbers from *HMS Hindostan* and *HMS Impregnable* (both of which had been dismantled by Castle's) were used on the distinctive exterior of Liberty's department store in Regent Street.

Castle's Vauxhall Bridge yard also enjoyed a local reputation for its distinctive exterior, which was decorated with ships' figureheads and its 'museum' which displayed a collection of maritime curiosities reclaimed from old ships. The historian Richard Hunter visited the site and described, 'Numerous Old Salts … walking around the yard looking up at the figureheads, dreaming of past times and glories.' Although Henry Castle died in 1865, his sons continued to operate the company, eventually passing control to their own children. The Castle & Beech shipbreaking yards continued to occupy the Thames wharves until World War 2, by which time the Castle family no longer retained links with the business.

While the old wharves close to central London were being used by shipbreakers and merchants, sites further east were developed by industrial companies, two of which survive (albeit in an amalgamated form) on the same site to this day, still producing the products that made them household names over 100 years ago. The founder of the first company, Henry Tate, was born in Chorley, Lancashire, in 1819, the 11th child of William Tate, a Unitarian minister, and his wife Agnes. After leaving school at the age of 13, Tate was apprenticed as a grocer to his elder brother Caleb and after being granted his freedom at the age of 20, opened his own grocer's shop in Old Haymarket, Liverpool. It soon transpired that he had a flair for business and over the following 15 years Tate expanded his retail empire to include five more outlets, all in Liverpool and the surrounding towns. The profits from his shops gave Tate the opportunity to diversify into other business fields and in 1859 he founded a partnership with a sugar refiner named John Wright. The two men established their own refinery three years later, by which time Tate had sold his retail premises to finance this new venture. Wright and Tate's sugar refinery proved so successful that a second site was opened in 1864 and on Wright's retirement in 1869, the company name was changed to Henry Tate & Sons.

As chairman of this new company, Tate was constantly searching for ways to improve the productivity and economy of the business and during his research into new refining techniques, he came across a process developed by a German engineer named Eugene Langen that compacted sugar into small cubes. At the time, sugar was purchased in 'loaves' – tall compressed cones from which the required amount of sugar had to be chipped. These loaves were expensive to buy and frustrating to use, especially if a specific amount of sugar was required, and Tate immediately recognised the commercial possibilities of a process through which sugar could be sold in smaller, weighed quantities. He bought the rights to Langen's invention in 1875 and immediately began looking for a suitable site at which the revolutionary cubes could be manufactured. After an exhaustive search, Tate found an old derelict shipyard on the Thames, south of the Albert Dock, which was suitable for development. The site was duly purchased and the new refinery opened in 1878 under the leadership of Tate's son, Edwin. Henry Tate & Sons' sugar cubes were an immediate success and afforded the family enough profit to purchase luxurious residences and sufficient time and resources to indulge their passions. In Henry Tate's case, this was undoubtedly art. From his plush London residence on Streatham Common, he enthusiastically encouraged new artists to develop their talents, entertained luminaries from the Victorian art world, including Sir John Everett Millais (then director of the Royal Academy), and acquired an impressive collection of 19th-century paintings. Shortly before his death in 1899, Tate decided to bequeath his art collection to the nation and had a new gallery built to display it at Millbank. This new gallery opened in 1897 as the National Gallery of British Art but was generally referred to as 'The Tate' – the name that it retains to this day.

Shortly after Henry Tate opened his Thames-side premises, a Greenock-based ship owner named Abram Lyle began to show interest in developing a neighbouring site for his own sugar refinery. Lyle had experience of the industry through a previous business venture in Scotland, where he had developed a highly popular brand of golden syrup and when he was unable to find suitable premises for a refinery in his home town, he widened his search to London. Lyle's sugar refinery opened in 1883 on a site previously known as Plaistow and Odam's Wharves, close to the premises of Henry Tate & Sons. The golden syrup that the refinery produced proved instantly popular with consumers. It is still sold today in a tin bearing Lyle's original logo depicting a lion and a swarm of bees surrounded by the legend, 'Out of the strong, came forth sweetness.' This phrase is taken from the 'Book of Judges', Chapter 14, and was personally selected by Abram Lyle, who was a deeply religious man. In the biblical story, Samson kills a lion while journeying to the land of the Philistines. On his return he sees the dead animal by the roadside and notices that bees have created a honeycomb inside the animal's carcass. Whether the legend is a metaphor for the industrial methods used to produce the syrup or a comment on the strength of Lyle's religious faith is a moot point.

The Tate & Lyle refineries operated independently for nearly 40 years until 1921, when the two firms amalgamated. The company went on to become the largest sugar refiner in Britain and still operates from its east London site to this day.

16

LIFE IN THE VICTORIAN DOCKS

By the second half of the 19th century, the entire area of east London that lay adjacent to the river and the southern districts of Rotherhithe and Deptford was dominated both geographically and economically by the docks and the related industries that relied on them.

Socially, these areas provided homes for thousands of unskilled workers whose low and erratic pay meant that they simply could not afford to live in the more commodious suburbs favoured by dock management and skilled workers. It was imperative to these men and women that work could be found within walking distance of their homes. Their household budgets did not stretch to the luxury of rail travel and the men in particular had to be available to work from a very early hour in the morning, when they would queue up at the dock gates hoping to get selected to help unload a ship.

These areas were also the resort of sailors in search of entertainment while their ship was in port. Consequently, public houses, music halls and other more seedy establishments such as brothels and opium dens could all be found within walking distance of the docks.

In the streets surrounding the St Katharine and London Docks, the longstanding prevalence of brothels serving the ships had, by the 1890s, forced the local police to give up any thoughts of getting rid of them altogether. Instead, most officers favoured the introduction of state regulation. A researcher working for the social investigator Charles Booth toured the area north of the St Katharine Docks with a local policeman in 1898 and noted, 'seeing as I do down here how much illness and trouble is caused by inherited syphilitic tendencies, it is a marvel how anyone can persist in favouring non-regulation.'

In addition to the brothels, the area around the St Katharine Docks attracted casual labourers and their families who, if not working at the waterside, were employed by Hoare's Red Lion Brewery in Lower East Smithfield, which was particularly noted for its excellent stouts and sparkling ales. These people lived either in old housing stock or, if they were lucky enough to have regular employment, one of the new model dwellings that had been constructed following the destruction of many dilapidated rookeries in the 1850s and 60s. One such block, which lay between Glasshouse and Cartwright Streets offered three-room apartments for 6s 9d per week, two rooms for 4s 6d and one room for 3s 3d. Their location made the one-room apartments very popular with young girls who worked in the City and the strict rules of admittance ensured that an air of respectability was maintained.

A little further east, the area gradually deteriorated. From the 1870s, Eastern European Jews, who had arrived at the docks virtually destitute after escaping pogroms in their homelands, began to settle in the houses surrounding Wellclose Square, which lay immediately north of the London Docks. The south-west side of this square was taken up by the Joel Emmanuel Alms Houses, which had been built specifically to house Jewish immigrants by one of their wealthier predecessors. The remaining perimeter of the square was occupied by private houses (most of which were let to Jewish families, who crammed in as many people as they possibly could in order to make the rent affordable), a brewery and, incongruously, a Roman Catholic Mission whose raison d'être was to convince sailors to eschew the perils of the demon drink in favour of a life devoted to Christ.

Six narrow roads radiated out from Wellclose Square leading to the main thoroughfares of Cable Street and St George's Street. Most combined more cheap lodgings for poor Jews with brothels. North East Passage was lined with common lodging houses, which provided squalid accommodation that was paid for by the night and had a 'no questions asked' admission policy. One of these dubious establishments was closed down in the 1890s after it was found to be a popular place for street prostitutes to take their clients. Close by, on the corner of Neptune Street, what had once been the sessions house for the area had by the end of the century become a second-hand furniture dealers. Inside, a jumble of old chairs, tables and bed frames were stacked up beside the original dock and judge's seat.

On the east side of Wellclose Square lay Pell Street, a popular residence for families of Irish descent, many of whom had come to London following the great famine in their homeland in the 1840s. These families, despite being poor, did not present too much trouble to the police, although in 1897 divisional Inspector Reid did report a row breaking out in the street after mourners at a wake got very drunk and set fire to the coffin frills.

East of Pell Street was Princes Square, the appearance of which gave clues to a more illustrious past. The 18th-century houses had elaborately carved wooden lintels and doorways leading to expensively panelled rooms that had once been the homes of prosperous Scandinavian merchants who made their fortunes trading in timber. In the centre of the square was a Swedish Protestant church dating from 1728, which still attracted a small congregation through its doors on a Sunday and retained a special pew for the Swedish Ambassador, on the rare occasions he attended a service. In its 18th century heyday the church had attracted some illustrious parishioners, not least the philosopher Emanuel Swedenborg, author of numerous theological and mystical works, who died in London in 1772.

By the late 19th century, the once prosperous area frequented by Swedenborg and his peers had descended into iniquity. Close to the church, Mayfield Place was generally regarded as the worst street in the locality. This shabby slum was inhabited by London's underclass of common criminals and prostitutes who for a variety of reasons had long since given up the search for honest work. Nearby, on Princes Square, the disciples of the Ratcliff Highway mission hall embarked on a largely unsuccessful quest to convert the fallen women of Mayfield Place and its like, while the St George's public baths ensured that the slum residents could at least bathe occasionally for an affordable price.

Running along the high north wall of the London Docks lay Pennington Street, bordered by six short streets that led up a hill to the main thoroughfare of St George's Street. By the 1880s, this area was a mishmash of warehouses serving the docks, new apartment blocks and old houses with ornamental doorways that were a relic of times before the construction of the dock complex. The streets were inhabited by casual dock labourers, many of whom were Irish, and a few prostitutes who specialised in serving the crews of German ships arriving at the port.

To the south of the London Docks lay a small residential area that was somewhat cut off from the rest of east London by the docks' basins. In the early 1850s, the area had a distinctly maritime atmosphere. Henry Mayhew visited during this period and wrote, 'The open streets themselves have all, more or less, a maritime character. Every other shop is either stocked with gear for the ship or for the sailor. The windows of one house are filled with quadrants and bright brass sextants, chronometers and huge mariners' compasses, with their cards trembling with the motion of the cabs and wagons passing in the street. Then comes the sailors' cheap shoe-mart, rejoicing in the attractive sign of "Jack and his Mother". Every public-house is a "Jolly Tar", or something equally taking. Then come sail makers, their windows stowed with ropes and lines smelling of tar. All the grocers are provision agents, and exhibit in their windows tin cases of meat and biscuits, and every article is warranted to keep in any climate ... Now you meet a satin-waistcoated mate, or a black sailor with his large fur cap, or else a Custom-house officer in his brass-buttoned jacket.'

By the 1880s, most of the old shops had disappeared and the men of the area were employed either at the docks and neighbouring wharves or at the London Hydraulic Works, which stood on the banks of the Thames by the north side of the dock bridge. Their women folk largely found home-based work making sacks for coal and other commodities, for which they received a pittance. In Star Street (later renamed Monza Street), lightermen advertised their services on small brass plaques fixed to the front doors of their homes, while many of the surrounding streets' old housing stock had been demolished in the mid- to late 1800s to make way for more model dwellings. A large recreation ground on the corner of Red Lion Street had been furnished at the council's expense with a see-saw, swings and a large slide. Although the local authorities had done their best to improve the area, by the 1890s this part of Wapping still had some notorious streets, the worst of which was Whitethorn Place, which was tenanted mainly by poor Irish families who lived off the streets, picking up work where they could, and Lowder Street, which was a popular resort for thieves and casual prostitutes.

Two roads – Old Gravel Lane and New Gravel Lane – connected the streets on the south of the London Docks to those on the north via two bridges, each known colloquially as the 'Bridge of Sighs', owing to the large amount of suicides committed there by desperate individuals who threw themselves into the waters of the dock canals below. By 1896, the bridges had garnered such a terrible reputation that a policeman was stationed on them between 3pm and 7am each day to prevent further deaths.

Across the river from Wapping lay the streets that led from the vast complex of the Surrey Commercial Docks. When he visited the area in 1898, Charles Booth's research assistant noted, 'London south of the Thames strikes you as a sea port. Glimpses of large ships sailing at the end of streets, narrow streets with small shops ... men in jerseys with clean shaven upper lips and goat beards; notices on doorways of mast and oar and pump and block makers, half rubbed out and meaning very little now, but still there – all proclaim that shipping or sea faring is or has been the main business of the people.'

The streets bounded on their north side by the Thames were almost exclusively the residences of the area's poorest inhabitants, many of whom had moved from the city some years previously in search of cheaper rents. The region between Jamaica Road and the river was occupied mainly by Irish immigrants who took casual labouring jobs at the docks and wharves; further east, Albion Street and its environs housed a good many gas works labourers and their families. The area surrounding Braddon Street was occupied by workers employed by local flour mills and Danish shops and restaurants in Derrick Street catered for mariners from the timber ships. Many of the women of Rotherhithe found employment in Peek Frean & Co's nearby biscuit factory, which although the work was tedious and repetitive, was more pleasant than sack making or stuffing palliasses.

Casual labourers in search of work at the Surrey Commercial Docks congregated on the corner of Rotherhithe New Road and Lower Road early in the morning in the hope that they would be selected. From the 1870s, the closure of the royal shipyards resulted in many labourers travelling from Deptford to Rotherhithe every day to queue up for work, thus creating a huge amount of competition between the labourers, with the result that only the very fittest-looking would be fortunate enough to secure work regularly.

Besides the immense dock complex, the most notable structure in the area was St Mary's which stood (as it does today) close to the Thames at the end of Marychurch Street. The church was built in 1714/15 by the architect John James, a colleague of Sir Christopher Wren, on the site of an earlier place of worship at which in 1622, Christopher Jones, the captain of the *Mayflower*, was laid to rest. By the mid-19th century, the church had lost its commanding view of the Thames to several flour mills that had been built along the bank and its churchyard had grown into a wilderness in places, giving sanctuary to flora and fauna in an area that was largely industrial.

Although Rotherhithe was a distinctly working-class area by the latter part of the 19th century, it did not have the same pockets of destitution that so blighted areas such as Wapping. There was little crime in the district, owing to the large amount of available work and, when Tower Bridge was completed in 1894, the opportunities for employment increased massively as residents of Rotherhithe could easily journey across the river to the St Katharine and London Docks. Work prospects were further improved for the inhabitants in 1899, when the Greenland Dock was enlarged to accept larger steam vessels.

While Rotherhithe in the latter part of the 19th century was an area on the up, across the water Limehouse had descended into one of the most vice-ridden and poverty-stricken places in the metropolis. The area lay conveniently midway between the London and West India Docks but the location was anything but prosperous. The streets were principally made up of decaying housing stock let out to multiple occupants at cheap rents and common lodging houses described by the local police as 'thieves' kitchens'. The Congregational Refuge Hall in Medland Street was one of the few 'respectable' lodging houses in the district and consequently was full to capacity, even in summer months when sleeping rough was an option worthy of contemplation by many destitute poor. The hall consisted of a ground floor and gallery along which were lines of wooden boxes used by the incumbent men as beds but closely resembling coffins. Men were admitted by the night on a first come, first served basis. Once the hall's capacity of 300 was full, those who had not secured a bed had to take to the streets in search of an alternative place to sleep. The inmates were given a meagre evening meal consisting of bread and water and usually took to their hard, uncomfortable beds early as they were turned out at 6am the next day so the place could be cleaned and aired before the next night's intake arrived. Apart from keeping them reasonably warm and fed, the refuge could do little more to help its unfortunate guests, although it did offer around 100 places on ships each year to men who wished to emigrate to the colonies.

Limehouse had long since been a popular centre for Chinese and Japanese sailors waiting for ships in the docks. Consequently, there were several grocery stores selling foodstuffs to appeal to this clientele, certain pubs in the area became meeting places for Oriental crews and opium dens appeared, offering escapism to anyone prepared to pay for the drug.

Opium smoking was not illegal and, as long as the patrons of the dens caused no trouble, the police tended to turn a blind eye to the goings-on in the smoke-filled rooms along the Ratcliff Highway – the traditional location for opium dens. In 1879, Charles Dickens Junior wrote in his *Dictionary of London*, 'The best known of these "dens" is that of one Johnstone, who lives in a garret off Ratcliff Highway, and for a consideration allows visitors to smoke a pipe which has been used by many crowned heads in common with poor Chinese sailors who seek their native pleasure in Johnstone's garret. This is the place referred to in *The Mystery of Edwin Drood*. A similar establishment of a slightly superior – or it might be more correct to say a shade less nauseating – class is that of Johnny Chang, at the London and St Katharine Coffee House in the Highway itself.'

Although the opium dens were well known and even publicised in publications such as Dickens' *Dictionary*, a visit to one of these establishments was not for the faint-hearted and could be expensive. In the mid- to late 19th century, an opium pipe could be purchased new for only five or six shillings but by the time it was filled with the drug it was worth up to £5. This high price did not seem to act as a deterrent, however. The writer J. C. Parkinson visited a den while compiling his *Places and People, Being Studies From Life* (1869) and later wrote, 'As soon as we are sufficiently acclimatised to peer through the smoke, and after the bearded Oriental, who makes faces, and passes jibes at and for the company, has lighted a small candle in our honour, we see a sorry little apartment, which is almost filled by the French bedstead, on which half-a-dozen coloured men are coiled long-wise across its breadth, and in the centre of which is a common japan tray and opium lamp. Turn which way you will, you see or touch opium smokers. The cramped little chamber is one large opium pipe, and inhaling its atmosphere partially brings you under the drug's influence.'

During the first half of the 19th century, the opium dens, public houses and prostitutes in the Limehouse area enjoyed good business from the constant influx of sailors arriving at the Port of London. Henry Mayhew spoke to Sergeant Prior from H (Whitechapel) Division of the Metropolitan Police while writing the fourth volume of his *magnum opus* – *London Labour and the London Poor* (1862) – who told him that until recently, 'when sailors landed in the docks, they drew their wages, they picked up some women to whom they considered themselves married pro tem, and to whom they gave the money made by their last voyage. They live with the women until the money is gone.' The pubs and music halls also benefited from the sailors' willingness to be parted from their hard-earned wages. Sergeant Prior continued, 'There are perhaps 12 or 15 public-houses in St George's Street and Ratcliff Highway: most of them a few years ago were thronged.'

These lavish spending sprees were beginning to die out by the mid-1800s due to two factors. Firstly, in a bid to stop the sailors' heavy drinking and use of prostitutes, several missions and the Board of Trade introduced sailors' saving schemes, whereby money could be easily deposited and distributed, thus reducing the need for the mariners to get rid of their cash before their next voyage. Secondly, foreign ships' captains began to insist on their men returning to their vessels by 7pm, thus drastically reducing the amount of time these men could spend in the public houses. This had a detrimental effect on licensed premises throughout the areas surrounding the docks. Charles Booth's researcher in Limehouse was amazed to report that by 1898, one local pub had even turned into a coffee house in bid to survive. That said, the majority of pubs managed to stay in business despite the reduced patronage of sailors by appealing to the native dock workers and other professions connected with the Port of London.

By the end of the 19th century, there were 105 licensed premises in Limehouse alone, made up of 50 fully licensed pubs, 49 beer houses, two off-licences and four licensed grocers' shops. The East India Dock Road and the streets surrounding it were lined with licensed premises, all of which thrived due to the huge amount of traffic going in and out of the docks that passed their doors. Some prospered by catering for a certain type of customer. For example, the Aberfeldy Tavern on Aberfeldy Street was a popular meeting place for marine engineers, while the Great Eastern was popular with ships' captains. The dock workers, who made up the largest proportion of clientele for the pubs, were extremely well catered for. On West India Dock Road, there were no fewer than five public houses just outside the dock entrance, one of which sent a member of staff onto the quay every day to serve beer to the dockers *in situ*. This arrangement proved popular with the dock management who reasoned that if they made the workers go off site for their lunchtime pint, they might never return for the afternoon shift.

To the east of Limehouse was the district of Poplar, which also included the Isle of Dogs. The geographic and social status of the northern part of this area closely resembled that of its neighbour. However, on the Isle, which until recently had been largely undeveloped, the visual environment changed significantly. The residential part of Millwall comprised a handful of streets running off the northern end of West Ferry Road and was occupied almost entirely by dock labourers and foremen whose homes were sandwiched between the riverside wharves and the Millwall Docks site. Until the 1840s, the eastern perimeter of the island remained semi-rural, the yards of its wharves leading into open fields. However, burgeoning trade at the West India Docks made the area an attractive proposition for housing developers, in particular, one William Cubitt.

William Cubitt was born in 1791 in the village of Buxton, near Aylesham in Norfolk. His father Jonathan, who was a carpenter by trade, relocated his family to London shortly after William's birth and found work in the building trade. As William and his brothers Thomas and Lewis reached adulthood they all followed their father into building-related professions and in about 1820 they formed a partnership that was destined to become one of the largest building firms in London by the 1830s.

As William Cubitt was busy with his construction business in central London, the owners of the land on the eastern side of the Isle of Dogs – the Countess of Glengall and William Mellish – were struggling with several problems. The constant passing of ever-larger ships making their way into the Port of London meant that their estate was quite literally being washed away. In order to stop the erosion, it was necessary to construct an embankment around the eastern perimeter of the Isle. However, this was an expensive project that the countess and Mellish were loath to undertake as the rents from the wharves and warehouses on the estate were insufficient even to partially cover the costs. Thoughts of selling some of the land to a railway company initially came to naught (although the Millwall Extension Railway did eventually run a line to North Greenwich in 1872) and the two landowners had virtually given up hope of ever rejuvenating their rapidly deteriorating estate when their agent, John Hooper, opened up discussions with William Cubitt.

In 1842, Cubitt agreed to purchase leasehold a strip of land that lay behind the rapidly crumbling river wall on the tip of the peninsula. In return for a 99-year lease, Cubitt agreed to undertake some major improvements to the area including building an embankment to stop the advance of the river, the construction of several new wharves and the laying out of some residential streets, the cost of which would be shared between the freeholders and himself. Once the rents acquired from the new properties covered the annual cost of the lease, the remaining monies could be taken by Cubitt.

Building work commenced. Between 1847 and 1853, Cubitt acquired a further 34½ acres slightly further inland from the Countess of Glengall in order to construct more housing and also acquired eight acres of land from William Stratton so the housing estate could extend up to the southernmost entrance basin of the West India Docks. The resulting development became known as Cubitt Town.

Cubitt Town was (and still is) divided into two estates connected by Manchester Road, which ran from Ferry Street in the south to the West India Docks in the north. By the end of the 19th century, the area had become largely self-sufficient with the exception of a shopping district. To remedy this, special transport was provided on Saturdays to convey the townsfolk to Chrisp Street in Poplar where groceries could be obtained. Cubitt Town had its own schools, several places of worship and even a library which had been financed by the great philanthropist Andrew Carnegie, after whom it was named. The library was not the only building financed by philanthropic sponsorship. In 1854, Christ Church on Wharf Road was opened as part of the Bishop of London's plan to protect his parishioners from 'irreligion and vice' and St John's church in Roserton Street was built in 1873 with money donated by a Mrs Isabelle Laurie of Maxwelton in Scotland to replace the earlier St Paul's Mission, which had been located in a hut close to Millwall Docks since 1866. Mrs Laurie's money also paid in part for the erection of a mission hall (1885/86), homes for the verger and the senior curate and a workmen's club house (built 1897).

Cubitt Town also had numerous pubs to serve both the builders and the residents, the most famous of which was the Newcastle Arms on the corner of Newcastle Street. Built by William Cubitt in 1853, the pub once claimed to have the largest stock of Scotch whisky in the East End. In 1962, it was purchased by the writer and television personality Dan Farson, who set about recreating the house's original Victorian interior and renamed it the Waterman's Arms. On reopening, the pub quickly became a popular watering hole and received press attention in late 1963 when Farson staged an exhibition of photographs by Stephen Ward, who had committed suicide on 3 August that year following his involvement in the Profumo scandal.

Another popular pub in the vicinity was the George Hotel, close to the Millwall Docks. This establishment catered for merchants and suppliers with business connections to the area and offered meeting rooms, a dining hall and an impressive billiards room. In 1889, the pub's owner William Clark was involved in Millwall Rovers football club's relocation to a new ground close to the George Hotel. The club subsequently changed its name to Millwall Athletic and the George Hotel became its headquarters.

From the development of its first streets, Cubitt Town attracted residents that largely comprised dock and waterside labourers and their families. Consequently, the area was poor compared to districts further west but by no means as destitute as places such as Limehouse. On visiting the area, Charles Booth's researcher observed, 'The chief vices of the island are drink, gambling, betting and thieving. There are more juvenile thieves found here than in any other part of (the Metropolitan Police's) K Division. Lots of things to thieve – old iron, goods from leaky sacks; there is a market for everything. Once anything is found lying about and portable, not a boy would not try to remove it.' Illegal bookmaking was also a lucrative sideline for the residents. The policeman accompanying the researcher told him that a bookmaker had been caught the previous week arranging bets in the middle of the street and when searched, the police found he had taken £50 in cash from his enterprise.

Despite the presence of a relatively benign criminal element, the majority of Cubitt Town's residents were quiet and law abiding. Allotments were laid out on the south side of Glengall Road, which proved to be very popular and jealously guarded by the lessees, who even set up a 'mutual protection society' to guard against thieves stealing their flowers while they were at work. Further recreational attractions were provided on Sundays when the county council band arrived to play at Island Gardens and on balmy summer days residents would stroll along the perimeter of Millwall Docks' south quay, which provided a surprisingly picturesque setting and was known humorously as 'East-End-By-The-Sea'.

Like Cubitt Town, the small residential area to the south of the Royal Albert Dock was also inhabited almost exclusively by dockers' families and employees of the industries located in the immediate vicinity. In 1852, Samuel Winkworth Silver opened his India Rubber Works on the north bank of the Thames, directly opposite the royal dockyard at Woolwich. The area was remote at that time, so Silver constructed small terraces of houses for his workers close to the site. The development subsequently became known as Silvertown.

By 1886, Silver's rubber works had expanded its operations to include a large electric telegraph works and had been joined by several additional works a little further along the riverside dealing with petroleum, gas and soap. Two railway stations – Silvertown and North Woolwich – served the area. The line divided at Silvertown to run either side of the Victoria Dock and in between lay the church of St Mark which had been built in 1861/62 to serve the local population. An ecclesiastical parish of St Mark was formed two years later, which included Silvertown and North Woolwich, along with parts of East and West Ham, which lay along the northern border of the Victoria Dock.

The area had two schools, both of which were well attended. The primary school – which had places for up to 320 infants – was run by the

West Ham School Board, while St Mark's National School provided a good basic education for older children. Opportunities for academic betterment in Silvertown did not end with childhood. In 1885, the members of the Primrose Library Society, who were mainly employees of Knight & Sons' soap and oil works [situated south of the Victoria Dock], opened Primrose Hall in Knights Road to provide recreational facilities for the local population. According to the 1886 edition of *Kelly's Directory*, the hall was 'a handsome building, containing a fine hall for lectures and public entertainments, capable of sitting 500 persons [with] an extensive library and reading room, billiards, bagatelle, coffee and smoking rooms; attached are hot and cold baths.'

In 1873, the population of the parish of St Mark had grown to the extent that an additional parish in the north of the district was needed. The area within it became known as Canning Town – named after either Sir Samuel Canning, a wealthy manufacturer who had business links to Samuel Silver, or George Canning, an engineer who was heavily involved with the development of both the railways and the docks in the area. Over the following decade, the population of the new parish exploded from 1,455 in 1871 to over 4,000 in 1881 as the opening of the Royal Albert Dock and the arrival of numerous new businesses created copious employment opportunities. In order to cater for the sudden influx of families to the area, streets lined with hastily built terraces were thrown up by speculative builders, many pubs appeared on street corners, two music halls – Relf's and the Royal Standard – opened to entertain the populace and six schools were built to provide education for their children.

Although establishments like Relf's Music Hall and Primrose Hall provided some escapism, life for the families of Silvertown and the other dockside areas of London was tough but did offer a wealth of employment opportunities, many of which were quite specific. For example, those employed to unload British timber ships (foreign vessels were unloaded by their crew) were known colloquially as lumpers. These men worked exclusively on the water and would either load the ship's cargo onto the dock's own barges inside the complex or, if a ship was too heavily laden to enter the dock (or if the cargo was destined for one of the wharves), they would transfer the merchandise onto lighters which carried it ashore. Occasionally, if a small craft arrived, the lumpers would offload the timber directly onto the quayside, where it would be carried to storage ponds or warehouses by porters.

Timber arriving at the docks was classified as either 'landed' or 'rafted'. The landed goods were items such as railway sleepers, deals (planks) or battens, which were stored in warehouses before being taken off to their final destination. Rafted goods were untreated, unadulterated lengths of timber which could not be allowed to dry out as the wood would often split, rendering it useless. These goods were handled by the rafters, a skilled group of men who were responsible for sorting the timber by length, quality and customer and then moving it to storage ponds ready for collection. The rafters learned their trade through a seven-year apprenticeship with the Watermen's Company before finding work at docks such as the Surrey or Commercial. Their pay depended on the size of ship they unloaded: 'short hour' ships, which could be emptied in under eight hours, offered pay of four shillings a day; 'long hour' vessels, which took up to 12 hours to unload, offered an extra shilling per day. The busy season lasted from July to October each year and during this time, the rafters were employed virtually every day. However, during the quieter winter and spring months, they often had to take on other jobs to make ends meet. Henry Mayhew spoke to some of the rafters at the Commercial Docks in the mid-19th century and one told him how financially difficult their lives were: 'There are about 16 rafters at the Commercial Docks ... They none of them save any money during the busy season. They are in debt when the brisk time comes, and it takes them all summer to get clear, which perhaps they does by the time the fall-ships have done, and then of course they begin going on in the old strain again. A rafter's life is merely getting into debt and getting clear of it ... and that is a great part of the life of all the labourers along-shore.'

Once timber cargoes had been deposited at the quayside, the porters took on its removal to the nearby warehouses. Their job was skilled, exhausting and highly dangerous as they were responsible for carrying huge planks of deal (pine or fir wood), which could measure up to 27ft long, by hand to their dockside destination where it was stacked in high piles ready for collection by the timber merchants. A deal porter at the Commercial Docks told Mayhew, 'Ours is very dangerous work. We pile the deals sometimes 90 deals high ... and we walk along planks with no hold, carrying the deals in our hands, and only our firm tread and our eye to depend upon. We work in foggy weather, and never stop for a fog; at least we haven't for eight or nine years ... In that sort of weather accidents are frequent. Last year there was, I believe, about 35 falls but no deaths. If it's a bad accident the deal porters give 6d apiece on a Saturday night to help the man that's had it. There's no fund for sickness.'

The stave porters worked alongside the deal porters, transporting thin, shaped pieces of wood that were used to make barrels to store beer, wine and other commodities. These men were highly skilled in loading the wood in such a way that the maximum load could be carried without being dropped. A stave porter interviewed by Henry Mayhew explained, 'We pack the bigger staves about our shoulders, resting one stave on another, more like a Jack-in-the-Green than anything else, as our head comes out in the middle of 'em.'

Like all jobs at the Port of London, work was inconsistent and so in particularly busy periods workmen such as the lumpers, rafters and porters were assisted by labourers. A small proportion of these unskilled workers were permanent but the vast majority were employed on a casual basis. Henry Mayhew investigated the workers at the London Docks in the 1850s and noted, 'This immense establishment is worked by from one to three thousand hands, according as the business is either "brisk" or "slack". Out of this number there are always from four to five hundred permanent labourers, receiving upon an average 16s 6d per week wages, with the exception of coopers, carpenters, smiths, and other mechanics, who are paid the usual wages of their crafts. Besides these there are many hundreds – from one thousand to two thousand five hundred – casual labourers, who are engaged at the rate of 2s 6d per day in the summer, and at 2s 4d per day in the winter months. Frequently, in case of many arrivals, extra hands are hired in the course of the day at the rate of 4d per hour. For the permanent labourers a recommendation is required, but for the casual labourers no "character" is demanded. The number of the casual hands engaged by the day depends of course upon the amount of work to be done, and I find that the total number of labourers in the docks varies from 500 to 3,000 and odd.'

The casual labourers were a disparate group who for reasons of ill health, domestic obligations, bad luck or pure indolence could not find permanent work. Mayhew described the men he saw at the London Docks thus: 'men of all grades, looks, and kinds; some in half-fashionable surtouts, burst at the elbows, with the dirty shirts showing through; others in greasy sporting jackets, with red pimpled faces; others in the rags of their half-slang gentility, with the velvet collars of their paletots worn through to the canvas; some in rusty black, with their waistcoats fastened tight up to the throat; others, again, with the knowing thieves' curl on each side of the jaunty cap; whilst here and there you may see a big-whiskered Pole, with his hands in the pockets of his plaited French trousers.'

At the Surrey and Commercial Docks the casual labourers were known as 'pokers' because they were always poking about the docks looking for work. The pokers and their compatriots at the other docks in the Port of London had little hope of escaping from their lives of relentless, grinding poverty. One sad soul interviewed in the early 1850s lamented, 'I've never stole, but have been hard tempted. I've thought of drowning myself and of hanging myself; but somehow a penny or two came in to stop that. Perhaps I didn't seriously intend it.' Over the following 20 years, the situation changed little. The writer Richard Rowe visited the home of an impoverished dock labourer named Sears in 1871 and later wrote of their meeting, 'I asked Sears whether being out in search for work would not be better than nursing his despair at home. "Haven't I been?" he retorted fiercely, with many epithets, which I need not repeat. "Wasn't I down at the Docks this morning? And wasn't I turned away, with hundreds more, because this horrid east wind keeps on blowing, just to keep the ships out? I'm not afraid of work. Why don't you give me some, instead of talking about it? Whatever it is, I'll do it ... Where can I get work now except at the Docks? And this beastly wind has done me out of the chance of that. I'm a likely-looking fellow for any one to hire, ain't I? You'd rig me out and be my reference, wouldn't you?" And the man, as he said it, burst into a laugh, half of mockery, half of remorseful pity, all of utter misery, and clutched at the breast of his tattered, napless, greasy frock-coat with such violence that the string which supplied the place of buttons broke, and I saw that, as I suspected, he was shirtless.'

Although work for many was scarce, one source of almost constant employment for the casual labourers and skilled dock workers alike was the unloading and storage of coal, which by the 19th century had become one of the principal cargoes at the Port of London. In 1805, when the city was beginning to feel the effects of the Industrial Revolution, 1,350,000 tons of coal arrived at the docks. By 1848, that amount had risen to 3,418,340 tons, which was brought in throughout the year by 2,717 vessels employing over 20,000 seamen. Once a coal ship had moored at one of the docks, a gang of 'coalwhippers' was requested by the captain to haul the cargo from the ship's hold by means of pulleys. Their unusual name came from the sudden jerk with which the men whipped the cargo onto the deck. Once the coal had been extricated from the hold, it was loaded either directly into trucks at the quayside or onto lighters and barges which would then convey the coal to its storage place.

Whether unloading timber, coal or any other commodities, the dock workers generally organised themselves into gangs of up to 13 men to complete the work. These gangs were usually comprised of individuals who had either known each other for some time or were related, as good working relationships were essential to ensure that the sometimes dangerous work was completed without any mishaps caused by arguments or misunderstandings. The gangs were well known to the contractors at the docks, who would negotiate the price at which a ship would be unloaded and then arrange for the appropriate number of gangs to complete the work.

The gangs' work was arduous and repetitive, mainly due to the fact that cargoes were generally packed in units that could be carried by hand such as sacks, boxes or barrels. Large cargoes were often lifted from the ship by crane and deposited on the quayside where they would be transported by workers known as 'truckers' to carts and warehouses. Efficient management of the dockside warehouses was overseen by a senior warehouseman who had several workers in his employ, all of whom enjoyed far more stable employment than the labourers on the quayside. The warehouse staff were responsible for marking up cargo destined for export, storing other goods in the appropriate spaces until the owner requested delivery and organising the collection of goods by merchants' agents. They also had to deal with requests for inspection by customs officials and 'box knockers' were employed in the warehouses specifically to open up cargoes and then reseal them once the customs officers were satisfied with the contents.

Remuneration for working at the docks varied widely depending on the worker's status. By the 1880s, permanent employees, for example the warehouse staff, could earn between 20 and 30 shillings per week. However, the casual labourers were paid an average of only 5d per hour and work was by no means guaranteed. One of the better-paid groups of workers were the men who undertook the highly skilled work of loading the ships destined for overseas markets. These men were known as stevedores, from the word 'estibador', which was used to describe their Spanish counterparts. The stevedores' profession was placed in high regard at the docks, not least because it took a good deal of experience to load a ship without causing it to become unbalanced. In addition to this, the cargoes had to be loaded in the order in which they would be taken off once the vessel reached its destination.

Like the men that unloaded the ships, the stevedores organised themselves into gangs headed up by a master, who would direct proceedings to make sure that goods were being loaded in the correct order. Compared with the dockers that dealt with the unloading, the stevedores were more organised, better paid and had more regular work. This was reflected in the fact that their homes were generally located in the more salubrious streets around the docks. These homes could often be identified by a brass plaque on the outside wall advertising the stevedore's services.

The unpredictable, hard and ultimately uninspiring nature of the dockers' work meant that cheap and temporary escape from their mundane lives was essential to many. As a group, the dockers had a reputation for enjoying a drink which, until an Act of Parliament was passed to stop the practice in 1843, was exacerbated by the fact that many were habitually paid in public houses. Henry Mayhew noted, 'Under this system none but the most dissolute and intemperate obtained employment – in fact, the more intemperate they were the more readily they found work.' A worker from the Surrey Docks agreed, stating, 'I can't say that we are compelled to take beer – certainly not when at our work in the dock; but we're "expected" to take it when we're waiting [to be paid]. I can't say either that we are discharged if we don't drink; but if we don't we are kept waiting late on a Saturday night on an excuse of the publican's having no change, or something like that; and we feel if we don't drink, we'll be left in the background.'

The landlords of these establishments were often related to ship owners and were responsible for selecting and remunerating the gangs chosen to work on their relatives' vessels. Realising that they had to keep a high profile to be in with a chance of employment, the men crowded round the bar, ordering ever larger rounds of drinks in a bid to attract the publican's attention. It was also necessary to spend long hours at the pubs in order to be first in line when a ship came in. As a result, many dock workers suffered from alcohol-related illnesses, including cirrhosis of the liver, delirium tremens and heart complaints.

The parliamentary act that ended the publicans' lucrative business may have partially solved the problem of widespread heavy drinking among the dock community. However, it unknowingly caused another as the men looking for work were now forced on to the streets surrounding the docks when seeking employment. From dawn, the area outside the dock gates would throng with casual labourers waiting to be selected at what was colloquially referred to as the 'call-on.' As an unprecedented amount of poverty-stricken families flooded into the East End looking for work in the latter part of the 19th century, the way casual labour was employed at the docks proved to be a catalyst for the improvement of employment rights and empowered the embryonic trades union movement.

17

BOILING POINT

On 15 June 1888, a young journalist by the name of Annie Besant attended a meeting of the Fabian Society, a left-wing debating group that met regularly to discuss and publicise the pressing social issues of the day, particularly those affecting the poor. The Fabians had been founded some five years previously by Edith Nesbit (who would later enjoy international recognition for her popular children's books) and her husband Hubert Bland. Initially, membership of the society was small, enabling meetings to be held in the front parlours of private individuals. However, by the end of the 1880s, the group was beginning to attract the support of such luminaries as George Bernard Shaw, Ramsay MacDonald and H. G. Wells.

During the course of the June 1888 meeting, the dealings of London match company Bryant & May were discussed in some depth. It appeared that despite huge yearly profits, the company was paying its workers a pittance in wages. More worryingly, horror stories had begun to emanate from its Bow factory concerning the company's inhuman treatment of its impoverished employees, many of whom were naïve and vulnerable teenage girls. Besant resolved to visit the factory and interview some of the workers in an attempt to establish whether there was any truth in the damning accusations. Her subsequent clandestine discussions with some of the company's staff uncovered a shocking state of affairs. The majority of the girls employed by Bryant & May came from a background of familial neglect caused by extreme poverty and felt completely alone in the world. Besant commented, 'born in slums, driven to work while still children, undersized because under-fed, oppressed because helpless, flung aside as soon as worked out, who cares if they die or go on to the streets...?' At first, the match girls were reluctant to speak out against their employer for fear of being sacked. However, once assured that their identity would not be revealed, they confirmed Annie Besant's worst fears.

Bryant & May was indeed running a highly profitable operation with shareholders receiving yearly dividends of over 20%. The impressive profits were, however, gained at the expense of the workers, who were treated in a quite abominable manner. The girls were expected to present themselves at the factory at 6.30am in summer or 8am during the winter months and work until 6pm. During that time, they were forced to stand exhausted at benches making and filling match boxes for literally hours, only resting briefly when breakfast and dinner was eaten. The work was extremely hazardous – the phosphorus used in match production being carcinogenic – and poorly paid. The average teenage employee received just 4s a week for her toil, half of which immediately disappeared into the grasping hands of either her landlord or parents, leaving her very little with which to buy food let alone go out and enjoy herself. In addition, the management regularly docked the girls' pay for what today would be considered extremely minor misdemeanours.

Annie Besant interviewed employees who had been fined for such grave transgressions as having dirty feet (for many had no shoes), talking or having an untidy bench. More worryingly, Bryant & May seemed more concerned about the welfare of its machinery than its workers. Besant wrote, 'One girl was fined 1s for letting the web twist round a machine in the endeavour to save her fingers from being cut, and was sharply told to take care of the machine, "never mind your fingers". Another, who carried out the instructions and lost a finger thereby, was left unsupported while she was helpless.' In addition to the swingeing fines, the girls also had to endure physical abuse from the foremen. Besant noted, '[the girls'] wage covers the duty of submitting to an occasional blow from a foreman; one, who appears to be a gentleman of variable temper, "clouts" them "when he is mad".' The directors were no better than their staff. A few years previously, Theodore Bryant had decided to demonstrate his admiration for the Liberal politician William Gladstone by erecting a statue of the great statesman. However, unwilling to fund the project single-handed, he decided to dock his workers' pay to the tune of 1s to help pay for the statue. To add insult to injury, the girls suffered further financial loss when half a day's (unpaid) holiday was announced so they could attend the unveiling of the statue. Annie Besant noted, 'So furious were the girls at this cruel plundering, that many went … with stones and bricks in their pockets, and I was conscious of a wish that some of those bricks had made an impression on Mr Bryant's conscience.'

Utterly appalled at the plight of the Bryant & May match girls, Besant resolved to do what she could to improve their lamentable working conditions. On 23 June, she published a damning article on the company in *The Link* newspaper entitled 'White Slavery in London'. Slamming the management and shareholders as barbarous profiteers, she shamed the men responsible, stating: 'Oh if we had but a people's Dante, to make a special circle in the inferno for those who live on this misery, and suck wealth out of the starvation of helpless girls.' She then organised distribution of the article outside the gates of Bryant May's factory, thus showing the girls that they were at last receiving support from someone with the power to help them.

Besant's inflammatory article was the catalyst for an event that was to have a profound effect on the working classes throughout the country. Eager to cleanse their sullied reputation, Bryant & May tried to force its employees into signing a statement refuting the claims made in the newspaper article. The match girls hastily dispatched an anonymous letter to Annie Besant, telling her of this latest turn of events. It read, 'Dear Lady, They have been trying to get the poor girls to say it is all lies that has been printed and trying to make us sign papers that it is all lies; dear Lady nobody knows what it is we have put up with and we will not sign them. We thank you very much for the kindness you have shown to us. My dear Lady we hope you will not get into any trouble on our behalf as what you have spoken is quite true.

However fearful of the possible repercussions, the match girls held their ground and refused to sign their employer's hastily written statement. In response, Bryant & May sacked three girls who they presumed to be the main 'informers'. Their arrogant refusal to bestow any sympathy on their beleaguered workers proved to be a fateful error of judgement. Following publication of the white slavery article, the match girls had been pleasantly surprised (if not shocked) at the amount of public sympathy it generated and, feeling newly empowered, the entire factory went out on strike. No doubt feeling responsible, Annie Besant determined to assist the girls in any way possible. She vehemently defended their actions in *The Link* newspaper and persuaded fellow editors William Stead of the *Pall Mall Gazette* and Henry Hyde Champion of the *Labour Elector* to support the strike. The newspapers encouraged a boycott of Bryant & May products and organised fundraising campaigns to sustain the girls while they were not working. In turn, the match girls set up their own union and elected Annie Besant as its leader. Furious at what they considered to be meddling, the Bryant & May management were unsurprisingly scathing about the union's new commander-in-chief. On being asked about the strike by *The Star* newspaper, the following exchange took place between the reporter and one of the directors, Bartholomew Bryant:

The Star: 'What is the cause of the strike?'

Bryant: 'Why, a girl was dismissed yesterday; it had nothing to do with Mrs Besant. She refused to follow the instructions of the foreman, and as she was irregular anyway, she was dismissed.'

The Star: 'Is it not very unusual that all the girls should strike because of one?'

Bryant: 'Yes, but I've no doubt they have been influenced by the twaddle of one.'

Despite Bartholomew Bryant's protestations, public support for the match girls continued enthusiastically and after an enforced shutdown of three weeks, the company's management were reluctantly forced to not only re-employ the sacked women but also to abolish their harsh system of fines.

The victory of the match girls over their employers was an important one. Prior to their dispute, unskilled workers had been loath to consider industrial action, mainly because they felt the only result would be the loss of their jobs. The match girls proved that collective action by unskilled workers could be as successful as strikes by less easily replaced skilled workers. Soon, unions of casual and unskilled workers were forming throughout the country and, in particular, the London docks.

At the time of the match girls' strike, the dock owners relied heavily on casual labour to unload the ships and perform menial tasks on the waterside. The arrival of ships into the docks was notoriously unpredictable. Sometimes, vessels would be held up for days or even weeks due to bad weather, leaving the quays and wharves relatively empty. Then hundreds would arrive within the same week and the race was on to unload the cargo as quickly as possible. A dock worker told Salvation Army founder William Booth how the inconsistent work affected him, 'I would earn 30s a week sometimes and then perhaps nothing for a fortnight. That's what makes it so hard. You get nothing to eat for a week scarcely and then when you get taken on, you are so weak that you can't do it properly.' It is unlikely that the dock workers blamed the management for the inconsistent nature of their work, but they most certainly bore grievances regarding the way they were employed.

In 1883, the writer George R. Sims investigated working life on the docks and was staggered by what he discovered. One morning he ventured down to the West India Dock to observe the morning employment ritual known colloquially as the 'call-on' and was amazed to find well over a thousand men waiting at the gate. Sims described the ensuing selection process in vivid detail:

'It is generally about six o'clock that the quay-gangers ascend the rostrums or elevated stands which are placed all along the outside wall, and survey the huge crowd in front of them, and commence to call them out for work and send them into the different docks where the good ships lie, with their vast cargoes, waiting for willing hands to unload them ... Many of (the men) are called "Royals" and are pretty sure to be taken on, their names being on the ganger's list and called out by him as a matter of course.'

Once the Royals had been selected, the ganger surveyed the crowd and picked out the hardiest-looking individuals to fill his first quota of men, a process that often provoked desperately violent behaviour as the hungry labourers jostled for a good, visible position. A contemporary report described them as 'men who, in their eagerness to obtain employment, trample each other under foot, and where like beasts they fight for the chance of a day's work.'

Unsurprisingly, the power wielded by the gangers often went to their heads and many took sadistic delight in standing aloft in their pulpit-like grandstands surveying the hundreds of men beneath them hanging on their every word and movement. These avaricious opportunists were also not averse to taking bribes. One docker noted, 'There is a chance of getting regular dock work, and that is, to lounge about the pubs where the foremen go, and treat them. Then they will very likely take you on the next day.' Dock worker Ben Tillett (who was to play a pivotal role in the events about to unfold) despised the gangers' swaggering demeanour and unethical hiring practices. He noted in his memoirs, 'as a brute would throw scraps to hungry wolves to delight in the exhibition of the savage struggle for existence, with beasts tearing each other to pieces, so these creatures would delight in the spectacle.'

The second call-on took place about ¾ of an hour after the first and was followed roughly an hour later by a third selection. By the time the gangers reappeared for a fourth and final time, an air of quiet desperation hung over the cobbled streets at the dock perimeter. At this stage, much of the crowd was comprised of older, less able men, standing proud but with an anxious look in their eye, knowing full well that this was their last opportunity to earn any money. As the final selection of the day drew to a close, Sims noted, 'You can almost hear a sigh run through the ragged crowd. There comes into some of the pale, pinched faces a look of unutterable woe – the hope that welled up in the heart has sunk back again. There is no chance now. All the men are engaged. As you turn and look at these men and study them, these unfortunate ones, you picture to yourself what the situation means to some of them. What are their thoughts as they turn away? It must be with a heavy heart that (a dock labourer's) wife towards midday hears the sound of her husband's footsteps on the creaking stairs. This advent means no joy to her. That footstep tells its sad, cruel tale in one single creak. He has not been taken on at the Docks.'

For the fortunate men selected by the gangers, life within the dock walls was tough, arduous and unrewarding, both mentally and financially. By presenting themselves for selection at the dock gates, the men automatically made themselves available to undertake any unskilled job that the dock owner or wharfinger (wharf manager) decided to give them. While much of the work involved the unloading of goods from ships, labourers were also expected to tidy and restock the warehouses that lined the dock quays, clear decaying and reeking rubbish, unload railway trucks, replenish all manner of supplies in the storerooms; in fact do their masters' bidding, regardless of how exhausting or degrading their bidding was. Much of the work was outdoors and the men were expected to continue their labours whatever the weather, be it driving rain, freezing sleet or burning midday sun. The day was long and interrupted only by mealtimes and short rest breaks, which gave rise to a cunning ploy created by the dock owners of which the Bryant & May management would have been proud. In a bid to reclaim some of the dock labourers' pay before they had even left the premises, their employers laid on beer carts, which would appear at regular intervals throughout the day. Of course, the beer brought round on the carts was not free, but the labourers were only too pleased to part with some of their hard-earned cash to receive a few minutes' respite from their relentless toil. In turn, the management were delighted to see their money returning to them sometimes less than 24 hours after it had been paid out.

Unfortunately, the drinks on the beer cart were luxuries that most labourers could ill afford. Remuneration for unskilled labour ran at a paltry five pence per hour at the East End docks, while rents for accommodation in even the cheapest areas ran at around 5s a week. Sometimes, the work would take only a couple of hours to complete, which meant that the labourers had to either rejoin the mob outside the dock wall in preparation for the next call-on or return home with a pathetic sum of money in their pocket. Earlier in the 19th century, labourers had been rewarded for unloading ships quickly by receiving a bonus from the dock owner, which was known as 'plus money.' However, by the 1880s, competition between rival docks had seen bonuses cut back to the point where they were barely worth having. Instead of welcoming the 'plus money' as an incentive to work fast, the dock labourers simply saw it as another method of denying them a living wage. Even labourers with 'Royal' status who earned regular bonuses found it very hard to make ends meet, especially if they had a family to support. The ridiculously low pay received by the dock workers was perpetuated by the ease at which the dock owners could employ men. By 1888, supply of casual labour in London massively outstripped demand. The Mansion House Committee estimated 20,000 Londoners were unemployed and philanthropists such as William Booth noted, 'this vast reservoir of unemployed labour is the bane of all efforts to raise the scale of living, to improve the condition of labour.'

The early hour of the first call-on combined with the erratic working schedule meant that commuting to the docks by train or bus from the more affordable suburbs of London was impossible. Therefore, dock labourers had to live within walking distance of their workplace in districts that were among the most run-down and squalid in the capital. However, then as now, the property mantra 'location, location, location' prevailed and the proximity to both the docks and the city meant that rents in areas such as Limehouse, Poplar and Wapping came at a premium despite the parlous state of the housing stock. George Sims wrote, 'It is scandalous that having done all they can, risked life and limb (for dock accidents are numerous and keep a hospital busy), and done their duty in that state of life to which it has pleased God to call them, they should have to creep home to fever dens and pestilential cellars – half the money they pay ought to go for food for themselves and their children, instead of into the well-lined pockets of those who are making fortunes out of the death-traps they call House Property.'

There is no doubt that the constant battle to make ends meet took a serious toll on the dock labourers' mental health – they were notorious for drinking to excess and reports abound of vicious domestic abuse. The journalist Thomas Wright noted that many labourers regarded wife-beating as 'the commonest of marital rights, and to judge from the manner in which the women take the beatings, they would seem to hold the same view. There can be no doubt indeed – strange as the assertion may sound – that some of the wives would regard with suspicion a husband who never laid his hand upon them save in the way of kindness.' Additionally, many dock labouring families were malnourished due to a diet that consisted almost exclusively of bread and cheese. While compiling his book *In Darkest England*, William Booth interviewed a casual labourer at the docks who told him that he and his family 'had only 1lb of bread between us yesterday.' In addition, Booth discovered that the docker was 'six weeks in arrears of rent, and is afraid that he will be ejected. The furniture which is in his home is not worth three shillings and the clothes of each member of his family are in a tattered state and hardly fit for the rag bag.'

By the summer of 1889, the dockers' miserable life of low pay and dreadful living and working conditions meant that something had to give. The breaking point finally came on 14 August, when the *Lady Armstrong* sailed into the West India Docks with a hold full of cargo. Keen to get the ship unloaded as quickly as possible, but reluctant to pay much extra for doing so, the dock management offered the labourers a pathetic amount of 'plus money' and instructed them to look lively. This proved to be the last straw. The exhausted, hungry men finally decided that they were no longer prepared to put up with blatant exploitation and under the leadership of fellow worker and unionist Ben Tillett they packed up their belongings and walked out of the dock. This was an incredibly brave move on behalf of the men: they would almost certainly be blacklisted by the dock management and if events did not go according to plan, it was doubtful they would ever find work on the docks again. However, Tillett passionately believed that a walk-out was the right course of action and reminded the men of the match girls' noble achievements down the road at the Bow factory of Bryant & May.

The West India Docks labourers' walk-out had a stunning effect on the Port of London. Two days later, labourers from the East India and Surrey Commercial Docks joined them on strike and by 19 August the action had spread to the Millwall, Royal and Tilbury Docks. The dock owners faced another unexpected blow when the Amalgamated Stevedores' Union (the members of which were essential for loading vessels) decided to come out in sympathy with the labourers. By 20 August, the strike had extended to the entire Port of London, *The Times* noting, 'men of almost every branch of work came out and joined the movement on behalf of the labourers.' Contemporary estimates suggest that as many as 100,000 men were on strike at this point and the streets of east London teemed with dockers busily organising picket lines and delivering tub-thumping speeches to rapt and enthusiastic audiences.

Empowered by the unprecedented support received from their fellow workers, Ben Tillett's fledgling Dock, Wharf, Riverside and General Labourers' Union rapidly received thousands of new members and it soon became clear that a manifesto detailing the dockers' demands needed to be drawn up as quickly as possible. Realising that he would need expert assistance to bring the strike to a satisfactory conclusion, Tillett called on the services of several colleagues whose experience and knowledge would be crucial. Tom Mann, a member of the Social

Democratic Federation with experience of drumming up support during the match girls' strike, was drafted in to organise relief for the striking workers and their families. Trade unionist John Burns was brought in to assist in both the creation of the strike manifesto and negotiations on the workers' behalf. Tillett, Mann and Burns were ably abetted by several other key figures in the trades union movement including Will Thorne, the founder of the National Gasworkers' Union, Joseph Havelock Wilson of the National Sailors' and Firemen's Union, and socialist publisher Henry Hyde Champion. Now the strike committee was in place, the manifesto was drawn up and presented to the dock owners. The key demand from the workers was an advance in pay to 6d for daytime work and 8d overtime (they were currently paid 5d). In addition, the insulting 'plus money' was to be abolished and workers were to be employed for a minimum of four hours per day, thus reducing the need for so many of the despised call-ons, which were to be reduced to just two per day. Finally, the workers demanded that their union was recognised by the dock owners.

Of course, the dock owners rejected the demands out of hand, dismissing them as totally unworkable schemes that would drive the London docks out of business. They argued that any increase in labourers' wages would have to be passed on to the ship owners, who in turn would dock at cheaper ports elsewhere in the country. Talks broke down and the two sides reached a stalemate, leaving many of the workers with grave misgivings about continuing. On 30 August, a journalist from *The Times* visited east London and encountered the striking men who stood, 'in clusters on the pavement, now listless, and now listening to the observations of a casual speaker. They sit in rows with their backs to the street walls, patient and without occupation. In effect, some 80,000 of the poorest men in London, the men who can less than others afford to be out of work, are doing nothing and, in spite of the help they are receiving from outside, the sight is one of the most pitiable upon which the human eye could rest.'

The *Times* writer was absolutely correct in his observations. Although the dock workers were receiving financial assistance from other unions and sympathetic members of the public, supporting around 80,000 families was an extremely tall order. The strike committee attempted to attract as much publicity as possible by organising rousing daily rallies in order to drum up more support and keep the causes of the strike in the newspapers. Workers were instructed to assemble at a pre-ordained spot in the morning and then march to the rally destination where men such as John Burns would give inspiring speeches, imploring the men not to lose their resolve. These rallies were quite a sight to be seen along the East End streets. On 20 August, *The Times* reported that men with 'banners of various descriptions and brass bands, marched round the docks and wharves and through a number of streets. The procession was between one and two miles in length, the men walking seven deep.'

In deference to the French Revolution a century before, the bands' favourite refrain was the 'Marseillaise'. In addition to the inspiring rallies, the strike committee did their best to ensure that all donations were put to good use and distributed fairly. Monies received were converted into meal tickets and distributed among the dockers, who redeemed them at local shops. Moreover, the Salvation Army provided indispensable help in the form of hastily set up soup kitchens. Union members were issued with vouchers for these makeshift refectories and could also purchase extra food at the highly reduced rate of one halfpenny for a large piece of bread and a 'basin' of soup. Some of the Salvation Army soup kitchens were so well attended that up to 9,000 loaves of bread were ordered on a nightly basis to feed the hordes of hungry dockers that streamed through their doors every morning.

Although East End bakers were evidently kept busy by the strike, many other businesses suffered greatly from the sudden mass unemployment. The pubs, which were generally heaving at the end of the afternoon dock shifts, stood empty. Shopkeepers complained at the severe downturn in trade and the much-criticised landlords tightened their belts as rents were left unpaid. Although much maligned by both their tenants and social commentators, it appears that many property owners accepted that the strike would inevitably mean a loss in revenue. A journalist who visited the East End on 30 August wrote, 'I came across a strange phenomenon in the shape of a notice, set up by the lessee or owner of a house, to the effect that although he disapproved of strikes generally as tending to produce a permanently deleterious effect on trade, he was yet so firmly convinced of the justice of the dock labourers' cause that he had determined to let his tenants occupy their rooms rent free until the strike came to an end.'

As negotiations continued between the dock owners and the strike committee, the ship owners were becoming increasingly restless. By the end of August, the Thames was full of vessels waiting to unload their freight. This veritable blockade of ships provided a spectacle never before witnessed in the great River Thames. Elegant sailing ships with elegantly carved bows and tall canvas-wrapped masts rocked silently in the water, their elaborate figureheads surveying the abandoned waterside landscape. Close by, colossal ocean-going steamers, their holds packed with rapidly decaying cargo, sat low in the docks, waiting for their massive loads to be discharged onto the dockside. Below deck, sailors wandered the narrow, airless passages, listlessly searching for sleeping quarters that were not heavy with the stench of foodstuffs gradually rotting in the heat of the August sun. On deck, crew lounged around in a state of ennui, finding temporary excitement in trivial occupations and apparently endless games of cards. Many of these sailors were regular visitors to the London docks and proved indispensable to the striking labourers as they used some of their seemingly infinite spare time identifying any 'black-legs' who entered the dock incognito and relaying their intelligence to the picket lines.

Outside the docks, smaller ships waited patiently by the city's ancient network of wharves, their captains and crew growing increasingly anxious as each day saw little change to the strike deadlock. Many of the ships that used the wharves were owned by small firms who could ill afford to have their ships inactive for any length of time and, by the end of August, some were beginning to contemplate the prospect of bankruptcy. In an attempt to discharge their goods so they could once again set sail, some ship owners began to negotiate with the lightermen, who were responsible for taking 'overside' deliveries of cargo onto smaller open-topped craft and carrying it over to the wharves where it could be unloaded. Some discussions resulted in a successful deal being brokered and a few vessels were unloaded, but this was nowhere near enough to clear the congestion on the Thames.

By 1889, there were around 300 wharves dotted along the banks of the Thames between the city and the border with Kent. These historic quays (many of which had existed long before the docks were built) were responsible for unloading around 50% of the shipping entering the Port of London. Therefore, the successful unloading of a handful of ships made precious little difference to the overall picture. By the beginning of September, the passenger steamers that carried thousands of commuting Londoners back and forth along the Thames were having to negotiate a veritable slalom course of tall ships, cargo steamers and empty lighters as they picked their way up and down stream. It was clear to all involved that a resolution had to be reached, but still the dock management refused to bow to the workers' demands, preferring instead to try other methods of getting their docks back to work. Striking labourers and stevedores were enticed back into the docks with promises of anonymity and large 'bonuses'. However, sympathetic sailors tipped off the strike committee who in turn planted their own men in the 'black-leg' gangs and achieved great success in persuading their fellow workers back out on strike. The dock owners also employed the help of young men from the city, who would come to work in the docks after finishing their normal day's employment. This practice met with some success and a few ships were unloaded, but the men's enthusiasm did not compensate for their inexperience and progress proved ridiculously slow.

By the beginning of September, matters were reaching breaking point for all involved. The strike committee was rapidly running out of money and the resolve of many workers began to dissipate as they realised that, sooner or later, the strike fund was going to run dry. The wharfingers were particularly frustrated with the situation, especially as many of them argued that they paid the striking labourers the six pence per hour already. In a bid to extricate themselves from the strike action, some wharf managers began to negotiate separately with the workers and a few were successful in getting their wharves back to work fulltime. The tolerance of the ship owners was also wearing thin. With many of their ships stranded in the Thames and crews sitting about with nothing to do, they began to devise ways to persuade their own men to offload the goods so they could free up their vessels. Luckily for the dock workers, the majority of the sailors refused to jeopardise the strike.

As the war of attrition continued between the dock owners and the workers, the scent of insurrection pervaded the East End air. Slowly, industrial action began to break out in other sectors as several trades became inspired by the bravery and commitment of the dockers. By 4 September, 6,000 tailors from the notoriously decrepit sweatshops of the East End had gone on strike and meetings were being held by cigar makers and boot finishers to discuss the creation of their own manifestos. The authorities began to realise that there was a very real threat of a general strike if they did not succeed in bringing the action at the docks to an end quickly. In response, the Lord Mayor of London, James Whitehead, formed a Mansion House Committee in an attempt to improve the dialogue between the dock owners, managers and workers. Aware of the antipathy that existed, Whitehead wisely searched for an unbiased third party to mediate between the warring factions. The man he chose was to have a profound effect on the outcome of the strike.

Cardinal Henry Manning was an elderly Catholic bishop who, on the face of things, appeared to be an odd choice of mediator. In fact, Manning was an extremely well-qualified man for the job. The son of a West India Company merchant, he had personal experience of the work that went on in the Port of London, particularly from the point of view of the dock owners and shipping companies. That said, his work with the church had also given him valuable insight into the deprivation faced by the poor and he had developed a keen interest in the growing trade union movement, the objectives of which he approved of wholeheartedly. Drawing on his knowledge of both sides of the disagreement, Manning managed to convince the dock owners to take the unprecedented step of giving the dockers' demands serious consideration. While the dock workers had a strong ally in the shape of Cardinal Manning, they also found their position suddenly strengthened due to an unexpected turn of events.

The international nature of the dock trade meant that news of the strike had gradually spread across the globe. The dockers had been pleasantly surprised to receive donations from as far afield as New York and Philadelphia, but America's financial assistance was about to be dwarfed by the generosity of men and women living on the other side of the world. As talks at the Mansion House continued, donations from Australian dock workers began to arrive at the strike committee headquarters. Many ex-East End dockers had either emigrated or been transported to Australia in the earlier part of the 19th century, and so felt a strong bond with the men they had left behind in London. Once news of the strike filtered through to the Australian dockyards, the men really got behind the cause and the initial trickle of donations to the strike fund became a veritable torrent. In total, the Australian dock workers sent over an incredible £30,000 in relief money. Suddenly, their colleagues in London realised they could continue their strike indefinitely. Admitting defeat and enthusiastically encouraged by Cardinal Manning, the dock owners agreed to the following crucial terms:

1. The 5d rate per hour to be raised in the case of all labour ... in and after November 4th next to 6d per hour, and 8d per hour overtime.
2. Men called in not to be discharged with less than 2s pay, except in regard to special short engagements in the afternoon.
3. The hours of overtime at the docks and up-town warehouses shall be from 6pm to 6am.

The dockers had achieved their objective. In victorious mood, they returned to work on 16 September to better pay, improved conditions and, most importantly, new-found respect from their employers.

The dock strike of 1889 was a watershed in the development of the labour movement as it bonded unskilled and previously unorganised workers into a union. Men and women across the country watched the activities of the dock workers and realised that they did not need a skilled trade to protect themselves from exploitation. In turn, employers were shocked into realising that men and women whom they had previously perceived as being powerless could collectively present a real threat to the efficient running of their businesses. Ben Tillett's Dock, Wharf, Riverside and General Labourers' Union, which had been at the centre of the strike, rapidly grew in numbers. In 1910 it amalgamated with the National Union of Dock Workers and the National Sailors' and Firemen's Union to form the National Transport Workers' Federation, which in turn became part of the Transport and General Workers' Union (now known as Unite) in 1922. These unions continued to play a major part in the development of working practices throughout the 20th century and marked the end of an era when working men and women were at the mercy of the whims of their employers.

18

THE BEGINNING OF THE END

The great dock strike of 1889 was just one of a series of problems that afflicted the Port of London in the late 19th century. One of the major causes for concern was that many of the enclosed docks were becoming totally inaccessible to the increasing number of huge vessels now arriving in the port. Not only were the basins too small, the Thames was too shallow in places for large steamers to safely negotiate. The London and St Katharine Dock Company's bold decision to build the Royal Albert deep-water dock paid off as the new complex took trade away from the older, smaller sites further down the Thames. In contrast, the East and West India Dock's response – Tilbury – had been a financial disaster. This distant new dock had cost double the projected amount to construct and failed to attract sufficient custom. The company was forced to sell off assets to offset the cost of keeping its white elephant, which given the general state of trade put it in a financially precarious position.

The East and West India Docks Company's predicament was made worse by the wharfingers who, in addition to boycotting Tilbury, also lowered their warehousing rates to levels at which the enclosed docks simply could not compete. The once bustling quaysides gradually degenerated into conveniently sited moorings from which cargoes were transported to independent wharves. The huge warehouses that surrounded them stood half empty. Joseph Conrad described the West India Docks in 1897 thus:

> The stony shores ran away right and left in straight lines, enclosing a sombre and rectangular pool. Brick walls rose high above the water – soulless walls, staring through hundreds of windows as troubled and dull as the eyes of overfed brutes.

By the mid-1880s, the enclosed docks companies realised that their warehousing rates would have to be cut if they were to have any hope of remaining solvent. This proved to be the final nail in the coffin for the East and West India Docks Company. In 1887, the board dramatically cut salaries and maintenance budgets in a last-ditch attempt to remain in business, but the outlook remained bleak. In March 1888, the company was forced to go into receivership and was facing liquidation when the London and St Katharine Docks Company (which had been interested in acquiring the site for some time) offered it a lifeline. Their board offered to buy the East and West India Docks and allow its directors to continue managing the site, although overall control would pass to the London and St Katharine Docks Company. The India Docks board had little option but to accept the offer and on 1 January 1889, the London and India Docks Joint Committee was formed

Realising that co-operation with other dock companies was now imperative to their survival, the joint committee quickly opened up talks with the Millwall and the Surrey Commercial Docks. The three companies agreed that each dock should specialise in handling specific cargoes, thus reducing competition and hopefully stabilising trade. The scheme proved to be temporarily successful and by the 1890s, the enclosed docks' financial fortunes had recovered sufficiently for a series of improvements to be implemented that made them more attractive and accessible to large steamships. Entrance locks were enlarged and basins deepened, while many of the adjacent warehouses installed refrigeration plants to compete with those at Hay's Wharf. However, despite the dock companies' best efforts, trade at the Port of London continued to decline. Competition from rival sites, in particular Liverpool, combined with the problems caused by the 'free water clause', which constantly threatened the enclosed docks' warehouse trade, eventually prompted state intervention. A royal commission was set up to identify and address the root causes of the difficulties facing the port and after an exhaustive inquiry, the commission concluded in 1902 that there was only one way to save the enclosed docks – nationalise them.

The dock companies were horrified at this suggestion but were in no position to argue. The Port of London Bill passed through Parliament in 1908 and on 31 March 1909, the state assumed control of the enclosed docks, assigning to them a new governing body – the Port of London

Authority (PLA). The new authority's remit was huge. It took control of almost 3,000 acres of prime commercial land, 32 miles of quays and a body of water twice the size of Hyde Park. In addition to running the docks, it was responsible for the Thames from Teddington to the estuary and immediately set about dredging the river to allow larger ships access to the docks closer to the city centre. In a bid to eliminate competition between the once rival docks, it also reduced and then fixed the rates for berthing vessels, a move that was welcomed by the merchants and ship owners, who had grown frustrated at having to barter constantly with the individual dock companies.

The PLA's action produced the required results. By 1912, the London docks had re-established themselves as Britain's premier port, with foreign trade being valued at almost £400 million per annum. Major imports included tea, timber, grain, meat, sugar, tobacco and wines. In April 1914, a journalist from *The Times* visited the docks' vast warehouses in which these commodities were stored and wrote:

> The wine and spirit vaults at the London Docks, interminable labyrinths of gas-lit darkness – the gangways that run between the piers supporting the roof, thickly grown, where wine is stowed, with masses of fungus – are 28½ miles in length. Of the annual import of wool, 20 million pounds in value, shorn from the backs of 90 million sheep, a third passes through the warehouses of the Authority, which provides for this one trade a floor space of 32 acres. It can also store at one time a million of the 10 or 11 million carcasses of mutton and the 120,000 tons of beef that Australia, New Zealand and South America send to London in the course of a year. These ... are enough in themselves to show how all important is the ... duty that the Port Authority is called upon to fulfil.

The effect that the PLA's improvements had on trade created surplus capital to make additional improvements to facilities, which in turn attracted more shipping. By 1939, London held a 38% share of British sea-borne trade, up from just 29% in 1909, and over 60 million tons of cargo was handled by the port. As early as the mid-1910s, trade had increased to such an extent that the docks were finding it hard to cope with the endless cargoes arriving at their quays. Some merchants began to blame the slow rate at which ships were dealt with on the dock labourers who quickly issued a response via the secretary of the Dockers' Union, Alderman W. Devenay, who stated, 'It is true that docks and wharves are crowded with shipping, that there are a number of vessels lying off Gravesend awaiting berths, that there is plenty of work for us dockers, but we cannot get it to do, for there are not sufficient berths, sufficient lighters, nor sufficient warehousing space for the enormous traffic on the Thames these days.'

In reaction to the dilemma, the PLA set about building additional warehousing for 600,000 tons of goods, drew up plans for improving access to some of the older basins and began construction of a massive extension of the Royal Albert Dock. However, many of the new storage facilities were commandeered in 1914 by the War Office, which was hastily forced to divert hundreds of vessels to the Port of London following Britain's declaration of war on Germany on 4 August.

Despite the disruption caused to the port following the outbreak of war, the PLA continued with some of its improvement works throughout the remaining months of 1914 and the following year. The entrance lock to the East India Docks was widened to accommodate steamers of up to 8,000 tons, more warehouses were built at the London and West India Docks, and excavation continued at the Royal Docks' extension. However, by the beginning of 1916, the majority of these works were forcibly put on hold when it became impossible to obtain the necessary machinery to complete the projects.

The docks were not the only district where commercial activity was restricted by the advent of war. By 1916, thousands of factories throughout Britain and the Continent had been requisitioned by governments. Production of all manner of goods was severely disrupted and, consequently, so were the activities of the merchants at the docks. In a bid to bolster the economy, the Board of Trade set up an annual British Industries Fair in 1914 at the Pennington Street warehouses of the London Docks. The fair, which ran for 10 days in March, promoted British goods that were still being produced, including pottery and glassware, stationery and toys. Publicity for the event in 1918 reported, 'Much has been done by the Commercial Intelligence Department of the

Board of Trade since the outbreak of war to assist British firms to capture trade from their German and Austro-Hungarian competitors, and our manufacturers are now reaping the reward of their enterprise and are ousting many enemy-made goods from the world market.'

While luxury goods manufacturers were displaying their wares at the trade exhibition, others had been forced to engage in the altogether more dangerous business of producing munitions for the British military. When Britain declared war on Germany, she was totally unprepared for a long conflict and ammunition supplies quickly began to run out. In an attempt to rectify the situation, the Ministry of Munitions started to search for suitable sites in which to produce the various components of ammunition, including the volatile explosive known as TNT. One of the sites investigated for this purpose was the Brunner Mond chemical works at Crescent Wharf in Silvertown. On learning that the ministry wanted them to work with a highly explosive chemical, the directors at Brunner Mond expressed their grave reservations. Their works were situated in a heavily populated area and any accidents that might occur could prove catastrophic. However, despite their protestations, the government refused to search for an alternative site and production of TNT began in September 1915.

The staff at Brunner Mond were instructed to treat the highly volatile substance with utmost care and for the first 14 months work continued with no major mishaps. However, on the evening of 19 January 1917, the unthinkable happened when a fire broke out at the works, causing a massive explosion that blew both the factory and several adjacent streets literally to pieces. Some 900 houses were totally destroyed and up to 70,000 more were badly damaged by the blast. Commercial premises at the Royal Docks had their windows blown out and many Silvertown wharves were consumed by the numerous fires that broke out in the wake of the explosion.

Under normal circumstances, an event as calamitous as this would have attracted the scrutiny of the national press. However, desperate to avoid news of the disaster reaching the enemy, the government forced the papers to run a hastily prepared statement that simply read, 'The Ministry of Munitions regrets to announce that an explosion occurred last evening at a munitions factory in the vicinity of London. It is feared that the explosion was attended by considerable loss of life and damage to property.'

Although the horrific events at Silvertown suffered from a news blackout, the local authorities responded effectively to the disaster. The day after the explosion, local councillors visited the devastated site and set up an explosion emergency committee to oversee the clearance of debris, organise temporary housing and provide medical assistance for those injured. The committee also set up a relief office in Canning Town where affected residents could apply for aid and seek compensation, which eventually amounted to a massive £3 million. In total, 73 people died in the Silvertown explosion. Although this figure was dreadful, it could have been much higher if the fire had broken out while workers were still in the factory. The resulting inquiry into the tragedy concluded that, while the fire had started by accident, the Ministry of Munitions was at great fault for locating such a dangerous works in a heavily populated area. It also criticised Brunner Mond's management for not taking greater care in protecting its workers by installing a 24-hour security team to watch for fires. The government chose not to make the inquiry's damning findings public and the report was locked away in a filing cabinet until the 1950s. Due to the lack of press coverage, the explosion and its terrible aftermath passed quickly from public memory and most of the residents of Silvertown chose not to speak of the awful night. That said, the site of the fated Brunner Mond works was conscientiously avoided by developers throughout the following decades and is today a car park for visitors to the Thames flood barrier.

Explosions in munitions factories were not the only threat Londoners had to live with during the dark days of World War 1. In April 1914, Colonel Louis Jackson published a paper entitled *The Defence of Localities against Aerial Attack* in which he expressed his severe concerns that London, and particularly the docks, had no defence against an attack from the air. Aware of the rising tensions in Europe, Jackson presciently warned, 'I have no wish to be alarmist or to make anyone's flesh creep, but … it seems to me that we cannot help accepting the fact that in three years or less, London will be exposed to the form of attack I have indicated.'

Following the declaration of war that August, London prepared itself for attack as best it could. On 19 August, the *Berliner Tageblatt* newspaper – who still had a correspondent in London – wrote, 'All public buildings, the General Post Office, the chief telegraph and telephone offices are barricaded and double steel wire nets and iron posts protect them from bombs.' At the docks, the Admiralty's requisition of ships and warehouses for military use made it sometimes impossible for commercial vessels to find moorings. This produced a shortage of some imported goods, particularly foodstuffs, and to make matters worse, the public embarked on a frenzied wave of panic buying, reducing supplies even further. The *Berliner Tageblatt* took delight in reporting, 'Fresh eggs cost 2½ pence apiece; sugar costs three times as much as before; butter is scarce. The provision of food will probably create difficulties for England.'

Although Londoners braced themselves for air raids, for the first months of the war Colonel Jackson's prediction remained unfulfilled. In October 1914, *The Times* reported, 'London just now ... is curiously like a stout-hearted householder who suspects the presence of a burglar under his roof and goes forth, candle in hand, to reconnoitre. There is no fear, but there is anticipation – anxious anticipation.' This anxiety made the continuation of business impossible for German merchants and ship owners who were forced to close their operations after being banned from the Baltic Exchange and several other markets' subscription rooms. Other businesses run by people of German extraction were regarded with suspicious eyes, regardless of how long the proprietors had been living amongst them. Animosity towards these people sometimes descended into violence. In October 1914, a group of men were arrested following anti-German disturbances at Deptford, during which a bakery run by a Mr Gobel was smashed up by a mob, causing £400 worth of damage. In nearby Evelyn Street the Harp of Erin pub, which had a landlord of German descent, was also badly damaged when a gang strode in and threatened the staff.

In a bid to allay fears of a German air strike on the British mainland, the fledgling Royal Flying Corps embarked on a series of raids on enemy airfields with some degree of success. However, by the closing weeks of 1914, the public's worst fears were realised when a German aeroplane appeared over the Kent coast on Christmas Eve and dropped a single bomb into a private garden close to Dover Castle before hastily retreating across the Channel. The next day, the inhabitants of towns along the Thames estuary were alarmed to see another German plane, which daringly followed the course of the Thames as far as Erith in Kent before being forced to turn back by a British biplane.

Although the two enemy planes caused little damage, the threat of a German air strike on civilians turned from being a remote possibility to a very real threat – the first time that the British mainland had been jeopardised in this way. In order to calm the atmosphere of dread that was rapidly pervading the streets, the government published safety advice on what to do in the event of an air attack, along with repeated assurances that such an assault was still extremely unlikely. The instructions warned people to stay indoors if an enemy aircraft was spotted, stating, 'The chances of any given building being struck by a bomb from an aircraft are extremely remote and, though a bomb might do much damage and cause injury and perhaps loss of life in a particular building, it is held that many more casualties would result if people flocked into the streets, where they would be exposed to bullets and flying fragments of shell from anti-aircraft guns.'

While the government was correct in assuming that relatively little damage could be inflicted by a single German aeroplane, it failed to mention in its safety advice that considerably more devastation could be wreaked by a full-scale organised raid involving fleets of planes or Zeppelin airships, which were capable of speeds up to 85mph and could carry two tons of bombs.

The first Zeppelin to appear in British skies during the conflict arrived in January 1915 when an air raid was launched on the coastal towns of Great Yarmouth and King's Lynn. Following the attack the *United Press*'s Berlin correspondent, Karl H. von Wiegard, asked the airship's creator, Count von Zeppelin, 'Is it planned to make an aerial attack upon London?' To which the count chillingly replied, 'That is a question that you should direct to the Admiralty or the General Staff.'

Over the months following the raid on the Norfolk coast, German air attacks became more frequent, more destructive and strayed closer to the capital – one raid on 31 May even reaching the outskirts of the city. The previously relaxed advice on the course of action during an air assault was rewritten and the public were advised that, in addition to staying indoors, householders should keep a supply of water and sand on the upper floors of their homes so that any small fires that broke out as a result of a bomb blast could be extinguished. Doors to all rooms should be closed at all times to 'prevent the admission of noxious gases' and makeshift gas masks should be made by tying gauze containing cotton pads soaked in a strong solution of washing soda round the nose and mouth. In addition to this, Londoners were urged to turn off their gas supply every night in case the mains were struck by a bomb.

The revised warnings were timely. On 8 September, the Port of London and the districts surrounding it were bombarded by explosive and incendiary bombs dropped from one of Count Zeppelin's airships, causing a huge amount of damage to business and private property and resulting in significant casualties. The German military were jubilant about their first onslaught on the city, Count Reventlow bombastically threatening, 'The coming days of autumn and early winter, with their ever-lengthening nights, will, we hope, provide plenty of opportunities to show London, the "heart" of the money world, what we think of its sanctity, and we hope that every visit will be more emphatic and thorough than the one before it.'

Londoners were understandably incredulous at the unprecedented threat of assault from the skies. The journalist William G. Shepherd of the *United Press* was in London during the 8 September Zeppelin raid and vividly described the scene on the streets.

> Among the autumn stars floats a long, gaunt Zeppelin. It is dull yellow – the colour of the harvest moon. The fingers of the search lights, reaching up from the roofs of the city, are touching all sides of the death messenger with their white tips. Great bombing sounds shake the city. They are Zeppelin bombs – falling – killing – burning.

In an attempt to reduce the devastation caused by any future raids, the government ordered a blackout of the city every night and insisted that the dock warehouses, many of which stored inflammable goods, should be guarded at all hours by a member of staff trained in fire-fighting.

As the residents and businesses at the docks defended themselves as best they could, the Zeppelin raids on London continued. On 13 October, a particularly destructive raid on the docks produced extremely large losses. A huge warehouse full of ammunition at the East India Docks suffered a direct hit and was razed to the ground. Further west, at the London Docks,

German bombs succeeded in destroying another warehouse along with several ships that were moored at the quayside. A cotton warehouse in the Royal Victoria Dock was also destroyed. Numerous workers lost their homes as terraces along St George's and Leman Streets were hit, the railways running through East Ham were badly damaged by explosives and the Woolwich Arsenal was also partially destroyed.

By the end of 1915, the people of London were becoming weary of the bombing raids. What had first been a novel and somewhat exciting spectacle had now taken on a much grimmer significance as the number of deaths and severe injuries increased with every attack. Even children, who had first greeted the arrival of the Zeppelins with naïve excitement, had come to understand the horror of the raids. An 11-year-old girl interviewed by Dr C. W. Kimmins, the Chief Inspector for Schools for the London County Council, told him that the air attacks 'make one realise what war is; and yet dropping bombs on harmless people is not war. That night [after a raid] I felt bitter towards the Germans. I felt I could fly to Germany and do the same thing to them.' The children interviewed by Dr Kimmins were not just angry at the raids. Many, particularly the older girls, were very scared of them. One told him, 'I could have seen the Zeppelins, but I thought if I do, I shall always see them when I look up into the sky, so I would not look at them.'

Despite the ongoing efforts of the anti-aircraft gunners and the Royal Flying Corps, the huge Zeppelins proved surprisingly difficult to shoot down. This was largely due to two factors. Firstly, they travelled at a height that was out of reach of the guns on the ground. Secondly, the British fighter planes, which were manned by two people at the most, were faced with the task of attacking a massive, heavily armed adversary with a far more stable and effective fighting platform, operated by considerably more men. From the Zeppelins' first appearance over the British mainland, rich rewards had been offered to the first person who succeeded in bringing one of them down but until September 1916 all attempts had failed. However, on Sunday 3 September, a 16-strong Zeppelin fleet emerged from the clouds along the east coast *en route* to a mass bombing raid on various English locations, including the Royal Docks. In response, planes from the Royal Flying Corps were scrambled, one of which was piloted by Captain William Leefe Robinson of No 39

Squadron, based at Sutton Farm in Essex, not far from the docks. Captain Robinson and several colleagues headed for the Thames where they encountered one of the Zeppelins preparing to leave the scene of destruction and return to its base. The British fighter pilots pursued the airship and began bombarding it with gunfire, forcing its crew to change course and head north in a bid to escape. By this time, the aerial battle was causing quite a scene on the ground. A writer for *The Times* excitedly wrote, 'The bombardment was at its height and the shells were bursting round the Zeppelin in a wonderful pyrotechnic display … we guessed our airmen were engaged in a duel with the enemy. It must have been a dangerous and nerve-trying fight, for the shells were still mounting and exploding, and the wonder was that none of the aeroplanes was hit.' As the airship desperately tried to escape its pursuers, Captain Robinson managed to get his aircraft under the Zeppelin and then swooped up towards it, riddling its side with gunfire. To everyone's amazement, the airship staggered a short distance before bursting into flames and crashing into a field behind The Plough public house in the rural village of Cuffley in Hertfordshire. All hands were lost.

Captain Robinson quickly became a national hero for proving that the previously invincible Zeppelins could be overcome. He was awarded the Victoria Cross for his valiant efforts and also received a prize of £1,000 from Lord Michelham. Most importantly, Captain Robinson's strategy for attacking the airship was taken up by other pilots and within weeks another Zeppelin had been shot down, this time over Essex, by Second Lieutenant Frederick Sowrey. Following these two losses, the German military decided to scale down the amount of airship raids on the British mainland.

Back at the docks, the nature of trade had taken on a very different form since the outbreak of war. By 1917, many of the younger dock workers had gone to fight and many were destined never to return. The PLA war memorial alone lists 403 employees who lost their lives in the Great War. It is impossible to calculate how many other dockers, sailors, wharfingers and merchants also laid down their lives for their country. In addition to the sudden dearth of workers, the business at the docks changed from being almost exclusively commercial in early 1914 to being increasingly military in nature. However, despite these changes, the dock workers became caught up in the fervent patriotism that prevailed throughout the United Kingdom during the dark days of World War 1. On Sunday 27 May 1917, a huge rally was organised in Hyde Park by the British Workers' League to show support for the military effort. The main event of the day was a series of rousing speeches given by a number of influential individuals connected with the labour movement, including Ben Tillett of the Dockers' Union. Following the speeches, the congregation proceeded to the French Embassy at Albert Gate where they were received by the ambassadors of several allied countries including the USA, Japan, Russia and Italy. Many unions connected with the docks were represented, including the National Unions of Sailors and Firemen, who carried a banner that provoked loud cheers from the watching crowd as it proclaimed, 'We are men of the sea who are not afraid of the Hun pirates. We meet them daily.'

Although events such as the British Workers' League march raised morale, the resolve of Londoners, particularly those living and working near Germany's prime target of the docks, was tested to the limit. Throughout the remainder of 1917, air attacks continued along the banks of the Thames. On 13 June, a particularly destructive raid on the East End succeeded in killing over 40 people (10 of whom were children in a school), and injuring hundreds more. The deaths of young innocents were impossible to justify. A sailor who went to help with the rescue effort was on the verge of tears as he explained, 'I could have stood it, if (the victims) had been grown men … But these little children – it is too much.'

Despite the horrors facing them on a weekly basis, the workers at the docks pressed on with fortitude, although the amount of commercial goods they handled was now greatly diminished. By March 1918, the amount of commercial shipping entering or leaving the port had reduced by approximately 35% compared with figures from March 1914. However, following the German request for armistice negotiations in November 1918, the necessity for a military presence at the docks lessened. As warehouses were gradually returned to commercial use, the PLA became anxious to get the Port of London back in business. It need not have worried. The restrictions on commercial shipping imposed throughout Europe during wartime had resulted in a huge backlog of cargoes at the Continental ports. As soon as trade restrictions were lifted, the Port of London became overrun with shipments – to the point where the warehousemen found it difficult to cope. In response, the PLA quickly resumed the improvements to the port that had been put on hold during the war. Building work on new warehousing recommenced and, most importantly, the extension to the Royal Albert Dock could now be completed.

Work on the new dock had begun in 1912 and for the first two years carried on apace. Inevitably, the outbreak of war brought construction practically to a standstill, leaving a vast basin lying unfilled and redundant on the Royal Albert's southern perimeter. However, virtually as soon as the war came to an end, work recommenced and by February 1919 the site was ready to accept shipping.

The new dock was named the King George V in deference to the monarch who had succeeded to the throne in 1910. Its vast perimeter walls towered over neighbouring Silvertown, reminding one visiting journalist of 'some monument of Assyrian or ancient Egyptian architecture.' The dock's entrance basin, which measured a colossal 800ft long by 100ft wide, was accessed from the Thames by a great lock and could also be reached via a cut that led from the Royal Albert Dock. Beyond this lay the main dock, its deep waters capable of holding up to 15 of the largest steamers. On its southern edge, seven concrete jetties lay parallel with the quay along which ships' cargoes could be discharged by electric cranes which lifted the goods into barges moored alongside the vessel or conveyed them directly onto the quay for transferral to one of the huge transit sheds that lay close by. At the western end of the main basin was a dry dock measuring 750ft by 100ft, with a depth of 35ft – capable of accommodating a 25,000-ton ship.

In order to construct this majestic new dock complex, the PLA had to demolish a cluster of dock workers' cottages in Silvertown. To replace these homes, it built 204 new houses opposite Beckton Road recreation ground and on the west side of Prince Regent's Lane. This new estate was designed using the fashionable 'garden village' model that had first been created by Sir Ebenezer Howard in 1898 and became the template for developments such as Welwyn Garden City in Hertfordshire and Hampstead Garden Suburb in north-west London.

The King George V Dock was officially opened on Friday 8 June 1919 by the King, who arrived by royal yacht amid much pomp and ceremony.

After touring round the new premises, the monarch officially declared the dock open to cheers from the assembled crowd, which were drowned out by the deafening noise of a gun salute fired from the Woolwich Arsenal, across the river. In retrospect, the elaborate celebration that surrounded the dock's opening was fitting, as unbeknownst to the guests that attended the lavish event it would be the last great enclosed dock ever to be built in London.

19

CRASH, DEPRESSION AND CONFLICT

As Britain slowly recovered from the devastating effects of World War 1, the docks experienced a brief period of stability as international trade, particularly with the USA, increased. As the roaring twenties dawned, Europe's need to relax after the anxieties and tremendous loss sustained in the previous decade combined with American prosperity to create an international trade bubble during which rash US investors ploughed money into the European manufacturing industries like never before. However, in September 1929, the US stock market entered a dangerously erratic period of wildly fluctuating commodity values that was rapidly followed by what became known as the Wall Street Crash – a total market collapse that began on 24 October. As the bubble burst, investors desperately tried to recoup their losses by selling their shares in European companies. Many British firms connected with the docks were severely jeopardised as their share values dramatically fell in a matter of days. On 16 November, *The Times* noted, 'There is no denying that recent events (on Wall Street) will, over an indefinite period of months, affect the purchasing power of the American people, and that this will most immediately be felt in the luxury trades, with a repercussion upon foreign exporters to the United States.'

The reduction in cargoes being sent to America was not the only problem facing the docks by the end of the 1920s. Between 1927 and 1929, the amount of goods imported into Britain grew, while exports dwindled. The biggest drop occurred in the 're-export' market whereby goods were shipped into a British port and then split up and distributed to their final overseas destinations. D. J. Owen, the general manager of the PLA, blamed this downturn on the fact that it had recently become much cheaper for ship owners to use the docks at Antwerp, Rotterdam and Hamburg than those in London or Liverpool. Statistics from the period reinforced Owen's theory. In 1929, the cost of berthing and discharging a ship in one of the English ports varied between 4s 9d and 12s per ton. The aforementioned Continental ports charged between 1s 5d and 2s 6d per ton. In addition to the expense of berthing at the UK ports, ship owners using the London docks still had to queue, sometimes for days, in order to obtain moorings, thus losing even more money.

In order to stop the decline of trade in London, the PLA reduced dock rates and devised an advertising campaign to attract new business. Half-page adverts appeared in the press showing impressive aerial photographs of Tilbury and the Royal Docks over the headline 'Take Advantage of London's Advantages.' The copy below urged ship owners and merchants to exploit London's unique status, proclaiming:

> It has the largest consuming population in the United Kingdom. There are 8,000,000 people within 10 miles and 16,000,000 within 100 miles of the docks of London as well as a large floating population on business or pleasure bent.

> London has the best selling and distributing organisation in the World and the Port of London Authority employ their own expert staff for sampling, grading, weighing, bulking and preparing for sale the cream of the world's merchandise entrusted to their keeping in the Port's vast warehouses.

The PLA's efforts paid off. By the time the Authority reached its 21st anniversary in 1930, the declining fortunes of the port had begun to reverse. The long-term figures made particularly satisfying reading. The value of overseas trade had grown from £322,614,363 in 1909 to almost £700 million 21 years later, while the tonnage of shipping handled at the port had increased from 38,510,989 in 1909 to 57,518,355 in 1929. In comparison, the Liverpool docks handled just under 35 million tons of shipping in 1929, while Bristol dealt with just seven million. To celebrate the returning prosperity of the port, the PLA organised a 'London Docks Week' in September 1930, which was designed to show outsiders the incredible waterside facilities the port had to offer. Boat trips down the Thames were organised, stopping off at the enclosed docks, where visitors could disembark and marvel at the huge steamships moored beside enormous warehouses full of rich cargoes. All proceeds from these river trips were donated to the London Hospital in Whitechapel and a charity set up specifically to help the inhabitants of the docks – the Dockland Settlements mission.

The Dockland Settlements had originally been set up by wealthy students of Malvern College in 1895 when the enclosed docks were in severe financial difficulties, causing great hardship for the workers. The first mission opened in Canning Town, close to the Royal Docks. The premises included a nursery, pre- and after-school clubs, workshops where the unemployed could learn new skills, a gymnasium that specialised in boxing, and even a dental surgery. The Canning Town Settlement proved so successful that in 1923 a second building was opened on the Isle of Dogs. Further missions were later established at Poplar, Dagenham and Rotherhithe.

For the remaining years of the 1930s, the docks continued to work profitably despite the ever-present competition from the foreign ports. However, the steady rise of national socialism in Europe resulted in yet another period of disruption and threat for the Port of London when Britain declared war against Germany on 3 September 1939.

As had been the case at the outbreak of World War 1, areas of the docks and many merchant ships were immediately commandeered by the government and by January 1940 the sheer amount of facilities required for the war effort resulted in the government imposing rationing on certain imported commodities. W. S. Morrison, the Minister of Food, explained, 'We must not ask [our seamen] to run unnecessary risks. Having decided to take less [imported goods], there must be perfect fairness in distribution – no first-come-first-served or anything of that kind. We must divide what we have and share out equally, and that can only be done by rationing.'

At first, rationed items comprised bacon, ham, butter and sugar, the majority of which came from overseas. Shortly afterwards, restrictions were extended to all meat and also petrol. As the war progressed, more items were added to the list, including tea (July 1940), cheese (May 1941), eggs (June 1941) and clothing (June 1941). All households were provided with a ration book for foodstuffs (a separate book was issued for clothing). Each time restricted items were purchased, the book was handed over to the retailer, who would remove or deface the relevant coupons. Rationing of the first commodities began on 8 January 1940. Unsurprisingly, in the days prior to its enforcement, shoppers went on a spending spree, buying up as much as they could of the soon to be scarce items. This resulted in severe shortages in the first few days of rationing combined with long queues at the shops as the staff struggled to get to grips with the coupon system. The prospect of further purchasing restrictions prompted some unscrupulous retailers to inflate the prices of non-rationed items on the premise that they might soon be in short supply. This blatant profiteering prompted the government to hastily pass the Prices of Goods Act, which controlled the retail cost of a wide range of merchandise including clothes, tools and utensils, cutlery, textiles, pottery and glass, torches, sandbags and batteries.

The onset of rationing also brought out the creativity of the British public. Calls were made to extend the shooting season so more game could be caught and a raft of new cookery books appeared with titles such as *Ration Recipes for Restricted Repasts* and *How You Can Help Win the War*, which gave instructions on how to make such culinary delights as sugar-free puddings and meatless stews. Families turned parts of their gardens over to vegetable patches and many purchased chickens and even pigs to be bred for food. Ironically the greater effort involved in creating food coupled with the restrictions on fat, meat and sugar resulted in a healthy population for whom the modern medical concern of obesity was virtually unheard of.

While vegetable plots and chicken coops were viable for families living in the suburbs and the countryside, inhabitants of the dockside districts simply did not have the space to embark on such ventures, although some allotments were made available and a few boroughs even set up their own ventures into farming. On 30 December 1940, the *Stratford Express* reported, 'The formation of a Pig Club is East Ham's contribution to the national effort. It is hoped to make a start in the New Year with three sties and 24 pigs, at the Sewage Works, and the proposal is to purchase from the Council some of the kitchen waste which is collected daily from households in the Borough. When ready for the market, the animals will be sold to help increase the nation's bacon supply.'

Despite positive responses to the war such as East Ham's pig club, the older inhabitants' memories of the World War 1 air attacks on the docks gave them uneasy feelings about the coming months. Both the government and its people were under no illusions that London was likely to suffer bombing from enemy planes, the destructive power of which would be far greater and more deadly than anything unleashed by the Germans during the Great War. Consequently, plans were drawn up to evacuate children from all the metropolitan boroughs of London, plus most of Middlesex, the northern towns of Surrey and the Thames-side districts of Essex.

At the beginning of September 1939, London children became part of a three million-strong group of people who were evacuated from towns and cities across Britain to the relative safety of the countryside. In the East End, Myrdle Street School on the Commercial Road was one of the first to be evacuated on 2 September. The *Daily Mirror* recorded that, 'Two hundred children, aged from three to 13, assembled before dawn. Each child carried a gas mask, food and a change of clothing and bore three labels. "Don't suck or eat your labels," the head teacher, Miss D. L. Herbert, told them ... While waiting to be taken away – they did not know where they were going except "to the country for a holiday" – the children had community singing. As dawn was breaking the children marched to Aldgate Metropolitan Station, where they entrained.'

During the months following the children's departure, London suffered no air raids and people began talking of the 'phoney war.' Some bereft parents even went to collect their children from the country after the empty schools and silent streets became too much to bear. William Wood, who lived with his family in Silvertown, had been evacuated to a farm in rural Essex in September 1939 and was surprised to see his mother appear at the house just before Christmas. 'She had come to take me back to London,' he later explained, 'as she couldn't stand being alone in the house without her children. She knew there was a risk in bringing us home, but she was prepared to take it.'

William Wood's mother was not alone in reclaiming her children. By the first months of 1940, many London families had been reunited and the streets once again filled with the noise of youngsters at play. However, that summer the German military shifted their attention from France and on 10 July the Battle of Britain began. The first bombing raid on London took place on the night of Friday 23 August when several German aircraft managed to evade the city's anti-aircraft batteries and succeeded in destroying two cinemas, a bank and numerous houses in east and north London. The following evening, the bombers returned, this time targeting the heart of the city, where incendiary devices started a fierce fire. The inhabitants of the East End were about to become the recipients of the most brutal and relentless assault on British civilians for centuries. Frank Lewey, the mayor of Stepney, later wrote, 'We knew we were in the front line. We have two miles of docks and wharves and vital riverside warehouses; we have almost a hundred miles of roads in less than two thousand acres, and those roads are essential to England's existence; and we have the most cosmopolitan population of any comparable area in the world, offering – as was supposed – a good target for panic.'

In addition to the evacuation of school-age children, gas masks had been issued to the inhabitants of all London boroughs and the whole of the city was put under a 'blackout' curfew to inhibit night-time visibility for any hostile aircraft. The result of all lights in London being obscured or extinguished was impressive. On the first night of the blackout, a journalist from the *Stratford Express* wrote, 'I was somewhere on Silvertown Way when zero hour struck, admiring the distant lights on the river, the panorama of shipping, the lighting effects in the sky caused by the searchlights, and their efforts to fix raiding bombers, when it was practically all snatched from before my eyes and I was almost groping in the darkness.'

Despite the arrangements for civilian protection, nothing could have prepared the residents of the East End for what was about to be unleashed on them. On 7 September 1940, Germany began an unyielding campaign of destruction on the East End of London intended to bring widespread disruption to Britain's centre of commerce and literally to bomb its people into submission. In the late afternoon, the sky over the Port of London filled with an enormous fleet of German bombers accompanied by several hundred fighter planes. Over the following hours, the docks and their surroundings were bombarded. Cyril Demarne, a writer and sub-officer of the West Ham fire brigade later recalled, 'Shortly before five o'clock … the Air Raid Warning Red message was received and the sirens began their wail … Suddenly, squadrons of bombers appeared all over the eastern sky, flying very high and escorted by hundreds of fighter aircraft … Now came an avalanche of bombs raining on the East End of London from an estimated 300 bombers. Flames erupted from the great factories and warehouses lining the River Thames from Woolwich to Tower Bridge. In the crowded dockland streets, massive warehouses and tiny dwellings alike came crashing down under the impact of high explosives, burying under the debris their occupants and any luckless passer-by.' The raid proved devastating as in addition to the damage sustained by the properties surrounding the docks, 436 people lost their lives. The following night, the bombers returned and once again the docks were subjected to heavy bombardment during which numerous fires broke out in the riverside warehouses, destroying thousands of pounds worth of merchandise. In the nearby residential streets, another 300 people were killed. The German press responded hubristically to the first wave of attacks on London – the *Volkischer Beobachter* announced that 'Germans modestly regard this merely as the battle of London from which the battle of Britain will develop.'

The German 'modest' battle tactics proved utterly devastating for the inhabitants of the districts surrounding the docks. Prior to the outbreak of war, many had taken advantage of the government's distribution of Anderson shelters – corrugated steel sheds available in various sizes accommodating up to 10 people. These were designed to be partially sunk into the earth of back yards and gardens, thus providing a relatively sturdy shelter for up to six people during an air raid. The Anderson shelters could be obtained free of charge to any households earning less than £250 per year and otherwise cost between £6 14s and £10s 8s to purchase. Over the course of the war, over 2¼ million of these shelters were erected across Britain and many lives were saved through their construction. However, being inside an Anderson shelter during an air raid could be a terrifying experience. For obvious reasons, the shelters had no windows and so those inside became entombed in a claustrophobic metal box while they heard the sound of bombs detonating around them. For many, the worst part of the experience was emerging from the shelter after the 'all-clear' sirens had sounded, not knowing whether their homes were still standing. R. J. Rice, who lived at 27 Sydney Street at Tidal Basin in Canning Town, later recalled retreating to the family Anderson shelter during the 7 September raid:

'My family, mother and five sisters (my father had gone out for a drink), were not long in the shelter before loud explosions were heard. The light in the shelter went out and the shelter rocked from side to side. My mother, thinking that we were all about to be suffocated, pushed the door of the shelter down, letting in all the dust raised by the bombs which had demolished a number of houses in the street including ours.'

The family were forced to resort to public shelters, first at Silvertown Way and then at a local school before being rehoused in an empty property in Finchley.

Displaced people from the docks were not always welcomed into new communities during the war. Harry Mann's family were also re-housed in an empty property in Finchley after their home in Portland Road, Canning Town was destroyed in an air raid. Later, Harry recalled, 'at first our new neighbours were suspicious and didn't want anything to do with us but one night, incendiary bombs fell on the nearby railway line and the men from our house risked their lives trying to put them out. After that, the neighbours' opinion of us changed.'

The bombing of London continued throughout the week following the first raids. During this short time, the city suffered nearly 40 air attacks during which 2,000 tons of bombs were dispatched. The docks continued to take a severe battering along with Downing Street and Buckingham Palace. With thousands of Londoners now homeless, the Lord Mayor set up a Mansion House Fund to provide food and shelter for the displaced residents. The response to the fund exceeded expectations. Within days, money was pouring in not just from Britain but from benefactors as diverse as the citizens of Port Elizabeth in South Africa, the mayor of Kingston in Jamaica and the Cuban American Allied Relief Fund. A proportion of the monies collected was used to set up 'communal feeding centres' throughout the capital, the awful name of which prompted prime minister Winston Churchill to write to the Minister of Food, 'I hope the term "Communal Feeding Centres" is not going to be adopted. It is an odious expression, suggestive of Communism and the workhouse. I suggest you call them "British Restaurants". Everybody associates the word "restaurant" with a good meal, and they may as well have the name if they cannot get anything else.' However, despite their 'odious' title, by the beginning of October 1940 the centres were providing refuge for up to 25,500 people who had either had their homes destroyed or had been temporarily evacuated while unexploded bombs were diffused.

While the feeding centres dealt with the homeless, yet more bombs rained down on London. On 16 October, a particularly heavy raid was launched when, according to the German High Command, 'Bombs of all sizes were dropped on targets of military importance on both sides of the Thames. The glow of the ensuing fires on the ceiling of clouds above London was visible at a great distance.' During the raid, the Royal Albert Dock suffered great loss of war supplies from its warehouses when fire from incendiary devices engulfed them.

The alarming frequency of the air raids prompted a hasty recruitment drive by the overworked emergency services, to which the public responded with alacrity. By November 1940, the London ambulance service, which before the war had 400 personnel, employed nearly 10,000 people. Similarly, the fire service grew from employing 3,000 firemen in 1939 to having nearly 30,000 employees by the end of the following year. These men and women often found themselves at the centre of bombing raids and showed great courage and dedication to their work. Unfortunately, the nature of their jobs meant that their own lives were often at risk. During the September 1940 raids, 27 emergency services personnel were killed in action, while over 100 more were severely wounded. Occasionally the deaths occurred beyond the front line of the bombing. Cyril Demarne recalled a tragic event in Gainsborough Road, West Ham, on 5 September 1940:

'The firemen attached to No 16 Station in Gainsborough Road were a cheerful bunch of lads. Two firemen were in charge, the remainder composed of auxiliary firemen volunteers with a sprinkling of World War 1 veterans ... On 5 September 1940, the men returned to their station after 48 hours of hard, slogging work; cold, hungry, wet and exhausted. They grabbed a hasty meal, hung out their wet uniforms to dry then turned in to catch up on sleep. But not for long. From that evening and for almost every night for the following three months, the number 16 boys were heavily engaged in fighting the Blitz fires. Then came the night of 8 December 1940. Fred Dell, their officer in charge, had learned the value of snatching every opportunity for sleep that became available. He advised his lads to turn in early in case Jerry decided to continue his nightly visits and they were in their dormitory when the bomb struck. Their mates from Stratford Fire Station and the Civil Defence Rescue teams recovered 10 bodies from the debris and removed the remainder of the watch to hospital.'

Despite the deaths of friends and colleagues, the emergency services had no option but to keep pressing on with their work. Bombing raids persisted into the early months of 1941 and on the night of 19/20 April the docks endured the heaviest bombardment yet when more than 1,000 tons of explosives were dropped in one raid. The attack began at 9.15pm and continued until just before dawn. *The Blitz Then and Now*, edited by Winston G. Ramsey, later noted, 'Enormous fires were visible in and around the Royal Victoria Dock, the East and West India Docks, in large granaries in Millwall Docks, in the vicinity of the Greenwich power station and along the north bank of the Thames and over adjacent districts … Altogether 1,460 fires were started, more than 1,200 people were killed and more than 1,000 seriously injured. Considerable damage was done to warehouses, sheds, silos, timber yards, barges, a variety of dock installations and the Royal Naval College at Greenwich.'

Following the raid, the inhabitants of the East End were confronted with a scene of utter ruin. The shocking effect of the assault provoked both incredulity and anger in all quarters of the capital and even prompted an unscheduled visit to the areas worst hit by the King and Queen, who were greeted by a surprisingly upbeat and stalwart crowd. The *Stratford Express* reported, 'By the time the King and Queen arrived, there was a large crowd to greet them. Cheers were raised and a stentorian voice cried, "Are we downhearted?" and the unanimous shout of "No!" in reply brought big smiles from their Majesties. When they left their car and had greeted the Mayor and Town Clerk they were quickly surrounded by men, women and children, and, as they rubbed shoulders with these subjects who have shown that they can "take it", they talked to them and shook hands.'

The East Enders' response to the nightly raids was truly extraordinary. The residents showed camaraderie, courage and generosity of spirit that was a true credit to the nation. Even youngsters joined in the effort to keep London working through the darkest days of the Blitz. One of the most remarkable of these youths was one Patsie Duggan, a teenage dock worker who organised a wartime gang known as the 'Dead End Kids' whose valiant exploits were published by Frank Lewey in *Cockney Campaign* in 1944.

Following his experiences as a volunteer shelter marshal, Patsie Duggan decided to form his own air raid patrol comprised of friends and siblings. The group found headquarters at Watson's Wharf in Wapping and immediately set about organising themselves into an effective unit. Frank Lewey explained, 'They were split into sections of four. Each section was responsible for a district on Wapping Island, which is connected with the mainland only by two bridges … None of these baby-fighters was paid … The Kids had their own hand-truck; some sand-buckets and spades completed their equipment. These Kids did things that were not in the official book of words. For instance, there was an unbreakable law that time-bombs were not to be touched by adult fire-fighters until Bomb Disposal personnel from the Royal Engineers could attend to them. Two time-bombs came down in the Watson's Wharf area. "To hell with this!" Patsie Duggan said. "We'll rope them and get them into the water." And they did.'

The Dead End Kids' organisation was terrifyingly efficient. A sentry was posted on the roof of Watson's Wharf buildings to watch out for fire bombs and once one was spotted, a team of teenagers were dispatched to the site to help extinguish it. The youngsters showed exceptional bravery. On one occasion, one of the older boys, Ronnie Eyres, led his team into a burning stable block where they managed to rescue up to 30 horses from the flames. Later that night, the boys saw incendiary devices dropping on a terrace of nearby houses. They quickly ran towards to the site but as they approached, three bombs came down almost on top of them. Ronnie Eyres and another boy, Bert Eadon, were killed instantly. Ronnie was 18 years old when he lost his life. Just before he died he had been delighted to learn that he had been accepted into the RAF but never got the chance to follow his dream. Following the tragic deaths, Patsie Duggan tried to obtain a posthumous honour for his friend, with little success. Frank Lewey surmised, 'Perhaps these suggestions are not given the same weight when they come from a youngster of Patsie's age. The authorities were not to know that these children, under fire, had grown as careful and critical as serving officers.'

The incredible resilience and bravery shown by people like Ronnie Eyres and Patsie Duggan during the bombing raids was a contributory factor in the German military reconsidering their tactics. The Blitz continued until mid-May 1941, when a 500-strong bombing raid damaged several important buildings including the British Museum and the Houses of Parliament. Six days later, a raid on Birmingham proved to be the last aerial assault on Britain for over a year and the inhabitants of the districts around the docks were able to start rebuilding their shattered home. However, by late 1943, reconnaissance aircraft flying over German airfields began to spot launch ramps, many of which seemed to be aimed at London. General Ismay hastily issued a memorandum, warning the government that Germany was experimenting with 'long-range rockets' and was ordered to respond by attacking any sites found to possess the ominous ramps. During the first six months of 1944, the RAF dropped over 2,000 tons of bombs on the targeted sites but to little avail. On 13 June, the first V1 rocket – an early cruise missile often referred to as the 'doodlebug' – fell on the village of Swanscombe in Kent. This initial attack was followed by hundreds of V1 attacks on the South-East, many of which were aimed at London and in particular the docks. By July, V1 rockets had killed 2,500 people and caused a massive amount of damage to property. The weapons terrified Londoners like never before. In his book *The Doodlebugs* Norman Longmate recalled, 'The noise is what everyone remembers best: the distant hum, growing to a raucous and deafening rattle, which either diminished as the aircraft disappeared into the distance or jerked abruptly to a stop, to be followed by an explosion. It was this interval that was the hardest to bear. It seemed interminable but … it was actually about 12 seconds. When the engine stopped it seemed that everything stopped.' 'It was,' thought a 12-year-old girl in East Ham, 'as if the world stood still and held its breath.'

The doodlebugs had taken warfare to a new level, but as they wreaked havoc in London during the summer of 1944 Germany put the finishing touches to its most technologically advanced weapon of destruction – the V2 long-range rocket – a shockingly sophisticated device with a one-ton warhead that shot up through the earth's atmosphere before descending at such a rate that it was impossible to intercept. The first V2 rocket to hit east London arrived on 14 September 1944 and succeeded in destroying almost an entire street in Walthamstow. During the following months, the space-age weapons reached the docks, obliterating vast areas in Poplar and West Ham. The arrival of one of these rockets was rapid and decisive as they hit the ground at a rate of 2,000mph. The devastating V2 raids were described in darkly humorous terms in December 1944 by George Orwell who wrote, 'People are complaining of the sudden unexpected wallop with which these things go off. "It wouldn't be so bad if you got a bit of warning," is the usual formula. There is even a tendency to talk nostalgically of the days of the V1. "The good old doodlebug did at least give you time to get under the table", etc. Whereas, in fact, when the doodlebugs were actually dropping, the usual subject of complaint was the uncomfortable waiting period before they went off. Some people are never satisfied.'

Luckily for the people of London, the V2 rockets were launched as war was drawing to a close. Had the Germans been in possession of the necessary technology earlier on in the conflict, its final result might have been quite different. By the time the war in Europe ended on 8 May 1945, the Port of London and its valiant people had been tested to the limits of their endurance. In total, nearly 30,000 Londoners had lost their lives in air raids and literally thousands of homes and businesses had been destroyed. In the East End, damage to property had been greatest in the districts of West Ham and Poplar, while 30 people out of every thousand in Bermondsey were either killed or severely injured during the Blitz.

The docks themselves also suffered greatly from the onslaught of air raids and attacks from the V1 and V2 rockets. The wharves and warehouses surrounding Blackfriars Station were damaged beyond repair, as were the wharfingers' properties that lay either side of Cannon Street Station. Close to the Tower, a large section of the old legal quay and the eastern end of the Custom House were destroyed by bombs. The ancient maritime settlement of Wapping where the Dead End Kids did their sterling work suffered severe damage, the properties lining

Hermitage Wall, Wapping High Street and Tench Street being particularly badly damaged. Across the river in Rotherhithe, the warehouses connected to the Albion, Quebec and Russia Docks were totally destroyed, as was the docks' railway yard. To the west of the site, whole streets containing dock workers' cottages were damaged beyond repair. The Isle of Dogs fared no better. Half the buildings on the north side of the West India Docks' northernmost basin were demolished by bombs and the warehousing at the Millwall Docks was almost totally destroyed. The dock workers' estate of Cubitt Town was also badly hit, with terraces destroyed on Galbraith Street following a direct strike from a V1 rocket. Areas of Canning Town and the central part of Silvertown were irreparably damaged.

By the end of World War 2, the sheer number of residential streets damaged or destroyed by enemy bombs resulted in a severe housing shortage in London, which was about to be exacerbated by the arrival of thousands of servicemen back from their tour of duty. During and immediately after the conflict, temporary housing had been provided in the form of 'Nissen' huts (named after their inventor, Mr P. Nissen) and prefabricated buildings. The 'prefabs' as they became known, were low bungalow-type dwellings constructed from cheap, easily obtainable materials and could be erected quickly, by unskilled workers, on cleared bomb sites at a cost of around £500 per unit. They comprised a kitchen, living room, bathroom and two bedrooms and cost approximately 15 shillings per week to rent. Directly after the end of the war, the government planned to construct millions of prefabs to house Londoners until more substantial new homes could be built. Consequently, the dwellings were built to last only an estimated maximum of 10 years. However, the solid design and careful construction of these 'flat pack' homes proved to be more durable than expected and some have even survived into the 21st century.

While the prefabricated homes temporarily solved the housing crisis in the East End, the government was keen to draw up plans for a long-term solution. Prior to the war, many residential areas surrounding the docks had become run-down and in many cases unfit for human habitation due to damp, infestations of vermin and dilapidation. Realising that now was a perfect time to clear these slums, the government appointed Professor Patrick Abercrombie to devise a new layout and infrastructure for London and the surrounding counties. Professor Abercrombie divided the region into rings that ran around the ancient cities of Westminster and London. The areas immediately adjacent to the city centre became the Inner Urban Ring. These were bordered by the Suburban Ring followed by the Green Belt, which covered most of Middlesex and parts of the Home Counties closest to London. Finally, the Outer Country Ring reached into more rural districts that were still a commutable distance from the city.

Within the outer ring, Abercrombie and his team laid plans for new satellite towns that would be connected to the capital via a new rail network. It was intended that these new towns would provide homes and employment for thousands of displaced inhabitants of inner London once the slums had been cleared. The government's brave new plans were not well received by residents of the East End, many of whom felt a strong allegiance to their city. Dorothy Nicholson wrote in *The Londoner* in 1944, 'Local patriotism is strong; people who had lost their homes in the Blitz would refuse to leave the district. "Why should I let 'itler get me out of Poplar?" they would say, or it might be Bermondsey, or Stepney.' Nicholson's interpretation of the general mood proved right. In April 1949, when the redevelopment of the East End was in full swing, the *Stratford Express* reported, 'There were some remarkable scenes in Beatrice Street, Plaistow, for about six hours on Friday afternoon and evening when efforts were made to evict the family of Mr Arthur Siddle. With their furniture piled high against an open doorway of Hut number 48 which they were occupying – the door having been forced off at the first attempt at eviction – Mrs Siddle and six neighbours sat on furniture and defied all efforts of police, council officers, a bailiff and workmen to remove them. They were watched by a big crowd. Eventually, after several skirmishes during which a chair was broken, the family were persuaded to leave the premises quietly. They were given three days to accept the council's offer of new accommodation on another site.'

Despite the attitude of the people they were rehousing, the authorities pressed on with the redevelopment and resettlement plans. New towns with labyrinthine housing estates and soulless shopping centres were constructed over previously rural market towns and farming villages in Hertfordshire and Essex, one of the first being Harlow, which was laid out in 1947 to plans by Sir Frederick Gibberd. Harlow New Town comprised several residential districts, each with their own shopping facilities set around a central precinct that included a theatre, town hall and a railway station that connected the town with Liverpool Street, close to the City. From 1951, Harlow also boasted a structure that was to become the scourge of London in future decades – a residential tower block, which was inappropriately named 'The Lawn'. Over the following 15 years, The Lawn spawned hundreds of imitations, not only in the new towns but also in the bombed-out areas of the capital. Tower blocks made perfect financial sense to the councils that erected them. They could be built quickly and cheaply and, most importantly, they could house hundreds of people while taking up very little acreage of land. Architects dreamt up ideas of 20th century communities in the sky, while the accompanying publicity material promoted a new and modern style of living, without the need for gas lamps, tin baths or outside WCs. However, for the inhabitants of these colossal structures, life inside one of the new tower blocks often did not live up to the expectations promoted by the advertising agencies. While most residents appreciated the inclusion of hot running water, sparkling new kitchens and indoor toilet facilities, they found their high-rise flats isolating and lonely. One of the main features of pre-war East End streets was the almost constant presence of people. Adults chatted to their neighbours across front steps or back yards while children played in the street. The high-rise blocks offered no such opportunities for sociability. There were no open spaces beyond the residents' doorsteps where children's play could be unobtrusively supervised. Lifts to the upper floors regularly broke down, leaving the inhabitants with the choice of either climbing up and down numerous flights of stairs in order to access the outside world or remain housebound – a particular problem for the elderly or infirm. In 1951, H. V. Morton surveyed the redevelopment of the East End for his book *In Search of London* and wrote of the new housing in Limehouse: 'Walking towards the Causeway, I saw at a glance that Limehouse has had its full share of bombs. Hundreds of terrible little houses had been swept away and an energetic local authority, or perhaps the London County Council, had already erected several large and shining blocks of flats, every flat apparently occupied. I met at a street corner two tough old salts, and I told them what a great difference I noticed since I was last there, and how glad I was to see such fine blocks of flats. One of the men gave me a glance of the deepest contempt, and the other removed the pipe from his mouth, spat angrily, and said they weren't a patch on the good old houses with their back gardens where the kids could play. "And stairs," he said angrily, "always blinkin' stairs!" I tried to put in a good word for the flats, but he told me they might be all right for some folks, but as far as he was concerned anybody could have the flats and their baths and their "ruddy little window boxes".

20

THE DEMISE OF THE DOCKS

In addition to coping with the loss of their homes and personal belongings during bombing raids, the dock workers were also subjected to new methods of employment as the authorities desperately tried to keep the docks working through the war. In 1941, the government established the National Dock Labour Corporation, which was given the onerous task of attempting to regulate the historically chaotic way that men were selected for employment at the docks.

For centuries, dockers had enjoyed the freedom to work when they wished. If they decided they could afford to miss a morning call-on, they were perfectly free to do so. However, while this state of affairs was beneficial to the workers, it could cause huge problems at the docks. As the war progressed, the devastation inflicted on East London by German bombers inevitably led to a great deal of absenteeism as the men skipped work to help clear damaged buildings, come to the aid of neighbours or mourn the dead. This situation led to the docks being regularly undermanned and began to disrupt the distribution of military supplies and urgently needed foodstuffs.

The National Dock Labour Corporation devised a scheme which it hoped would bring order to the Port of London and ensure that there would always be enough manpower available. Under its new regulations, all dock workers were given an incentive to turn up to work each day by the offer of 'attendance pay' – an allowance given to every man who appeared at the morning call-on, regardless of whether work was available or not. In order to facilitate the distribution of the allowance, the corporation erected new meeting halls within the dock complexes in which the men were required to assemble in order to be selected for work.

Although this new system seemed efficient and practical on paper, it provoked a furious response from the dockers, many of whom saw it as a threat to their freedom and only a step away from becoming employees of the PLA. By November 1944, the stevedores at the Surrey Commercial Docks had walked out on strike in protest. *The Times* reported, 'It does not make sense that men should prefer to stand in the street in the dark and cold and rain of early winter mornings rather than wait in a brightly lighted, though austere assembly hall. But so it is; and they have their reasons ... they "fought for" and won the right to be engaged as free men on free territory, and not on the dock company's ground. They are holding to that right.'

The stevedores' action prompted such a backlog of ships waiting to leave the docks that, within days, the management were forced to give in to their demands and allow the selections to be undertaken in the street, outside the dock wall, while their bright, new hall stood empty.

Encouraged by the stevedores' success, workers at other docks began to rail against the corporation's new employment policies. When one of the dreaded assembly halls was erected at the Royal Docks in early 1945, both the Stevedores' and the General Workers' Unions organised a mass walk-out involving up to 7,000 men. The government was forced to bring in the army to unload the ships and W. Mabane, parliamentary secretary to the food industry, noted, 'A strike such as this creates difficulties that grow more substantial with every passing day. We have ships that we want turned round in order that they may bring in more food, and if they are not turned round, we don't get supplies as rapidly as we would wish. We have other goods, some of them perishable, such as oranges and shell-eggs, in transit sheds, and there is a danger of deterioration if these perishables are not moved on.' Mr Mabane's prosaic words were undoubtedly correct. In peace time, the 'deterioration' of produce lying in warehouses would at worst result in financial loss for the merchants to whom they belonged. During the war, the inability to distribute goods due to a disagreement over employment rights was a wanton waste of resources. Despite this, the government refused to back down and by the following day the strike had spread to Tilbury. It was to be a full week before the dockers were persuaded to return to work, following the promise of an inquiry into their grievances (which ultimately found in the corporation's favour).

Despite the return to work, the trouble at the docks was far from over. At the end of 1945, the 'Western Front Agreement', which had given dockers a higher rate of pay during the western offensive of the war in return for them accepting the change in call-on policy, was withdrawn. The workers, many of whom had suffered great personal losses during the hostilities, were in no mood to take a pay cut and promptly went on a 'go-slow' strike until the PLA agreed to a basic rate of pay of 25 shillings per day (as opposed to the 16 shillings they had been offered), plus a revision of piece-work rates. Soon after the go-slow began, a journalist from the *Daily Telegraph* visited the docks and described the scene. 'In everything they did, the men were unhurried in a way that looked deliberate ... True, the cranes were working and goods were passing from the dockside to the ship, but there was a leisureliness about the proceedings that made everything seem half-hearted.'

The go-slow had a paralysing effect on the Port of London as the ships took up to treble the normal amount of time to unload. The *SS Norwegian*, which had arrived at the port just as the strike began, laden with a cargo of sugar and timber, took a massive 30 days to unload. Normally, her cargo would have been discharged in just nine days. Further along the river, unloading of the *Tecumseh Park*'s general cargo began on 6 June and was expected to be completed in 14 days. By 10 July, the ship was still not empty. This state of affairs naturally angered the merchants and ship owners who had to bear the cost of the delays, which were often substantial – unloading of the *Norwegian* ended up costing £1,900 instead of the expected £850. Consequently, as the strike wore on, the ships began to dock at ports unaffected by the action. Under intense pressure to end the strike, the National Dock Labour Corporation opened talks with the unions in early July but their discussions failed to end the strike. Frustrated at the unions, the corporation began to round up the men who they considered to be the ring-leaders and threatened them with suspension or dismissal if they failed to justify their actions. The armed forces were once again brought in to unload the rapidly increasing number of vessels waiting in the Thames and the dockers' attendance money was stopped. In response, the unions sent representatives to other British ports such as Cardiff and Liverpool with the express intention of persuading the incumbent workers not to unload any ships that had been redirected from the Port of London. Their plan worked and soon action was being taken at docks throughout the country. However, despite the widespread go-slow strikes, victory evaded the workers. The presence of the military at the docks ensured that the ships would continue to be unloaded, albeit slowly, for an indefinite period of time. This, combined with the lack of attendance pay and little support from the war-weary British public, finally forced the men back to work on 14 August with their demand for a better rate of pay refused. However, the strike action further afield carried on apace and by October 1945 the docks and wharves at Liverpool, Manchester, Preston, Middlesbrough, Hartlepool, Hull, Grimsby and South Shields were at a standstill. Empowered by this, many workers at the Port of London resumed their strike. Faced with national disruption, the government agreed to negotiate over pay and conditions and on 5 November the men returned to work, pending an investigation into their demands. By 11 December, the investigating committee returned its verdict, recommending a pay rate of 19 shillings per day – a figure that the unions urged their members to accept. The docks returned to normal work, but strike action was destined to afflict the Port of London for the rest of its days.

The combination of relatively low pay and irregular work for the dockers with the valuable nature of many cargoes meant that theft had been a problem at the docks from their inception. Ever since the creation of the enclosed docks at the end of the 18th century, it had been clear to the management that the sites' high perimeter walls and spot checks did little to deter workers from helping themselves to some of the goods they handled. In November 1808, James Darrett, a warehouseman at the West India Docks, was indicted for stealing 2½lb of coffee while at work. His ensuing trial at the Old Bailey revealed that on 8 October, James Knight, an export marker working in the same warehouse as Darrett, saw him take several handfuls of coffee from an open sack and surreptitiously put them in his pockets. Knight reported what he had seen to his superiors and the luckless Darrett was duly arrested. At the time of the theft, coffee was a hugely valuable commodity and this was reflected in the harshness of the sentence handed down by the judge – Darrett was found guilty and sentenced to transportation for seven years.

Initially, crime prevention and detection at the enclosed docks were handled by the military. The dock companies employed soldiers to man the site entrances and keep an eye on cargoes. However, it soon became clear that the soldiers were not averse to accepting bribes from the thieves and in some cases would even make off with goods themselves. By the end of the 18th century, it was estimated that out of every £12 million worth of cargo brought into the port, up to £500,000 was stolen. Additionally, a census of 37,000 workers employed on the Thames suggested that up to 11,000 of these people had at some point been involved in illegal activity at their place of work. Consequently, a marine police force was set up to deal with crime on the river in 1798. The foundation of this constabulary was wholeheartedly welcomed by the merchants, who hoped that the increased security would ultimately reflect in their profits. In August 1798, *The Times* proclaimed that, 'The River Thames never in the memory of man was so favourably circumstanced as it has been since the establishment of the Marine Police. All river pirates, and other suspicious persons who used to infest it, are now completely banished, and nothing can be conceived more still and quiet than every part of the river is in the night.'

While the merchants were pleased with the diligence of the new police force, others thought the officers rather too eager to make arrests. Later that same year, the marine police's detention of Charles Eyres – a coal heaver who had been accused of making off with some of the goods he conveyed – provoked a riot during which the police headquarters were besieged by an angry mob. *The Times* reported, 'a most furious and outrageous mob assembled round the Marine Police Office, and after shouting, instantly attacked the windows, broke the outside shutters, threw large stones, and did a great deal of damage. As soon as it was possible for the magistrates and officers to force their way to the street, the Riot Act was instantly read; but before this was effected, while the mob were trying to break into the house, the officers, who were by this time armed, fired one or two pistols, but the mob continued notwithstanding to be very outrageous, nor was it possible to make the least impression until one of the mob, a coal heaver, was shot.'

The marine police did much to curb crime on the river, but the enclosed docks did not fall within their jurisdiction. Consequently, the dock companies had to organise their own security. Private individuals were employed to watch the dock workers, the first of whom was Captain Robert Bartlett, who was appointed Captain of the Watch at the West India

Docks in 1802. Bartlett was in control of a team of seven constables and his appointment proved so successful that the model was eventually duplicated in all enclosed docks throughout the Port of London. The dock companies continued to employ their own security officers until the late 19th century, when the decline in trade obliged them to disband the forces.

When the PLA took over the enclosed docks, the question of security was once again brought to the fore. Talks with the Metropolitan Police over assigning a number of their officers to the docks ended in failure and so the authority was compelled to create its own security team, which became known as the Port of London police force – one of the largest forces in the country.

Employment as a dock policeman provided steady work but was poorly paid and arduous. Officers were required to work 12-hour shifts that began at either 6am or 6pm. These shifts often ran into overtime, which was unpaid. There were no official breaks so the officers resorted to grabbing a quick bite to eat while holed up in one of the police boxes situated around the dock to which they were assigned. Days off were rare. First-class officers were supposed to get one day off in seven, but staff shortages often meant that this was denied. Second-class officers received only one day off every six weeks. Taking account of the overtime worked, the dock policemen's average wage was 4d per hour – at least 3d less than the dock workers earned. Consequently, theft from the docks continued, often with the police constables in cahoots with the thieves in return for a slice of the profit. In 1955, the PLA reported that £10,500 worth of property had been stolen from their docks that year. In truth, the figure was almost certainly much higher as the dock workers evolved ever more crafty ways of removing cargoes without arousing the authority's suspicions. Howard Collins, who had many acquaintances at the docks during the 1950s and 60s, remembered dockers smuggling meat out of the gates under their hats. On a particularly hot day, blood from the meat began to run down one of the smugglers' faces as the contents of his hat overheated. His quick-thinking companions told him to clutch his temple as if in agony and quickly whisked him off the premises, telling the police at the gate that he had suffered a most terrible accident.

The dockers could be exceptionally ingenious when thinking up ways to hide their contraband. Just after World War 1, the dock police confiscated no fewer than 150 hot water bottles from workers who had been using them as receptacles for rum. Stealing from crates was particularly popular with the resourceful men in the warehouses, who would remove a slat from the crate, take out some of the contents and then replace the stolen goods with something worthless of a similar weight. The slat was then replaced with such expertise that often the theft remained undetected until the cargo reached its final destination.

No cargo escaped the smugglers' attentions. Alan Richardson, who worked as a tally clerk checking cargoes at the Surrey Commercial Docks in the early 1960s recalled, 'we had a lot of general cargo coming in one day and we had some gangs [of dockers] working from another dock. While we were unloading, a tally clerk from the West India Dock came in and said, "You want to watch this lot, they're dodgy." I watched them but nothing went on. At the end of the week, once the gang had gone back to their normal berth, the tally clerk came over and said, "Well, did you find anything?" I replied, "No, everything was clean as a new pin." "Wrong!" he said. "They were smuggling every day!" It turned out that the gang had been smuggling underwear from one of the consignments. Every day, they would break open one of the crates and put on four or five T-shirts and several pairs of underpants before leaving the dock. They did this for two weeks so they made off with a fair amount of stuff!'

Despite this experience, Alan Richardson did not begrudge the dockers' antics. 'If you were there at the time and you saw how the guys worked, you wouldn't mind them taking a little bit here and there because they earned it.'

The docks were even used as a distribution point for counterfeit currency. In December 1950, the dock police noticed unusual labels on some cases of Spanish oranges at the East India Docks. On closer inspection, it became apparent that the labels were actually facsimiles of £1 notes, which could be easily detached and passed off as the real thing. Officers were hastily dispatched to Covent Garden Market in an attempt to retrieve any of the crates that had already been taken out of the docks, but met with no success.

By the 1960s, the Port of London had also become a distribution point for drugs and weapons of terrorism. In May 1964, enough hemp to make 11¼ miles of reefer cigarettes was found in the possession of Fatick

Halder, Nani Ghose and Bhabani Mitra, all crew members of the ship *City of Gloucester*. Five years later, the Israeli ship *Kineret* was stormed by police following intelligence that a bomb had been secreted on board by Arab terrorists.

Problems with smuggling and more serious crimes notwithstanding, the docks recovered from the ravages of World War 2 and entered their final period of prosperity. As ships from all over the world arrived in the Thames, employment was plentiful and although their working days were physically demanding and sometimes dangerous, the majority of workers at the Port of London thoroughly enjoyed the post-war period. To many who witnessed the port during this period, the secret cities behind the docks' high walls were fascinating. Alan Richardson became fascinated by the port in 1948, following a childhood trip with his father. He recalled, 'My Dad was a lorry driver for Cherry Blossom Boot Polish, (which was based in Chiswick), and made regular trips to the docks. When I was five, he took me along one Saturday morning. We left about 6am and I remember there was nothing on the road except a few vans and the odd saloon car or trolley bus. Sitting in the lorry, I got a grandstand view as we drove through London – it was like watching a film through the windscreen. The magical part was when we got to Canning Town. By the time we arrived there, the sun was rising over the Royal Docks like a big, red ball. The entrance to the docks had huge, iron gates and hundreds of dockers were pouring through them on their way to work along the cobbled road. A policeman was waiting at the gate with a clipboard. He looked at Dad's shipping order and then opened up the back of the lorry to have a quick look, although all he could see was this mass of boxes – he hadn't got the time to search them – then he closed the doors of the lorry, gave back the shipping notes and waved us through. It was exciting for a small boy to go into this forbidden city. We drove into the sheds with cranes towering over them and that's where I got my first glimpse of the ships. Their funnels were the most impressive thing because they were all different colours. It was a magical experience. I was only five years old and seeing the cranes, the ships, the dockers and everything else just blew my mind and I decided that one day I'd like to work in the docks.'

The docks were not only pleasurable for young visitors; many of the workers within them thoroughly enjoyed their jobs, not least because of the rapport that existed among them. Brian Metherell, who worked as a 'perm' (a docker on a permanent contract with the PLA) at the Royal Albert Dock from 1958-1977, remembered, 'The camaraderie was very good down at the docks. If you were put to work on a ship, you were with the same gang until you'd finished. If there was heavy rain, we'd stop work and have a game of cards. If our ship wasn't due in for a few hours, we used to go and have a round of golf over at Hainault.'

Part of this comradeship was born from the fact that many of the dockers came from a long line of port workers who obtained work for younger members of their family when they left school. Brian Powell, who worked for Wilson Meats (whose headquarters were at the Royal Victoria Dock) from 1956 to 1973, explained how he came to work there:

'I was born and bred in Bethnal Green. My uncle worked for the shipping lines. When I came out of National Service, I didn't want to go back to my original job and my uncle said to me, "do you fancy working in the docks?" He spoke to someone he knew at Wilson Meats and I got employed.'

Brian worked in distribution for the company and although the hours could be long, the job gave him a great deal of independence. 'When I first started, my working hours were 8am till 5pm with overtime until 7pm. Then Lord Devlin split the working day into two shifts, so it started at 7am and that shift worked until 2pm, then another shift came on from 2pm till 9pm. What Lord Devlin didn't take into account was someone like me, who was the lone representative, was left with a working day that stretched from seven in the morning until nine at night. Well, you couldn't do that so you put your priorities in the right order. I sometimes used to wake up and wonder where I was going to work that day. It could be Sheerness, Tilbury, London, I just had to make my mind up. Where I went every morning was up to my judgement.'

The dock workers' camaraderie did not end with the working day. There were numerous pubs both inside and outside the dock walls that were packed at lunchtimes and early evenings. These pubs did not only provide refreshment after a hard day's work, they also served as meeting places for the unions. One of the most popular union pubs was the Connaught at the Royal Docks. It is still there today, serving chilled New World wines to suited visitors from the nearby ExCel exhibition centre.

However, back in the 1950s and 60s, it had a very different clientele, the most famous of whom was Jack Dash, a trade union activist who strived to improve the wages and working conditions of the dockers during the docks' final boom period. Brian Powell recalled, 'The dockers had their meetings at the Connaught. The speaker was often Jack Dash, who was the unofficial union leader. Dash was a really eloquent man and clever with it. He would get enthusiasm going by speaking at the Connaught and the ship owners would go absolutely mad but they could never nail him down for doing anything wrong. He was an amazing character who spent his life trying to help other people and being hated by officialdom for it because he invariably cost them money.'

Some pubs around the docks attracted a surprisingly diverse clientele. Dick de Kerbrech, who experienced the docks from 1961 to 1966 while serving his apprenticeship with the merchant navy, remembered a particularly unusual pub at North Woolwich. 'Behind the railway track, there was a pub called the Kent Arms. I'll never forget it! It looked derelict because it had boarding on the windows. It was full of dockers – rough buggers – during the day, but at night it was frequented by gay blokes! I'm talking about 1965 – before homosexuality was declared legal – I suppose it was a sort of safe haven for gay men.'

Over on the south bank of the Thames, tally clerk Alan Richardson made an intriguing discovery about one of his regular haunts. He recollected, 'on a Friday afternoon, a friend and I would get on our motorbikes and go down to a pub called The Angel in Bermondsey. It was down a road called Paradise Street. I used to chuckle because at that time it was a bomb site. We would have a meal there – cod, chips and peas, freshly made, and a pint of Guinness. We used to go outside and sit on the balcony, which overlooked the Thames. Looking upstream you could see Tower Bridge and downstream you could see Deptford Buoys. When the tide came in, the river ran right underneath the balcony. Years later, a friend bought me a book on Whistler, the American artist who lived and worked in Britain in the 1880s and 1890s. In this book was an illustration of the balcony I knew so well. It was nice for me to make that connection – that I'd actually had my lunch in the same place as the great Whistler used to paint and draw.'

The early 1960s heralded the final heyday for the docks. By the time the decade drew to a close, the Port of London's once massive workforce had begun to drastically reduce as trade at the port was affected by a new development in transportation that would eventually cause insurmountable problems for the Port of London – containerisation.

Containerisation of goods had begun nearly 200 years previously, when barge operators on Britain's canal network began to use wooden boxes to carry consignments of coal. As the railways developed in the second half of the 19th century, their operators began to use similar containers to those on the coal barges. Containers had many advantages for freight transportation, not least because the time spent loading and unloading the goods was cut down immeasurably. Once a consignment had been packed into a container it would not need to be unpacked or reloaded until it reached its final destination, regardless of how many times the goods were transferred to another vehicle. Large cranes and winches were designed that could not only convey large containers from one train to another but could also transfer the goods from rail to road transport. In addition to this, containers could be securely sealed, thus radically reducing any opportunities for theft.

As the use of containers in road and rail haulage increased in popularity, it became clear that this method of transporting goods could be made significantly more space- and cost-efficient if the size of the containers was standardised. Thus, in the 1920s, the Railway Clearing House, which handled the distribution of revenue for several major railway companies, standardised the size of containers carried on Britain's rail network. The new containers were available in lengths of 5 or 10ft and fitted neatly onto rolling stock, thus allowing huge amounts of goods to be transported during one single journey.

The use of containers revolutionised the way goods were distributed throughout Britain. However, the system was unworkable for ships because their holds were simply not designed to accommodate bulk-packed goods of this size. Consequently, railway containers bound for overseas had to be painstakingly unpacked at the docks before their contents could be transferred to waiting vessels. The frustrated ship owners saw how beneficial containerisation could be for their businesses. Since the days of Isambard Kingdom Brunel, it had been eminently possible to design a ship with a hold large enough to accommodate numerous containers. However, with the notable exception of Tilbury, the Port of London was incapable of receiving such large vessels. Consequently, the slow and labour-intensive process of unloading goods at London's enclosed docks prevailed into the middle of the 20th century, while ports on the coastlines of Europe began to upgrade their facilities to cope with the imminent arrival of gigantic container shipping.

During the last year of World War 2, the US Army began to use large metal containers to ship supplies to its troops overseas and realised that, with some alterations and improvements, this system could work for post-war commercial purposes. Over the ensuing five years, the US, Canada and Denmark began to construct prototype container ships and, by the early 1950s, the first vessels were operating in Scandinavia and North America. Back in London, the PLA realised that the economics of containerisation of sea-borne goods were too compelling to be ignored. Aware that all bar one of its enclosed docks were incapable of receiving container ships due to their inaccessible location, it set about upgrading the one site that could keep them in business – Tilbury in Essex. In 1963, work began on a massive new dock that stretched for nearly a mile northwards from the port's centre. Six years later, a colossal grain terminal was constructed on nearby Northfleet Hope and, in 1978, land adjacent to this site was used to build a terminal specifically designed to accommodate container ships. The PLA's investment in Tilbury paid off. Today, along with Southampton and Felixstowe, it remains one of Britain's busiest ports.

While Tilbury prospered, the arrival of container ships signalled the end for London's enclosed docks and ancient wharves. These initially speculative enterprises, which had survived the numerous fluctuations in trade for 150 years and even managed to rally after the devastation caused by two world wars, finally fell victim to a combination of economics and inaccessibility. From 1965, London's port went into a rapid and unstoppable decline as the docks' outmoded and expensive methods of discharging and loading ships prompted even smaller vessels to berth elsewhere. Additional decline in shipping was caused by Britain's newly independent former colonies developing their own markets, which often bypassed the Port of London altogether.

The ancient wharves that lined the banks of the Thames in inner London were among the first to succumb to the port's decline in trade. Between 1967 and 1971, all the major wharves closed including the sprawling Hay's Wharf – the former 'larder of London' – which until the 1950s had been handling 1,750,000 tons of produce every year. Hay's had been experiencing financial difficulties for some time. The once 1,000-strong workforce had been gradually dismissed and by June 1969 the company was forced to close down its Mark Brown Wharf after a walk-out by workers over pay drove away precious trade from a number of regular customers. News of the closure spread fast. Fearing that the rest of the wharf might soon follow suit, anxious ship owners deserted Hay's in droves. On 22 October, the wharf's board announced that the entire operation would shut down on 28 November due to lack of trade.

At the enclosed docks, the situation was no better. By the 1960s, the declining fortunes of the PLA had prompted it to reassess the way the inner London docks operated. As early as 1962, a committee was set up by the government to investigate the long term viability of keeping the docks in London operating. The committee's verdict read, 'We think that the port activity should be moved away from the centre of London ... We are aware that at present the docks perform a useful and to some extent specialised function, but we think it at least possible that the traffic could be catered for elsewhere in the port, especially if pressure can be eased by development at Tilbury.'

Throughout the 1960s the decline in trade was made worse by an increase in industrial action by the workers over pay and conditions. In July 1967, representatives from the docks at Liverpool, Manchester, Southampton, Hull and London met secretly to discuss the possibility of putting the increasingly militant workers on permanent contracts. Although these contracts would greatly simplify the running of the docks and help to minimise labour costs, the respective authorities knew from bitter experience that the idea would be energetically resisted by the workers. However, when the proposal was presented to the unions, their response was not as bad as some had expected. While the unions were understandably loath to relinquish their members' longstanding right to casual employment, they were also aware that the post-war exodus of many erstwhile dock workers to the leafier surroundings of the new towns in the provinces had left the PLA with a much smaller pool of labour from which to draw. Thus employment (in the short term at least) would be guaranteed for the vast majority of their members. The unions were also fully aware of the threat posed by containerisation and knew that London's docks might not be in business for much longer. With this in mind, they responded to the PLA's call for decasualisation of the workers by demanding a healthy minimum wage of £17 per week, a pension of £8 10s per week at the age of 65 and, crucially, redundancy pay of £5,000 for each worker should they be laid off. The PLA was unable to meet the unions' demands and a series of strikes were subsequently planned for the autumn.

Ultimately, the authority's plans to revive the declining fortunes of the docks and the dockers' demands for financial protection in the event of redundancy came too late. Soon after the secret meeting in 1967, the PLA announced that the East India Docks would cease to accept shipping from 1 October and all workers engaged there would be offered transfers to either the West India or Millwall Docks. This was not the end of the bad news. When questioned by the press on the future of the other docks in the Port of London, the director general of the PLA, Dudley Perkins, admitted that the London and St Katharine Docks had recently been losing approximately £1 million per year but concern for the local economy had prevented any action being taken thus far. His statement read, 'A strictly commercial decision would be to close down the docks completely. On technical grounds this could be justified, but I have declined to treat 800 dock workers as if they were ciphers. They are men whose livelihood is at stake.'

Despite Perkins' concerns over his workers' future, the dockers continued with their strike plans and mass walk-outs were organised for the week commencing 16 October, threatening to bring the port to a standstill. As work ground to a halt, ships began to queue in the Thames, waiting for a berth in the enclosed docks. By 26 October, 44 vessels were lying idle in the river as nearly 6,000 dock workers continued the strike. As it transpired, their action was futile. The strike ended in stalemate and the dockers returned to work with no assurances regarding their financial security should more docks be forced to close. By January 1968, their fears were realised when the PLA announced the closure of both the St Katharine and London Docks, citing the strike as one of the factors that expedited their demise.

Despite their concerns for the future, London's dockers showed little prudence when it came to managing their personal finances, preferring to spend any money they earned rather than save some of it for the inevitable 'rainy day' that now loomed on the horizon. In January 1970, Jeremy Bugler interviewed Harry Simmonds, a crane and fork-lift truck driver at the Surrey Commercial Docks, who earned (excluding overtime) a healthy £50 per week. In his resulting article, which appeared in *The Guardian*, Bugler wrote of Simmonds, 'The way he puts this (£50) money out again is like a one-man campaign for a scheme called "Spend-As-You-Earn". When he says "Me and money don't get along very well together; we part very quick," it is a confession of faith ... Harry Simmonds refuses to have anything to do with a budget. Money comes in and money goes out. Thus, despite his consistent high earnings, all the Simmondses have saved is £45 knocking around in the current account at the bank. The family never go on holidays: "When it comes round holiday time, there's never enough to go away on. I suppose I ought to put a quid or two aside every week, but I can't do it."' Harry Simmonds' spendthrift proclivities left him in severely straitened circumstances later that year when the PLA closed the Surrey Commercial Docks at the end of September.

Initially, the Authority hoped that the closure of the innermost enclosed docks would enable it to save those that remained. However, this began to seem impossible after trade at the Port of London (with the exception of Tilbury) continued to decrease over the following years. Following a dramatic reduction in traffic at the port in 1975, the PLA decided to close both the West India and Millwall Docks in a desperate bid to reverse the downward slide of its fortunes, which had plummeted from a £500,000 profit in 1974 to a £5 million loss a year later.

Sadly, the closure of these two docks was not enough to stem the tide. The last remaining enclosed docks in London – 'The Royals' – staggered on, aided by the government, through the last years of the 1970s, but by 1981 the loss suffered each year by the vast complex was simply too great to sustain. The Royal Docks closed at the end of October that year.

The rapid demise of almost the whole of the Port of London radically altered the geographic and economic landscape that surrounded them. Between 1966 and 1976, over 150,000 jobs were lost in the dock boroughs, which represented 20% of the total jobs in the area. By 1981, the once bustling streets surrounding the docks were a depressing sight. Those that could afford to move out to the suburbs did so, but the population that remained found it almost impossible to find work as their skills were now useless. They eked out a living where they could and relied on benefits to keep a roof over their heads. By the middle of the 1980s, 95% of the docks' residential areas were comprised of social housing. *The Times* vividly described a 'Dockland in the Doldrums' in a leader article that read, 'Derelict warehouses, overturned ironwork and unvisited sheets of water stretch for miles, and the willow herb flourishes as freely as it did on the bombed sites after the war. A dwindling population live here and there in terraces half boarded up and grim tower blocks. The cause of the trouble is, of course, that the occasional training ship is almost all that does come by, apart from colliers and rubbish barges bound farther upstream. The Port of London has moved closer to the sea, leaving behind the largest area in need of wholesale redevelopment anywhere in Europe.'

One thing the redundant docks did not suffer from was a lack of ideas regarding their redevelopment. Following the closure of the London and St Katharine sites, a consortium calling itself the Thamesside Research and Development Group put forward grand plans for a 200-acre 'Venice' on the two docks. Under its ambitious scheme, the sites would be linked by a new waterway and then connected to the nearby Tower of London via its moat which, after over 100 years of lying empty would once again be filled. In the dock basins, new housing would rise majestically out of the water, commanding enviable views across the London landscape. At St Katharine Docks, the warehousing surrounding the new complex would be given over to a 'folk museum' commemorating the docks' heyday, with re-creations of Dickensian streets and workshops, while the area adjoining the quayside would become a floating art gallery. Over the river at Hay's Wharf, planners envisaged a 'New West End'.

Further east, the disused dock sites attracted less interest from developers, largely because they were considered too far away from the centre of the capital to attract hotel and retail trade. By 1970, the remaining residents of the Isle of Dogs were despairing of ever getting their ignored and isolated community back on its feet when a group of locals came up with an idea that would at the very least guarantee publicity for the Isle. Taking inspiration from the classic comedy *Passport* to *Pimlico*, at midnight on 9 March 1970, the residents of the Isle of Dogs declared independence from the rest of Britain! Ray Paget, the chairman of a local tenants' association, explained the motivation behind their actions: 'We are grappling with a really vast problem, that of ordinary people trying to overcome bureaucracy. All the ammunition and resources are on the side of the authorities. They have the money and the power. But we want some measure of say over the running of our island.'

The council of the new 'republic' set up headquarters at Glengall School in Cubitt Town, which had lain empty for two years following the closure of the West India and Millwall Docks, and appointed councillor Ted Johns as its chairman. They immediately demanded financial assistance from Tower Hamlets council so they could begin to regenerate the area and threatened to take their press campaign to an international level if their demands were not met. Although the Isle of Dogs campaign was never meant to be serious, the publicity it attracted worked wonders. Two years later, David Eversley, chief strategic planner for the Greater London Council, remembered that the islanders' 'half serious, half comic "declaration of independence" drew attention both to the needs of the area, and to the possibilities. Within a few months of this demonstration, developers were bidding for potential building plots in Millwall.'

By 1972, the sheer number of schemes being submitted by developers for areas of the docks prompted the GLC to temporarily call a halt to any plans for piecemeal development and instead begin to consider the dock area as a whole. The region subsequently became known for the first time as 'Docklands' and planners Travers Morgan & Partners were asked to submit proposals for the wholesale redevelopment of 6,000 acres of dockside land – an area that comprised all the enclosed docks – working on the depressing but accurate assumption that all the sites would soon be closed. The resulting report suggested five different proposals for regeneration, all of which combined new housing with commercial premises in various different layouts, none of which were particularly controversial. However, the report was published in the middle of the 1973 GLC election campaign and soon provided ammunition for opposing factions. Rumours abounded that the relevant authorities had not been properly consulted before the plans were drawn up and that none of the schemes met the needs of the local populace. Consequently,

Travers Morgan's carefully thought-out schemes never got further than the drawing board. The concept of tackling the regeneration of the docks as a whole prevailed, however, although the nuts and bolts of how this monumentally large project would be tackled remained unaddressed.

By 1981, when the last of the enclosed docks closed, virtually nothing had been agreed concerning the future of London's Docklands. During this uncertain period, Michael Heseltine, the then Secretary of State for the Environment, flew over the abandoned docks and was horrified by what he saw on the ground beneath him. He later wrote in his memoirs, 'I had found myself in a small plane, heading [towards] London's East End. My indignation at what was happening on the south bank was as nothing compared to my reaction to the immense tracts of dereliction I now observed. The rotting docks – long since abandoned for deep-water harbours able to take modern container ships downstream – the crumbling infrastructure that had once supported their thriving industry and vast expanses of polluted land left behind by modern technology and enhanced environmentalism. The place was a tip: 6,000 acres of forgotten wasteland.'

Heseltine determined to address the wanton waste of the dock sites and in order to effect the necessary regeneration works he set up the London Docklands Development Corporation in July 1981. This new body, which subsequently became known as the LDDC, was given the remit to oversee the development of the docks and their surrounds. In order to make the process as uncomplicated as possible, the corporation was given access to munificent financial resources, the power to acquire land from public sector authorities and, most importantly, total control over the project without the need to seek approval or agreement from the London boroughs in which the land was situated.

With the power to do whatever it saw fit, the LDDC began to draw up a programme of redevelopment, concentrating on the Isle of Dogs and beginning with a new transport infrastructure. By the early 1980s, the Isle had become very difficult to access. Many areas were connected by drawbridges over the old locks. Once the docks were abandoned, all maintenance on the bridges had stopped and, consequently, they were constantly breaking down or getting stuck, forcing vehicles to take circuitous routes in an attempt to reach their destinations. The lack of transport infrastructure gave the island a remote atmosphere that was unlikely to attract investors and it was clear that this needed to be quickly rectified. In response, the LDDC built several new roads to bypass the problem hotspots near the lock entrances and introduced the 'Docklands Clipper', a shuttle bus service that connected the island with Mile End underground station.

Obviously, a few new roads and a bus route were not sufficient to transform the fortunes of the docks. It soon became apparent that a new rail network connecting the area with the centre of London was required and following discussions with London Transport, the LDDC submitted a proposal to the government for a light railway, costing an estimated £65 million. The resulting Docklands Light Railway was constructed between 1985 and 1987, using the existing infrastructure of old lines that had served the docks when they were still operational. The railway had three branches with termini at the Tower (Tower Gateway Station), Stratford and Island Gardens on the Isle of Dogs. Although it suffered lengthy teething troubles and became notorious for delays and cancellations, it succeeded in connecting the docks to the rest of the capital. By 1991, the service had become so well used that the line was extended via a tunnel to Bank Station in the heart of the City. At the same time, a fourth branch line was opened connecting Poplar to Beckton via Canning Town and in 1999 a further line was built running from the Isle of Dogs to Lewisham via Greenwich. Finally, in 2009, the railway was extended once again, this time to Woolwich via the Royal Docks and one of the LDDC's grandest schemes – London City Airport.

The airport was first proposed in 1981 as a way to transform public (and investor) perception of the docks from a defunct wasteland to a prospective centre for international trade. The site selected for the runway was the broad quayside that lay between the Royal Albert and the King George V Docks, the location of which was sufficiently close to the City to attract the attention of wealthy bankers and brokers who had the funds to jet off to the south of France at a moment's notice. Although many residents of nearby Silvertown were opposed to the airport on the grounds of the noise and fumes it would create, plans were approved by Parliament and, on 29 May 1986, the foundation stone was laid by the Prince of Wales. The first aircraft landed almost exactly a year later, on 31 May 1987, and commercial flights commenced in October the same year.

In addition to the construction of a transport infrastructure for the docks, the LDDC set about creating premises to attract small businesses, along with new housing schemes. The first commercial premises were concentrated on the Isle of Dogs and took the form of either small warehouses or low-built office complexes designed primarily to attract service industries. The majority of new housing comprised affordable homes for families, complete with driveways and small gardens, built on demolished industrial sites close to the Royal Docks at Beckton and at the Surrey Commercial Docks.

The initial development projects undertaken by the LDDC could not have come at a better time. In 1986, the London financial markets were deregulated by the government in a bid to compete with foreign exchanges. This deregulation, which became known as the 'Big Bang', significantly strengthened London's status within the international money markets and was responsible for re-establishing the City's position as one of the most dominant banking centres in the world, second only to New York. This in turn created an economic boom during which banks looked for new schemes in which to invest. The LDDC's initial speculation at the docks paid off when the corporation was approached by US bank Credit Suisse First Boston with a proposal to build a 10 million sq ft office complex on the quayside at the West India Docks. The site the bank had in mind had been known since 1936 as Canary Wharf, when shipping company Fruit Lines Ltd built warehousing there to store produce from the Mediterranean and the Canary Islands. At the time the site was surveyed by the American bankers it was being used as a television studio.

Initially, plans to develop Canary Wharf into a showpiece office complex were handled by an entrepreneurial US developer named G. Ware Travelstead. However, as the size of the project emerged, it became clear that Travelstead did not have the necessary resources to see it through to completion. The scheme was subsequently taken over by one of the largest developers in North America – Olympia & York – and on 17 July 1987 the building agreement for a 12.2 million sq ft financial centre was signed.

The first plans for the development featured three tall tower-blocks, which caused much concern for Londoners who feared that the skyscrapers would ruin views from Greenwich Park and block television reception. Several boroughs along with the GLC attempted to press for a review of the proposals but failed to stop the development. It is worth noting that the majority of people living closest to the site were largely in favour of the scheme, having been convinced that the massive amount of construction work involved would bring much-needed employment and the activity surrounding the finished complex would breathe new life into the area.

Construction of Canary Wharf began in 1987. The site was spread over a long, thin strip of land that stretched between the centre of the West India Docks' basins, thus surrounding the complex with water. This island site was accessed by Trafalgar Way in the east, which ran across the docks' old entrance basin, and Westferry Road in the west. At the junction with the site entrance, an underground roundabout named Westferry Circus was constructed to convey traffic to and from the new development. This subterranean entrance led into West India Dock Avenue, which in turn opened out into a huge rectangular expanse divided into five sections – Cabot Square, the North and South Colonnades, Canada Square and Churchill Place. The perimeter of Canada Square was dominated by a soaring structure (the first of three) known colloquially as Canary Wharf Tower. This magnificent edifice was designed by the architect Cesar Pelli, who wanted to create 'a sky scraper, not simply a high rise building.' Pelli succeeded in realising his dream, despite having to take off five floors in order to comply with air traffic safety regulations. The resulting tower was 824ft high and provided 1.3 million sq ft of office space within its stainless steel-clad walls. The remaining land around the central square at Canary Wharf was eventually flanked by medium-height office buildings overlooking a grassy park under which a shopping complex and car park lay concealed from view.

Although the Canary Wharf development transformed the West India Docks, it was slow to take off commercially. However, as the tower slowly rose from the quayside, other investors began to show interest in the Isle of Dogs. In 1989, a vast new headquarters for the *Financial Times* was completed at the East India Docks and a year later Reuters moved into new premises built across the remains of the former graving dock at Blackwall. Further east, the independent industries that had long since been located at Leamouth continued to prosper. This sustained interest in the area prompted further improvements to its transport links, including the construction of the Limehouse Link Tunnel, which provided a much-needed alternative route across the top of the Isle of Dogs without the need to suffer the regular gridlocks on the East India Dock Road. In addition to this, a riverbus service began to operate and finally the decision was made to extend London Underground's Jubilee Line to the island.

The Jubilee Line had first opened in 1979 and originally connected north-west London with the West End. However, following their redevelopment of Canary Wharf, Olympia & York began to press for a new railway line connecting their site to the mainline station at Waterloo, even offering to build the line themselves. Their proposal was considered by London Transport, which was not convinced that the line followed the most practical route and, subsequently, a study into a new railway for east London was conducted. The recommendation that came out of this investigation was to extend the Jubilee Line from Green Park to Waterloo via Westminster and then to the Docklands via a line that would run from Southwark across the river to the Isle of Dogs and through Canning Town before terminating at Stratford. The extension was authorised in 1990 and the line opened nine years later after a difficult and lengthy construction period, which ultimately cost £3.5 billion.

As businesses gradually began to move into the Isle of Dogs, the residential population began to change. New housing estates were built across the island to accommodate workers, but although some of the old housing stock was improved, the development of Canary Wharf ultimately did little to help the indigenous population of the island. Despite the total number of jobs available in the area rising from an estimated 5,500 in 1981 to a staggering 37,300 in 1997, unemployment fell only from 14% to 11.2% over the same period, suggesting that the vast majority of new jobs were not taken by the old residents. That said, the sheer amount of money ploughed into improving the Isle of Dogs during the 1980s and 90s certainly had an effect on the quality of life for original inhabitants that remained on the island. Millions of pounds were invested in the improvement of local shopping facilities, including a £1.3 million refurbishment of Chrisp Street Market, which although not officially part of the island, had served its population for generations. In addition to these facilities, new riverside walkways and parks were laid out over the wharf sites along the bank of the river, a sailing club was established at Millwall Docks and Mudchute Park and Farm was opened on land adjoining the old Cubitt Town estate.

Although the LDDC initially concentrated its energies on regenerating the Isle of Dogs, the other dock areas also benefited greatly from its attention. Over on the south bank of the Thames, Hay's Wharf and the surrounding labyrinth of residential streets and looming, empty warehouses were transformed. The corporation drew up plans to convert the central part of the area between Tower Bridge and London Bridge into a diverse commercial centre with a mixture of offices, shops and tourist attractions, while the eastern portion of the site was earmarked to contain live/work units, residential blocks and restaurants. The area's proximity to central London soon attracted the attention of investors and, by 1986, several of the riverside wharves and warehouses had been converted into modern business accommodation while still managing to retain some of the character of the area. The original buildings of Hay's Wharf formed a centrepiece to the development and were renamed Hay's Galleria. Part of the old dock was covered over with a high glass roof and the surrounding warehouse space was divided into offices and flats with shops and restaurants beneath. Beyond the wharf a riverside walk was laid out, giving commanding views over the city. The area quickly became a popular destination for visitors with the arrival of the London Dungeon on Tooley Street and *HMS Belfast*, which was moored in the Thames east of Hay's.

Just past Tower Bridge lay the empty warehouses of Butler's Wharf, which formed much of the eastern part of the LDDC's regeneration area. This 25-acre site had originally been named after a grain importer who rented the warehouses during the late 18th century. By 1873, the wharf had expanded to comprise what remains to this day the largest development of Victorian warehouses in London. During its heyday, in the late 19th and early 20th century, Butler's Wharf specialised in the storage of a huge range of foodstuffs including grain, sugar, tea, cinnamon and tapioca. When the warehouses began to close in the 1970s, some parts of the empty buildings were rented out as artists' studios to such luminaries as David Hockney, but by the time the LDDC took over the site most of the creative tenants had moved on and the buildings had become derelict. Their interesting heritage caught the attention of Terence Conran, however, and in 1981 the Conran Group put forward a proposal to renovate and develop the main Butler's Wharf building and five of the surrounding warehouses as workshops and studios for designers and artists, with a ground-level complex of restaurants and shops bordering the river.

The remaining part of the LDDC's Southwark site lay east of Butler's Wharf around the ancient thoroughfare of Mill Street. During the 19th century this area was known as Jacob's Island, described by Charles Dickens as 'the filthiest, the strangest, the most extraordinary of the many localities that are hidden in London.' Jacob's Island was arranged around a thin, crooked stretch of murky water known as St Saviour's Dock. Along the dock's perimeter lay tall, forbidding warehouses and rookeries whose most infamous fictional resident was the evil Bill Sykes and his doomed paramour Nancy. By the 1980s, Jacob's Island was, like so many other Thames-side sites, deserted and decaying. The nearby residential streets that had escaped the bombing raids of World War 2 housed a rapidly decreasing population of impoverished ex-wharf labourers and dockers. Despite the area's reputation, the local council were keen to retain its industrial character and consequently deemed it a conservation area, thus halting any plans for clearance of the site. However, despite the restrictions facing developers, the area's location was too good to be ignored and by the time the LDDC took control of the area, New Concordia Wharf – an old warehouse at the rear of St Saviour's Dock – had already been purchased by a young entrepreneur named Andrew Wadsworth who, at the age of just 23, became the creator of the first 'loft conversion' in the docks. Wadsworth's conversion of the warehouse combined modern practicalities with the retention of character so effectively that New Concordia Wharf became the blueprint for warehouse conversions throughout London.

A little further along the Thames, the former site of the Surrey Commercial Docks received a very different and even more radical programme of redevelopment. Following the closure of the docks, the PLA and Southwark Council had filled in all the basins in the complex bar the historic Greenland and neighbouring South Docks. Envisaging the area becoming largely residential, with a smattering of small warehouse-based trades bordering the Thames, the council built a new road around the tip of the peninsula, a few riverside commercial units were erected and a wooded park was laid out over what had once been the Russia Dock. Following these initial improvements, the council waited for tenders from developers keen to build housing on the remaining portions of the site. They didn't come. By the time the LDDC had taken control of the area in 1981, the old Surrey Commercial Docks were in a truly lamentable state. Huge swathes of concrete wasteland stretched over the old basins, flanked by crumbling warehousing and temporary business units. The surrounding residential area comprised mainly post-war council estates that had been allowed to degenerate, so convinced were the authorities that the area would soon be snapped up by investors.

Inspired by the successful regeneration of Butler's Wharf, the LDDC commissioned the Conran Group's property division to draw up plans for the redevelopment of the area surrounding the Surrey Commercial's two remaining dock basins, creating a mixture of business properties and residential estates. The remaining site was given over to affordable housing. Attracted by the successes further along the river at Hay's and Butler's Wharves, financiers gradually began to show interest in the Surrey Commercial site. Speculative residential estates were laid out and, as these reached completion, the LDDC introduced a scheme whereby the local residents were given the right to enjoy first refusal on the new homes, which they could purchase at an exclusive, discounted rate. This deal proved extremely popular with the local population, who were eager to escape their ghastly council accommodation. At the Nelson's Reach estate on the eastern side of the peninsula, people queued overnight in order to stake their claim on one of the new homes. At the Lavender Quay development, nearly all the property was sold before the builders had time to finish the show home.

By 1996, the Surrey Commercial Docks had changed beyond recognition – 5,500 new houses had been built on the site and were now occupied. The neglected council estates nearby had been given a multi-million pound overhaul and were once again decent places to live and the prevailing atmosphere was one of optimism. The area now also benefited from over five acres of parkland and riverside walks, along with three acres of enclosed water at the two remaining docks, which had found a new use. The South Dock had become a marina with berthing for 200 craft, while the historic Greenland Dock had turned into the Surrey Docks watersports centre. To the west of the site, the old Canada Dock was covered by Surrey Quays shopping centre (built in 1988). The small portion of the old basin that remained was renamed Canada Water. In 1997, land adjacent to this site was also redeveloped to form the Surrey Quays leisure park, which included a cinema complex, bowling alley and bingo hall along with several restaurants and a pub.

Today, there are few clues that the land beneath the Surrey Quays estate was ever one of the largest enclosed docks in the country, as the layout of the site has almost completely changed. In an attempt to retain at least a small link with the past, the LDDC commissioned a series of sculptures depicting scenes from the area's history. The most evocative of these works of art is perhaps Philip Bew's 'Deal Porters', which commemorates the men who for centuries worked with the Surrey Commercial Docks' most lucrative cargo.

Across the river from the Surrey Commercial Docks, the ancient maritime district of Wapping presented new problems for the LDDC. Like their counterparts in Southwark, Tower Hamlets Council had started to fill in the London Docks' basins and demolish the surrounding warehouses shortly after their closure in order to avoid maintenance costs. In their place, new housing had begun to be built and plans for a new sports centre were reaching the approval stage. Over at the St Katharine Docks, 'London's Venice' had never materialised. Instead, the old ivory warehouse had been converted into shops and offices, the Tower Hotel had been built on the area adjacent to the approach to Tower Bridge and the anachronistic Dickens Inn had been erected on the docks' north quayside, using the framework of an ancient timber brewery that the developers stumbled upon while demolishing one of the warehouses. The resulting site was an uneasy mixture of old dock structures, modern buildings and expanses of concrete reminiscent of the Surrey Commercial site. In an attempt to save some of the character of the area before the bulldozers totally eradicated it, the LDDC stopped all demolition and infilling works and began consultation with the local people in order to ascertain what should be done with the undeveloped sections of the two sites. The results of the consultations were revealed in 1983 at an exhibition entitled 'The Future For Wapping'. The plans on display showed a mix of new private housing that would either be built from scratch or converted from old warehouse space using a similar model to the highly successful development at St Saviour's Dock in Southwark. In addition, the area between the two docks would be given over to a large commercial development and a new river walk would link the two sites.

As at the Surrey Commercial Docks, local inhabitants were encouraged to invest in the new residential properties. However, the central location of Wapping meant that house prices were, by the mid-1980s, at levels that most of the original residents could never hope to afford. In response, the LDDC gave the locals interest-free loans to cover up to 20% of the purchase price. While this undoubtedly helped some families, many others still could not afford to (or did not want to) purchase one of the new homes and, as a result, new properties to rent were built at Hermitage Wall, the London's Western Dock and Wapping Wall. The old St Katharine and London Docks evolved into a mixture of commercial, light industrial and residential developments. At St Katharine's, some evidence of what had been there before still remained, but over at the adjacent site almost all trace of the London Docks was swept away. Today, all that remains of the once great shipping complex is a slim, canalised strip of water that originally formed part of the great Tobacco Dock.

The LDDC's final major regeneration project centred around the Royal Docks at Silvertown. This area had been particularly badly hit by the closure of the Royal Docks. Much of the industry that surrounded them, with the notable exception of the Tate & Lyle plant, had moved northwards to Essex following World War 2, causing huge unemployment and economic strife. Following the commencement of the regeneration works, the LDDC noted, 'It is hard to convey the sheer desolation of the area in the period after the closure of the Royal Docks; so close to the City and West End, yet so remote.'

The main problem faced by the LDDC at the Royal Docks site was the sheer amount of land that needed redeveloping. These docks had been built on a massive scale. To try to surround them with small business and housing developments similar to those at the older docks would have been futile as literally thousands of tenants would have been required to fill them. In addition to the problems caused by the scale of the project, the transport links from the Royal Docks to central London were inadequate, so the LDDC drew up a new system of roads along with a proposal to extend the Docklands Light Railway to the area. Work on both these projects began at the end of the 1980s.

Plans for the Royal Docks' regeneration were blighted by a property recession in the early 1990s. This, coupled with the vast size of the project, meant that at present the redevelopment of the last of London's enclosed docks is still not complete and, despite improved transport links, the area still has an air of isolation. To date, the Royal Docks have provided locations for three major developments. London City Airport is up and running in between the Royal Albert and King George V Docks; over at the Royal Victoria Dock, the south-west end of the basin borders a modern residential estate, while the North Quay houses the ExCel exhibition centre – a cavernous warehouse that hosts all manner of fairs and special events. Further east, on the north quay of the Royal Albert Dock, lies the first phase of the Royals Business Park.

To the erstwhile workers and residents of the docks, the area is now unrecognisable and provokes mixed emotions. Some are disappointed that the Port of London's maritime character has been swept away and almost all mourn the loss of the once-thriving industry that existed in and along the banks of the Thames. Retired tally clerk Alan Richardson summed up the opinion of many by stating, 'the old warehouses have been turned into millionaire flats overlooking the Thames, but the show's over.' Others reflect that while the nature of work has changed in the docklands, the area's *raison d'être* has not. As merchant seaman Dick de Kerbrech noted, 'in the 1960s, the docks were the centre of commerce and they still are, except now its money that's traded, not goods.'

In 1998, the LDDC closed down its operations and control over the future of London's Docklands was handed back to the relevant local authorities. By this time, London's role as an international sea port had been forgotten by many and it is inconceivable that the docks will ever be returned to their original use. Nevertheless, many of the vast basins, deep locks and tall warehouses that once formed the great Port of London remain part of the city landscape. They now serve only as a visual reminder of a once vital part of the capital that has now become London's lost quarter.

SELECT BIBLIOGRAPHY

Ackroyd, P. *Thames: Sacred River* (2007) Chatto & Windus

Ackroyd, P. *London: The Biography* (2001) Vintage

Balen, M. *A Very English Deceit* (2002) Fourth Estate

Booth, C. *Descriptive Map of London Poverty* (1984) London Topographical Society

Booth, W. *In Darkest England* (1890) Salvation Army

Braudel, F. *Civilization and Capitalism, 15th-18th Century: Perspective of the World* (1985) Fontana Press

Brigham, T. and Woodger, A. *Roman and Medieval Townhouses on the London Waterfront* (2001) Museum of London Archaeology Service

Brown, D. *Anglo Saxon England* (1978) Bodley Head

Burgon, J. W. *The Life and Times of Sir Thomas Gresham* (1965) B. Franklin

Collis, M. *British Merchant Adventurers* (1942) Collins

Crick, M. *Michael Heseltine: A Biography* (1997) Penguin

Defoe, D. *A Journal of the Plague Year* (2001) Dover Publications

Demarne, C. *The London Blitz: A Fireman's Tale* (1991) London

Dickens, C. *The Uncommercial Traveller* (2002) Weidenfeld & Nicholson

Dickens, C. *Oliver Twist* (2003) Penguin Classics

Dickens, C. Jnr. *Dickens's Dictionary of London 1888* (1995) Old House Books

Dickens, C. Jnr. *Dickens's Dictionary of the Thames 1887* (1995) Old House Books

Dollinger, P. *The German Hanse* (1970) Macmillan

Dyer, C. *Standards of Living in the Middle Ages* (1989) Cambridge University Press

Elton, G. R. *England under The Tudors* (1991) Routledge

Englund, S. *Napoleon: A Political Life* (2005) Harvard University Press

Evelyn, J. *The Diary of John Evelyn* (2006) Everyman's Library

Fisher, D. *Anglo Saxon Age* (1973) Longman

Foister, S. *Holbein in England* (2006) Tate Publishing

Frere S. S. *Britannia* (1967) Routledge & Kegan Paul

Goldman, N. and Nyenhuis, J. E. *Latin via Ovid* (1982) Wayne State University Press

Hobley, B. *Notes on Lundenwic and Lundenburh: two cities rediscovered*

Herzl, V. *Life in Saxon and Viking Britain* (1982) Nelson Harrap

Hutchinson, G. *Medieval Ships and Shipping* (1994) Farleigh Dickinson

Harvey, I. M. W. *Popular Revolt and Unrest in England* (1987) University College of Wales

Heseltine, M. *Life in the Jungle* (2000) Hodder & Stoughton

Jackson, L. *The Defence of Localities against Aerial Attack* (1914) London

Lewey, F. *Cockney Campaign* (1944) Stanley Paul & Co

Kerr, R. *A General History and Collection of Voyages and Travels* (1824) Blackwood

Lillywhite, B. *London Coffee Houses* (1963) George Allen & Unwin

Lingelbach, W. E. *The Merchant Adventurers of England* (1971) Franklin

Londinium – A Descriptive Map and Guide – Ordnance Survey

Longmate, N. *The Doodlebugs* (1981) Hutchinson

Lyle, H. M. *The Rebellion of Jack Cade* (1950) George Philip & Son

Maddicott, J. R. *Simon de Montfort* (1996) Cambridge University Press

Martin, D *Olaudah* (2008) Soham Community History Museum

Mayhew, H. *London Labour and the London Poor* (1965) Oxford University Press

Milne, G. *Port of London* (1985) Batsford

Milne, G. *Book of Roman London* (1995) Batsford

Mogg, E. *Mogg's New Picture of London* (1845) London

Morton, H. V. *In Search of London* (1956) Methuen & Co

Ormrod, M. (ed.) and Lindley, P. (ed.) *The Black Death in England, 1348-1500* (1996) Paul Watkins

Parkinson, J. C. *Places and People, Being Studies from Life* (1869) London

Pepys, S. *The Diaries of Samuel Pepys* (2003) Penguin Classics

Porter, S. *The Great Fire of London* (2001) Sutton

Postan, M. M. and Miller, E. *Cambridge Economic History of Europe* (1963) Cambridge University Press

Quennell, M. and C. H. B. *Everyday Life in Roman Britain* (1952) Batsford

Quennell, M. *Everyday Life in Anglo-Saxon Times* (1972) Transworld

Ramsey, W. G. *The East End Then and Now* (1997)

Reynolds, G. W. M. *The Mysteries of London* (1846) Vickers

Rodger, N. A. M. *The Safeguard of the Sea* (1997) HarperCollins

Schofield, J. *Medieval London Houses* (2003) Yale University Press

Shore, T. *Anglo Saxon London* (1902) London

Starkey, D. *Elizabeth* (2001) Vintage

Starkey, D. *Reign of Henry VIII* (2002) Vintage

Stow, J. *A Survey of London: Written in the Year 1598* (2005) History Press

Sutton, J. *Lords of the East* (2000) Conway Maritime Press

Thomas, H. *The Slave Trade, 1440-1870* (2006) Phoenix

Thornbury, W. *Old and New London* (1897) Cassell

Thrupp, J. *Anglo Saxon Home* (1862) Longman

White, J. *London in the 19th Century: A Human Awful Wonder of God* (2007) Jonathan Cape

Whitfield, P. *London: A Life in Maps* (2006) British Library

Whitfield, P. *Sir Francis Drake* (2004) British Library Publishing

Williams, G. A. *Medieval London* (2006) Routledge

Young, H. W. *Roman London* (1962) HMSO

Zacks, R. *The Pirate Hunter* (2003) Hyperion

SELECTED ONLINE RESOURCES

Charles Booth Online

Ancestry.com

Dictionary of National Biography

Newgate Calendar

Old Bailey Online

Dictionary of Victorian London

SELECTED NEWSPAPERS AND DIRECTORIES (ARCHIVE)
The Times
Kelly's Directory
The Daily Mirror
The Telegraph
The East London Advertiser
A-Z of Georgian London
A-Z of Victorian London
The East London Observer
The Manchester Guardian
Who's Who/Who Was Who

INDEX

1066   11, 55, 56

Abigail Lloyd   See Lloyd's
Albion Dock   204, 294
Anglo-Saxons   See Saxons

Baltic Docks   201, see also Commercial Docks
Baltic Wharf   229
Baynard Castle Ward   67
Baynard's Castle Wharf   58
Bear Quay   114
Beare Kaye   See Legal Quays and Bear Quay
Billingsgate Dock   177
Billingsgate Ward   67, 82
Black Death   12, 88-90, 91, see also plague
Black Eagle Wharf   229
Blackwall   15, 126-128, 129, 175, 183, 197, 199, 200, 201, 318
Blackwall Dock   126-128, 166
Bridge Ward   67, 82, 93
Broken Wharf   66, 145, 149
Brunswick Dock   199
Bull's Head Dock   229
Busshers Wharf   114
Butler's Wharf   320-321, 322
Buttolphe Wharff   See Legal Quays

Cabot Square   318
Canada Dock   204, 220, 323

Canary Wharf   317-319
Cannon Street   18, 147
Cannon Street railway bridge   27
Cannon Street station   12, 24, 214, 293
Captain Kidd   See William Kidd
Chamberlain's Wharf   228
Cnut (King Cnut)   53-54
Cocks Kaye   See Legal Quays
Commercial Docks   201, 220, 246,
Commercial Docks Company   201, 202, see also Surrey Commercial
    Docks Company
Connaught (pub)   306
Cotton's Wharf   227, 228
Crescent Wharf   271
Crowne Kaye   See Legal Quays
Custom House   82, 112, 149-150, 156, 160, 184, 213, 236, 293
Custom Howse Kaye   See Legal Quays
Custom Quay   225

de Gisor (family name)   68
Dockland Settlements   283
Dowgate Ward   67
Dyse Kaye   See Legal Quays and Dice Quay

East Country Dock   202, see also South Dock
East India Dock Company   199
East India Dock Road   200, 201
East India Docks   15, 199-200, 211, 270, 275, 304, 311, 318
Eastern Dock   205
Edgar the Aethling   56
Edmund (King of England)   54, 56
Edward (the Confessor)   54-55, 57
Edward Howard, Sir   99
Edward III   72, 81-82, 90
Edward IV   58
Edward Lloyd   162, see also Lloyd's

Edward VI 100, 110
Ethelred 46, 51-52
Ethelred II (the Unready) 52-54
Execution Dock 178-179, 181, 182, 215

Fish Wharf 75
Fresh Wharf 146, 225
Freshe Wharff See Legal Quays

Galley Quay 94, 113, see also Legal Quays
Gaunts Kaye See Legal Quays
Gibsons Kaye See Legal Quays
Great Harry (ship) 97-98, 104
Greenberys Kaye See Legal Quays
Greenland Dock 170, 175, 182, 201, 202, 238, 323
Gun & Shot Wharf 229

Hanseatic League 12, 61-63, 66, 69, 71, 72, 73, 76, 80, 84, 86, 107, 109,
    110, 114, 123-124, 127, 130, 147, 151, 214
Hardacnut 54
Hardel's Wharf 76
Harold Godwinson (King Harold) 11, 55, 56
Harold Harefoot 54
Hay's Galleria 24, 175, 228, 320
Hay's Wharf 175, 226-229, 268, 310, 313, 320
Henry Castle (& Sons, Shipbuilders) 229-230
Henry Hyde Champion 255, 261
Henry I 46
Henry II 62
Henry III 12, 58, 68-69
Henry Manning, Cardinal 265
Henry Mayhew 225, 236, 240, 246-248, 250
Henry Tate 230-232
Henry VI 92, 95
Henry VII 98
Henry VIII 12, 58, 89, 97-99, 107, 108, 115

Hermitage Dock   196
Hermitage Wall   294
Howland Great Dock   168, 170, see also Greenland Dock

Irongate Wharf   229
Isle of Dogs   14, 15, 127, 183, 186, 214, 215, 216, 241, 283, 294, 313-314, 315, 316, 317, 318, 319, 320

John Cabot   13, 110
Joseph Conrad   223, 267

kiddles   75
King George V Dock   279, 316, 325

Lavender Quay   322
Legal Quays   13-14, 112, 114,-115, 127, 150, 166, 167, 170, 175, 183, 195, 213, 224, 226, 293
Lloyd's (of London, insurers and underwriters)   14, 164, 209
Lloyd's Coffee House   14, 162-164, 166
Lloyd's List   14, 163, 209
Londinium   11, see also Romans
London and India Docks Joint Committee   268
London and St Katharine's Docks Company   221, 239, 267/268, 311, see also London Docks Company and St Katharine's Docks Company
London Bridge   11, 15, 53, 145, 193, 225, 227, 229, 320
London Docks   15, 195, 197, 198, 200, 206, 214, 233, 238, 247, 248, 269, 270, 275, 282, 311, 323, 324
London Docks Company   195, 220, see also London and St Katharine's Docks Company
London Stone   18
Lundenburh   11, see also Saxons

Mark Brown Wharf   310
Mary Rose (ship)   98-100, 103, 104
Mercer's Company   See Mercers
Mercers   91-92, 115, 156

Merchant Adventurers   12 13, 92, 106, 109 111, 115, 124
Merchant Staplers   12, 91 see also Merchant Adventurers
Millwall Docks   15, 214-216, 217, 218, 220, 241, 243, 244, 260, 268, 290, 294, 311, 312, 314, 320
Millwall Docks Company   216-217, 218

New Concordia Wharf   321
North Quay   10, 325
Norway Dock   202

Old Thrustons Kaye   See Legal Quays
Olde Wollkaye   See Legal Quays

PLA   See Port of London Authority
plague   12, 88-90, 143, 145, 186-187, see also Black Death
Pomegranate (ship)   98
Port of London   9, 11-13, 15, 16, 45, 60, 63, 72, 97, 105, 107, 112, 113, 126, 140, 151, 153, 163, 170, 182, 183, 186, 187, 188, 190, 195, 197, 198, 199, 204, 206, 210, 213, 218, 221, 223, 224, 226, 240, 242, 247, 248, 249, 260, 264, 265, 267, 268, 270, 275, 278, 283, 286, 293, 298, 300, 301, 303, 304, 305, 307, 308, 309, 311, 312, 313, 325
Port of London Authority (PLA)   16, 282, 299, 300, 303, 306, 309-312, 321
Port of London Bill   268
Port of London police force   303
Puntack's Head   162

Quebec Dock   204, 294
Queenhithe Ward   82

Raffs Kaye   See Legal Quays
Regent's Canal Dock   189
Roman London   See Romans
Romans   11-41
Rome   See Romans
Royal Albert Dock   9, 15, 223, 225, 244, 245, 267, 270, 279, 289, 306, 316,

325, see also Royal Docks

Royal Docks   9, 270-271, 276, 282-283, 299, 305, 306, 312, 316, 317, 324-325, see also Victoria Dock and Royal Albert Dock

Royal Victoria Dock   See Victoria Dock

Russia Dock   294, 322

Sabbes Kaye   See Legal Quays

Saxons   11, 38-41, 43-54, 57

Sebastian Cabot   12, 110, 111

Simon de Montfort   12, 68-71

Smart's Quay   150

Smarts Kaye   See Legal Quays and Smarts Quay

Sommers Kaye   See Legal Quays

South Dock   202, 204, 321, 323

South Quay   10

St Katharine Docks   15, 204, 206, 207, 214, 233, 234, 238, 311, 313, 323, 324

St Katharine's Docks Company   220, 221, 267, 268

St Saviour's Dock   321, 324

Steelyard   12, 92, 94-96, 107, 108, 110, 114, 123, 127, 147, 214

Surrey [and] Commercial Docks   15, 202-204, 237, 246, 248, 260, 268, 299, 304, 312, 317, 321, 322, 323, 324, see also Surrey Docks, Commercial Docks

Surrey Commercial Docks Company   202, 220

Surrey Docks   202, 250, 323

Surrey Docks Company   202, see also Surrey Commercial Docks Company

Surrey Quays   203, 204, 323

Tate & Lyle   232, 324

Tate (& Sons)   231-232, see also Henry Tate and Tate & Lyle

Thames Quay   157

Three Cranes   See Legal Quays

Thrustans Kaye   See Legal Quays

Tilbury Docks   15, 223, 224, 260, 267, 282, 299, 306, 308, 309, 310, 312

Tobacco Dock   324

Tower Ward   67, 02
Tower Wharf   89, 150
trades unions   15, 251, 255, 260-262, 265-266, 270, 278, 299-301,
    306-307, 310-311
Trinity House   104-106, 225

unions   See trades unions

Victoria (London) Dock Company   124, 214
Victoria Dock   9, 10, 213, 214, 217, 220, 222, 244, 245, 276, 290, 306,
    325, see also Royal Docks
Vintry Ward   67, 69, 72, 82

Wapping   15, 178, 182, 183, 195-196, 201, 202, 203, 215, 229, 236, 237,
    238, 259, 291, 293, 294, 323-324
Wapping Dock   195
Wapping Wall   324
wards   52, 67-69, 73, 81-82, 144
Watson's Wharf   291
West India Docks   14, 15, 183-185, 187, 198, 199, 200, 206, 214, 215,
    216, 223, 238, 241, 242, 256, 260, 265, 267-268, 270, 290, 294, 301,
    302-303, 304, 311, 312, 314, 317, 318
Western Dock   324
wharfingers   184, 224, 226, 257, 264, 267, 277, 293
wharfs   113, 192, 216, 224-227, 229, 310, 320, 321
William Fitz Stephen   60
William Kidd   179-182
William, Duke of Normandy (the Conqueror)   55, 56-58, 68
Wool Quay   71, 82

Yong's Quay   113, 114
Yongs Kaye   See Legal Quays and Yong's Quay